Rivalry and Alliance Politics in
Cold War Latin America

Rivalry and Alliance Politics in Cold War Latin America

CHRISTOPHER DARNTON

Johns Hopkins University Press

Baltimore

© 2014 Johns Hopkins University Press
All rights reserved. Published 2014
Printed in the United States of America on acid-free paper

2 4 6 8 9 7 5 3 1

Johns Hopkins University Press
2715 North Charles Street
Baltimore, Maryland 21218-4363
www.press.jhu.edu

Library of Congress Cataloging-in-Publication Data

Darnton, Christopher Neil, 1980–
    Rivalry and alliance politics in cold war Latin America / Christopher Darnton.
        p. cm.
    Includes bibliographical references and index.
    ISBN 978-1-4214-1361-7 (pbk. : alk. paper)—ISBN 978-1-4214-1362-4
(electronic)—ISBN 1-4214-1361-2 (pbk. : alk. paper)—ISBN 1-4214-1362-0
(electronic) 1. Latin America—Foreign relations—20th century.
2. Cold War—Political aspects—Latin America. 3. Latin America—
Politics and government—1948–1980. 4. Latin America—Politics and
government—1980– I. Title.
    F1415.D334 2014
    980.03—dc23   2013036554

A catalog record for this book is available from the British Library.

*Special discounts are available for bulk purchases of this book. For more information,
please contact Special Sales at 410-516-6936 or specialsales@press.jhu.edu.*

Johns Hopkins University Press uses environmentally friendly book materials,
including recycled text paper that is composed of at least 30 percent
post-consumer waste, whenever possible.

CONTENTS

ACKNOWLEDGMENTS

This book began a decade ago in a directed reading course with Paul Sigmund on Latin American international relations, an intellectually intense experience that reoriented my thinking in several ways. My background had been in US foreign policy toward Latin America, but I began to explore a larger terrain of regional interactions. My native Californian focus on Mexico and the Caribbean Basin shifted to account for South America. And my readings in international relations theory and regional diplomatic history often seemed irreconcilable. One puzzle in particular transfixed me: What caused the transition in Argentine-Brazilian relations from centuries of rivalry to the Mercosur era, why did this change happen when it did, and to what extent do these dynamics and their policy lessons apply to other protracted conflicts within and beyond Latin America?

That course came midway between two mentorships that profoundly shaped my approach to international politics. Among the many lessons I drew from Abraham Lowenthal at the University of Southern California and Andrew Moravcsik at Princeton are these: to understand what transpires between states, look within them, and to explain what drives organizations and individuals, think hard about interests. To both advisors I am indebted for motivation both by example and by expectation to pose, investigate, and prepare for difficult questions, to bring theory and evidence to bear on significant international problems, and to get swiftly to the point.

Over the last several years I have benefited from the instruction and inspiration of many teachers. I thank David Andrus, Nancy Bermeo, John Borneman, Christina Davis, Richard Dekmejian, Kent Eaton, Mark Fischle, Joanne Gowa, Jeffrey Herbst, Robert Hutchings, Norman Itzkowitz, Dominic D. P. Johnson, Robert Keohane, Atul Kohli, Steve Lamy, Evan Lieberman, Abraham Lowenthal, Dan Lynch, Kathleen McNamara, John Odell, Michael O'Hanlon, Kristopher Ramsay, William Rosenau, Anne Sartori, Paul Sigmund, Deborah

Yashar, the faculty of the 2006 Institute for Qualitative Research Methods, the staff of Princeton's McGraw Center for Teaching and Learning, and above all my dissertation advisors, Andrew Moravcsik, Tom Christensen, Jeremy Adelman, and Jason Lyall.

For comments on parts of what became this book, I thank Jeremy Adelman, Nora Bensahel, Tom Christensen, Jason Davidson, Matt Green, Ron Hassner, Evan Lieberman, Dan Lindley, Abraham Lowenthal, Jason Lyall, Ana Margheritis, Sean McEnroe, Jon Mercer, Andrew Moravcsik, Karl Mueller, Rebecca Szper, Wallace Thies, the anonymous reviewers of the book manuscript and the articles in *Security Studies* and *Latin American Research Review* that came out of it (versions of chapter four and of one section of chapter three, respectively), and the participants at numerous conference panels, talks, and workshops. I especially thank my editor, Suzanne Flinchbaugh, for her astute suggestions and unstinting support.

For hiring me and supporting my work, thanks go to my chairs and deans, Darius Rejali and Peter Steinberger at Reed College, and particularly Phil Henderson and Larry Poos at Catholic University. For intellectual havens and welcomes in new places, I thank Carlos Escudé, Ivonne Jeannot Laens, Gustavo Lamouret, and Diana Mondino in Buenos Aires; Jon Mercer and Beth Kier in Seattle; and Tom Cohen, Mario Ortiz, and Enrique Pumar in Washington. Research funding came from the CUA School of Arts and Sciences and Politics Department as well as the Princeton Institute for International and Regional Studies, Program in Latin American Studies, Bobst Center for Peace and Justice, and Department of Politics.

For documents, assistance, and patience, I thank the librarians at Catholic University and the Washington Libraries Research Consortium, Princeton University, the University of Washington, Reed College, the Universidad del CEMA, the Fundação Getúlio Vargas (Rio de Janeiro and São Paulo), and the Universidade Nacional de Brasília as well as Argentina's Biblioteca Nacional and Biblioteca del Congreso. I am particularly grateful to the dedicated staff of the US Library of Congress (Hispanic Division and Law Library), the Archivo Histórico de la Cancillería Argentina, and the Arquivo Histórico do Itamaraty (Brasília).

During graduate school and on the tenure track, I have deeply appreciated the comradeship of Will Barndt, Pam Bromley, Sarah Chartock, Ian Chong, Leo Coleman, Andrew Erickson, Jennifer Fleeger, Matt Green, Jaime Kirzner-Roberts, Elizabeth Kittrell, Mareike Kleine, Philip Lipscy, Austin Long, Sean McEnroe, Valeria Palanza, Alex Russo, Min Ye, Andrew Yeo, and Rafi Youatt. And in part because Latin American international relations can feel at times like a scholarly no-man's-land, I have greatly appreciated conversations with fellow travelers Mariano Bertucci, Miguel Centeno, Tom Long, Robert Pastor, João Resende-Santos, Michael Shifter, Arturo Sotomayor, and the foreign policy experts and practitioners who granted me interviews in Argentina and Brazil.

Ultimately this book is for my family: my parents, who encouraged me to read and write; my grandfather, with whom I wish I could have shared this book; and especially my wife, Jessica, who has sustained me all along, and our son Henry, who arrived four days after I completed the manuscript and who celebrated his first birthday on the day I wrote this text. Acknowledgments are not enough.

*Rivalry and Alliance Politics in
Cold War Latin America*

CHAPTER ONE

Explaining Rivalry and Rapprochement in Cold War Latin America

> The grandeur of history lies in the perpetual conflict of nations,
> and it is simply foolish to desire the suppression of their rivalry.
> —*Heinrich von Treitschke*

> In England we have come to regard as fellow-citizens between
> whom there can be no sort of conflict of interest scores of tribes
> that spent their time mutually throat-cutting at no very distant
> period, as history goes. We recognize, indeed, that profound
> national differences like those which exist between the Welshman
> and the Englishman, or the Scotchman and the Irishman, not
> only need involve no conflict of interest, but need involve even no
> separate political existence.
> —*Norman Angell*

Why do international rivalries persist despite incentives to cooperate, and how can states resolve these conflicts? Conventional wisdom in international relations identifies a common enemy as the most prominent source of cooperation between adversaries, but external threat only rarely delivers lasting reconciliation.[1] Why then does a common foe provoke rapprochement between some rivals, but not others, and why do some conflict resolution efforts between allies fail while others succeed? To answer these questions, this book analyzes a series of rivalries in Cold War Latin America and derives broader lessons for alliance politics and conflict resolution. During the Cold War, rivalries within the Western Bloc undermined alliance coordination, particularly in the Americas. The shared threat of Communism and related insurgencies helped some US allies, but not others, to transcend their rivalries with one another. Similar rivalry dynamics now subvert US coalition-building efforts in the ongoing global struggle against al-Qaeda and its insurgent affiliates.

I argue that rivalries frequently persist because of parochial interest within states, not mistrust between them. In particular, the armed forces and other state agencies maintain rivalry to protect their organizational interests in the continued preparation for conflict, defending the status quo by obstructing attempts at major policy change. Rapprochement occurs if two conditions are met in both countries: an alternative mission that assures these agencies continued benefits and state resource constraints that compel tradeoffs among policies. In Cold War Latin America, the combination of leftist insurgency and economic crisis in rival countries created political space for presidents to achieve rapprochement by persuading guardian agencies to abandon rivalry and focus on internal security missions. This argument explains the broad pattern of conflict and cooperation within Cold War Latin America and is directly relevant to persistent rivalries in the Islamic world during the current era of global counterterrorism.

This analysis offers some novel and counterintuitive conclusions. First, though necessary, statecraft is overrated. Peacemaking requires neither genius nor sainthood, and rapprochement can fail even when gifted leaders do their utmost to make it work. In contrast, extensive research on conflict resolution and rapprochement emphasizes the importance of costly signaling, symbolic and transformative gestures, and diplomatic engagement.[2] In *How Enemies Become Friends*, Charles Kupchan argues that carefully orchestrated gestures of self-restraint and reciprocal accommodation are essential to break out of mistrust and rivalry.[3] However, I show that these efforts often fail and that the obstacle to cooperation is more often the interests of the bureaucracy than the diplomatic shortcomings of leaders. Second, the drivers of protracted conflict often involve greed rather than grievance, and the state rather than society. This contrasts with the majority of research on protracted conflicts, which emphasizes ideational factors like identity, culture, and social learning.[4] Third, and relatedly, aid to allies is often counterproductive, reinforcing rather than undermining existing rivalries. This speaks directly to current policy debates, since US coalition-building efforts involve calls for ever more military assistance. Fourth, Latin American "dirty wars" had silver linings: by creating a new vested interest for the armed forces, they opened the door to international rapprochement. This contrasts with studies that attribute Latin American peacemaking primarily to democratic and neoliberal governments.[5] Finally, to proponents of several international relations perspectives, the book offers uncomfortable observations. Realists have to contend with systematic bureaucratic obstruction of the national interest, constructivists with political actors' response to incentives rather than ideas, and liberals with the apparent insignificance of regime type for conflict resolution.

In this chapter I frame the problem of protracted rivalry and rapprochement; introduce my parochial interest argument; outline the empirical puzzle of intra-bloc Cold War rivalries and the research design, emphasizing the value of Latin American cases; derive six alternative arguments from prominent international relations theories; and discuss the potential role of US foreign policy in this analysis and in resolving or perpetuating historical and contemporary rivalries among allies.

Purpose of chapter

The Problem: Rivalry and Rapprochement

This book is about the persistence of international rivalry and the emergence of rapprochement. Rivalries are enduring, conflictual relationships between states. They are characterized by mutual anticipation of hostility, which is reinforced as both sides act on these expectations, but not by constant or unrestrained violence.[6] Rivalry defined previous eras in international politics, from struggles between Athens and Sparta, Rome and Carthage, and Byzantium and the Ottomans to the Cold War between the United States and the Soviet Union, and it remains a source of danger. Rivalries account for a disproportionate share of international crises and wars, and they underpin several ongoing flashpoints of international security, such as Kashmir, the West Bank, and the Taiwan Strait, increasing the likelihood of regional wars and nuclear proliferation.[7] To identify such cases, I follow William Thompson's definition of a "strategic rivalry" as an international relationship in which "the actors in question . . . regard each other as (a) competitors, (b) the source of actual or latent threats that pose some possibility of becoming militarized, and (c) enemies."[8] Knowledge of the conditions under which tension between rival states can be de-escalated, thereby defusing those flashpoints, is essential for policymakers in those countries as well as for potential outside mediators, including the United States.[9]

DEF Strategic Rivalry

"Rapprochement" is a diplomatic term for the significant improvement of previously hostile relations, a reconciliation between adversaries.[10] It is analytically distinct from cooperation (since even rivals can act on common interests, as the United States and USSR did during the Cold War), détente (a temporary de-escalation of tensions), and normalization (the formal establishment of diplomatic relations).[11] It precedes and leads to the complete termination of rivalry.[12] Because rapprochement offers an essential first step from hostility to stable peace and security community, we need to understand why it emerges in order to build toward those loftier goals. Also, as a major change in relations between

DEF Rapprochement

countries, it offers important tests for theories of international cooperation.[13] A critical inflection point at which a bilateral relationship shifts from an arc of conflict to an arc of cooperation, rapprochement between rival states provides an important research puzzle. How do rivalries end? Several paths are possible, but some risk a human cost perhaps even greater than continued conflict. The conquests of Carthage, Athens, and Constantinople by their adversaries are particularly sobering examples, as is the contingency of the Soviet Union's comparatively peaceful collapse. However, many conflicts end without terminating either opponent, and rivals can achieve peaceful reconciliation.

Under what conditions does rapprochement occur? Dozens of plausible factors have been identified, while investigations of rapprochement have proceeded through quantitative analyses of the correlates of rivalry termination, case studies of trust-building between particular adversaries, and, increasingly, comparative-historical research.[14] Unfortunately, there is often little engagement between these approaches, and gaps often separate political science from conflict resolution and studies of protracted domestic conflicts from those of international rivalries.[15] No single variable is likely to be determinative, and several possible pathways may lead to successful rapprochement.[16] The search for a silver bullet is not only misguided but also counterproductive, harming the development and testing of theories and precluding useful policy lessons. A quest for the necessary underlying condition can sweep multiple factors into overly broad categories (making arguments hard to disprove), while a search for the optimal policy can lead toward causes not far removed conceptually from rapprochement itself (raising the question of where a hypothesized "cause" actually comes from).[17] Thus, a central premise in this book is that the causes of peace, like the causes of war, should be investigated through comparative hypothesis testing across multiple cases.[18]

One of the most important problems rivalries pose for policymakers and scholars alike is their persistence. From either a policy-oriented or an area studies perspective, the proposition that prior conflict at least partially drives rivalry would seem an unquestionable and even defining element of intractable conflicts.[19] Similarly, most quantitative work on rivalry agrees that early conflicts breed future hostility and conflict.[20] However, neither a statistical correlation nor an article of faith based on regional knowledge is the same as a specified theory backed by evidence of causation. A given string of conflicts between two states might simply be a "hot hand": if whatever factors caused the first conflict in a series also directly caused subsequent conflicts, then the enduring nature of many rivalries might be epiphenomenal, while arguments that history matters might be spurious.[21] Although there is strong evidence that the more conflicts two rival countries endure, the higher the probability that they will undergo an additional one, it is still important to question assumptions of path dependence.[22] This matters for the study of rapprochement because, as Paul Pierson argues, if vague "path-dependent arguments degenerate into little more than a description of stability," then major changes "are usually attributed . . . to 'exogenous shocks.' "[23] Conversely, a "clear understanding of the mechanisms of reproduction provides an instrument for the investigation of change."[24] Although external shocks or catalysts may produce cooperation by breaking apart a rivalry's stasis or inertia, it is not clear in advance which events count as shocks and how they affect outcomes.[25] Therefore, a second major premise of this book is that hypotheses on rapprochement should flow logically from a theory of rivalry maintenance.

The most frequently identified source of international cooperation among adversaries is the emergence of a common foe.[26] Intriguingly, such claims come from several international relations perspectives that provide very different models of rivalry maintenance, mechanisms through which a common foe contributes to cooperation, and conditions under which these are most likely to function successfully. In the widely debated case of France and West Germany after World War II, to what extent did a common Soviet enemy contribute to Franco-German rapprochement, and why did cooperation persist while other alliances of convenience (such as the United States and USSR against Nazi Germany) quickly collapse?[27] For that matter, why does a common foe often fail to cause cooperation at all, leading to underbalancing?[28] Discussing the broader pattern of peaceful relations among industrialized countries in postwar Western Europe, Bruce Russett and Harvey Starr observe that "if we could understand why such a large set of peoples, who only recently fought bitterly and bloodily, now live at peace with one another, we would know something very important."[29] The consequences of a common foe for relations among adversaries are central to contemporary security policy as well. With the post–Cold War rise of new security threats, including transnational Islamist terrorism, whether international cooperation against these threats might mitigate existing international rivalries, particularly in the Islamic world, or whether rivalries will undermine counterterrorism coalitions is a vital but unanswered question.

Research on alliances identifies several consequences of intra-bloc rivalry but little about the causes of conflict resolution among allies, which is the central focus of this book. Intra-bloc rivalry can make cross-bloc violence more likely by undermining the effectiveness of coercive diplomacy and contributing to mutual misperceptions.[30] It can weaken alliance cohesion when states weigh threats internal to the alliance against those external to it.[31] And it can provoke difficult situations of "pivotal deterrence" for a bloc leader just to keep the peace among nominal allies.[32] More broadly, because states form alliances for several reasons beyond balancing external threats, including "tethering" threatening states by allying with them, bandwagoning "for profit" with rising revisionist powers, and restraining prospective allies' aggression toward third parties, it should not be surprising that rivalries sometimes persist among allies.[33] As Paul Schroeder argued, "The internal rivalries and cross-purposes that all alliances contain are no secret."[34] Clearer understanding of what drives these internecine rivalries, however, would enhance our knowledge of both alliance politics and conflict resolution.

Why do some rivals, but not others, overcome their mutual antagonism in the context of a common foe?[35] This book seeks an answer by analyzing the pattern of rivalry and rapprochement among non-Communist Latin American governments allied with one another and with the United States through the Rio Treaty of 1947.[36] By explaining the variation across intra-bloc rivalries in Cold War Latin America, this book contributes not only to existing knowledge about conflict resolution and alliance politics but also to studies of Latin American foreign relations and of the global history of the Cold War.[37] Why, given a common foe, did some Latin American rivals achieve rapprochement at particular historical moments while others did not?

The Argument: Parochial Interest

I argue that the major obstacle to rapprochement lay in the vested interest of agencies within the state apparatus (particularly the armed forces) and that the combination of an alternative mission for those agencies and resource constraints compelling policy tradeoffs caused rapprochement. As Stephen Stedman suggested regarding civil wars, "Instead of thinking generally about the possible threats to peace . . . ask, '*Who* are the threats to peace?' "[38] Existing research has begun exploring the effects of domestic political processes on international rivalry, but this book offers the first systematic investigation of the possibility that domestic proponents of rivalry might be coherent governmental organizations rather than diffuse factions and that these groups might maintain conflict for reasons of parochial interest rather than ideology, beliefs, or socialization.[39] A satisfactory explanation of rapprochement, like any theory of policy change, needs to identify the mechanism that maintains the status quo and to indicate the conditions under which it can be dismantled or overcome. To do so, I draw on analyses of other policy changes, especially the termination of civil wars, retrenchment from imperialism, and domestic policy reform.[40] A major lesson from this research is that bureaucratic agencies can act as "veto players," as "agents" that resist the instructions of their "principals," and ultimately as guardians of the status quo.[41]

I assume that government agencies charged with carrying out the policies associated with rivalry derive parochial benefits from those policies and thus develop a vested interest in maintaining rivalry and blocking rapprochement. Agencies charged with implementing particular policies tend to develop recognized expertise in those issue areas, giving them the power to define policy problems and solutions, as well as a vested interest in making sure those policies reinforce their own dominance.[42] Beyond any general bureaucratic resistance to change, government agencies are likely to resist changes that threaten their policy portfolios and parochial benefits.[43] Conversely, agencies are likely to accept or even to advocate for policy change only when they stand to benefit from those changes. Protracted conflict and preparation for war tend to increase the size and power of the security apparatus, but the possibility that the security apparatus would act to maintain this relationship needs further investigation.[44] Continued international hostility can serve several organizational interests: resources in the form of budgets for training and procurement, autonomy from interference by societal and other bureaucratic groups over the design and implementation of security policy, and political power to influence national leaders' security decision making. When international threats are highly salient, such as in rivalries, agencies charged with addressing them are likely to enjoy high levels of resources, power, and autonomy. Because rapprochement threatens these privileges, these agencies will generally oppose rapprochement initiatives to protect the flow of parochial benefits. The fundamental question to ask about protracted conflicts is, who benefits? To be clear, I am not arguing that state agencies create rivalries or that they prefer to escalate existing disputes to crisis or war.[45] I do claim, however, that the policies associated with rivalry benefit the government agencies that implement them and therefore that these actors will tend to oppose efforts by national leaders to overcome international rivalry.

If parochial interest perpetuates rivalry, then under what conditions will rapprochement occur? A common foe can present the relevant government agencies with a clear and parochially beneficial alternative mission and is most likely to induce rapprochement between rival states when national resource constraints force agencies to choose among possible missions rather than simply expanding their policy portfolios to encompass both tasks. Here, cooperation emerges not when leaders defeat, persuade, or outflank guardian agencies but rather when they satisfy agencies' core interests with acceptable substitutes in the context of economic pressure. Without an alternative mission, rapprochement threatens the interests of guardian agencies. Thus, resource constraints in the absence of an alternative mission are unlikely to produce rapprochement—if anything, they might compel a tooth-and-nail defense of the existing mission of rivalry against possible budget cuts and other restrictions. Resource constraints can come from several directions, including a stagnating or declining gross domestic product, a high or increasing imbalance of payments, a high or increasing national debt burden, and monetary instability such as hyperinflation. Conversely, an alternative mission in itself is insufficient to produce rapprochement. State agencies tend to be fundamentally conservative, more interested in defending existing missions than in unfettered expansion (they might well decline new missions that conflict with core values), and they are unlikely to give up existing missions except under duress. If an important new mission emerges, agencies would rather add it to their existing policy portfolio than displace existing missions, if possible.

The fundamental hypothesis of this book is that the combination of an alternative mission and resource constraints compels guardian agencies to accept a policy tradeoff, keeping the new mission while sacrificing the old mission of rivalry. In other words, mission and constraint are jointly sufficient to cause rapprochement, while the absence of one or both of these factors causes rivalry persistence (table 1.1). These two factors might not emerge at the same moment in time, though. If we look at a brief period of relations among rivals, what sorts of changes should precede and produce rapprochement? If an alternative mission already exists, then economic decline should produce rapprochement. Conversely, if a country is already experiencing resource constraints, then the emergence of an alternative mission should cause rapprochement. Both factors need to be present in both rival countries. Even if the entire government of one country is convinced that peace is desirable, the rival country's intransigence (and the first country's knowledge of this) will continue conflict; although appeasement might be one path to cooperation, this is not the path I investigate. Put another way, even one guardian is sufficient to veto rapprochement.[46] As Helen Milner observes, when domestic vetoes are taken into account, international cooperation looks even less likely than in a purely state-to-state model of world politics.[47] As noted above, this is about sufficiency rather than necessity: I do not claim to uncover the only path to rapprochement, since the causes of peace are surely plural, but I do argue that the combination of alternative mission and resource constraints causes rapprochement between rival states.

TABLE 1.1
The argument

		Resource constraints	
		No	Yes
Alternative mission	Yes	II. Continued rivalry	I. Rapprochement
	No	III. Continued rivalry	IV. Continued rivalry

How can we tell whether parochial interest affects rival states' foreign policies? In addition to the overall hypothesis about initial conditions and rivalry outcomes, parochial interest offers testable predictions about the behavior of actors within each government. Where state resources are unconstrained or no alternative mission is available, guardian agencies are likely to undermine rapprochement initiatives by presidents or other national leaders. At the extreme, punishment of leaders deemed soft on rivalry might include coup or assassination, but more frequently, it will involve subtler and less openly confrontational means of policy sabotage. This ongoing but often unstated threat by powerful government agencies to defend the status quo may be strong enough to dissuade pro-rapprochement leaders from seeking the presidency, to influence the public against electing them (or authoritarian elites from appointing them), or to prevent presidents from trying to implement international cooperation, at least through normal channels.[48] Although agencies may have de facto veto power over major policy changes, presidents still have means of their own to execute policy and may reach out to the rival government personally or through trusted envoys, conducting end runs around the obstructionist bureaucracy.[49] During failed rapprochement efforts, we should see not only the absence of alternative missions or resource constraints (or both) but also some combination of sabotage by guardian agencies and end runs by presidents. Conversely, in cases of successful rapprochement, we should see not only the presence of both causal factors but also presidential reliance on fully cooperative agencies. As presidents give up end runs and agencies decline sabotage, rapprochement should emerge through routine diplomacy.

This argument offers a clear alternative to existing work on the effects of domestic politics on rivalry behavior. Early research on rivalry and rapprochement often treated the state as a black box, framing the central problem as one of reconciling two adversaries rather than of overcoming domestic opposition to policy change and cooperation.[50] However, later studies, drawing on models of "two-level games," argue that domestic conflicts between hawks and doves heavily affect rivalry behavior, and vice versa.[51] Michael Colaresi, for example, links the socialization process of rivalry to the mechanisms of diversionary conflict, arguing that prior conflict and the rivalry relationship make the public feel insecure and unwilling to support cooperative overtures toward the rival, such that opponents of a dovish leader whose cooperative attempt was not reciprocated by the rival can exploit this public sentiment to attack the leader as weak or treacherous.[52] Similarly, Kenneth Schultz focuses on the signaling dimension of foreign policy for electoral politics: hawkish leaders who advocate cooperation wind up looking like moderates, while dovish leaders pushing the same policy look extreme; thus, the leaders who most prefer cooperation are least able to deliver it, while those more capable of ensuring cooperation are less interested in doing so.[53] In contrast, I offer an explanation of the origins of pro-rivalry preferences, and a corollary hypothesis about the causes of rapprochement, based on state actors rather than society and on interests rather than ideology. Fundamentally, I argue that alternative mission and resource constraints are jointly sufficient to produce rapprochement between rivals.

The Puzzle: Cold Wars within Cold Wars

To test this argument, I analyze a series of cases drawn from Cold War Latin America, offering controlled comparisons of successful rapprochements with negative cases (where cooperation seemed likely but did not occur) and tracing causal processes using primary sources.[54] Why the Cold War? The global, bipolar struggle between the United States and the Soviet Union reduced the range of possible alignment options. Although these realignments sometimes paved over a host of regional rivalries, the prior conflicts often bubbled to the surface, providing an ideal setting in which to evaluate the effects of a common foe on relations between rival states. Given the prominence of common foe hypotheses, we might expect similarly aligned states to achieve rapprochement, as with France and West Germany. Conversely, if local rivalry is more salient than the global struggle (or if rival states disagree about the direction of global threat), we might expect each rival to side with a different superpower patron rather than going it alone. In turn, opposing alignments would exacerbate and prolong rivalries such as India-Pakistan or North Korea–South Korea.[55]

The historical record, however, raises a number of puzzles. First, what explains the prevalence of intra-bloc rivalries during the Cold War (table 1.2)?[56] Second, all of these occurred within the Western alliance system, with no rivalries on the Eastern side (as of 1955). How did US allies assess the Communist threat, and why did so many rivalries persist among them? The relative dearth of Eastern Bloc rivalries may reflect a data problem rather than a historical reality, requiring further research on the Cold War foreign relations of Soviet allies.[57] However, including additional rivalries in this category would only enhance the historical puzzle of intra-bloc rivalries. Furthermore, the West's common foe manifested differently across regions and periods of the Cold War, from the prospect of invasion by Soviet troops in Western and Central Europe and Central Asia to armed conflict with other Communist states in East Asia, to leftist insurgencies with possible Communist sponsorship in Latin America, Greece and Turkey, and beyond. This makes detailed examination of specific regions and historical episodes particularly valuable. Third, what explains the low rate of rivalry termination in the Western Bloc compared to the mixed and cross-bloc rivalries?[58] Fourth, two-thirds of the intra-bloc rivalries in the historical record (8 of 12) pitted Latin American states against one another, making Latin America the best single region in which to evaluate the effects of a common foe on the emergence of cooperation among rivals during the Cold War. How can we explain ongoing Cold War rivalries among non-Communist Latin American states? And what explains the variation between allied rivals that achieved rapprochement at particular moments in time and those that did not? These are the core research questions I address in this book.

After outlining the research project in chapter one and fleshing out the parochial interest argument in chapter two, I turn to the case studies, which are designed as a series of controlled comparisons. Chapters three through five each address one of the three successful cases of rapprochement among longstanding Latin American rivals during the Cold War, in comparative perspective. Table 1.2 lists the dates of full rivalry termination; generally, the turning point of rapprochement precedes this by a year or more, much as transitions from authoritarianism precede democratic consolidation. And as with regime change, early reversals are certainly possible. For that reason, and in order to avoid independently coding success and failure in the cases in a way that might bias the study, I treat rapprochement efforts as successful only if they led to rivalry termination. Working backward from rivalry termination, using secondary sources as well as each country's published diplomatic records, I identify the successful cases of rapprochement as follows. Between Argentina and Brazil, an early sign of cooperation came in 1979 with the Tripartite Accord that resolved a major hydroelectric dispute, and rapprochement occurred in 1980 with reciprocal presidential visits and a bevy of bilateral accords (with rivalry terminating in

TABLE 1.2
Strategic rivalries in 1955 by bloc alignment

Country A		Country B		Rivalry		
State	Alliance/ Alignment	State	Alliance/ Alignment	Begin	End	Bloc
Thailand	SEATO	North Vietnam	USSR	1954	1988	Cross
North Korea	USSR	South Vietnam	USA	1954	1975	Cross
China	USSR	Taiwan	USA	1949		Cross
China	USSR	USA	USA	1949	1978	Cross
West Germany	NATO	East Germany	Warsaw Pact	1949	1973	Cross
Israel	USA	Syria	USSR	1948		Cross
North Korea	USSR	South Korea	USA	1948		Cross
Iraq	CENTO	Syria	USSR	1946		Cross
USSR	USSR	USA	USA	1945	1989	Cross
Albania	Warsaw Pact	Greece	NATO	1913	1987	Cross
Britain	NATO, SEATO, CENTO	USSR	USSR	1816	1956	Cross
Egypt		Iran	CENTO	1955	1971	Mixed
Indonesia		Netherlands	NATO	1951	1962	Mixed
USSR	USSR	Yugoslavia		1948	1955	Mixed
China	USSR	India		1948		Mixed
Egypt		Israel	USA	1948		Mixed
Israel	USA	Jordan		1948	1994	Mixed
India		Pakistan	SEATO	1947		Mixed
Afghanistan		Pakistan	SEATO	1947	1979	Mixed
Jordan		Saudi Arabia	USA	1946	1958	Mixed
Jordan		Syria	USSR	1946		Mixed
Egypt		Jordan		1946	1970	Mixed
Egypt		Iraq	CENTO	1945		Mixed
Hungary	Warsaw Pact	Yugoslavia		1918	1955	Mixed
Turkey	NATO, CENTO	Yugoslavia		1878	1957	Mixed
Greece	NATO	Turkey	NATO, CENTO	1955		West
Iraq	CENTO	Israel	USA	1948		West
Costa Rica	Rio Treaty	Nicaragua	Rio Treaty	1948	1992	West
Iraq	CENTO	Saudi Arabia	USA	1932	1957	West
Honduras	Rio Treaty	Nicaragua	Rio Treaty	1895	1962	West
Argentina	Rio Treaty	Chile	Rio Treaty	1843	1991	West
El Salvador	Rio Treaty	Honduras	Rio Treaty	1840	1992	West
Bolivia	Rio Treaty	Chile	Rio Treaty	1836		West
Colombia	Rio Treaty	Venezuela	Rio Treaty	1831		West
Ecuador	Rio Treaty	Peru	Rio Treaty	1830	1998	West
Argentina	Rio Treaty	Brazil	Rio Treaty	1817	1985	West
France	NATO, SEATO	West Germany	NATO	1816	1955	West

Source: List of rivalries, participants, and dates adapted from Colaresi, Rasler, and Thompson, *Strategic Rivalries.* For other sources on alliances and alignments, and bloc coding, see note 56 to this chapter.

1985; see table 1.2). Argentine-Chilean relations slowly began thawing after a 1978 militarized crisis over the Beagle Channel dispute; rapprochement occurred in 1984 with the Treaty of Peace and Friendship, and rivalry terminated in 1991. After signs of possible cooperation began in 1957, Nicaraguan-Honduran rapprochement occurred in 1961 with a presidential meeting on the border, and rivalry ended the following year.

Chapter three analyzes the relationship between Argentina and Brazil from 1945 to 1980, from postwar rivalry to successful rapprochement, which paved the way for the formation of Mercosur (the Common Market of the South, Mercosul in Portuguese) a decade later. Brazil and Argentina, Western Bloc allies under the Rio Treaty, had maintained the region's most prominent rivalry, dating back to New World colonial competition between Spain and Portugal. Why did Argentine-Brazilian rapprochement succeed in 1980 when previous efforts, marked by presidential summits, had failed? Attempts at cooperation are valuable negative cases, and they generate a rich documentary trail, which I pursued in the archives of the Argentine and Brazilian foreign ministries as well as through published government records. I test my argument in the four Cold War cases of attempted rapprochement between Argentina and Brazil: in 1947 and 1961, both under democratically elected governments, and both of which failed, and in 1972 and 1980, both under military governments, when the first attempt failed and the second successfully shifted the Argentine-Brazilian bilateral relationship from its centuries-long pattern of conflict and competition to one of cooperation.

I argue in chapter three that the key proponents and beneficiaries of the policies associated with rivalry were the armed forces and the foreign ministries of the two countries, that these agencies sabotaged all cooperative efforts between presidents until the late 1970s, that presidents attempted to conduct diplomatic end runs around the bureaucracy that ultimately failed, and that the combination of economic crisis and the alternative mission of counterinsurgency during the 1970s shifted state agencies' interests from favoring rivalry to supporting cooperation. This thesis contrasts with much of our received knowledge of Argentine-Brazilian cooperation and the origins of Mercosur, which prominent scholarship often attributes to regional democratization, the spread of neoliberal economic ideas, and the end of the Cold War. Although such arguments contribute a great deal to our understanding of the deepening of integration and stable peace, they cannot account for the origins or the persistence of rapprochement between the two countries. Parochial interest explains the preceding stage of cooperation on which these later achievements were constructed.

Chapters four and five present controlled comparisons of additional cases, each holding one of my independent variables constant to assess the effects of the other (as against alternative hypothesized factors) on the perpetuation of rivalry or the emergence of rapprochement in a particular subregion over the span of a few years. In other words, each addresses a specific empirical puzzle. Chapter four examines three rivalries among Central American countries at the time of the 1959 Cuban Revolution, which, along with the transnational insurgencies that followed it, presented a clear threat and a compelling alternative mission for the security forces of all of these states. Why, given these incentives, did Honduras and Nicaragua, but not El Salvador and Honduras or Costa Rica and Nicaragua, achieve rapprochement? Among states with available alternative missions, I argue that economic resource constraints provide the key that differentiates outcomes (in table 1.1, I compare pairs of states in cells I and II). Specifically, the dearth of US aid provided a window of opportunity, stretching from Castro's 1959 guerrilla victory to the Kennedy administration's 1961 launch of the Alliance for Progress, in which the small countries of Central America could cooperate against a common threat and set aside their longstanding rivalries. Salvadoran and Costa Rican prosperity mitigated these pressures, and so no policy tradeoff was necessary, while Nicaraguan and Honduran resource constraints caused those countries to make (and, critically, their security agencies to accept) the sacrifices necessary for rapprochement.

Chapter five reverses this structure, addressing four rivalries among Andean countries during the debt crisis of the 1980s, which spurred numerous regional cooperation efforts. Why, given these incentives, did Argentina and Chile, but not Colombia and Venezuela, Ecuador and Peru, or Bolivia and Chile, achieve rapprochement? Among states with serious resource constraints, I argue that prior mission development by the armed forces determines whether these guardians of the status quo will accept rapprochement (in table 1.1, I compare pairs of states in cells I and IV). Argentina and Chile had adopted internal security missions against the threat of leftist insurgency, as had Colombia and Peru, but not Venezuela, Ecuador, or Bolivia. The lack of an alternative mission by one rival country explains why economic crisis did not cause rapprochement between Venezuela and Colombia, Bolivia and Chile, and Ecuador and Peru. Similarly, the timing of the debt crisis explains why Argentina and Chile, with their internal missions, achieved rapprochement in the early 1980s but not in the late 1970s (when they nearly went to war).

Chapter six discusses the prospects for counterterrorism cooperation to mitigate international rivalries in the contemporary era. To do so, it draws on and critically evaluates the common analogy between the Cold War and the Global War on Terrorism, identifies the most likely cases for rapprochement on this basis, and presents a case study of the ongoing rivalry between US counterterrorism partners Morocco and Algeria. Finally, chapter seven summarizes the main empirical findings, identifies theoretical contributions to the study of international relations, suggests avenues for future research, and offers foreign policy suggestions for the United States and leaders of rival states.

Like policy choices, research designs are full of tradeoffs. The focus on Cold War Latin America offers several advantages beyond framing and solving the Argentine-Brazilian, Central American, and Andean puzzles. First, a regional emphasis permits a researcher to explore a greater depth of primary sources and to detect and correct for biases and gaps in the historical literature. Latin American international relations is an emerging field, and this book engages existing works in debate on cases that are increasingly popular (e.g., Argentine-Brazilian cooperation and Argentine-Chilean rapprochement in the 1980s) and seeks to stimulate new research and future debate on cases for which virtually no work exists (e.g., the 1950s Central American relationships and the 1972 Argentine-Brazilian summit).[59] Second, focusing on one region in a particular historical era helps to hold constant factors like culture, colonial history, and great power involvement. Because many of the hypotheses under consideration originated in studies of European and North American foreign relations, this offers a valuable out-of-area test. Third, the controlled comparisons offer added leverage beyond the value of each individual case study. For example, the synchronic comparisons in chapters four and five sequentially isolate the effects of each of my independent variables so that alternative arguments can be fairly tested. They also ensure the strongest possible comparability across cases within each chapter, and the different decades and subregions in the two chapters enhance the generalizability of the findings. The diachronic comparison of Argentine-Brazilian summits in chapter three assesses the effects of my variables over time and especially tests the behavioral predictions about presidents and guardian agencies.

These advantages come with a few limitations, of course. I treat relationships among US allies in Cold War Latin America as a universe of cases, and my primary empirical goal is to explain the variation in rivalry and rapprochement within this domain. Even if this explanation is successful, however, scholars of conflict resolution and alliance politics might raise questions about the conceptualization of rivalry itself and the population of cases to which it applies as well as the relationship between these and the Latin American cases in this study.

First, why identify rivalries by their political relationships rather than by a be-havioral indicator, such as conflict frequency, or by the actual stakes being dis-puted? Most scholars agree about the basic concept of rivalry as a conflictual relationship with an ongoing probability of militarization. However, disagree-ments over how to operationalize the prospect of violence have led scholars to establish competing rivalry datasets.[60] Although much of our interest in rival-ries comes from their propensity to generate crises and wars, if we exclude rela-tionships that go several years without violence, we might overlook rivalries that have not yet escalated and confuse cease-fires with rapprochement.[61] Alterna-tively, defining rivalries by the disputed stakes (especially territory) would con-flate rapprochement with the resolution of a particular issue dispute, although a rivalry might involve several disputes and the stakes might change over time.[62] Although unresolved disputes often contribute to rivalry endurance, the rela-tionship between rivals can also affect the perceived value and indivisibility of the stakes.[63] "Ripeness" studies of conflict resolution identify several factors beyond the inherent characteristics of the stakes that contribute to moments of opportunity for negotiation.[64] As Richard Haass observes, the persistence of conflicts usually does not stem from the absence of a negotiable formula to resolve substantive disputes.[65] Thus, I focus on a change in the political rela-tionship, rather than the resolution of particular disputes or de-escalation from particular episodes of violence.

Second, within the strategic rivalry framework, how does Cold War Latin America relate to the broader set of cases? After all, if our mental image of rap-prochement is that of post-1945 France and West Germany and our image of rivalry that of Germany and France punctuating a century of competition with devastating wars in 1870, 1914, and 1940, Latin America hardly seems cut from the same cloth. As Miguel Centeno observes, Latin American interstate wars have been fewer and less destructive than those of Europe, and most violence has been intrastate.[66] Severity and representativeness are two different ques-tions, however. Latin American rivalries in the twentieth century may be a bet-ter guide to contemporary rivalries among developing countries than the great power interactions that pervade existing research on rivalries, for example. Thus, I argue in chapter six that the conclusions ought to travel to contempo-rary rivalries in the context of global counterterrorism. Future research is wel-come to test the argument elsewhere and to verify scope conditions, which in turn would contribute to further theory building. For qualitative research, a clear universe of cases is valuable for unbiased case selection, while drawing on existing datasets should facilitate a conversation between findings from qualitative and quantitative studies.[67] Because rivalry concerns mutual perceptions of hostility, studies of rivalry should demonstrate fidelity to the complex "political histories of individual states' foreign policy activities"; thus, new comparative case study work should complement existing quantitative scholarship, as I hope the present volume will.[68]

Alternative Arguments

Under what conditions does a common foe produce rapprochement? I derive six alternative hypotheses from major works in international relations theory, based on three implicit mechanisms of rivalry maintenance corresponding to realist, liberal, and constructivist worldviews. I articulate multiple hypotheses within each school of thought because these are rich perspectives within which competing theories can and should be developed.[69] All of these theories posit that the presence of a common foe has the potential to cause rapprochement among rivals. However, each hypothesis offers different predictions about the conditions under which a common foe is most likely to produce successful cooperation as well as the mechanisms through which it is likely to do so (table 1.3). For each of the three perspectives, I outline the basic model of rivalry maintenance; for each hypothesis on rapprochement, I clarify why and how a common foe ought to contribute to cooperation, identify the major predicted condition under which rapprochement is likely to emerge, and demonstrate the plausibility of that prediction for rivalries in Cold War Latin America.

A Realist Perspective on Rivalry

Realist arguments about rivalry begin with an assumed situation of international anarchy and uncertainty, which breeds the necessity of self-defense against other states, whose power represents a constant possibility of war.[70] For realists, security relationships—whether allied or adversarial—are tenuous, readily altered through shifts in the distribution of power or other sources of threat. As Hans Morgenthau argues, "the balance of power . . . creates a precarious stability in the relations between the respective nations, a stability that is always in danger of being disturbed."[71] Underlying this view that today's ally may be tomorrow's adversary is a fundamental uncertainty about other states' capabilities and intentions, which incentivizes worst-case assumptions for the purposes of defense planning and, due to the fear that the other side will cheat (and the magnitude of the consequences should this occur), makes it difficult to commit credibly to cooperate.[72] Thus, many arguments about the effects of incomplete, asymmetric, or misrepresented information on war termination and conflict bargaining are

TABLE 1.3
Seven hypotheses on rapprochement

	If a common foe provides:	Then the condition most likely to cause rapprochement is:
Balancing	Alternative source of threat	High level of common threat
Bandwagoning	Reassurance for weaker rival	Power asymmetry between rival states
Democratic peace	Opportunity to signal trustworthiness	Democratic or democratizing regimes in rival states
Counter-revolutionary ideology	Revisionist opposition to dominant regimes	Parallel authoritarian regimes in rival states
Norm diffusion	Opposition to regional hegemon's agenda	Regional hegemon promoting cooperation
Identity spillover	Opportunity for self-reinforcing cooperative behavior	Subregional institutions or operations
Parochial interest	Alternative mission for guardian agencies	State resource constraints

compatible with the realist model.[73] How might realists explain enduring rivalry? Conflict persists either because the distribution of capabilities has not changed or because prior conflict and arms races have altered capabilities and enhanced the threat each state poses to its rival.[74] I evaluate two hypotheses on rapprochement consistent with the realist model described above.

First, a prominent realist argument holds that even rival states are likely to band together to balance a common threat. Cooperation is generally proportional to the degree of threat: only major threats can bring rivals together, alliances are unlikely to endure once the threat dissipates, and a commonality of interests can produce cooperation but not vice versa.[75] Furthermore, states can counter threats either by mobilizing and building armaments or by recruiting foreign allies (perhaps less costly, though also less reliable, than arming), and rivals with a history of conflict are unlikely to view one another as particularly reliable allies.[76] Thus, for a common foe to induce rapprochement among rivals, it needs to be particularly threatening to both rivals, and the prospective cooperation between the rivals needs to have particular utility for defeating the foe that alternative strategies (e.g., external allies or domestic arms production) would not provide. The balancing argument's fundamental prediction is that rapprochement is most likely when common threat levels are highest. There is evidence that shared, external military threats tend to induce rivals to resolve their issue disputes.[77] Since Third World states constitute the majority of all rivalry participants and since internal and non-material threats often dominate the security concerns of Third World governments, however, a fair test of the realist balancing argument should look at domestic threats.[78] For much of Cold War Latin America, the major threat came from leftist insurgent groups inspired by the Cuban Revolution.[79]

A second realist hypothesis emphasizes bandwagoning.[80] A longstanding argument among realists concerns whether a preponderance or a balance of power is more amenable to peace. In both perspectives, the middle ground is dangerous: power shifts are likely to produce not only windows of vulnerability and opportunity in which declining states have incentives to launch preventive wars but also gaps between power and prestige such that rising states are likely to launch wars to seize what they perceive as their due status.[81] The possible stability and pacific consequences of power preponderance have earned a new look, and sparked new debate, given the sustained failure of other powers to balance the United States after the Cold War.[82] In the context of rivalry rather than international order and systemic war, the primary determinant of rapprochement is a stark asymmetry of power between the rivals, such that the weaker side capitulates to the stronger one's demands rather than facing the disastrous consequences of conflict.[83] However, surrender is a terribly risky business, and the weaker side likely fears exploitation or destruction unless it has additional and credible assurances, such as security guarantees by outside powers.[84] These problems may be more acute in civil wars than in international conflicts.[85] However, rivalries, with their prior history of conflict and often an aversion by outside powers to engage in mediation, may be more like civil wars in this respect than like other international disputes. Here, a common enemy might help to persuade the stronger state that it has more important problems than maintaining rivalry while also reassuring the weaker state that the power of the stronger will likely be directed elsewhere.[86] Furthermore, to the extent that the stronger state is distracted by the common foe, the weaker state has an opportunity to promote the common struggle and to seek side payments for its assistance.[87] The fundamental claim of the bandwagoning hypothesis is that in the context of a common foe, the achievement of marked material superiority by one rival is the most likely condition to produce rapprochement. In Cold War Latin America, troop counts and levels of defense spending, as well as the overall size of national populations and economies (potentially and partially convertible into troops and military hardware, respectively), offer a useful approximation of relative power.[88] Variations in rates of development and levels of military mobilization present important tests of this hypothesis.

A Constructivist Perspective on Rivalry

Many studies of protracted conflict rely, implicitly or explicitly, on a social-psychological or constructivist mechanism to connect prior conflict with present hostility.[89] Common images of rivalry maintenance include feuds and vendettas between Shakespeare's Capulets and Montagues, the Hatfields and McCoys in post–Civil War Appalachia, or clans in contemporary developing countries such as Albania. Much work focuses on the reproduction of adversarial images, although how much of this is driven by affect and emotion as opposed to updating and information processing (often labeled "hot" and "cold" cognition, respectively) remains unclear.[90] Alexander Wendt argues that interactions affect state identities and interests through a process of social learning—these effects are deeper than just constraining behavior and actually change what the states are.[91] In particular, conflictual interactions develop and sustain hostile relationships as each state acts based on its perception that the other is aggressive; failure to learn the rules and roles in a nascent Hobbesian system "could be fatal."[92] Some of the clearest articulations of learning mechanisms come from scholars who are not necessarily constructivists but who apply psychological findings in their work. Deborah Larson, for example, explains that expectations of other states' behavior come from "previous experience" and that acting on the basis of those expectations can be "self-fulfilling," since this provokes the other side to "act accordingly."[93] Furthermore, some of the strongest versions of these claims come from studies on the construction of intrastate ethnic conflict, where a history of violence and discrimination polarizes group identities, such as in Rwanda.[94] Constructivists recognize that social learning hardly yields optimism about peace and cooperation given the existing cultural and institutional content of international politics.[95] Given constructivist sensitivities to the deep roots of the status quo and its mechanisms of perpetuation, what conditions might cause rapprochement between rivals? I evaluate two hypotheses consistent with this rivalry mechanism.

The first, which I label identity spillover, emphasizes the self-reinforcing character of cooperative deeds against a common foe.[96] To shift cultures from a Lockean mode of rivalry toward a Kantian one of friendship, Alexander Wendt explains that a "common fate" (including situations involving a common foe) can induce states to act "as if" they believed in a shared identity, which ultimately can come to pass through repeated cooperative behavior, the "ideological labor" of leaders to communicate to one another the existence of a common fate and the necessity of cooperation and common identity, and the practice of self-restraint.[97] Such arguments draw on a long tradition in the social psychology of conflict resolution, in which the repeated pursuit of superordinate goals, even by groups recently in conflict, tends to produce a recategorization of group identity at a higher (shared) level.[98] Although the emergence of a common enemy "activates and makes more salient the cohesive bonds between the conflicting parties" and contributes to mutual trust, the key to sustaining cooperation is indirect, stemming from the rivals' actions against that enemy, since "characteristic processes and effects elicited by a given type of social relationship (cooperative or competitive) tend also to elicit that type of social relationship."[99] The key identity spillover claim is that a common foe induces cooperative behavior that in turn undermines the existing culture of rivalry and replaces it with one of friendship; cooperation ultimately becomes disproportionate to the initial common threat and is likely to outlast it as well. Looking for the development of subregional institutions or joint security operations by the rival countries seems the best way to operationalize the identity spillover hypothesis about the effects of initially limited security cooperation. In Cold War Latin America, several cooperative institutions emerged, from counterterrorism efforts to trade pacts, providing crucial opportunities for rival states to develop new relationships.[100]

A second constructivist argument concerns norm promotion, the ability of "entrepreneurs" to build new collective identities, define shared adversaries, and prescribe appropriate behavioral rules. One of the attractions of the norm promotion thesis is that its introduction of third parties addresses the agency problem of the identity spillover argument. Cooperative behavior and shared identity may be self-reinforcing, but the emergence of a common foe might not always be sufficient to cause the first cooperative move in a series of interactions between adversaries.[101] Even materially weak nonstate and transnational actors such as professional groups and advocacy networks have transformed state security behavior, either by constraining states from using certain weapons and military tactics or by encouraging states to pursue particular policies, such as humanitarian intervention.[102] However, power still matters, because among the myriad actors promoting their chosen norms, not all voices carry equal weight.[103] Thus, the promotion of new norms may involve a substantial element of coercion by powerful or even hegemonic actors.[104] Ultimately, in the context of a common foe, the most likely condition for rapprochement driven by norm promotion is that an authoritative third party clearly articulates a set of security norms that identifies the common foe as a pressing threat, calls for collective action against that adversary, and seeks to minimize disputes among the members of the emerging coalition. In Cold War Latin America, the United States was the most viable candidate; it disseminated a game plan to the region, with clear preferences regarding hemispheric security and counterinsurgency, relations with the Communist world, and economic strategy.[105]

A Liberal Perspective on Rivalry

In contrast to the realist emphasis on material threats and the constructivist focus on external and relational determinants of identity and norms, liberal claims prioritize the domestic sources of state preferences.[106] Enduring conflict, like stable peace, is less a function of military power or constructed trust than of national regimes' compatibility in political institutions and reigning ideologies.[107] How might liberals account for the entrenchment of rivalry over time? Bruce Russett and John Oneal introduce a temporal dimension of "Vicious Circles and Virtuous Circles," in which the mutually reinforcing effects of democracy, interdependence, and international organizations on peace and on one another "are apt to become stronger, and the system itself more stable over time."[108] Certain regimes might benefit either from conflict or from peace—authoritarian states can find external enemies useful for maintaining a grip on the population, while regional peace can strengthen existing democratic rule.[109] Although liberal arguments can account for protracted conflict or cooperation, they clearly depart from constructivist emphases on the feedback of international interactions on state identity. Russett and Oneal deny that democracy is primarily a byproduct of peace, or authoritarianism of conflict, although they do call for future research on these "reciprocal effects."[110] I address two liberal hypotheses.

First, the democratic peace hypothesis claims that liberal democracies are uniquely able to refrain from going to war with one another.[111] The idea that leaders of similar regimes might cooperate more frequently and more deeply than leaders of incompatible systems is so pervasive that several scholars offering primarily realist studies of alliances, alignment, and rapprochement bring this claim into their analysis.[112] Joint democracy might strengthen peace through two mechanisms: liberal values might enhance norms of peaceful conflict resolution and international cooperation, and democratic institutions could constrain potentially bellicose leaders from launching unnecessary or unpopular wars. These mechanisms are mutually reinforcing: without democratic institutions for aggregating preferences and selecting leaders, it is unclear how a liberal populace would achieve its policy objectives, while in the absence of a foundation of liberal values, the simple existence of "[m]ajority rule begs the question of *what the majority wants*."[113] How might a common foe matter? A common foe could help liberal democracies resolve signaling problems, improve mutual perception, and deepen their cooperative agenda. First, to overcome the fundamental mistrust impeding international cooperation, states need to signal credibly their trustworthiness to one another, and a critical mechanism for doing so involves taking advantage of domestic audience costs, for which democratic institutions make a particularly useful tool because they hold leaders accountable for their commitments.[114] If these perceptions are only barely sufficient to contain crises and war, how could they possibly induce states to overcome a pattern of lower-level rivalry? A useful extension of existing democratic peace work would investigate the conditions under which joint democracy produces simply the absence of war and the conditions under which it actually leads to the "virtuous circles" described by Russett and Oneal. A common foe might catalyze these mutual perceptions of shared regime type and foreign policy preferences by providing a salient initial test of cooperation's viability. In other words, the antecedent condition of a common foe provides a most likely case for the democratic peace to produce cooperation above and beyond the mere avoidance of war. A variant of this hypothesis is also important to test, especially because in Cold War Latin America, dyads of fully consolidated democracies were almost nonexistent. Joint democratization itself, by creating a shared sense of political vulnerability among the leaders of rival states, might contribute to peacemaking.[115] In Cold War Latin America, two waves of democratic transitions (the "twilight of the tyrants" in the late 1950s and the "third wave" in the 1980s) provide ample opportunity to test this argument.[116]

A second liberal argument suggests that a concert of counterrevolutionary regimes is likely to form against revisionist threats. Assessing the nineteenth-century Concert of Europe, Mark Haas argues that the very low level of "ideological distance" between the region's monarchical, imperial, multinational governments, which in the wake of Napoleon's attempts to revolutionize the European states system along nationalist lines remained both objectively vulnerable and subjectively afraid of insurgent challenges to their legitimacy, allowed them to form a collective security organization.[117] Aside from the specific content of ideology, difference causes a "fear of subversion" sponsored by the other state, a perception that the other state has fundamentally opposing interests and thus an "increasing belief in the inevitability of conflict" and a different symbolic language resulting in "inability to communicate effectively," raising the probability of conflict.[118] Similarly, there is evidence that pairs of authoritarian regimes tend to refrain from war with one another more successfully than mixed pairs of one democracy and one authoritarian state, particularly if one disaggregates authoritarianism into different regime subtypes.[119] In part, this shares the initial logic of democratic peace arguments that similar regimes will tend to trust one another.[120] Thus, rather than looking at liberal ideologies (themselves quite rare in Latin America during this period), I focus on counterrevolutionary ones. The counterrevolutionary claim is that similar but illiberal regimes are likely to perceive one another as being vulnerable to the common foe and thus as having a credible shared interest in cooperating to defeat it. Here, a common foe is even more important than for the democratic peace argument: authoritarian regimes generally lack the institutional ability to signal their common preferences to one another, so a common threat is critical for helping them discover their mutual interests in self-preservation. Additionally, a common foe, as opposed to unrelated internal threats in the two countries, should help each rival overcome its fear that the other might be sponsoring an insurgent force against it.[121] For Cold War Latin America, the armed forces' fears of another Cuba (a regional revisionist in the decade after the 1959 revolution), and a subsequent wave of "bureaucratic-authoritarian" coups, rooted in national security doctrines emphasizing counterinsurgency and anti-Communism, should have stimulated rapprochement.[122]

How well do these hypotheses explain the pattern of rivalry and rapprochement in Cold War Latin America? All yield useful insights in specific cases, but a parochial interest account (which I develop further in the following chapter) offers the best overall explanation of the three cases of rapprochement in comparative perspective.

Regional Rivalries and United States Foreign Policy

The primary empirical goal of this book is to explain the pattern of conflict and cooperation among Latin American countries during the Cold War. However, each of the comparative case study chapters devotes a penultimate section to reflections on US foreign policy, for three reasons. First, leaders in the Americas have faced an international environment of tremendous asymmetry since at least the 1898 Spanish-American War, which starkly demonstrated the overseas power projection capability of the United States of America as a regional hegemon. In former Guatemalan President Juan José Arévalo's metaphor, if Latin American countries are a school of sardines, then the United States is a shark in the same water; even if the smaller fish act autonomously and interactions among them are significant, they invariably account for the predator.[123] Although this asymmetry is often a poor guide to the effects (and origins) of US foreign policy in the hemisphere, a study of inter-American relations that omitted the United

States as an actor would be as flawed as one that explained hemispheric outcomes solely as a function of US preferences and initiatives.

Second, the United States might affect factors critical to all of the available hypotheses. Norm promotion, of course, directly assesses a regional hegemon's ability to shape the values and agenda of the smaller states, but the potential impact of US actions is far broader than this. US aid, arms sales, and training missions might shift the balance of capabilities in several bilateral relationships, affecting the prospect that a weaker state might bandwagon with a stronger one. US interventions in a region might provoke or eradicate local rebellions, altering the severity of internal threats to rival governments. Recurrent US democracy promotion efforts might nurture an emergent democratic peace. Alternatively, US support—tacit or active, overt or covert—for military coups, along with other signals to the armed forces, might enhance the likelihood of a counterrevolutionary concert among authoritarian regimes. Although identity spillover is primarily about the self-reinforcing effects of bilateral cooperative interactions, it is entirely possible that US restraint or inaction—particularly by not addressing mutual problems—provides an opportunity for such early gestures to emerge and take hold in response to those issues.

Finally, this book is not only about foreign policy in Cold War Latin America but also about the enduring principles of alliance management and conflict resolution. To derive from historical Latin American cases useful lessons for contemporary security policy, and particularly to apply those lessons to US counterterrorism coalition-building efforts after September 11, 2001, we need a clear picture of what US leaders sought, what they achieved, and which policy options they considered, neglected or discarded, and ultimately chose. Especially, we need to address the potential unintended consequences of US foreign policy for relations among its ostensible regional allies, whether in the contemporary Islamic world or in Cold War Latin America.

CHAPTER TWO

Parochial Interest and Policy Change

Nor is the task of the President in the leadership of federal administration simply one of the issuance of directions to subordinates: the arts of compromise, of negotiation, of persuasion have as great a relevance in the White House as in Congress.

—*V. O. Key Jr.*

Although I should have known better, I only slowly developed a sense of unease that something was seriously wrong with the premise of the information-analysis-directive approach to the management of the public sector. Briefly, this approach fails to account for the institutions of bureaucracy and representative government. By 1964 I came to realize that there is nothing inherent in the nature of bureaus and our political institutions that leads public officials to know, seek out, or act in the public interest. Cynics and a few political scientists could have told me this earlier—but without effect, prior to my personal experience in the bureaucracy.

—*William A. Niskanen Jr., Assistant Director for Evaluation,*
White House Office of Management and Budget

In this chapter, I develop a parochial interest theory of international rivalry maintenance and the prospects for rapprochement. I argue that government agencies with vested interests in the policies associated with rivalry will act to prevent national leaders from achieving cooperation with the rival country, except when two conditions are satisfied: first, the emergence of an alternative mission for those agencies in the form of a common foe, and second, state resource constraints that force budgetary tradeoffs among policy priorities.[1] This argument resolves the empirical puzzle raised in chapter one by explaining why a common foe induces rapprochement between some rivals but not others. Rivalry, like other stable government activities, is essentially a bundle of public policies that is deeply resistant to change. This resistance, as studies of policy termination, major policy change, and institutional reform on both domestic and foreign fronts have noted, largely comes from the intransigence of organizations with vested interests in the status quo.[2] If bureaucracy is "the least understood source of unhappy outcomes," then the relationship between state actors and the unhappy outcome (from the national interest standpoint, at least) of protracted international rivalry clearly merits new research.[3]

Parochial interest also sheds light on additional puzzles of protracted conflict. First, rivalries often exhibit several failed attempts at cooperation and many instances of thawing and subsequent re-freezing of relations; this suggests that leaders are neither socialized into hatred or mistrust of the other state nor especially afraid of being voted out of office by an outraged, nationalistic populace.[4] Although it is possible that these cooperative overtures fail through poor diplomacy or a refusal by leaders to engage one another, it is also plausible that rapprochement fails because it is dragged down intentionally from within each state, a line of argument I take up in this book.[5] Studies of civil wars have demonstrated the role of spoilers in making conflicts intractable and in torpedoing compromise attempts by leaders, and I see little reason why international rivalries would be immune to these dynamics.[6] In fact, the organizational apparatus of the state and its position atop a steady stream of resources through taxation and expenditure might make parochial interest dynamics even stronger in interstate rivalries than in civil wars or ethnic conflicts. Furthermore, if conflict ripeness matters for timing successful cooperative initiatives, then for interstate rivalries, we need to know more about the domestic obstacles to rapprochement and about the institutional sources of ripe moments for conflict resolution.[7] Second, rivalries often exist for decades without a war or even a major crisis, suggesting a degree of stability, domestic functionality, or even tacit bilateral collusion in the propagation of low-grade interstate conflict.[8] As Harold Lasswell argued in his classic essay on the garrison state, the ceremony of national defense—the policies, behaviors, and attitudes of preparation for militarized conflict—can substitute for war itself in perpetuating the political dominance of the specialists on violence.[9]

While articulating this source of rivalry persistence and this road to rapprochement, I readily concede that others may exist and that, like any model of the foreign policy process, my argument will fit some classes of countries and conflicts better than others.[10] Psychological factors of hatred and mistrust may predominate in some conflicts, for example, and naked competition for power resources may drive others. Likewise, democratic transitions and the development of economic interdependence may create cooperation in some cases. However, as I argued in chapter one, the prominence of a common foe as a causal factor in international relations scholarship, the inadequacy of our understanding of how a common enemy should produce cooperation between adversaries, the shortage of research on whether these effects actually occur, and the unexplained variation in the effects of anti-Communism on intra-bloc Western rivalries during the Cold War all warrant this study's investigation of the conditions under which a common threat can produce effective and lasting cooperation between rival states and the book's focus on the intrastate politics of international rivalry and rapprochement.

Attention to the autonomous policymaking role of government organizations is not new (although it has fallen out of favor in recent years), and my argument draws on and combines the insights of others in order to apply them to the issue of protracted interstate conflict. First of all, my work recalls the bureaucratic politics approach to foreign policy analysis, most notably Graham Allison's *Essence of Decision*. Although bureaucratic politics has been widely criticized for its lack of parsimony and its dearth of general and falsifiable propositions, I attempt to avoid these pitfalls by developing limited, testable hypotheses rather than outlining a general theory of bureaucracy.[11] Additionally, rather than relying solely on the bureaucratic politics literature, I borrow from work in the fields of American, comparative, and international politics on public policy formation and particularly on government agencies' resistance to policy termination or major policy change.[12] I also draw on studies of the distorting effects of parochially interested groups on conflict behavior, especially the effects of spoilers in civil wars, of coalitions in the foreign policy of empire, and of vested interests on militarism.[13]

To be clear, none of this suggests that interest groups manufacture threats and conflicts out of thin air for their own purposes—a staple of conspiracy theories.[14] Countries (or, more accurately, national leaders) do not necessarily choose to become rivals, nor do government agencies such as the armed forces create rivalry for their own ends.[15] Nor do I argue that vested interests push the state to escalate conflicts into outright violence and war. Rather, I suggest that rivalry, like militarism, displays a pattern of excess—a greater policy emphasis on national security and the armed forces than would be warranted by threats alone—that is primarily driven by the policy pressure of vested interests.[16] After all, President Dwight

Eisenhower's 1961 farewell address, the source of the oft-cited and frequently mis-interpreted "military-industrial complex" phrase, neither blames the complex for starting the Cold War nor calls for dismantling it but instead advocates for public vigilance against statist excesses. Specifically, Eisenhower warned against "the acquisition of *unwarranted* influence, whether sought or unsought, by the military-industrial complex."[17] Thus, some degree of military influence on policy may be warranted, perhaps by virtue of issue-specific expertise, and some development of excessive influence might well be unsought—an unintended consequence of bureaucratic expansion to address the real external threat posed by the Soviet Union. Eisenhower was primarily concerned with the emergence of a lobby, a set of vested interests that might distort policymaking and undermine the efficient allocation of resources for a long-term struggle with the Soviet Union. The military-industrial complex as a political and cultural "trope," as a critique of defense preparations and warfare itself, came later, during the Vietnam War in the late 1960s.[18] Certainly, the politics of enduring threat serves the interests of the groups in charge of responses to threat, which usually include the armed forces.[19] However, this feedback loop faces political and economic constraints. Although rivalry between the United States and the Soviet Union bulked up the civilian and military wings of the state apparatus in both countries, in neither country can the complex accurately be accused of driving the Cold War rivalry. Furthermore, US defense buildup was limited domestically by anti-statist ideological and institutional forces and might have been restricted further if the economy not grown so spectacularly, shielding society from its costs.[20]

Nor are the effects of parochial interests on national security always nefarious. Much of the aggression and spiraling of militarism may not be due to the pressure of concrete groups within government, let alone the armed forces, but rather to civilian hawks, jingoistic public discourse, and mass acquiescence—in short, to society rather than the state, and to ideology rather than interests.[21] Furthermore, agencies' adherence to standard procedures can be adaptive and efficient given human information-processing and problem-solving limitations.[22] Because bureaucrats have a more accurate understanding of the consequences of different policy options within their area of expertise than politicians do, latitude for agencies to make their own decisions may result in more optimal outcomes than would micromanagement or excessive constraint by national leaders.[23] Leaders may make better decisions by listening to advisors from different agencies with different interpretations of problems and menus of solutions, including a voice playing devil's advocate.[24] Lastly, soldiers, diplomats, and bureaucrats are generally both professional and patriotic.[25] Heads of agencies may honestly believe that the best interests of their organization and the nation as a whole are, if not identical, at least complementary.[26] They may even be correct, in which case principled defense of their preferred policies may serve the national interest.[27] In the particular context of rivalry, even if bureaucratic or other domestic factors prolong the situation of hostility, the possibility of confrontation could still be very real or at least could have been quite significant at the outset. When agencies oppose cooperation with a rival country, they might make a sensible and persuasive argument from a national security standpoint, even if it happens to sustain their parochial interests.

However, vested interests do systematically distort policymaking, and this is the dynamic that I explore in this chapter. For example, militarism constricts the range of policy options available to presidents: even when presidents oppose particular policies, they are mostly reactive, since problem definition and policy options are largely dictated for them.[28] Agencies' mission development may contribute to simple, unintentional policy inertia (agencies oppose shifting to a new set of tasks because "that's not how we do things"), but it also produces concerted, active opposition to policy change, in defense of the existing stream of parochial benefits from the central government.[29] Policy continuity might be helpful as public opinion vacillates, overt threat manifestations vary, and national leaders rotate through office, but an unwarranted continuity—one that applies old tools to new situations, interprets new signals as part of established patterns, expands existing programs rather than replacing them, and opposes new thinking and the prospects of change—is counterproductive and may indicate the influence of vested interests on the policy process.[30] After all, one of the core insights of scholarship on vested interests and national security policy is that seemingly irrational or at least inefficient policies from a national standpoint are often desirable from the parochial standpoint of powerful government agencies.[31] In a chess metaphor from Graham Allison, "the black rook's move might contribute to the loss of a black knight with no comparable gains for the black team, but with the black rook becoming the principal guardian of the palace on that side of the board."[32] Parochial and national interests are not necessarily incompatible, but when they clash, the parochial imperative is likely to predominate. The most demonstrable case of such distortion, as well as the most theoretically puzzling instance of policy from perspectives other than that of parochial interest, is the propagation of rivalry in the face of more salient threats, including particularly a common foe.

The first task for a parochial interest theory is to explain how organizations develop both their attachment to particular policies and their ability to protect those policies in the decision-making process. In *Myths of Empire,* Jack Snyder identifies an inverse relationship between the power and motive of cartelized groups to achieve excessively expansionary imperial policies.[33] Although this contradiction may fade in stable rivalries that impose fairly low costs on the rival states, we still need to explain how self-interested narrow groups come to dominate policymaking in a particular issue area. The second task is to identify conditions under which major policy change is most likely, given the dominance of vested interests. For Snyder, as for theorists of the democratic peace, this means exploring national capacities for overpowering the parochially interested groups; for me, it involves investigating the possibility of redirecting the vested interests of state agencies onto new missions in order to permit leaders to achieve international rapprochement. Thus, the goals of this chapter, which I address in sequential sections, are to identify the origins and consequences of state agencies' parochial interests in rivalry, to specify observable and testable implications of parochially driven rivalry, to explain interest realignment through the emergence of alternative missions and resource constraints, and to assess the limitations of the argument.

State Agencies, Vested Interests, and the Reproduction of Rivalry

In this section, I outline a three-step process through which initial conflicts between states create self-sustaining rivalry (figure 2.1). First, conflict provides a policy problem which is distributed to government agencies in the form of missions. Missions bring parochial benefits for those agencies, including budgets, political power and prestige, and autonomy. Second, benefits alter the incentive structure of agencies, becoming ends in themselves that should be defended (though not necessarily expanded or maximized), creating a vested interest. Third, agencies act to protect their vested interests in the continued flow of benefits by opposing successfully any policy change—particularly rapprochement with the rival country—that would threaten the mission from which the benefits are derived. In short, rivalry is path-dependent, displaying positive feedback between international conflict behavior and the power and prestige of pro-rivalry agencies.[34] After walking through this process of vested interest creation and rivalry maintenance, I turn to additional observable implications of this theory, using the logic of principal-agent models, and later present arguments about how to break out of this situation of policy stasis, virtual veto by the bureaucracy over presidential reform initiatives, and protracted rivalry.

International conflict—whatever its initial cause—tends to develop missions for state agencies.[35] Whether there is a particular issue dispute, a general insecurity

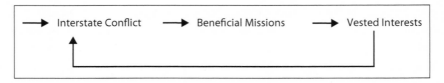

Figure 2.1. Rivalry maintenance

over the international distribution of power, or some other cause of conflict, national leaders are likely to designate the adversary country as a significant policy problem and to assign this problem to agencies of the national government for response.[36] Complex policy problems will usually be "parceled out" to multiple agencies, leading to "considerable baronial discretion" for the agencies involved.[37] This parceling of missions does not necessarily entail a clear, reasoned directive from the president in a cabinet meeting after deliberation of options. Rather, the assignment of missions related to the adversary may develop organically, as diplomats protest against the adversary's behavior, military commanders mobilize frontier units, and each side reacts to perceived provocations by the other. While presidents might prefer a coherent, productive policy, in practice government agencies often act independently to define and address what they perceive as their portion of a policy problem in the short run, often in overlapping and redundant ways.[38]

Mission creation inhibits future policy change, for several reasons. First, as veto player theories argue, the greater the proliferation of individuals or groups capable of preventing an agreement unless their demands are met, the lower the probability of major policy change, all else being equal.[39] Second, missions produce standard operating procedures within agencies. While these procedures are useful for stabilizing decision making and reducing uncertainty, they also change (for better or worse) an agency's incentives in favor of keeping the missions to which they are now "wedded" and which give them an "action-channel" with increased political power for future policy negotiations.[40] Thus, the more an agency depends for its core benefits on a particular mission, the more resistant to change its attendant procedures will be. Furthermore, the initial arrangement of tasks affects the policy process for subsequent decisions regarding the rival country. Not only are agencies unlikely to change their own missions but also they will fight attempts by outsiders to change them, and will usually succeed.[41] Third, as C. Wright Mills explains, other players leave the field: although part of conflict maintenance can be explained by the self-interested "thrust" of elite groups (like the state agencies I examine), much of it also comes from an overarching "drift" characterized by leaders' sequential attention to problems and by a generalized public apathy about foreign affairs, which cedes much of the decision-making terrain to the state apparatus.[42] Finally, and most importantly for my argument, missions create vested interests by distributing benefits along with responsibilities.

Missions provide benefits for the agencies to which they are assigned, thus creating vested interests. The most obvious parochial benefit is financial resources, both in absolute terms and the form of budget share. Although these resources are intended by national leaders as means to an end (agencies' implementation of tasks to fulfill assigned missions), they become a powerful motivation for the agencies that receive them. Bureaucracies are driven at least as much by the need to maintain "organizational health" as by the "formal mandates," constitutional and legal, intended to define their roles.[43] Of course, agencies care about several factors beyond budgets, such as public prestige, internal political power, and behavioral autonomy.[44] These benefits are often mutually reinforcing. When national leaders and the public perceive a policy problem as important, they correspondingly grant prestige to the agencies tasked with addressing that problem. Additionally, as agencies develop both real and perceived expertise on that class of issues, their views on policy in related areas gain influence over decision making, and thus the agencies gain political power.[45] Given their expertise and the importance of their tasks, agencies have an excellent argument that national leaders should grant them both autonomy (i.e., that other organs of government should not interfere with their operations) and sufficient resources to continue their work.[46] The symbiosis between all of these benefits is clear in William Niskanen's claim that the majority of a bureaucrat's objectives, such as salary and professional reputation, "are a positive monotonic function of the total *budget* of the bureau. . . . For these reasons, budget maximization should be an adequate proxy even for those bureaucrats with a relatively low pecuniary motivation and a relatively high motivation for making changes in the public interest."[47]

Agencies generally act to protect their benefits. This requires defending their mission against any threatening policy changes; in the context of rivalry, this means preventing rapprochement. In short, once missions create vested interests, these reinforce the rivalry that produced the mission in the first place. As in other areas of public policy, programs tend not to be cut, primarily because they develop self-interested defenders.[48] This does not mean that agencies will support escalating the rivalry, though: mission maintenance is not the same thing as the fabrication of crisis or war. Although national leaders may have reasons to prefer cooperation with the rival country, state agencies with vested interests in rivalry are likely to have both the motivation and the ability to oppose rapprochement. As with the origins of conflict, many different factors can incentivize international cooperation, such as common economic interests in expanding trade that would make both countries better off.[49] Even without such factors, leaders might prefer to dismantle rivalry solely to redirect the resources to new policy areas that rivalry would otherwise drain away—a classic guns-and-butter tradeoff. Whether redistributing these resources is the central goal of presidents' cooperation initiatives or merely an indirect result, the expected consequences are the same for the agencies presently benefiting from rivalry: the loss of parochial benefits. The prior decision to assign agencies to prepare for conflict with the rival inhibits the likelihood of cooperation at a later stage: one should not assume that "organizational options . . . can be created without also raising the probability that those options will be exercised."[50] That leaders might focus on national problems while agencies focus on parochial interest exemplifies the bureaucratic politics axiom, "Where you stand depends on where you sit."[51]

For vested interests to achieve their preferred policy outcomes, they need to be stronger than groups with opposing policy goals. If parochially interested pro-rivalry agencies constitute a hawk coalition within government, will they overpower dove groups? The main factor inhibiting the emergence of a powerful dove coalition is an asymmetry of motivation. Because of the prior enactment of rivalry, hawks have concentrated interests in maintaining conflict and the political power to back up their position, while doves have much more diffuse interests in rapprochement.[52] Groups with concentrated interests tend to win such policy debates.[53] I expect that the shift in national priorities—expressed as a distribution of benefits including budgets, autonomy, and influence, as discussed above—following the initial episodes of conflict will alter the domestic balance of power decisively in favor of hawks, who can put those benefits to use in future contests with their political opponents. Even though many prospective dove agencies might anticipate future gains from defeating the hawks and redistributing the hawks' former benefits, they would still have to consider the costs and risks of opposing the hawks and the distribution of gains after the fact among all the dove groups. A dove coalition would be likely to form only if its members could be assured that they would gain the bulk of the benefits. In terms of budget share, if the surplus resources from ending rivalry were redistributed across a spectrum of national budget policies or removed altogether through lower government spending across the board, individual agencies might not be able to overcome the free-rider problem of insufficient incentive to organize a dove coalition. As Jack Snyder observes, the diffuse costs of empire and the diffuse benefits of refraining from imperialism account for the usual absence (or at least weakness) of anti-imperialist coalitions.[54] In the following section, I examine some observable implications of this conflict between presidents and powerful vested interests over the implementation of policy towards the rival country.

Diplomacy and Principal-Agent Relations: Sabotage and End Runs

If this model accurately describes the process of rivalry maintenance, what behaviors should we observe in the conduct of diplomacy between the rival countries? What does the conduct of foreign policy look like in a rivalry affected by parochial interest? The logic of principal-agent models, frequently employed in studies of the relationship between bureaucracies and other political actors, suggests two behavior patterns within the conduct of diplomacy that should occur in rivalries driven by parochial interest—sabotage by state agencies of presidential rapprochement attempts and end runs around those agencies by presidents and their personal envoys.

These predictions of sabotage and end runs diverge from the expectations not only of realists but also of proponents of other theories of rapprochement that assume a unitary state (or at least that policy outcomes ultimately align with the expected behavior of a unitary state), who would predict routine diplomacy in rivalry. By "routine," I mean that diplomatic interactions between the two states, particularly on the issue of prospective rapprochement, will display two main characteristics: good-faith communications both with the rival and with national leaders at home (i.e., the opposite of sabotage) and the direct involvement of the bureaucratic hierarchy, particularly at the ministerial or vice-ministerial level (i.e., the opposite of end runs). Although realists do not assume that bureaucratic politics (or domestic politics more broadly) does not occur, they expect that the outcome of pulling and hauling over particular policies usually conforms to the national interest.[55] Additionally, studies that incorporate domestic politics in the analysis of rivalry usually argue that public nationalism, perhaps channeled through the legislature or the media, constrains any cooperative moves by the executive.[56] Routine diplomacy should characterize relations under rivalry for these theories as well.

Principal-agent models shed light on the clash of power and preferences within the executive branch of the government that is at the core of a parochial interest explanation of rivalry maintenance and support my predictions of sabotage by the bureaucracy and end runs by presidents and their envoys. Illustrating this approach, Amy Zegart and Peter Feaver employ principal-agent frameworks to show the power of national security agencies—civilian bureaus as well as uniformed service branches—to thwart presidential initiatives that would encroach on their parochial interests.[57] However, applications of principal-agent models to national security and diplomacy have tended to restrict unduly the menu of options available to both the principal and agent. Research on principals and agents in domestic public policy likewise suggests that we need a richer understanding of bureaucratic noncompliance.[58] Perhaps as a result of the predominant application of these models in economics, where the principal is usually an executive and the agent a manager, they tend to assume that the principal's task is to monitor compliance or impose sanctions to create incentives for the agent to work unsupervised and that the agent seeks above all to minimize his efforts and outputs under the constraints of sanctions and monitoring.

However, presidents implementing foreign policy have an additional option perhaps not available to heads of companies: they can appoint alternative agents or implement their agendas themselves, employing what I term "end runs." Additionally, by overlooking substantive policy preferences on the agents' part, such models tend to underestimate the potential breadth and depth of bureaucratic resistance to presidential policy change initiatives, and they tend to conflate sabotage with mere shirking. In the field of American politics and domestic policy, however, John Brehm and Scott Gates add an important dimension by allowing agents' preferences to vary across policies. When agents support a policy, they are likely to work even without supervision, but when they oppose a policy, they are likely to sabotage it, even if the sabotage takes just as much effort as working would have required; only when agents are indifferent and unsupervised is shirking likely to predominate.[59] This helps to explain real-world instances of overcompliance: the professional devotion, zeal, and vocation felt and practiced by many government employees including teachers, soldiers, police officers, and environmental regulators. Again, the effects of bureaucracy on policy, while systematic and consequential, are not always negative. I do not assume that bureaucrats are lazy or corrupt but merely that they are self-interested and that, although though they value the public interest, they are generally inclined (for reasons of prior self-selection into a given agency and socialization once having entered it as well as of prospective career advancement incentives within the hierarchy) to view the national interest through the prism of their parochial interest. A corollary of bureaucratic and military possession of expertise is that presidents generally lack it; it follows that state agencies are likely to receive periodically what they see as incorrect orders and to disobey these.[60]

Agencies have a variety of means to defend their parochial interests through opposing policy change, ranging from lobbying to coups. In lobbying, agencies have an advantage given their information monopolies and professional specialization, which enables not only the ability to recommend among policy options but also the power to set agendas, to define the realm of acceptable alternatives, within their area of expertise.[61] Agencies can also lobby indirectly by seeking allies in the legislature, elsewhere in the bureaucracy, or the public at large to counterbalance instructions from above. Thus, civilian control of the military (or presidential control of other agencies) does not necessarily mean that such agencies are entirely deferential on matters of policy.[62] However, national leaders are frequently resolute in their positions; if lobbying is unsuccessful, what options does an agency have left? The first option is to support the president's initiative: to "work," in principal-agent terms. At the other extreme, a coup is a possible response, but only as a "nuclear option," since coup attempts are risky for the perpetrators, and even when they succeed they can deeply destabilize the country and the perpetrators' parochial interests. Besides, not all agencies have equal coup-making capabilities, and not all countries have similar levels of historical precedent or public support for the possibility of a coup.

If a president is determined to push rapprochement, I expect a pro-rivalry agency to take an intermediate strategy to preserve its parochial benefits, neither working, fighting back openly through a coup, nor even "shirking" but rather actively sabotaging the proposed policy change. Sabotage sounds violent, or at least destructive toward infrastructure and property, but Thorstein Veblen explains that it should be construed more broadly, to include "deliberate malingering, confusion, and misdirection of work" and "tactics of friction, obstruction, and delay," pithily captured by the labor-activism concept of "conscientious withdrawal of efficiency."[63] Furthermore, Veblen argues that sabotage should be stripped of its derogatory connotation, since slowdowns or restrictions of production are perfectly natural, self-interested behavior not only for workers but also for firms seeking to restrict output in order to drive up prices, countries imposing tariffs to restrict competition, or governments levying taxes or prohibitions on consumption of goods or services they deem undesirable.[64] Sabotage in the industrial setting, and still more so in the bureaucratic one, is likely to be nonviolent, consisting more of slowing down production than of destroying the infrastructure and machinery of production.[65] In other words, bureaucratic saboteurs interfere with the operations of the policy machinery that it is their task to oversee.[66]

Sabotage is a useful tool for "weak" agencies (foreign ministries, for example) without direct monopoly control over the machinery of state violence that affords the leverage of threatening a coup against the head of government.[67] Such organizations can subvert cooperative policies by fouling up interactions with their counterparts in the rival country, by leaking information to the public, and simply by stalling, all while formally remaining compliant with instructions and retaining allegiance to the existing structure of authority and the national leadership.[68] Even for "strong" agencies, such as the military service branches, forms of nonviolent resistance to instructions from above are frequently more attractive than outright coup threats, particularly in democratic settings with clear civilian dominance.[69] Again, patriotic and moral imperatives may undergird this disobedience (though as I have argued, government employees' sense of the national interest and of their organizational self-interest frequently coincide): as leaders sometimes authorize soldiers to take immoral actions, subordinates can make unauthorized but morally correct decisions.[70] In the context of international rivalry, where risky overtures toward rapprochement might conjure images of appeasement or surrender, self-interested bureaucratic resistance to policy change finds a convenient justification.

Finally, much of this internal conflict over policy may not need to play out overtly, since both presidents and agencies can anticipate one another's behavior and alter their own accordingly. Knowing, for example, that the military might launch a coup over a rapprochement attempt with the rival country, or that the foreign ministry might scuttle such an initiative in the implementation phase, a president is unlikely even to contemplate the prospect out loud, let alone to make the initial overtures that would lay the groundwork for cooperation. Alternatively, knowing that a president (perhaps newly elected) expressed interest either in international cooperation or in a domestic agenda that might require sacrificing other policy priorities, agencies benefiting from rivalry are likely to signal quickly their opposition to such initiatives.

What are presidents likely to do if they prefer international cooperation but face the staunch opposition of their own bureaucratic agencies (whose participation would normally be critical to implementing any cooperative overture) and if, furthermore, they are unresponsive to those agencies' lobbying and are not unduly afraid of a coup? As noted above, I expect presidents to employ end runs—secret summits, hotlines and personal communications, unofficial personal envoys, direct relations with ambassadors (of their own country and of others), public diplomacy, and other such tactics—to circumvent the headquarters and hierarchy of the foreign ministry and the armed forces. Essentially, if a principal suspects his or her agent as a likely saboteur, the natural fallback should be to appoint a different agent or to handle the assignment personally.

Presidents have a variety of symbolic communication tools at their disposal, so they might be tempted to roll up their sleeves and implement their foreign policy agendas directly.[71] However, there are many reasons to expect these initiatives to fail. Chas Freeman points out that the "substitutes" employed during a suspension of diplomatic relations "are seldom as direct, efficient, secure, and reliable as resident ambassadors and embassies."[72] Some portion of blame for the 1938 Munich disaster falls on British Prime Minister Neville Chamberlain, who "felt that the regular mechanisms of diplomacy should be bypassed" and decided to take the reins of negotiation himself (aided by new technology—this was the first time a major head of state had traveled to a summit by airplane, and it was also Chamberlain's first flight).[73] Even setting aside the risks of being manipulated by the other state, the ability of presidents to interact directly with one another is often hampered because of the guardian role of the bureaucracy. This calls for end runs such as reliance on envoys, direct communication with ambassadors and foreign leaders without the intermediation of the foreign ministry, and public diplomacy.

Historically, the use of personal envoys long preceded the development of a foreign policy bureaucracy, and the rise of that bureaucracy largely absorbed the ambassadorial function.[74] End runs resemble therefore a reversion to the premodern era of diplomacy. The few functions for which special envoys are particularly well suited include "when the subject matter of a negotiation is highly technical, represents a radical shift in policy, or is of such scope and weight as to exceed the capacity of a resident ambassador or where there is no ambassador in place."[75] The use of special envoys may be largely restricted to efforts at radical change, such as rapprochement, because the threat of sabotage by parochially interested government agencies motivates cooperation-seeking presidents to employ end runs rather than simply relying on the existing diplomatic machinery.

Personal overtures by a president, or indirect efforts through an envoy, might still run up against the brick wall of the rival state's bureaucracy. Because rapprochement initiatives face guardians within both rival states, presidents or their envoys are likely to employ public diplomacy. Inverting Margaret Keck and Kathryn Sikkink's "boomerang model" of transnational activism, public diplomacy involves national leaders using foreign publics to bring pressure on the target state.[76] However, like other end runs, public diplomacy seems to have the deck stacked against it. Negotiation scholar Raymond Cohen notes that shutting out an official ambassador or envoy is a "sure sign" of cold relations, while "going public" usually is a last-ditch sign of desperation or a cheap attempt to score propaganda points.[77] In his seminal work, Sir Harold Nicolson largely denigrates public diplomacy, conflating it with support for a target country's domestic opposition, reducing it to propaganda and lies, and arguing that such tactics aggrieve the traditional spirit of diplomacy, are most successful when they appeal to the base emotions of the masses, and are liable to backfire.[78] Although the parochial interest of government agencies makes rivalry extremely difficult to overcome, interstate rapprochement is possible, so I turn now to conditions and processes that enable leaders to achieve these rare breakthroughs in cooperation among adversaries.

Common Foe, State Resource Constraints, and the Routine Diplomacy of Rapprochement

As I discussed in chapter one, the idea that a common foe can induce effective cooperation among adversaries is a prominent but largely untested and undertheorized argument in international relations scholarship. Under the parochial interest model of rivalry articulated above, what are the expected effects of an emerging common foe on relations between rivals? Again, the analysis proceeds in three stages (figure 2.2). First, a common foe provides a new policy problem and thus a source of new missions (and by extension, a new stream of parochial benefits) for government agencies. Second, this newly created vested interest alters agencies' incentive structures, creating the potential for rapprochement. Third, state resource constraints force sharp tradeoffs among policy priorities, also creating a potential stimulus for rapprochement. In the historical evolution of a rivalry, alternative missions and state resource constraints might emerge in different sequences. A common foe might arise first, in which case rival countries might persist in their conflict for decades before an economic crisis sets in and triggers rapprochement. Alternatively, rival states might face years of hardship, perhaps exacerbated by expensive arms races, until the emergence of a common foe removes the bureaucratic obstacle to rapprochement. Neither an alternative mission nor resource constraint alone is likely to induce the agencies with vested interests in rivalry to support rapprochement; however, their combined occurrence should cause agencies to focus on the alternative mission represented by the common foe and to jettison the old mission of rivalry.

From a parochial interest standpoint, the essential aspect of a common foe is that it creates a new policy problem that will be assigned to government agencies in the form of missions. As discussed above, the top government leadership will assess the new threat, determine some policy responses in military, eco-

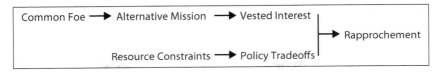

Figure 2.2. A path to rapprochement

nomic, and diplomatic spheres, and then distribute these to bureaucratic orga-nizations for implementation.[79] New missions generally bring additional bene-fits for the responsible agencies, increasing their influence over the policy process. As threat yields missions, and missions bring benefits, agencies in-crease their political power.[80] Thus, organizations not only are capable of main-taining multiple incompatible missions through sequential attention but also are likely to prefer to do so when such missions arise, in order to expand their parochial benefits.[81] This is not to say that agencies invent new missions willy-nilly; organizational conservatism predominates, and the defense of existing priorities is more important than acquiring new ones. However, ceteris pari-bus, adding new and important missions to an existing portfolio is an excellent way for an agency to increase its benefits as well as to enhance its ability to de-fend the status quo and its own role therein.

The expansion of benefits is desirable in absolute terms, but is even more important in relative terms: if prestige, autonomy, power, and budgetary re-sources constitute a governmental pie, agencies seek to protect their own slices and to widen them if possible.[82] Agencies do not always prefer budgetary expan-sion at the expense of other dimensions of organizational health. However, even agencies that might prefer not to absorb some new mission are likely to do so if a competing agency in the government appears likely to take over the mission otherwise.[83] Important problems such as new and salient threats need address-ing and will bring benefits to the agencies that take on those tasks, so even agencies that do not want to expand face compelling pressure to do so. Thus, an agency's acquisition of a new beneficial mission creates a vested interest in perpetuating it, even if the agency possesses other missions involving rivalry maintenance.

Unlike with some realist and constructivist views of rivalry and a common foe, I see no inherent contradiction between old and new adversaries. Nor do I necessarily expect new threats to displace old ones: the emergence of a new com-mon threat will be insufficient, on its own, to cause rapprochement among ri-vals. Realists or constructivists might expect a state in the presence of multiple adversaries to focus on its primary threat and to find common cause with secondary foes such as traditional rivals. After all, retaining multiple sets of adversaries rather than cooperating with one against the other is at best inefficient, and at worst it endangers regime and state survival. Realist arguments are not particularly optimistic about the chances for rapprochement, however, since only a high level of common threat should be sufficient to induce cooperation.

In contrast, parochial interest argues that where state agencies derive clear benefits from addressing both new and old threats, they are likely to have the power to dictate state policy, and they will generally prefer to continue rivalry even in the face of a new and salient threat unless they are forced by economic decline to make tradeoffs among their priorities. First of all, organizations can "thrive with considerable latent goal conflict" through "sequential attention" to whichever problem is most pressing at the moment.[84] Sequential attention may produce suboptimal policy outcomes from a public interest standpoint, but it enables agencies to maximize efficiency and activity, maintaining existing benefits. This ability and inclination of bureaucratic agencies to retain independent or even incompatible missions allows countries to maintain multiple adversarial relationships rather than committing to an effective alliance against a common foe. Second, this is not simply a time lag while a state shifts its confrontational posture from one adversary to the other—realists would readily anticipate that such policy changes require time for a state to redeploy its forces, mobilize domestic resources, and reshuffle alliance portfolios. Rather, it constitutes a preference for addressing both simultaneously, where economic conditions permit. In other words, I assume that state agencies will strive to defend their existing parochial benefits and, ceteris paribus, to expand those benefits when suitable opportunities arise in the form of new missions.[85] This does not necessarily make parochial interest more pessimistic than realism, however, since I argue that even a fairly low level of new common threat might contribute to rapprochement, provided that the relevant agencies have developed new missions from that threat and that economic pressures are acute. Because agencies are unlikely to replace of their own accord the old mission of rivalry with the new one proffered by the common foe, no matter how salient that new threat becomes, a common foe is insufficient to cause rapprochement among rival states. However, the new missions do create the beginnings of a possible path to cooperation by diluting agencies' preeminent focus on rivalry.

Does it have to be a common threat that produces rapprochement, or would any two simultaneous, but unrelated, new threats to the rivals serve this purpose? Furthermore, does the shared stimulus for cooperation have to be an adversary (a traditional security threat, whether internal or external), or might some other type of shared challenge be able to substitute for a common foe? The shared nature of common threat is important for two reasons. First, the expectation of some degree of burden sharing with the rival allows agencies to make the argument that they can address the new threat efficiently. Second, when rivals face separate threats, there might be a strong suspicion that the rival state is secretly in league with the new threat.[86] Thus, the failure to cooperate against a truly common foe is deeply puzzling, and the variation in cooperative or conflictual outcomes when faced with a common foe deserves explanation.

Regarding challenge rather than foe, several of the alternative hypotheses discussed in chapter one suggest that such a path to rapprochement might work.[87] Many other researchers also argue that emerging transnational challenges such as climate change, pandemics, migration and refugee flows, and financial crises constitute threats to national security, which in turn can create strong pressures for international cooperation (although they may also create new conflicts at home and abroad).[88] Each of these challenges might offer incentives for rapprochement, but they all fall outside the scope of my argument unless they provide a clear alternative mission for the state agencies previously focused on rivalry. Shifting from one adversary to another, and even from external to internal threats, is a less fundamental shift than from defense or foreign policy to some other category of activity. However, many types of armed groups, from terrorist networks to criminal gangs to insurgencies, can pose threats to states that are likely to create alternative missions for traditional security agencies, so my argument should apply fairly widely.[89]

If agencies could be forced to choose among missions rather than simply adding the new tasks to the old, then parochial interest could be diverted away from rivalry, though not eliminated.[90] Organizations generally prefer to avoid tradeoffs or "hard choices among goals," but some circumstances may force these tough decisions and thus spur policy change.[91] Theories of learning in international relations, in areas from military doctrine to imperial strategy to alliance policy, usually emphasize the imminence or aftermath of failure (particularly, undesirable war outcomes) as the impetus for policy change.[92] In the context of rivalry and rapprochement, the most commonly cited source of learning from failure is a military crisis between the adversaries.[93] Such arguments emphasize that the unacceptable prospect of disastrous war between the rivals, as they peer over the brink, can become the functional equivalent of a common foe, prompting, for example, détente between the United States and the Soviet Union after the Cuban Missile Crisis.[94] The spiraling expense of an arms race might perform the same function: acute tension and the perception of impending unacceptable costs could force adversaries to develop ways to manage their disputes and to contain the risks of escalation. Furthermore, a learning argument could address the bureaucratic hurdles to policy change: given policy "brittleness" and entrenched resistance to change, "when rigidity leads to failure—but only then—the policy becomes unstuck and sudden reversals become possible."[95]

I agree that a situation of failure is more likely than one of success to induce policy change. However, rather than focusing on psychological mechanisms of learning, correcting misperceptions, or loss aversion, I focus on material incentives. Specifically, I argue that state economic resource constraints can force tradeoffs among policy priorities and that constraint, in conjunction with alternative missions addressing a common foe, constitutes a sufficient condition for rapprochement between rivals. A declining economy exerts downward pressure on government spending, all else being equal.[96] Although governments often try to preserve existing programs in the face of temporary economic or security crises through deficit spending and incurring national debt, these measures are often unsustainable.[97] To address structural imbalances between spending commitments and revenue, particularly when the economy is contracting, governments have to cut spending, and that means sacrificing policies.[98] Although policy change can come either from budgetary feast or famine (the former enables leaders to set new priorities, while the latter "forces major retrenchment"), comparative research on bureaucratic reform and policy termination indicates that economic downturn is more effective than economic prosperity in causing major policy shifts.[99] Economic resource constraints make tradeoffs acute and reveal the unsustainability of current policy priorities.

However, even major economic crisis is unlikely to produce rapprochement among adversaries by itself, since that would entail cutting the policy of rivalry and harming the interests of the powerful agencies that benefit from ongoing conflict.[100] A shrinking pie heightens competition for relative gains: facing budget cuts, each agency is likely to emphasize its most compelling missions to justify retaining as much budget share as possible. Without an alternative mission (and an attendant alternative stream of parochial benefits), resource constraints might even cause agencies to exacerbate rivalry, overemphasizing the threat in order to justify continuing their budgetary receipts. This parallels the logic of diversionary war theory, in which leaders facing the imminent loss of their core benefit (tenure in office) drum up international crises to secure popular support (the "rally round the flag" effect).[101] Like a common foe, economic decline offers a possible source of policy change but is insufficient on its own.

My central argument is that the combination of economic downturn and a common foe will produce rapprochement between interstate rivals. A common foe provides a potential alternative mission for the government agencies presently benefiting from rivalry, while state resource constraints force budgetary cutbacks that cause agencies to jettison the old mission in favor of the new. The new common foe is more intrinsically salient and a better justification for future resources, since dealing with new problems often requires new plans, new equipment and infrastructure, and new personnel and training. Policy termination studies show that termination efforts are most likely to succeed when they involve the simultaneous creation of new policies and significant concessions or side payments to co-opt actors disadvantaged by the death of the old policy.[102]

Why would powerful state agencies make any sacrifices, even when resources are constrained and an alternative mission is available? Again, bureaucrats, diplomats, and soldiers are generally patriotic, and their agencies are rather conservative. An agency with a single mission will usually see that mission as integral to the national interest and defend it against threatening policy changes, irrespective of the state's fiscal dilemmas. An agency with multiple missions is unlikely to sacrifice any of them unless it is forced to, and a prospering economy facilitates (without singlehandedly causing) mission expansion, organizational redundancy, and other forms of excess. However, an agency with multiple missions, in the context of serious national resource constraints, is quite likely to sacrifice an older, less politically salient mission in exchange for a newer and more attractive one. This consolidation of activity is a form of national shared sacrifice and contributes to the agency's political justification for continued power. Furthermore, to the extent that mission-related choices are made voluntarily, agency autonomy is protected. Organizations trim fat reluctantly, but they steadfastly refuse to carve themselves to the bone.

A core observable implication of this hypothesis is that, given an alternative mission and state resource constraints, rapprochement initiatives will not face parochial opposition and thus should exhibit routine diplomacy, with the bureaucracy declining to sabotage the process and presidents similarly refraining from end runs around the state apparatus. Successful rapprochement will include the substantial involvement of the foreign ministries and, at a minimum, the silent acquiescence of the armed forces. As noted above, routine diplomacy is conducted by the higher echelons of the foreign ministry; I expect that the active support of these bureaucratic elites is necessary for rapprochement to succeed. While presidents are still often needed to sign final agreements, and ambassadors will still have a direct hand in communications, the president-to-ambassador, president-to-public, and ambassador-to-public links characteristic of end runs should be much weaker, while the minister-minister, president-minister, and minister-ambassador links should be much stronger, than in failed rapprochement attempts. Also, the military should maintain a nearly single-minded focus on the alternative mission, rather than engaging in border incidents with the rival, warning ominously that the other side is going to take advantage of any concessions, or hinting at a coup.

The Limits of Parochial Interest

The central theoretical purpose of this book is to evaluate whether, how, and under what conditions a common foe can induce international rapprochement as opposed to persisting alongside rivalry among allies. The core hypothesis advanced in this chapter is that a common foe is most likely to provoke rapprochement in the context of state resource constraints, when the government agencies with vested interests in rivalry have both the motivation and the opportunity to redirect their parochial attentions to an alternative mission. In the case study chapters that follow, I demonstrate that this argument explains the pattern of rivalry and rapprochement in Cold War Latin America. Does it also offer a universal explanation of the path to peace between interstate adversaries, challenging existing interpretations of other historical cases of rapprochement? Does the argument apply beyond the Americas, in other historical eras, and to contemporary rivalries? And what could parochial interest tell us about the conduct of policymaking and international relations more broadly, beyond the context of rivalry among allies? In this concluding section, I address these potential limitations and extensions of my thesis.[103]

First, other paths to cooperation among adversaries surely exist. The potential origins of war are legion, and the causes of peace and cooperation, though far less studied, are likely numerous as well.[104] For example, the declining number of rivalries since the end of the Cold War is probably not driven by common adversaries and deserves future research.[105] Also, many historical instances of rapprochement appear well explained by other theories. Realists and constructivists continue to debate the peaceful end of the Cold War, with both sides presenting cogent and deeply documented cases.[106] Likewise, liberal arguments emphasizing shared democratic governments, economic interconnections, and membership in international organizations offer persuasive explanations of rapprochement between the United States and Great Britain in the late nineteenth century.[107] Although I argue in the following chapters that democracy was not an effective cause of rapprochement in Cold War Latin America, I make no claims about the possibility of a democratic path to peace elsewhere.

In fact, my parochial interest argument should be seen as fundamentally compatible with the democratic peace and other liberal theories that mistrust parochial groups' willingness and ability to hijack state policies on security issues for their own narrow ends and that suggest ways to subordinate these groups to elected leaders.[108] A change in group behavior can come either from a shift in relative power among factions with fixed but divergent preferences or from an alteration in the preferences of the dominant faction, with power remaining constant. The democratic peace literature has primarily focused on the former; I address the latter.[109] Presidents who prefer rapprochement, if they cannot beat their bureaucracy into submission through democratic consolidation, might be able to enjoin state agencies' acquiescence to policy change in a situation of common threat (leading to an alternative mission) and economic resource constraints (forcing acute policy tradeoffs among missions).

Second, the theory advanced in this chapter has discussed state agencies as though these were cast from the same mold in different countries and historical periods. This assumption should be interrogated before testing the argument in case studies, since the real institutions of government vary so widely.[110] There are good reasons to expect parochial interest to distort conflict behavior outside Latin America, and we should not assume that other classes of countries, such as advanced industrial democracies, are institutionally immune to these sometimes pernicious dynamics. For example, during the Cold War, the United States and the Soviet Union both experienced the buildup of bureaucratic organizations with vested interests in national expansion and bipolar rivalry. Although democratic institutions may have helped the United States to learn and retrench from strategic blunders and to resist the pull of statism, both learning and resistance were incomplete, uncertain, and uneven across time.[111] Scholars often consider the United States a relatively stateless society, but the state-building effects of security missions, and their empowerment of bureaucratic actors in the policy process, have had very real effects even in this case.[112] However, the apparatus of the state has unquestionably evolved over time, may still be changing, and emerged in different ways in different regions of the world.[113] The politics of end runs and sabotage, principals and agents, might look quite different in these different contexts, suggesting a few potential scope conditions of my argument. For instance, a focus on the bureaucratic trappings of the modern state may not apply well to premodern rivalries, such as the imperial struggles between the French and English monarchies, the empires of Rome and Carthage, or the city-states of Athens and Sparta.[114] Also, to the extent that the prototypical modern state is declining (as even advanced industrial countries increasingly delegate their authority to intergovernmental networks of civil servants, outsource government functions including combat operations, and devolve several aspects of global governance to nongovernmental organizations and a nascent global civil society), the contemporary relevance of the argument decreases.[115] And even within the modern era, parochial interest may not explain well the foreign policies of countries that lack many attributes of stateness but remain formally independent thanks to the agreement of great powers on global norms of self-determination and sovereignty.[116]

Third, parochial interest dynamics likely affect a range of other conflicts and policy decisions beyond the scope of this book. The argument so far has touched on rivalry between non-allies (for instance, observing that the absence of an alternative mission for state agencies constricts the prospects for rapprochement), but what about alliances between non-rivals? If the missions of the alliance filter into the state apparatus and create organized vested interests, these in turn might act to maintain international "special relationships" beyond the threat or provocation that initially brought states together. Parochial interest could thus offer an alternative explanation for cooperative relationship persistence—even, for instance, among NATO member states—other than threat levels, collective identity, or joint democracy. And it would present a perhaps necessary, though certainly insufficient, explanation for the deepening of cooperative relations after the initial rapprochement. In each of these areas, a parochial interest perspective would encourage a research focus on failed attempts to change those relations (to push for neutrality or abrogation of alliance, for example) in comparative perspective. I hope that scholars of domestic policy reform, foreign policy change, imperialism, and civil-military relations will find my work as helpful as I have found theirs. Although parochial interest arguments should have broad import for the study of the international and comparative politics of policy change in general and conflict resolution in particular, their persuasiveness depends upon the strength of evidence within a necessarily limited area of research.

In this book, I concentrate on interstate conflicts in Cold War Latin America: a set of relationships among developing countries in one region in the second half of the twentieth century. Working outward from this core, rather than inward from hypothetical limits of the argument, I should account for causal factors outside my theory that might contribute to the pattern of parochial interest and rivalry I explore. In particular, the political prominence of the armed forces across history in most of Latin America needs to be addressed. Although I maintain that part of this comes from a feedback loop between rivalry behavior and parochial benefits, interstate rivalry is clearly insufficient to explain the full extent of military authority in Latin America.[117] Three factors—in addition to regional rivalry—seem particularly important for the development of the modal pattern of Latin American civil-military relations during the first century of national independence.

First, the highly unequal structure of the domestic economy, primarily a legacy of colonial rule, in much of Latin America produced an alliance between the military and the ruling economic elites.[118] However, by the time of the Cold War, the modal Latin American armed forces had acquired a degree of professionalism and autonomy, which they vigorously defended against perceived civilian encroachment, and were not a mere tool of the oligarchy.[119] Over time, as elites empowered armed forces to suppress labor unrest, to quell regional rebellions, or to pacify the frontier, these agents of "order and progress" developed their own corporate interests and acquired increased bargaining leverage.[120] Second, the geographical challenges to state-building, especially the construction of borders during both the colonial period and the early independence years, left an internal frontier—vast, underpopulated, autonomous, and often racially distinct from the capital region—for the larger Latin American states. The forcible incorporation of these lands and peoples provided a critical stimulus for state-building and, concomitantly, the development of parochial interests and power by state agencies. In particular, Argentina's "Conquest of the Desert," Brazil's suppression of the Contestado and Canudos rebellions, and Mexico's wars against the Yaqui and other northern tribes all built the state apparatus, and the political role of the military therein, more than any international conflict did.[121] Third, foreign powers shaped the course of Latin American statebuilding. European military missions and arms sales helped build the Latin American armed forces in the nineteenth century, and for that matter, many of the officers in the armies and navies of independence were foreigners.[122] Meanwhile, external military interventions, increasingly but not exclusively by the United States, provoked Latin American defenses but also constrained political development. By coddling dictators the United States and other great powers often fomented revolution, by castigating reformers they frequently prompted reactionary coups, and through incessant interference and economic domination, they damaged state sovereignty and the prospects for democratic rule.

Although these historical experiences surely influenced Latin American states' national security policymaking processes during the Cold War, they do not make Latin American cases completely distinct from the rest of the developing world. We can draw useful, if limited, generalizations from the history of conflict and cooperation in Cold War Latin America to other regions, especially to rivalries among developing countries with at least a minimal state apparatus that has not yet been consistently dominated by democratic rule. Thus, one of the strongest indicators that a pair of countries should follow the pattern described in this chapter is the state of civil-military relations. Where government agencies, particularly but not exclusively the armed forces, are not stably subordinate to the policy preferences of the titular head of state, I expect that such agencies will have the motive and opportunity to perpetuate rivalry for their own ends. In more abstract terms, for the principal-agent relationship to operate, there needs to be a meaningful distinction between principal and agent, and there has to be a reasonable expectation that agents' behavior (to say nothing of preferences) will not conform systematically to principals' instructions. Twentieth-century rivalries not addressed here, but which fit this description, might include Greece and Turkey, India and Pakistan, and the intra-Arab conflicts. For such rivalries within the anticipated scope conditions of parochial interest, my argument should be accountable to the results of future studies by area experts. Thus, I examine in chapter six the prospect that the common foe of Islamist terrorism and insurgency might induce rapprochement among interstate rivals in the contemporary era.

My central hypothesis is that the combination of a common foe and state resource constraints will produce rapprochement between international rivals, while the absence of either of these will cause rivalry to continue. The parochial interest theory outlined in this chapter points to the macroeconomic limitations that force policy tradeoffs and to the alternative missions to which government agencies turn for sustenance in conditions of resource shortage. In addition to testing how well these factors explain the variation in outcomes of rivalry or rapprochement in my cases as against the explanatory power of the alternative arguments outlined in chapter one, I also look for an intermediate behavioral change, the shift of diplomatic conduct from sabotage and end runs to routine diplomacy. In the chapters that follow, I explore the unsteady balance in Cold War Latin America between the imperatives of regional rivalry and hemispheric anti-Communism, and I demonstrate that the latter mission only fully displaced the former under conditions of local insurgency and macroeconomic duress.

CHAPTER THREE

Antagonism and Anti-Communism in Argentine-Brazilian Relations

Nothing more censurable and strange than that two Heads of
State would exchange letters, about foreign policy, above and
without the knowledge of the diplomatic channels.

—*João Neves da Fontoura,*
former foreign minister of Brazil, 1954

In the case of Brazil-Argentina, the social character of relations is
especially important. What we find is a long history, not of
Hobbesian conflict, but rather of recurrent rivalry and conflict,
often with military overtones, combined with periods of cooperation. . . . Alongside the recurrent fears and suspicions, the
post-war period saw a number of previous moves to cooperation. . . . This is in itself something of a puzzle.

—*Andrew Hurrell, 1998*

Argentina and Brazil, the two largest countries in South America in terms of territory, population, and economic might, maintained a strategic rivalry from independence until 1980.[1] From territorial disputes and two wars in the nineteenth
century to conflicting hydroelectric energy projects and nuclear ambitions in the
twentieth, competition dominated the relationship. Meanwhile, leaders frequently
proposed regional economic integration schemes and united political fronts,
which routinely failed. In the 1980s, however, the two countries coordinated
sweeping changes to policies from commerce to nuclear research. They produced
166 bilateral accords that decade, matching the preceding half century's total and
more than tripling the yield of the century before that.[2] Rivalry, the central feature
of Argentine-Brazilian relations for centuries, had been overcome definitively.
The political breakthrough of rapprochement paved the way for strategic alliance

and regional integration: Mercosur, a customs union established in 1991, is now the fifth-largest economic bloc in the world. This transformation, a watershed in the history of Latin American foreign relations, has been gaining attention in international relations scholarship.[3] However, most of this research addresses the deepening of cooperation in the 1980s and 1990s rather than uncovering the roots of rapprochement in the late 1970s and the causes of an inflection point from protracted rivalry to more than three decades of cooperation.[4] This chapter therefore addresses a fundamental puzzle: Why didn't Argentina and Brazil cooperate sooner? More specifically, why did presidential summits in 1947, 1961, and 1972 fail to overcome rivalry, while those of 1980 succeeded?

A political cartoon in the Uruguayan newspaper *El Diario*, commenting in 1980 on the second Argentine-Brazilian presidential summit of the year, captures the stark change in the bilateral relationship from rivalry to cooperation. In it, Argentine President Jorge Videla and Brazilian President João Figueiredo calmly share a gourd of *yerba mate*, a tea indigenous to the borderlands their predecessors had contested since the imperial clashes between Spain and Portugal. The caption, in verse, uses *"mate"* to indicate both competition and friendship, playing on a second meaning ("checkmate") to suggest a transition from chess match to teatime:

> United, for it is their will,
> Go Argentina and Brazil.
> They ratify fraternity
> Meeting on a second date;
> The two forget their rivalry,
> And in this actuality,
> There is *"mate,"* but not checkmate:
> *"mate"* for a friendly tea.[5]

The cartoon's tranquil and lighthearted tone is particularly remarkable because the two leaders headed military regimes with a history of repression. Additionally, its place of publication underscores the transformation of regional politics, since small states like Uruguay had long feared Argentine-Brazilian cooperation (which had almost completely annihilated Paraguay in the 1860s War of the Triple Alliance) and often sought gains from maintaining their competition.

To explain this moment of transition, we also need to explain why rivalry persisted until that point. By the end of World War II, Argentina and Brazil had perpetuated their rivalry for nearly a century since their last war against one another and for a half century since resolving their final outstanding territorial

dispute.[6] Unlike some rivalries, Brazil's and Argentina's persisted at a low sim-
mer without boiling over into acute crises and wars, offering several lessons
about the dynamics of protracted conflict.

Rather than outright violence, two central mechanisms reproduced rivalry
over the decades: the "hypotheses of conflict" maintained by the two countries'
military high commands and competition for regional influence (particularly
in the smaller neighboring states of Uruguay, Paraguay, and Bolivia, though
also in dealings with other countries, including the United States), which was
carried out primarily by the foreign ministries.[7] Rivalry manifested not in
bloodshed but in the planning and preparation for potential warfare and in the
execution of conflict by diplomatic means. These missions provided parochial
benefits, including budgets, political prestige, and organizational autonomy,
for the state agencies that carried them out, creating vested interests in continued rivalry.[8] This chapter's four case studies of bilateral summits trace the
long road to Argentine-Brazilian rapprochement, one on which presidents, pursuing regional cooperation for security and development, confronted, circum-
vented, and finally co-opted the entrenched and powerful opposition of these
groups.

A series of disputes provided fuel for rivalry, from territorial issues in the
nineteenth century to alignment questions in the two world wars to nuclear and
hydroelectric power projects in the 1960s and 1970s. The most important dispute during the Cold War involved competing hydroelectric dam projects on the
Paraná River (which touches Brazilian, Paraguayan, and Argentine territory)
and other tributaries of the River Plate. Hydroelectricity became increasingly vital for industrial development, and major public works demonstrated regional
prestige. Moreover, the geography and topography of the dam sites raised issues
of national sovereignty and security. In particular, upstream projects had serious
ramifications for the downstream countries. Brazil's position, as an upstream
country, was that each state had the sovereign right to use the resources in its
territory, and it began developing a joint hydroelectric power project with Paraguay, eventually known as Itaipú. Downstream, Argentina passionately argued
in both regional and global forums that international rivers are shared resources,
the exploitation of which requires prior consultation of affected countries and
assurances that upstream developments would not harm them. Argentina also
had technical concerns, since it could not begin construction of its proposed Corpus dam (also a joint project with Paraguay) without confirmation of Brazil's plans
for Itaipú's height and number of turbines, which would affect downstream water
levels. Furthermore, there were geopolitical fears: Argentine leaders worried that

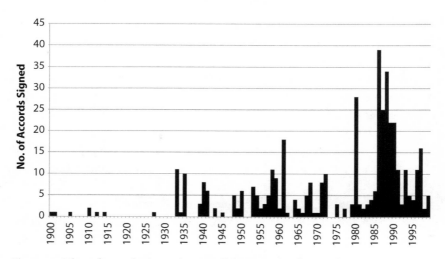

Figure 3.1. Bilateral accords, Argentina-Brazil, by year signed, 1900–1999.
Source: Compiled from Argentina Ministry of Foreign Relations, http://tratados.cancilleria.gob.ar/
busqueda.php, accessed in 2011

Brazil could use Itaipú to flood Argentina's Mesopotamian northeast, devastating its agricultural economy and endangering its population.

However, Argentine and Brazilian leaders met repeatedly, roughly once a decade, to seek bilateral cooperation on a range of common interests from economic development assistance to border infrastructure, from cultural exchanges to counterterrorism. In fact, one of the most striking attributes of the Argentine-Brazilian relationship is the trail of wrecked attempts at bilateral cooperation. Recently, several authors have revisited this record, identifying particular cooperative episodes as predecessors of Mercosur.[9] Presidential summits, in particular, are momentous occasions that present opportunities for significant policy change. They also offer researchers important negative cases for comparison with successful ones, and they yield troves of valuable documents including memoranda, speeches, and diplomatic cables.[10]

The summits of 1947, 1961, 1972, and 1980 produced strikingly different results.[11] Figure 3.1 shows the number of new treaties signed each year between Argentina and Brazil, an approximation of the increase in bilateral cooperation over the previous year. Some of the major spikes are associated with presidential visits (1961 and 1980), but there are also instances of temporary increases in cooperation in the absence of presidential meetings (1953 and 1968) and of presidential meetings without large spikes in cooperation (1947 and 1972).[12] Also, 1978 is the last year on record without at least one new treaty: The 1979 Tripartite Accord that resolved the hydroelectric disputes and the 1980 watershed of reciprocal presidential visits launched a new era of peace, cooperation, and integration.

Competing Arguments, Comparing Cases

How well do the realist, constructivist, liberal, and parochial interest arguments discussed in the preceding chapters account for this pattern of success and failure of rapprochement attempts during the Cold War? Parochial interest correctly predicts the outcomes of all four cases, while the bandwagoning argument and the identity spillover claims each predict three out of four. At the other end of the spectrum, the democratic peace argument gets only one case correct, and the norm promotion hypothesis strikes out altogether. In between, the common threat and counterrevolutionary alliance arguments correctly predict two of four.

To what extent did the common threat of Communism enable the military governments of Argentina and Brazil to transcend rivalry at the end of the 1970s? Why did this common foe, a clear theme in inter-American relations since the 1940s, not produce success in earlier Cold War attempts by Argentine and Brazilian leaders to achieve rapprochement? The core argument in this chapter is that the alternative security mission of anti-Communism only displaced rivalry when the postwar economic expansion faltered in the late 1970s, leading ultimately to the debt crisis of the following decade. The combination of mission and constraint best explains why Argentina and Brazil achieved rapprochement in 1980 and not before—the common threat of leftist insurgency, by itself, was insufficient for cooperation. Specifically, the emergence of leftist guerrilla groups at the end of the 1960s, the oil shocks of the 1970s, and human rights pressures from the United States beginning in 1977 combined to induce the Argentine and Brazilian armed forces and foreign ministries—the key proponents and beneficiaries of rivalry—to accept the rapprochement that presidents had sought for generations.

Argentine and Brazilian annual rates of economic growth, and total foreign debt, from 1945 to 1990 (figure 3.2), suggest the importance of macroeconomic conditions for rapprochement. Although growth rates fluctuate, particularly for Argentina, the most important observation is an upward trend from 1945 to the mid-1970s and then a general decline for the next decade and a half. Although analysts commonly peg the beginning of the Latin American debt crisis at August, 1982, when Mexico defaulted on its foreign debt, the origins of the crisis date to the 1973 OPEC oil shock, which hit the fuel-importing nations of Latin America squarely in the balance of payments. Even though Brazil and other Latin American countries managed to sustain (lower) growth for the rest of the

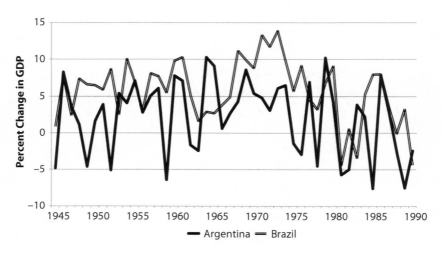

Figure 3.2. GDP growth rates, 1945–1990.
Source: Data from World Bank, World Development Indicators

decade, they funded this with the stopgap measure of foreign loans. This financial pressure pushed the bureaucratic actors invested in rivalry maintenance to accept stark policy tradeoffs and to focus solely on the internal mission of anti-Communism.

The first realist claim looks to a heightened common threat: in Cold War Latin America, the shift from nominal to actual threat involved the emergence of leftist guerrilla groups and the escalation of ideologically polarized political violence. Common-threat arguments are compatible with the failure of rapprochement in 1947 and 1961, prior to the spread of insurgency. However, the failure of the 1972 summit, after the guerrillas emerged in Argentina and Brazil in the late 1960s, strongly undermines this hypothesis. Furthermore, by the time rapprochement succeeded in 1980, the guerrillas (and thereby the common threat, overinflated as it might have been) had been effectively wiped out. If the two countries had overcome rivalry while ramping up their internal security missions, the common-threat argument would gain credence (see figure 3.3 for the annual number of disappearances in Argentina and of torture accusations in Brazil). However, because cooperation emerged after the threat had diminished, a parochial-interest emphasis on the ongoing (albeit less violent) countersubversive missions in supporting rapprochement seems superior.

The next realist argument concerns shifts in relative power. It contrasts Argentina's decline from wealth and prestige before World War I to pariah status by the early 1980s with Brazil's relative success in casting off the mantle of under-

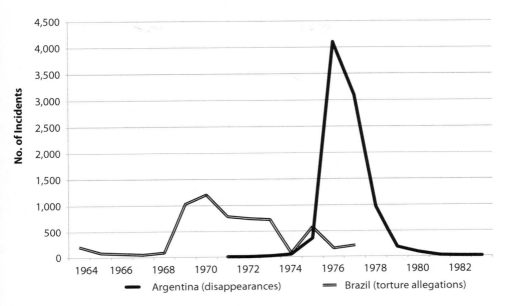

Figure 3.3. State repression, 1964–1983.
Source: Data from Wolfgang Heinz and Hugo Frühling, *Determinants of Gross Human Rights Violations by State and State-Sponsored Actors in Brazil, Uruguay, Chile, and Argentina* (The Hague: Martinus Nijhoff, 1999)

development and becoming a rising power by the late 1960s. This argument seems congruent with the failure of cooperation during a period of relative parity in 1947 and 1961 as well as the success of rapprochement after decades of Brazilian expansion and Argentina's inability to catch up. However, the lack of rapprochement in 1972 after years of robust Brazilian economic expansion is hard to reconcile with a bandwagoning thesis. Furthermore, despite a growing power disparity, Argentina stubbornly refused to perceive itself as a weak state until after the Falklands/Malvinas War in 1982, after rapprochement had succeeded, and the success of rapprochement in 1980 had at least as much to do with the Brazilian experience of absolute decline as with Argentine recognition of falling behind relative to Brazil.

Constructivist identity-spillover arguments look to a self-reinforcing process of cooperation between two countries, one not dependent on outside actors. In Cold War Latin America, governments created numerous subregional institutions for dispute resolution and collective action on common goals from infrastructure projects to intelligence sharing. By 1980 the governments of Videla and Figueiredo were embedded in a host of shared institutions, including the clandestine subregional security pact of Operation Condor. Conversely, the lack of institutional ties in 1947 may have contributed to the failed summit between Eurico Dutra and Juan Perón. However, the 1961 and 1972 summits are more troublesome. Many of the organizations present in 1980 had already been created by 1972 by the bureaucratic-authoritarian regimes (especially the Argentine-Brazilian Council for Economic Cooperation—CEBAC—and the periodic meetings of chancellors of the Río de la Plata countries, which also included Paraguay and Uruguay). And in 1961, the Argentine-Brazilian cooperation attempt followed years of regional diplomacy for development cooperation, including the Latin American Free Trade Association (ALALC) and Brazilian President Juscelino Kubitschek's Operation Pan-America. Furthermore, if Operation Condor produced a common identity that led to rapprochement, why did it take so long to emerge, why was Brazil such a reluctant participant, and why did the program's creator, Augusto Pinochet's Chile, nearly go to war with an equally enthusiastic partner, Videla's Argentina?

For norm promotion, the US government certainly acted as a norm entrepreneur, advancing ideas of collective security after World War II, National Security Doctrine in the 1960s, and human rights in the late 1970s. However, this is a completely unpersuasive account of the four summits and their outcomes. Perón and Dutra were on board with hemispheric security and the Truman administration's Rio Treaty agenda in 1947, Arturo Frondizi and Jânio Quadros strongly supported Kennedy's Alliance for Progress in 1961, and Alejandro Lanusse and Emílio Médici earned Nixon's backing in 1972, but all three summits failed. Conversely, Videla and Figueiredo delivered rapprochement while vehemently protesting Carter's opposition to their human rights practices and nuclear programs. In fact, the consistent divergence between Argentine-Brazilian relations and the relations of the United States with both countries might suggest that US opposition rather than US entrepreneurship unintentionally aided rapprochement (a point I address below).

Liberal claims take two main forms. First, a democratic peace argument suggests that rapprochement will be most likely when both countries are governed by liberal democratic regimes (or, more minimally, democratizing ones), thanks to a combination of improved signaling abilities, common identity, and externalization of pacific conflict resolution norms. This hypothesis might expect rapprochement to occur under elected governments in 1947 or 1961, or not until the more truly liberal democratic governments in the 1980s, rather than when it actually occurred, under repressive military rule. And although one can argue that Figueiredo's Brazil was already beginning to democratize before the 1980 summits, this cannot be said of Videla's Argentina. Democratic peace arguments would, however, correctly estimate the difficulties faced by the military leaders in 1972.

Finally, a counterrevolutionary alliance argument focuses on shared concerns with the ideological threat of Communism. Leaders focused on extirpating Communism from the hemisphere, and particularly military officers who had trained to oppose leftist subversion, should cooperate with one another. Although rapprochement did ultimately succeed under military rule in 1980 and fail under elected civilians with populist sympathies and restive officer corps in 1961, military officers (though elected presidents) and sincere anti-Communists Perón and Dutra failed to achieve rapprochement in 1947, and Generals Lanusse and Médici, both heading military regimes, failed to cooperate in 1972.

Assessing the rough congruence of each argument with the pattern of the four cases suggests that parochial interest seems superior to the alternatives. The economic contractions of the late 1970s, in conjunction with the ongoing missions of counterinsurgency even after the peak threat had been eliminated, appear to be the essential causes of successful rapprochement in 1979–1980 as opposed to the earlier efforts. However, a tougher test, and a more persuasive narrative, requires analysis of documentary evidence from the countries under study. In the four case studies of presidential summits, I present several types of evidence: scholarly sources from both countries, participants' memoirs and published government records, and documents from the foreign ministry archives of both Brazil and Argentina.[13]

Perón and Dutra, 1947: Damn the Torpedoes

The May 1947 summit between Presidents Juan Domingo Perón and Eurico Gaspar Dutra is one of the more obscure and perplexing cases of attempted cooperation in the long Argentine-Brazilian relationship. Both presidents were staunchly anti-Communist army officers, and both had been democratically elected, but despite a litany of proposals from trade to security and a broad array of common regional interests, no breakthrough was reached, and rivalry continued. Existing scholarship either overlooks this meeting or attributes its failure to international factors (particularly the United States) or to individual ones (such as the presidents' personal incompatibility, reinforced by their advisors' mistrust). Instead, parochial interest reveals the critical role of state agencies in perpetuating rivalry and sabotaging rapprochement. Rivalry between Argentina and Brazil after World War II, counterproductive for the two nations and no longer justified by any serious threat of war, benefited parts of the state apparatus, particularly the armed forces and the foreign ministries, enhancing their prestige, political autonomy, and budget share. To protect these benefits, state agencies routinely obstructed any attempts at rapprochement, while presidents attempted end runs around this blockade through personal contacts, summits, and envoys. The case proceeds in three sections: first critiquing existing perspectives on the failure of rapprochement, then outlining the historical context and consequences of the presidential summit, and finally analyzing documents from the Brazilian foreign ministry archives that indicate institutional, rather than individual or structural, opposition. In particular, I follow up on what Brazilian scholar Amado Luiz Cervo calls the "diplomacy of obstruction" in which cooperative initiatives by presidents and ambassadors were "torpedoed" by foreign ministries and other domestic groups.[14]

Contending Explanations for the Absence of Cooperation

The 1947 summit is surprisingly understudied, given the interest of scholars in Argentine-Brazilian relations and the prehistory of Mercosur. For example, the fourteen-volume *Historia General de las Relaciones Exteriores de la República Argentina* records that "the Dutra government tenaciously opposed Perón's project of re-floating the ABC bloc" (a vision of political cooperation and economic integration between Argentina, Brazil, and Chile) but does not mention the 1947 meeting between Dutra and Perón.[15] And yet the meeting was hardly a secret, since both *Time* magazine and the *New York Times* reported on it (though briefly and with apparent boredom).[16] Even basic facts about the event are still disputed: one Argentine analyst claims that "numerous accords" were signed but that these were never ratified by Brazil, while another argues that "the meeting did not translate into the signing of any agreements" but "acted as a positive antecedent for the pursuit of rapprochement" later on.[17]

Among works that do address the summit and more broadly analyze postwar Argentine-Brazilian relations, explanations of rivalry persistence generally blame individuals or international forces.[18] At the international level, a common explanation for the lack of rapprochement is the meddling of a hegemonic United States in relations among Latin American countries.[19] Gerson Moura (in his evocatively titled *Alignment without Recompense*) argues that the 1947 Rio Conference bolstered US power and scuttled Latin American proposals for regional cooperation against leftist subversion in order to keep the focus of hemispheric security on the conventional threat of the Soviet Union, while American foreign aid exacerbated regional insecurity by helping Argentina re-arm.[20] Similarly, for Mônica Hirst, a "combination of differences," principally regarding relations with the United States, to which Perón's foreign policy offered a "rebellion" and Dutra's an "unconditional alignment," kept Argentine-Brazilian relations "politically distant."[21] More broadly, Iuri Cavlak argues that Argentine growth in the 1940s created insecurity in Brazil, while the ideological and political contrasts between the conservative Dutra and populist Perón regimes were insurmountable.[22]

The case also bears examination at an individual level. According to Juan Archibaldo Lanús, Perón's enthusiasm for broad cooperation contrasted markedly with Dutra's hesitancy.[23] Similarly, Miguel Ángel Scenna observes "the coldness of the contact between the two soldiers."[24] Even primarily structural accounts recognize that personality and partisanship affected the diplomacy of the period.[25] Luiz Alberto Moniz Bandeira notes that Dutra's first foreign minister, João Neves da Fontoura, "was profoundly adverse to Perón," especially after the right-wing UDN party pushed Dutra to replace him with Raul Fernandes, who was "extremely anti-[ex-president Getúlio] Vargas and pro-USA."[26] Fernandes fired the Brazilian ambassador in Buenos Aires, replacing the pro-rapprochement João Baptista Lusardo with the reliably anti-Peronist Cyro de Freitas Valle.[27] In sum, Brazilian decision makers exhibited a "political and ideological animosity against the Perón government," while "The rivalry of Argentina, in Perón's perception, was not properly with Brazil but rather with the USA"—thus, personal biases contributed to the lack of rapprochement.[28]

There are problems with both of these accounts. At the international level, although the United States did not explicitly promote Argentine-Brazilian rapprochement, in 1947 it retained close relations with Brazil while simultaneously restoring a cooperative relationship with Argentina. The Rio Conference was initially scheduled for early 1946 and postponed because the United States refused to participate alongside Argentina, but from late 1946 through 1947, the United States earnestly sought to build hemispheric solidarity against Communism and to close ranks for the possibility of World War III.[29] Internal US disagreements over how to handle Argentina seemed resolved in June 1947 when Secretary of State George Marshall fired Spruille Braden, assistant secretary for American Republics Affairs, over Braden's ongoing hostility to Argentina and the Rio Conference postponements (although no-one replaced Braden at ARA until 1949).[30] Even before this, US records indicate not opposition to Argentine-Brazilian cooperation but rather a prevailing lack of attention to Latin America. For instance, the memoirs of Undersecretary of State Dean Acheson and Director of Policy Planning George Kennan describe the spring of 1947 as overwhelmingly focused on shoring up Greece and Turkey against Communism. Between Truman's speech on March 12 and Marshall's on June 5 (launching, respectively, the Truman Doctrine and the Marshall Plan), top US officials undoubtedly overlooked the meeting between Perón and Dutra in May.[31]

At the individual level, if Dutra was pro–United States and anti-Perón, it is not clear why he agreed to meet with Perón in the first place. Dutra's predecessor (and successor) Getúlio Vargas apparently never publicly agreed to a presidential summit, despite having a much greater affinity with Perón. Furthermore, why did two Brazilian foreign ministers with different partisan affiliations, Neves da Fontoura (closely linked to Vargas) and Raul Fernandes (strongly opposed to Vargas), take essentially the same stand against cooperation with Argentina? Why did Dutra keep a pro-rapprochement ambassador (Lusardo) in place upon taking office, and why did that ambassador's replacement (Freitas Valle) wind up advocating Argentine-Brazilian cooperation despite being appointed precisely because of his partisan leanings in the other direction?

A parochial interest argument, situated at an intermediate level of analysis and concentrating on state agencies, particularly the foreign ministries and the armed forces, helps resolve many of these puzzles. Although individual preferences and international influences affect the timing, intensity, and prospects for success of rapprochement attempts, a crucial determinant of decision makers' stances on rapprochement or rivalry is their institutional position. Especially, presidents are likely to take a broad view of the national interest and generally to favor overcoming sterile and counterproductive rivalries, and ambassadors in the field are likely to recognize and support opportunities for cooperation (and to be employed by presidents for precisely this purpose). Meanwhile, the senior officials of the foreign ministries and armed services are likely to strenuously oppose such cooperative overtures.

The Summit: Context and Consequences

The 1947 meeting between Perón and Dutra fit into the restructuring of regional and global order after World War II and the onset of the Cold War. In particular, the regional defense conferences at Chapultepec (Mexico, February–March 1945) and Rio de Janeiro (August–September 1947) established collective security arrangements between the American republics and the foundation for cooperation against common threats (initially the Axis powers, then the Soviet Union, and finally, in the 1950s, the prospect of leftist insurgencies).[32] Brazil had staunchly supported the United States since 1942 and sent an army division to fight in Italy for the Allies, but Argentina only declared war on the Axis on March 27, 1945 (in time to be eligible for UN membership, but too late to participate in the Chapultepec defense talks).[33] The Rio Conference, intended as a sequel to Chapultepec, had initially been scheduled for October 20, 1945, but was repeatedly delayed, and US relations with Argentina were extremely difficult in the immediate postwar period.[34] Perón won the presidency in part by rhetorically running against US interventionism (in the person of Spruille Braden, ambassador in Buenos Aires before his promotion to assistant secretary), but toned this down once in office; by August 1946 the Argentine congress was debating ratification of the Chapultepec treaty. Brazil advocated Argentina's reincorporation in hemispheric institutions, and the meeting between Perón and Dutra in May 1947 was closely connected to the upcoming Rio conference.

What did the summit cover, and what did it achieve? Beforehand, Brazilian Foreign Minister Raul Fernandes announced that the summit would address the date of the hemispheric conference of foreign ministers as well as a range of regional policy issues.[35] The two presidents untied a ribbon to inaugurate a bridge over the Uruguay River, with much pomp and an embrace, naming it after former Argentine President Agustín Justo. Afterwards, Perón and Dutra met privately, and "it was believed they discussed trade policies, Pan-American relations and Communist infiltration in the continent."[36] The bridge had been built two years earlier, "but Brazil and Argentina are South America's most powerful rivals, and many reasons of state had been found to delay the formal inaugural," as *Time* put it.[37] They also discussed the potential for jointly mediating the Paraguayan civil war, which had been running for eleven weeks, before the August Rio conference.[38] Meanwhile, the two foreign ministers met separately (and agreed to discuss further a bilateral treaty on hydroelectric power), as did the president of the Argentine Central Bank with Brazilian economists to finalize a bilateral trade agreement.[39] The summit seemed to end positively: Dutra announced, "The future will reveal the importance of today's meeting, which will be a landmark for true Americans," and Perón proclaimed it "a continental event."[40]

However, the meeting accomplished little in terms of building cooperation, let alone rapprochement, except for the symbolic significance of having occurred at all. As *Time* reported, "Brazil's press had almost nothing to say," while the mediation proposal "stalled" and a trade agreement "stood where it had before—on the shelf."[41] Furthermore, Dutra faced domestic opposition to any opening with Argentina. Three weeks after the summit, in a secret session of the Brazilian Chamber of Deputies, leaders of two major parties accused Perón of promoting "imperialistic policies" in and beyond Paraguay and raised concerns about the undefended state of Brazil's borders (which troops from both sides of the Paraguayan conflict had apparently crossed repeatedly) and the prospects of an Argentine attack.[42] Were these protests legitimately caused by international factors, or did they reflect personal and partisan agendas? An Argentine invasion was highly unlikely, but the individual explanation has a lot of merit: the protest came from UDN leader General J. A. Flores da Cunha (supported by Pereira Silva of the PSD), a lifelong political enemy of João Baptista Lusardo, the ambassador who had laid the groundwork for possible rapprochement (Flores had actually challenged Lusardo to a duel back in 1922, when both were small-town politicians in Uruguaiana).[43] An institutional argument, however, suggests that connections between state agencies and political parties work both ways—Flores was an army general and a co-partisan of Raul Fernandes, the foreign minister, so the congressional protest against cooperation with Argentina could be influenced by executive branch interests just as much as the actions of executive decision makers like Fernandes could reflect individual political commitments. Perón, in a much stronger political position domestically than his Brazilian counterpart, soon expressed frustration and mistrust of bureaucracy to carry out cooperative overtures. Calling in March 1948 for a "San Martín-ian" foreign policy, Perón proposed personal diplomacy, the interlinking of interests, and bilateral accords, explaining, "I believe that the time has passed for holding conferences, speeches, and lunches in foreign ministries, because this road leads to nothing."[44]

Tracing Torpedoes in the Archives

To understand why more was not accomplished, I turn to the archives, particularly to communications between the Brazilian embassy in Buenos Aires and the Brazilian foreign ministry in Rio de Janeiro. When João Baptista Lusardo arrived in Buenos Aires as the Brazilian ambassador in June 1945, he waxed rhapsodic about the prospects for rapprochement. After a meeting with then–Vice President Perón, President Farrell, and the foreign minister, Lusardo relayed back to Itamaraty (the Brazilian foreign ministry) his florid declarations of "collaborating with ardor in the maintenance of the old and traditional policy of ample and sincere friendship" and his call for "a solid system of understanding, that will permit putting aside the distrust by chance still existing between the two countries, as a vestige of the past military preoccupation."[45] According to Lusardo, both Perón and Farrell "approved of my words," and Perón explained that he wanted "to arrive at a broad understanding with Brazil, in which practical realizations will be studied that would solve the military problem and would come to facilitate and coordinate our commercial, political, and cultural relations."[46] However, Itamaraty swiftly shot down this optimism: "I submitted the issue to the President of the Republic who told me that it would have been preferable that Your Excellency, who was summoned, would have listened in first place to what the Argentines wanted to say. . . . Your Excellency preferred to take the word and speak in first place."[47]

Lusardo tried to set a date for a meeting between Perón and Dutra, and Itamaraty's opposition to rapprochement is clear in another rebuke he received, in October 1946: "according to instructions that I gave verbally to your Excellency here [a] date for the encounter between Presidents Dutra and Perón should not have been mentioned,"[48] and since the meeting's principal purpose was to inaugurate the already-constructed bridge, "it is not convenient to give the encounter other political and historical significance beyond that which it has and it is without doubt of great importance."[49] The foreign ministry recommended following the already-agreed program "without the signature of treaties . . . but solely visits to buildings related to the bridge."[50]

In January 1947, Lusardo expressed a detailed optimism about the upcoming summit, "to which I referred in official communications to that Ministry and in letters to the President of the Republic."[51] This is important from an institutional perspective: Lusardo communicated not only with his superiors in the foreign ministry but also through a separate channel to Dutra. Such back-channel diplomacy between Perón and Getúlio Vargas, with Lusardo as one of several intermediaries, caused a scandal in 1954 that brought impeachment proceedings against Vargas (unsuccessfully, although coup rumblings shortly thereafter contributed to his suicide) and terminated the prospect of a pact between Argentina, Brazil, and Chile.[52]

After several delays, the summit was scheduled for March, with an extensive agenda. Perón, according to Lusardo, "awaits that opportunity" to develop accords with Dutra on "various issues of common interest" including border traffic and hydroelectric developments.[53] Lusardo related that Argentine Foreign Minister Juan Bramuglia spoke to him "with much insistence" about "very elevated proposals" regarding the Rio conference, the bridge, the summit, a border transit accord, and hydroelectric projects at Iguassu Falls.[54] A further issue concerned implementing a 1946 trade treaty under which Argentina would export wheat to Brazil in exchange for fabrics and machinery. Lusardo reminded Itamaraty that "after so much struggle, the Argentine-Brazilian points of view were well articulated" in the 1946 treaty and urged the "practical execution" of the accord.[55] Lusardo's continual promotion of historic breakthroughs contrasted with Itamaraty's admonishments not to give the summit more importance than necessary.

Because Lusardo, who had helped arrange the presidential summit, was removed as ambassador in February 1947, an individual-level explanation for the lack of bilateral cooperation is tempting (Lusardo's replacement, Cyro Freitas Valle, arrived in April and actually participated in the meeting). Freitas complained that his predecessor continued to intervene in Argentine-Brazilian relations: "For the fourth time in the last 3 months Mr. João Baptista Lusardo arrived here yesterday," and according to a trusted informant "my predecessor has already managed to convince the governmental circles that I am [an] enemy of Peronism."[56] Freitas may not have been an enemy, but he clearly mistrusted Peronist designs, writing to Foreign Minister Fernandes that "the attempt at Peronist infiltration in Brazil is so dangerous for the relations of the two countries."[57]

Lieutenant-Colonel Mario Gomes da Silva, a Brazilian trade official, after visiting Buenos Aires in the wake of the presidential summit, confirmed both Lusardo's interventionism and Freitas Valle's suspiciousness while taking an intermediate position. Gomes noted that Freitas had warned him in advance that "I would be dealing with a rude and arrogant person" (Mr. Miranda, in charge of much of Argentina's economic policy), but "happily, however, the predictions of the Ambassador were not confirmed. D[om] Miranda remained within gentlemanly limits," courteous and deferential.[58] In Buenos Aires, Gomes was approached by Baptista Lusardo, who wanted to play a role in trade negotiations with Argentina, but "I declared frankly to the ex-ambassador of Brazil that the Brazilian Government would not permit intermediaries in that negotiation, with which he fully agreed."[59] Finally, Gomes observed, "It is not a proven thing, the friendship of Gen. Perón for Brazil, but the fact is that" Perón prevented Argentine newspapers from attacking Brazil or its leaders even though Brazilian papers frequently attacked him.[60]

At the international level, although it is hard to sustain the argument that the United States worked to undermine Argentine-Brazilian rapprochement, the same is not necessarily true of other Latin American countries.[61] According to the Brazilian ambassador in Santiago, the Chilean minister of foreign relations "did not dissemble his apprehension" about an upcoming meeting between Perón and the president of Bolivia, noting, "He has the impression that Argentine imperialism begins to decline although it still represents ponderous factors of possible complications, being convenient that we, Brazil and Chile, be attentive and use the utmost caution in our relations with Argentina."[62]

One critical document for evaluating and explaining the limited achievements of the presidential summit is a confidential letter from Freitas to Interim Foreign Minister Hildebrando Accioly, just three days after the summit.[63] Five main points in this memorandum support a thesis of institutional sabotage that explains the failure of rapprochement not only in May 1947 but also in the surrounding postwar period of Argentine-Brazilian relations. First, Itamaraty in general, not merely one minister or one ambassador, opposed the summit in the first place, and during the summit the ministry pursued victory in negotiation rather than bilateral cooperation as such. Freitas wrote, "That encounter was not in this moment pleasing to Your Excellency or to Mr. Raul Fernandes, nor to me. But, to fulfill the promises previously made, this had to be done."[64] Later, he observed the "personal triumph of Mr. Raul Fernandes on pulling out of Mr. Bramuglia the integral participation of Brazil" in Argentina's proposed hydroelectric developments. Similarly, when Bramuglia seemed amenable to Brazil taking the lead on mediation in the Paraguayan civil war, Freitas mistrusted Argentine motives: "So many and such sizable concessions (this is what it seems to me) will not have been made here without seeking something in return." However, the Argentines were not moving against Brazilian interests but rather "almost timidly" seeking US and regional recognition before the Rio Conference as well as Brazilian support in that regard. Although this issue was unresolved at the summit, both Brazil and the United States supported Argentine participation at the Rio Conference, so this cannot have been an obstacle to rapprochement.

Second, the visit exposed a far greater degree of common interest than is commonly recognized. The foreign ministers' hour-and-a-half conversation produced "a *tour d'horizon* that can only have surprised one or the other for the amenity with which it was done and for the harmony that it revealed."[65] The ministers discussed several issues, "arriving at agreement regarding each one of these," and later "the blessing of the heads of state was obtained" on those agreements. The presidents, too, found common ground: "The most active participation of the Heads of State in the meeting was concerning communism. The opinions of Their Excellencies on that issue almost coincided." The absence of serious disagreement between two countries with a history of rivalry, on a host of issues from trade to regional security to physical infrastructure for transportation and energy, is remarkable. It strongly suggests that the absence of cooperation in the years that followed cannot be blamed on structural conflicts or individual reluctance but rather is attributable to a concerted campaign to derail a developing relationship that seemed almost inevitable at the summit.

Third, the concrete issues discussed but not resolved at the summit (on cross-border traffic and the potential for joint hydroelectric projects) were delegated to the foreign ministries, presenting a clear opportunity for obstruction.

Several proposals brought by the Argentines "remained without greater difficulty, in agreement with the telegraphic instructions from Your Excellency, left to be negotiated here by the normal diplomatic channel," and Freitas requested new instructions on each of them. Miranda pushed vigorously to sign a trade agreement at the summit, but "with fineness but firmness, Mr. Raul Fernandes made him see that accords of such character demanded in Brazil the participation of we ourselves of Itamaraty, which has the right of decision in that respect."

Fourth, a radical proposal by Miranda for coordinated defense spending cuts exposed a stark tradeoff between integration and parochial benefits, indicating a motive for state agencies to oppose rapprochement and defend rivalry. Miranda announced ("in the presence of two Presidents who are Generals," as Freitas noted) that "more than half of the budget of each nation was consumed in military expenditures and that it seemed curious to him to say that Brazil does not have money to buy Argentine wheat, when it is with bread that one avoids communism, in the moment in which cannons are being purchased."[66]

Finally, Freitas's last observation underscores the gap between the leaders and citizens, who supported Argentine-Brazilian cooperation, and the representatives of the state apparatus, who routinely obstructed it: "I cannot conceal a disagreeable success in Uruguaiana. Upon arrival of the two Presidents, evidently purposefully prepared, the multitude approached the official stage to present General Perón a noisy and excessive demonstration." If the momentary scene of popularity and presidential diplomacy provided a "disagreeable success" for the agencies in charge of foreign relations, then surely the stalled bilateral accords and the ongoing resistance to rapprochement should be recorded, conversely, as a quite agreeable failure.

Frondizi and Quadros, 1961: The Spirit of Uruguaiana

When Presidents Arturo Frondizi of Argentina and Jânio Quadros of Brazil met in Uruguaiana, a Brazilian town across the river from Paso de los Libres, Argentina, in April 1961, "both were aware that they were protagonizing an exceptional episode in the history of bilateral relations" that promised to end the historic rivalry for good.[67] The commonality of Argentine and Brazilian interests and the compatibility of their leaders' foreign policy positions in the late 1950s and early 1960s were overwhelming. They emphasized regional cooperation, promoted economic development, and defended the vulnerable democracies of the hemisphere—goals that frequently resonated with those of the United States.[68] Unlike their less successful counterparts in the 1947 and 1972 summits, Frondizi and Quadros reached formal and informal agreements on a range of policy issues, from boosting trade and cultural exchanges to creating a system of permanent consultation and coordinating the two countries' approaches to the deepening regional problem posed by the Cuban revolution. One Argentine historian calls the Friendship and Consultation agreement "one of the most important accords signed by our country in its diplomatic history and even in the Latin American sphere."[69] Uruguaiana arguably marked the high tide of Argentine-Brazilian cooperation between the Paraguayan War in the 1860s and the Tripartite Accord of 1979, and scholars and policymakers continue to invoke the "spirit of Uruguaiana" as a precursor to the current era of strategic alliance and regional integration.[70]

However, this cooperative spirit was short-lived, and the underlying rivalry persisted. Two headstones mark Uruguaiana's ultimate end: the military coups, in 1964 in Brazil and 1966 in Argentina, that launched an era of bureaucratic authoritarianism in South America and redoubled the competition between Buenos Aires and Brasília.[71] However, like the Alliance for Progress to which it paid tribute, Uruguaiana was effectively over long before it was officially retired. The two mortal blows came in August 1961, when Quadros resigned the Brazilian presidency, and in March 1962, when the Argentine armed forces overthrew Frondizi. Quadros's unexpected resignation endangered the already fragile relationship.[72] His successor, João Goulart, was unable to deliver more than a rhetorical commitment to cooperation, expressed with Frondizi at Galeão airport in Rio during a brief refueling stop.[73] When the Argentine armed forces ousted Frondizi, although they installed his (civilian) constitutional successor, José María Guido, rather than taking power directly (as they would in 1966), the new Argentine regime abruptly ceased any effort to improve relations with Brazil and aligned itself strictly with the United States.

The failure of Argentine-Brazilian rapprochement in 1961 is even more puzzling than in the previous case. In 1947, Argentina and Brazil shared an opposition to Communism, but Latin America did not yet face a serious Cold War threat; Juan Perón and Eurico Dutra had been elected, but both were military officers who had served in wartime dictatorships, and neither regime could be considered a liberal democracy. In contrast, in 1961 both countries had elected civilian presidents, both countries faced mounting popular unrest, and both leaders were concerned about the regional spread of the Cuban revolution.

Why did the 1961 summit not achieve lasting rapprochement, despite clear common interests, presidential commitment, and a set of accords? Existing scholarship tends to attribute the end of Uruguaiana to US pressure, or to individual leadership and regime type. In the former case, the Kennedy administration's strict application of a Cold War template to the Americas and escalation of conflict with Cuba meant that the perceived neutralist tendencies of Frondizi and especially Quadros were anathema, so cooperation between these governments to thwart Washington's regional plans presented an unacceptable threat.[74] In the latter, cooperation was a strictly personal affair: for cooperation to have endured, Frondizi and Quadros would have had to stay in office to see their plans to fruition. Some argue that Frondizi and Quadros disagreed on issues like Cuba and in particular that Frondizi rejected several of Quadros's proposals; others hold Quadros responsible for the end of Uruguaiana, since his resignation destabilized Brazilian politics and foreign relations.[75] Still others suggest that the military coups beginning in 1962 produced a political sea change, sweeping away the shaky structures both of Uruguaiana and of representative democracy; without Frondizi and Quadros in office, their shared vision was simply no longer relevant.[76]

However, foreign policy, and especially Argentine-Brazilian bilateral cooperation and regional coordination regarding Cuba, had a much greater role in motivating both Quadros's resignation and the coup against Frondizi than is often acknowledged. Reflecting on the causes of his March 1962 overthrow only days afterwards, Frondizi explained that while Peronist electoral successes had been "a spark to produce the fire," "deep economic, social, ideological, and international causes," including his "independent policy" in foreign affairs (encompassing both Uruguaiana and outreach to Cuba) drove the military to launch a coup.[77]

The story of Uruguaiana is one of domestically vulnerable presidents executing their own foreign policies, working closely with one another but earning the wrath of their own governments. Four main points support this interpretation against the alternatives. First, the regional context of the summit undermines both international and individual explanations. The United States did not torpedo Uruguaiana, since US leaders barely paid attention. Moreover, the Kennedy administration was willing to work with both Quadros and Frondizi, while Uruguaiana's emphasis on the Alliance for Progress shows that Argentine and Brazilian presidents were not trying to balance the United States or declare neutrality but rather to enhance their bargaining leverage and achieve a more valuable hemispheric partnership. Furthermore, the continuity of diplomatic efforts during the Frondizi years belies an individual argument: Kubitschek, Quadros, and Goulart pursued a similar agenda with Argentina, despite their political differences.

Second, the primary opposition to rapprochement came from the military on both sides, before as well as after the summit (and well before the coups), driven by parochial interest. The armed forces opposed rapprochement, despite leaders' anti-Communism, because they had not yet developed an alternative mission and because economic growth, industrialization, and US assistance enabled an ongoing stream of parochial benefits. Third, presidential end runs around the state apparatus demonstrate far less trust in the foreign ministries than is often assumed. Finally, archival documents support each of these points, demonstrating the extreme fragility both of Argentine-Brazilian cooperation and of the authority of its presidential champions.

Uruguaiana in Historical Context

The summit's hemispheric and bilateral contexts strongly suggest that its failure cannot be attributed persuasively either to the United States or to Frondizi and Quadros, emphasizing instead the domestic opposition that both presidents confronted. Bilaterally, the stubborn continuity in pursuit of rapprochement in the late 1950s and 1960s is remarkable. Brazilian presidents Juscelino Kubitschek, Jânio Quadros, and João Goulart all supported cooperation with Argentina, especially during the Frondizi years, despite their other political differences and even variation in foreign policy visions.[78] Two bilateral meetings provide important bookends to the April 1961 Uruguaiana summit. First, Frondizi visited Brazil as president-elect in April 1958 and met with Juscelino Kubitschek. The Argentine was "warmly received," so much so that "the new government fostered unmeasurable relations between Buenos Aires and Brasília . . . a permanent accord of both nations, deepening it to unprecedented extremes."[79] Second, Frondizi met briefly with João Goulart as president in September 1961 during a refueling stop en route to the US, to reiterate commitment to the Uruguaiana principles.

Regionally, although Frondizi and Quadros sought greater influence and coordinated their approaches to engaging the revolutionary Cuban regime, this was hardly a rejection of alignment with the Western Bloc, let alone of cooperation with the United States, but rather a quest to maximize autonomy and bargaining leverage, and with these, US economic assistance.[80] In the weeks after Uruguaiana, Frondizi denied trying to form a new bloc with Brazil, and Quadros explained that Argentine-Brazilian cooperation, "reciprocally strengthening the international position of the two countries, would likewise serve to impose respect for the principle of self-determination of peoples and to introduce a new element of equilibrium on this continent."[81] Uruguaiana was a cornerstone of what Brazilians called "independent foreign policy" (a concept that fits Frondizi's foreign policy closely as well), which was primarily oriented toward enhancing national development and improving bargaining leverage with great powers. Frondizi observed that the United Kingdom (a stalwart US ally) maintained relations with the People's Republic of China; his government sought a similar degree of flexibility for Argentina but faced domestic and international "factors of obstruction," noting that "the problem was to distinguish clearly whether Argentina was a friend or a satellite of the United States."[82]

Both Quadros and Frondizi sought domestic political benefits from independent foreign policy gestures. Argentine journalist Gregorio Selser characterized the impending Uruguaiana summit as a "leftward gambit" intended to bolster Frondizi's support among the working classes and offset their opposition to his economic policies.[83] Brazilian Foreign Minister Afonso Arinos de Melo Franco, in a secret memorandum to Quadros shortly after Uruguaiana and the Bay of Pigs, recognized that "we should not oppose the American designs regarding the condemnation of communism" (in part to avoid the instability that Frondizi faced) but recommended continued opposition to any intervention in Cuba, not only out of anticolonial principle and for international prestige but also because this stance would boost domestic popularity and enable otherwise unpopular economic reforms.[84]

US decision makers clearly tolerated Argentine and Brazilian rhetorical gestures toward neutrality as a minor irritant intended for domestic consumption, and they deemed Quadros and Frondizi acceptable partners. The week before Uruguaiana, Treasury Secretary C. Douglas Dillon met with Quadros and reported to Kennedy Quadros's bottom line: that "there was no cause whatsoever for any political difficulties between U.S. and Brazil. He said that we should understand the situation in which he came to power. He did not have a fully free hand."[85] Dillon observed that Quadros "very obviously intended to give the impression that his neutralist political activities in the international arena were designed to strengthen his position against the Brazilian left in the battle over his domestic program," concluding that although Quadros "was sincere in his professions," "the fact that he looks on foreign policy primarily as a tool to help him out with his domestic problems can make for unexpected and at times unpleasant results."[86]

Furthermore, rather than undermining Argentine-Brazilian cooperation, Washington seems to have overlooked it. The Uruguaiana summit came only three days after the Bay of Pigs debacle, and high-level US attention was focused on Cuba, the Soviet Union, and domestic fallout. The only reference to the meeting in the *Foreign Relations of the United States* collection is brief and positive: Deputy Assistant Secretary of State for Inter-American Affairs Coerr reported, "In April, Quadros joined with Argentine President Frondizi in a statement that, inter alia, praised the Alliance for Progress and urged the repelling of 'direct or indirect interference of extra-continental factors.' "[87] Frondizi and Quadros were on the same page, and US leaders did not object, so what explains the failure of rapprochement?

Domestic Opposition

Governmental, and especially military, opposition to rapprochement long preceded the summit. As Frondizi recalled, his troubles with the armed forces predated his administration and were from the beginning connected to foreign affairs. When Frondizi traveled to Brazil and Uruguay as president-elect in 1958, the Argentine military regime refused to send any uniformed escort with him.[88] Internal resistance to foreign policy decisions was clearly part of Frondizi's mental model of how other countries conducted foreign affairs as well. In an interview shortly after his 1962 overthrow, Frondizi emphasized that Truman and Eisenhower had both recognized the corporate and military dangers that presidents faced in their foreign policymaking.[89]

Even agreeing to meet with Quadros in the first place proved difficult for Frondizi, given staunch resistance to the summit in both the foreign ministry and the armed forces.[90] In an April 13 memorandum to Frondizi, Argentine Naval Secretary Admiral Clement suggested postponing the summit so that "new and serious internal commotions in the country" would not arise.[91] Given the number of serious confrontations Frondizi had already navigated with his own military, this surely read more like a warning than a suggestion.[92]

The leaders reached agreements at the summit, but they did so under a cloud: the internal opposition that would doom Uruguaiana and rapprochement was visible immediately.[93] As an Argentine scholar and diplomat observes, "The conventions of Uruguaiana raised storms in the Argentine and Brazilian military high commands and in the diplomatic bureaucracy of our Chancellery, adhered to the theory of Argentine-Brazilian rivalry since a century ago."[94] Some Brazilian scholars place the blame fully on the Argentine side and in military rather than foreign ministry quarters.[95] However, Brazilian Foreign Minister Arinos's memoirs indicate widespread domestic opposition to Quadros's independent foreign policy, including "the infiltration of North American propaganda among the higher officers of the armed forces" as well as the "decorated frivolity of certain museum pieces of Itamaraty" who wanted to maintain strict allegiance to the United States.[96]

Even at the summit itself, there were warning signs. In his memoirs, Arinos recalls that Frondizi expressed support for one of the Brazilian proposals, and when Argentine Foreign Minister Diógenes Taboada interjected, "Is the President not going to consult?" Frondizi replied, "But consult with whom?"[97] According to Arinos's interpretation of this exchange, the silent but constant and very visible presence of armed forces representatives in the room implied an ongoing need for Frondizi to submit any decisions to the veto power of the military. Afterward, Jânio Quadros confided to Arinos that "a president should never have to submit himself to this."[98]

This opposition had swift and important consequences. Under pressure from the military and the Right, Frondizi replaced the bulk of his cabinet only days after Uruguaiana, including substituting Adolfo Mugica for Taboada as foreign minister. Second, Frondizi delivered the Uruguaiana accords to the senate in August shortly before Quadros's resignation, but the senate never voted to approve them. In November, Frondizi and Goulart opted to enact them through an exchange of notes instead.[99]

Internal resistance was even more severe regarding engagement with Cuba. Uruguaiana anchored a new approach to regional relations that included a coordinated effort to engage Cuba; although the accords did not directly provoke coups or sabotage, Cuba policy seriously destabilized both governments. In particular, both presidents' (separate) meetings with Ernesto "Che" Guevara galvanized their opponents. The Argentine military nearly overthrew Frondizi after his meeting and did force Mugica to resign, requiring Frondizi to bring in Miguel Ángel Cárcano as his fourth foreign minister.[100] In Brazil, Quadros resigned the presidency only six days after meeting with Che, in part due to escalating pressure from the Right (led by Carlos Lacerda and backed by much of the military and bureaucracy).[101] The Argentine military forced Frondizi to make additional foreign policy changes, including severing diplomatic ties with Cuba in 1962. US leaders applauded these shifts but recognized the risk to Argentine stability. Secretary of State Dean Rusk wrote to the US embassy in Argentina, "We welcome foreign policy changes brought about by internal pressures mainly from military," though "continued and extreme military pressure upon government would be contrary to US interests."[102] And yet Frondizi explained that his objectives in meeting with Guevara were hardly anti-American: "Great possibilities existed that the conversation with Guevara would be very positive for the solution of the problem between the United States and Cuba and

I could not dodge that possibility," but "unfortunately the internal reaction that the visit produced annulled the possibility of attempting that road."[103]

Although Quadros may have had a freer hand than Frondizi given his electoral mandate, his resignation provoked constitutional changes in Brazil that dramatically curtailed presidential power (particularly through the creation of a parliamentary system with a prime minister), so his vice president and successor, João Goulart, faced far tighter constraints.[104] Thus, unlike Quadros, Goulart had to rely more on the bureaucracy to make and implement policy. Afonso Arinos (who became Brazil's UN ambassador after Goulart's inauguration) admitted to Rusk in September 1961 that "the President, and now also the Prime Minister, were so involved with domestic problems and administration that they left the conduct of foreign affairs largely to the Foreign Minister."[105]

Frondizi's and Quadros's foreign policies, and especially their engagement with Cuba (on which the two leaders appear to have coordinated), was a major motivation for internal military opposition and a source of political instability. However, neither Quadros's resignation nor the coup against Frondizi can be reduced to divergent preferences over foreign policy. The absence of a dominant coalition in the Brazilian congress, the split among Radicals and the resurgence of Peronists in the Argentine one, and the polarized debate between nationalist and liberal approaches to economic policy were particularly divisive problems.[106] One domestic issue is particularly important from a parochial interest standpoint: the Argentine military increasingly wanted to focus on an internal security mission, but Frondizi rebuffed many of these proposals.[107] Frondizi might have had more success in gaining military support for his foreign policy overtures, including rapprochement with Brazil, had he accepted an alternative mission for the armed forces. Facing bureaucratic and military opposition, presidents went to great lengths to recoup foreign policy autonomy by employing end runs.

End Runs

Opponents frequently accused Frondizi and Quadros of arrogance, dictatorial tendencies, and erratic decision making. However, both presidents had made extensive efforts to circumvent bureaucratic obstruction in bilateral relations and a range of other policy areas, which naturally attracted criticism from those with vested interests in existing policies. A US National Intelligence Estimate two weeks before Quadros's resignation expressed confidence in his political prospects, observing that his main opposition came from the "largely pro-US armed forces," which "probably will tolerate a considerable degree of neutralism in his foreign policy," but which bridle at his "authoritarian bent."[108] Specifically, "his determination to impose his own policies, together with his high-strung temperament, could lead to some hasty action" that could provoke a coup, particularly if he were to "reduce the special position of the armed forces, or to abandon Brazil's ties with the West, or should he take definite steps to perpetuate himself in power."[109] Later, explaining the coup against Frondizi, US Ambassador McClintock observed Argentina's political "headlessness," the extreme degree of military tutelage, and the voluminous claims of corruption, lying, and immorality leveled at Frondizi.[110]

As president, Quadros used a technique he had developed as governor of São Paulo to rule through personal involvement rather than delegation: sending instructions through *bilhetes*, or short notes, rather than formal memoranda.[111] These notes, usually handwritten, were delivered not only to cabinet ministers but also frequently to their subordinates. To ensure compliance, Quadros had his messages read on the government-run radio station (critical for reaching the Brazilian masses, especially in rural areas with low literacy rates and slow newspaper delivery), often before the physical notes reached their targets.[112] As a journalist reported, the *bilhetes* creatively outflanked bureaucratic resistance: rather than "transmitting orders that are not fulfilled, or suggestions that are not followed," they provided public transparency, "a novelty that breaks with the routine of the bureaucracy, weighty and vain."[113] The *bilhetes* to Arinos reveal, according to the Itamaraty researchers who published them a half century later, "concise and willful instructions" and "curious testimony of the conceptions of his foreign policy, of the styles of the president and his relations with the media," which provided the notes' "political relevance, mobilizing public opinion in favor of the acts of government.[114]

Quadros also employed personal diplomacy with foreign envoys, negotiating directly with the Argentines prior to the Uruguaiana summit. A March 1 note to Arinos reported a "very good" meeting with the Argentine ambassador at which the "suggestions of Itamaraty [were] accepted and put into practice" and instructed Arinos to "receive him with the desirable interest and sympathy."[115] Quadros met the Argentine ambassador again on March 17, and although he told Arinos to set the agenda, he provided not only the central theme ("increase of economic relations") but also several subtopics including "a treaty of friendship and consultation, which will fortify continental solidarity."[116] As with Argentina, so with Cuba: after meeting with Che, Quadros told Arinos to follow up on the possibility for a Cuban trade agreement, noting: "The opportunity is excellent. I saw eye to eye, in that respect, with Minister Guevara."[117] Seeing eye

to eye with the Argentine-Cuban revolutionary, even in the interest of national autonomy and development, precipitated Brazilian military opposition and contributed to Quadros's resignation. It was also a breaking point even for Quadros's diplomatic allies: Arinos recalls that although he had signed off on Guevara's visit, he was not in Brasília at the time, so Quadros bears responsibility for the summit, including the decision to grant Che a medal.[118]

Frondizi, too, employed creative end runs. First, he relied heavily on advisers outside the cabinet, prompting criticism that he was running a parallel government.[119] Interviewed shortly after his overthrow in 1962, Frondizi denied this allegation but admitted to relying on like-minded advisors, much as Kennedy and FDR had.[120] Frondizi also implemented a "second-level strategy" of placing political allies and trusted advisors in subcabinet positions where they could execute his policy goals while bypassing the formal heads of the ministries. Thus, in foreign affairs, Frondizi minimized the involvement of his four foreign ministers in policymaking. Having met with Argentine decision makers in January 1962, Richard Goodwin reported "no doubt in my mind" that Frondizi's top political advisor, Rogelio Frigerio, "is at least the second most powerful man in Argentina. . . . In foreign policy his voice is the only one that counts while Cárcano is an intelligent sincere fellow with very little meaningful influence or authority."[121]

Frondizi also engaged in personal diplomacy. In 1961 alone, he traveled to Uruguay, Chile, Bolivia, Paraguay, Peru, Venezuela, and twice to the United States, in addition to meeting with two Brazilian presidents.[122] Three years earlier, Frondizi had visited Brazil as president-elect, met with President Kubitschek and his advisors, and set up an ongoing "policy of prior consultation" that made the 1961 agreements "nothing but a coda to the policy that both countries had put into practice much earlier."[123] After Quadros's resignation, Frondizi arranged a meeting with Arinos in New York; Arinos recalls that Frondizi "authorized me to write to him directly, when I had something to tell him (a thing that I never did)," even as Frondizi worried about the "militarist threat in South America" and "the command aspirations of the armed forces" in Argentina and Brazil that "covered themselves with the anti-Communist defense."[124] Frondizi's meeting with Che Guevara, which nearly provoked a military coup (and forced Foreign Minister Mugica's resignation) when officers realized after Guevara's departure that a visit about which they had not been previously consulted had been executed on their watch, illustrates the risks of this approach.[125]

Frondizi also tried to mobilize public support for foreign policy as a presidential prerogative as against military tutelage. In August 1961, after the Guevara

visit, Frondizi painted himself as the representative of national sovereignty, asserting a "totally coherent policy" based on an "undelegatable" and "indivisible" presidential authority: "One cannot demand energy and responsibility from the government to revitalize the internal front if at the same time one tries to immobilize it and undermine it in the conduct of foreign policy."[126] And in January 1962, Frondizi emphasized that Argentine sovereignty required his continuation in office, alluded to past national heroes, cited Eisenhower's warnings about the military-industrial complex, likened the groups calling for intervention in Cuba or for his overthrow to the old imperialist powers, and pledged the "honor and life of a ruler that will not ever preside over a titular government."[127] This speech offended military leaders, who overthrew him two months later.[128]

Archival Evidence of Presidential Predicaments

Documents from the Brazilian foreign ministry archives reinforce each of these arguments. First, they detail the constraints, particularly excruciating for Frondizi, under which presidents sought rapprochement. Quadros, too, faced hurdles to cooperation: to calm Chilean concerns that Brazil was embracing Argentina too closely, Foreign Minister Arinos explained that the Quadros-Frondizi meeting took place only on the Brazilian side of the river, because Quadros had not "judged the moment propitious to solicit authorization to leave the country."[129] Shortly before the Uruguaiana meeting, the Brazilian ambassador in Buenos Aires, Aguinaldo Boulitreau Fragoso, reported "strong pressure from the Army and from conservative groups" for Frondizi "to take measures against the alleged penetration of extremists in the Government . . . including the exit of the Minister of Foreign Relations," indicating a renewed "hard line" in the military.[130] Among Frondizi's advisors, Fragoso "noted recently a swift decrease in enthusiasm for the projected meeting of the Presidents" due to "the existence of a prior agenda" which "would remove the liberty of the Presidents, obligating them to arrive at public conclusions over each one of the pre-established items and would presuppose the presence of numerous delegations to debate technical questions."[131] Furthermore, "Certain sectors of the armed forces view the meeting with some distrust, for having been much linked to the case of Cuba, since it was announced shortly after the conciliatory gesture of Argentina in that case."[132] The Brazilian embassy repeatedly emphasized the constraints on Frondizi's foreign policy autonomy: "the practice of presidential explanations to the Armed Forces on acts of foreign policy seems to have become 'institutionalized,'" and "the necessity . . . of obtaining approval from the Armed Forces for international acts demonstrates that his foreign policy feels itself tightly over-

seen and submitted to an authentic military tutelage."[133] Thus, "it would be a difficult task for President Frondizi to execute a policy inspired by the accords of Uruguaiana, since he does not have sufficient ballast and liberty of action to be able to conduct this country on the same course that Doctor Jânio Quadros attempted to impress upon Brazilian foreign policy."[134]

Under these conditions, presidential reliance on end runs is understandable. A February 1961 memorandum from Arinos to Quadros expresses Frondizi's urging for direct presidential diplomacy to bypass the sclerosis of normal negotiations. Carlos Muñiz, the Argentine ambassador in Brazil, had sought out Arinos to relay Frondizi's position: "So decided is Argentina that it does not need any official instrument, nor a Treaty of Consultation for these objectives."[135] Frondizi had "told him that he did not need to send notes or telegrams, instead to telephone directly to Buenos Aires and speak with the Minister or with him himself" and urged Quadros to visit Argentina, following up on an earlier conversation.[136] Brazilian leaders used similar gestures: in January 1961, Vice President Goulart traveled to Argentina and met with Frondizi.[137] And Fragoso came to the same conclusion as US observers regarding Frondizi's outflanking of the bureaucracy: "of Chancellor Mugica the same can be said that is said with respect to the Queen of England: *reigns, but doesn't govern.*"[138]

Archival records also indicate that Quadros's resignation left the foundation of Uruguaiana badly cracked and that end runs sustained bilateral cooperation until the Argentine coup. The Brazilian embassy observed Argentine doubts of Brazil's commitment to Uruguaiana, due to "instability inherent in the functioning of the parliamentary system" under Goulart and because "certain principles assented in that meeting do not count on the sympathies of the groups that had pressured with most force in the peak of the Brazilian crisis."[139] The embassy also noted possible "hegemonic tendencies of Argentina given the supposed vacuum of influence or the apparent loss of power of international gravitation of Brazil due to the renunciation" of Quadros."[140] Much of the foreign policy continuity on the Argentine side, given the ministerial turnover, depended on "persons of the President's trust" in subcabinet positions, installed under Frondizi's second-level strategy.[141] On the Brazilian side, Goulart not only met with Frondizi in Argentina in January (and again in September at Galeão Airport in Rio) but also briefly visited Buenos Aires between Quadros's resignation and his own inauguration.[142]

Again, Frondizi's encounter with Guevara was the apotheosis of these end runs. In the Brazilian embassy's assessment, the Guevara visit was an ultimately futile "maneuver" by Frondizi "to feel the reaction of the military regarding a possible reexamination of the position maintained by this country in relation to Cuba."[143] Although Frondizi's Cuban initiative sought "reconciliation between the governments of Havana and Washington" and even though the dismissed foreign minister, Mugica, swore that Frondizi had merely followed US precedent and policy, military leaders expressed "complete displeasure and their disapproval" with Guevara's visit, since "for the Argentine Armed Forces there is no third position possible between Cuba and the United States of America."[144]

Finally, the documents emphasize the effects of foreign policy on Frondizi's overthrow, and in turn, the coup's destruction of Uruguaiana. According to Fragoso, the military's motivations included "the back-and-forths imprinted on the conduct of Argentine foreign policy."[145] Itamaraty's reaction to the coup, expressed to its ambassadors abroad, was "great apprehension" at "the virtual establishment of a military dictatorship in Argentina" and suspicion "that the forces today predominant in that country do not see with good eyes the policy of rapprochement with Brazil, as conceived in the Uruguaiana accords."[146] Brazil might "be forced to maintain correct relations with the Argentine leaders, but we fear difficult days for the fraternal collaboration between the two countries."[147] Fragoso worried that withholding diplomatic recognition from the new regime could provoke the "mistrust" and "animosity" that "the Guido Government seems to have latent, for Brazil," "atrophy or annihilate the so-called 'spirit of Uruguaiana,'" and even lead to "the revival of anachronistic rivalries."[148] Notwithstanding recognition, Uruguaiana was over: in May, Fragoso reported a "definitive" statement by the new Argentine foreign minister, Bonifacio del Carril, that presented "an occidentalist profession of faith" marked by "the manifest desire of following a strictly American international course of action" and "the total omission of the Accord of Uruguaiana."[149]

Lanusse and Médici, 1972: General to General

As the two preceding cases demonstrated, elected presidents seeking international cooperation faced staunch opposition from agencies within their own states, groups with vested interests in perpetuating the status quo of Argentine-Brazilian rivalry. After military coups in Brazil in 1964 and Argentina in 1966 dramatically altered the political landscape in both countries, the shared anti-Communist struggle became a top priority for the new bureaucratic-authoritarian regimes, raising the possibility that foreign policy change might finally be attainable. However, a March 1972 summit between two military rulers, Argentine President Alejandro Agustín Lanusse and Brazilian President Emílio Garrastazu Médici, not only failed to achieve rapprochement but even set back relations through scandal and acrimony.

The failed rapprochement attempt in March 1972 is both poorly explained by existing theories of rapprochement and generally overlooked or misinterpreted in the historical literature. From a theoretical standpoint, the lack of cooperation is puzzling, since the Argentine and Brazilian governments faced real threats from leftist insurgent groups (and perceived these threats as greater still), maintained kindred bureaucratic-authoritarian regimes, and received normative encouragement from their mutual ally, the United States. A broad consensus among historians of Argentine-Brazilian relations reduces the 1972 failure to the fallout from an ill-chosen remark, a gaffe by President Lanusse involving two phrases seemingly inserted into his dinner toast without vetting by Itamaraty, but these individual-agency accounts are methodologically questionable because of their uncritical reliance on participants' later memoirs.[150]

Instead, parochial interest offers a revisionist explanation of the 1972 case, supported by documents from the Argentine foreign ministry archives as well as on freshly declassified US government documents and published primary sources. Rivalry persisted despite a host of incentives, including common threat and shared regime type, because economic growth enabled state agencies (especially militaries and foreign ministries) to defend the parochially beneficial missions derived from ongoing international conflict.

Two sequential issues of the prominent Brazilian newsweekly *Veja* capture the stark contrast between the seemingly favorable environment for international cooperation that preceded the summit and the antagonistic recriminations that followed. Prior to the trip, *Veja* expressed optimism about its potential. For the March 15 cover story, the editorial page proclaimed "the opportunity for an accord between the two ancient and persistent rivals."[151] The main article recounted the failures of previous bilateral summits but predicted a "Future of Unity," expecting that "the two presidents know the errors committed by governments of the past and understand the opportunities lost by their peoples . . . if the future of South America depends on Argentine-Brazilian relations, it can be guaranteed that at least in the coming years this future will not be an exercise in abstract divisions."[152] On March 22, after the failed summit, the magazine could point only to the silver lining that the two countries had avoided turning the offensive verbal "shards" into a war. Had tempers flared,

Escalation was easy. Brazil would officially respond to the impertinence of the 'shards.' In turn, the Argentines would refuse to sign any joint communiqué. . . . Itamaraty would recall its ambassador. . . . Troops would be concentrated on the border and, finally, it would never able to be determined how, through fault of an accidental shot, war would begin between the Empire of Brazil and the Viceroyalty of La Plata, an old nineteenth-century dream nourished by amateurs camped on the two sides of the border.[153]

Both sides managed to avoid such escalation, but the drastic deterioration in bilateral relations and the failure of the summit seem deeply puzzling.

The case proceeds in three sections. First, I demonstrate that both countries were developing anti-Communist internal security missions during a period of plentiful and even increasing sources of state revenues. As a parochial interest argument would expect, resource availability mitigated policy tradeoffs, reducing the potential for new missions to displace old ones and making rapprochement less likely. Second, I critique existing historical interpretations of the 1972 summit's failure. Third, I offer new evidence to support a thesis of bureaucratic sabotage: published primary sources suggest that the "gaffe" was more a pretext than a true provocation, and archival documents demonstrate that prior opposition to cooperation within the state apparatus was far stronger than previously acknowledged. Overall, no amount of political will, and no degree of precision in public speaking, would have enabled Presidents Lanusse and Médici to achieve rapprochement in 1972.

In the late 1960s and early 1970s, a broad spectrum of insurgent groups (rural and urban, Communist and Peronist, Cuban-trained and homegrown) emerged in Argentina and Brazil, and they met with heightened repression from a proliferating array of state security agencies.[154] Both Lanusse and Médici came to power on the promise of restoring political order: Médici, when selected for the presidency by the Brazilian military in October 1969, was serving as head of the SNI (Brazil's national intelligence service); in Argentina, Lanusse's inauguration in March 1971 followed the ouster of two military presidents in nine months who had proven unable to respond effectively to a wave of bombings, mass protests, and high-profile kidnappings.[155] Security concerns were especially acute in early 1972 when Lanusse and Médici met in Brasília. In Argentina, the number of bombings jumped by more than 50 percent from 1971 to 1972.[156] In Brazil, the army uncovered a growing rural insurgency led by Chinese-trained guerrillas in the Amazonian hinterlands of Pará late in 1971 and began its counterinsurgency campaign (which lasted for two years and required at least

20,000 troops) on April 12, 1972, shortly after the Lanusse-Médici summit.[157] Furthermore, the Nixon administration encouraged such efforts and promoted Argentine-Brazilian cooperation to stem the tide of Communism in South America.[158] Why, then, did these expanding internal missions not lead to cooperation and rapprochement?

Parochial interest suggests that state economic prosperity enabled bureaucratic actors to retain their missions of rivalry even as they absorbed new missions of countersubversion. National economic growth had a dark side, enabling state agencies to take on new missions while defending their existing benefits against presidential encroachment. Because the peak years of Brazilian counterinsurgency coincided with the Brazilian "miracle" of high economic growth, which reached double-digit figures annually (see figure 3.3), they did not generate strong pressures for state agencies to accept conciliation with Argentina.[159] In the early 1970s, the Brazilian military regime could support its great power dreams, pursuing order, progress, and defense simultaneously. Brazil was so flush that it extended foreign aid to Bolivia, Paraguay, and Uruguay, countries in which it had long competed with Argentina for regional influence.[160] Cooperation with Argentina would have been useful to promote development, to combat leftist extremism in the region, and to establish a common front against economic discrimination by the great powers, but it would have been acceptable to Brazil only on Brazilian terms. Although Brazil was certainly outpacing Argentina, even the Argentine economy was functioning well overall during this period, growing at more than 4 percent annually, with industrial production increasing about 7 percent annually.[161] In 1972, Argentina was well into its longest postwar period without a recession; although growth rates had fallen over the previous three years, they had remained positive, and they began accelerating again over the final year of the military regime (see figure 3.3). Argentine manufacturing exports grew 19 percent a year from 1970 to 1975 (although Brazil doubled this rate).[162] Internal security operations based on the common foe of leftist insurgency did not displace interstate rivalry—rather, the absence of resource constraints prevented this tradeoff and enabled state agencies to maintain missions against both domestic and foreign adversaries.

An Avoidable Rupture? Reconsidering Diplomatic Historiography

Why did the presidential summit fail to achieve rapprochement? Secondary literature yields surprisingly few references to the 1972 summit and even fewer explicit interpretations of the sources of failure. Argentine diplomat Juan Archibaldo Lanús mentions obliquely that Lanusse visited Brazil and that at least one accord was signed, but he makes no reference to the trip's overall failure.[163] Roberto Russell and Juan Gabriel Tokatlian are absolutely right that the relationship between the Brazilian military regime and its Argentine counterparts from 1966 to 1976 was one of continued rivalry and that the turning point arrived only in 1979 "after many comings and goings."[164] The comings and goings matter a great deal, and the 1972 episode presents an important lacuna in our understanding of the tortuous path to rapprochement.

Two commonalities emerge from works that do relate the episode. First, they generally emphasize presidential agency, expressed either as the hubris or the accidental mismanagement of Lanusse's diplomacy. Second, they tend to rely rather uncritically on participants' memoirs. Two Brazilian authors of encyclopedic and well-sourced volumes claim that by departing from protocol, Lanusse ruined any prospect for cooperation—however, both refer only to the version of events in the memoir of Brazilian Foreign Minister Mario Gibson Barboza and to the text of Lanusse's speech in *O Estado de São Paulo*.[165] Argentine authors Andrés Cisneros and Carlos Escudé, in their monumental *Historia General*, suggest that Lanusse's comments may have been aimed at an audience of domestic nationalists rather than at his Brazilian hosts; their reading relies on *La Nación* and on Lanusse's own memoirs.[166] While disagreeing about Lanusse's intentions, Argentine and Brazilian scholars generally concur that the gaffes reflected his personal agency. This implies a clear counterfactual: had Lanusse remained on script, the summit would have produced bilateral cooperation and perhaps even rapprochement.

I disagree. Instead, I attribute the trip's failure to the continued emphasis by parochially interested bureaucratic and military agencies within each country on increasing their own power and influence at the expense of the national goals sought by presidents. In essence, because both the Argentine and the Brazilian economies were performing well from a bureaucratic standpoint (in the Brazilian case, extraordinarily well, at least in terms of GDP growth), state agencies on both sides refused to compromise despite national incentives for cooperation. Lanusse's misstatements make a convenient excuse for the failure of the trip, but state agencies would likely have seized upon (or provoked) any number of rhetorical pitfalls to sabotage the presidential rapprochement efforts.

Sources and Sabotage

Revisiting the memoirs casts four points of doubt on the agency interpretation. First of all, if the gaffes were an intentional move by Lanusse, either to strike a blow at Brazilian dreams of hegemony or to persuade Argentine nationalists that he was willing to do so, why did he not take credit for it in one of his several volumes of memoirs? Lanusse devotes just three pages of *Mi Testimonio* to his foreign policy strategy of "ideological pluralism" and confines the Brazil summit to one sentence; his later books, *Confesiones de un General* and *Protagonista y Testigo*, skip foreign relations altogether.[167] The one sentence we do have conflicts with our only other memoir account: Lanusse claims that the initial proposal for the trip came from Brazilian President Médici, which Gibson Barboza clearly disputes.[168]

Second, it appears that the Brazilian foreign ministry was predisposed to maintain rivalry and to mistrust any Argentine overtures. Gibson Barboza, relating the origins of the 1971 Declaration of Asunción, characterized his role in zealous terms: "I saw our diplomacy as a protective shield, behind which a great work would come to pass. It was a true diplomatic war."[169] Furthermore, Barboza states that he and President Médici were opposed to Lanusse's proposal to visit in the first place, reading in the Argentine president's regional activity an effort to encircle Brazil and undermine its hydroelectric projects.[170]

Third, the orchestration of the trip and the setting of the "gaffe" seem too clever for the statement to have been an accident, but it is hard to credit these moves to Lanusse himself. According to Barboza, Brazil was forced to accept the visit once Lanusse announced his intention to inaugurate in Brazil a new statue of José de San Martín.[171] Furthermore, the offending speech occurred in Itamaraty itself (in the new palace in Brasília, which had only been completed two years previously), and Lanusse spoke last, which by protocol precluded Barboza from replying. If the Argentine delegation were intentionally trying to provoke the ire of the Brazilian foreign ministry, this would have been the perfect setting, but the ploy with the statue and the setting of the gaffe seem quite clever moves for an Argentine president who (according to Barboza) blamed the fiasco on his lack of diplomatic skill.[172]

Fourth, it is unclear how exactly Lanusse's remarks scuttled cooperation. In Moniz Bandeira's version, Lanusse's speech "attacked Brazil . . . in a highly aggressive tone," implying a national offense; in de Mello Barreto's, the main problem was that it "left Médici irritated" suggesting a personal insult.[173] However, Barboza's language indicates that the real offense may not have been the content of Lanusse's last-minute additions to his speech but rather the fact that these violated the control of the foreign ministries over foreign policy—in other words, they posed a *bureaucratic* problem. Gibson Barboza states that the speeches "were reciprocally known, and thus had been discussed, phrase by phrase, word by word, by the chancelleries and embassies of the two countries . . . [with]

minute scrutiny," and asserts, seemingly on behalf of Itamaraty, that Lanusse "added to his speech, without our knowledge . . . if we had known beforehand . . . we might even have cancelled the visit . . . Lanusse surprised us."[174] Similarly, Barboza's stern rebuke of Lanusse's apology sounds more like opposition to rapprochement than dismay over failed negotiations—if a supposedly insulting gaffe had not destroyed the potential for cooperation, then accusing a visiting head of state of an ethical breach certainly would have.

Turning to the speech's context, a collection of published statements by both leaders during the visits reveals two indications that the gaffes were hardly the cause of rapprochement failure but rather a pretext for it. First, in his session with the Brazilian press, Lanusse made at least two strikes against the supposed spirit of amity and solidarity, either of which could have been seized on by Itamaraty. When asked what he thought of President Nixon's recent remark that "Where Brazil goes, so will the rest of Latin America," Lanusse claimed not to have been aware of the statement, but "with respect to your eventual interpretation I can say that the Argentine government only goes where the sovereign will of the people makes it."[175] Later, when a reporter asked for Lanusse's opinion on whether Brazil would accept the "prior consultation" principle in reference to the hydroelectric projects, Lanusse argued that both countries "naturally" have the right to pursue development, but he also stated his "conviction that that development should not be materialized in a way that would harm the interest of another nation or nations," referred to the rivers as "international," and seemed to challenge the Brazilian government to provide information on the possible impact of its hydroelectric projects on Argentina "as a clear and unequivocal expression of an authentic bilateral cooperation."[176] Given these statements, the "offensive" inserts to Lanusse's speech no longer seem either accidental or off message. Either Lanusse had received woefully inadequate preparation for the trip—which is unlikely, given that it was an official presidential visit to Argentina's main rival and that Lanusse was accompanied by his foreign minister—or provocation was part of the plan.

Second, departures from cooperative themes were not limited to the Argentine delegation. In his prepared speech, Médici constantly emphasized national sovereignty, which in the context of the summit is a clear allusion to the Brazilian position on the hydroelectric projects (i.e., that river resources can be exploited by the country in whose territory they lie, irrespective of problems this might cause for countries downstream). Also, questions from the Brazilian press seemed eager to entrap Lanusse as anti-Brazilian. One wonders whether these questions, which had been prepared in advance, had been pre-authorized by Itamaraty like the other texts during the visit: the Brazilian and Argentine foreign ministries had almost legendarily hand-in-glove relations with the press, making it easy to interpret several questions as having been carefully selected as weapons in a diplomatic war. In one of the starkest examples, Lanusse faced a three-part query: whether he accepted the thesis that Latin American militaries focused on internal threats because of an absence of external ones, how he would justify recent Argentine purchases of airplanes and naval ships, and whether in addition to its current tank program Argentina planned to develop other arms programs.[177] It would be difficult for any president to survive a series of such encounters without giving offense and thereby providing a pretext to abandon rapprochement.

Published primary sources offer a valuable corrective to the evasions and recriminations that often crop up in memoirs and echo in secondary literature, but a positive case for a revisionist interpretation of rapprochement failure should go further. Internal government documents from the archives, if they can be obtained, often provide starker assessments (and should be considered, all else being equal, more authoritative evidence) of preferences and expectations since they were not intended for public consumption.[178] A declassified telegram from US Ambassador to Brazil William Rountree a week before the summit, for example, expresses pessimism about the potential for rapprochement. Although Rountree argued, "It is clearly in US interest that Brazil and Argentina should play as effective a role as possible in supporting maintenance of Bordaberry and Banzer governments in Uruguay and Bolivia, and it is also desirable that they should if possible cooperate in such efforts," he saw prospects for cooperation as weak:

> Most serious problem is Brazilian-Argentine relationship itself. While fundamental relationship is better than it used to be, and relations between military and police leaders are quite good . . . Lanusse personally is disliked and distrusted by Brazilian leadership, and his visit viewed as an unavoidable distasteful necessity by both Presidency and Itamaraty . . . we seriously doubt that this would be the forum to kick off genuine cooperation.[179]

US documents also reveal information about Brazilian and Argentine intentions. Médici brought up the disputed hydroelectric projects with Nixon, explaining that "his greatest difficulty would be with the Argentines. He said that he intended to speak very frankly to President Lanusse when he came to Brazil.

He would speak not as President to President but as General to General."[180] Médici's "general to general" approach seems to underscore the security dimension and the importance of solidarity against Communism; while this quote does not necessarily imply confidence that the two leaders would be able to achieve rapprochement, it does suggest tolerance and even encouragement for unvarnished, blunt communications—hardly the attitude of a man who would be dissuaded from negotiations by a gaffe. Similarly, Lanusse explained to Nixon that his planned trip to China "was in line with the philosophy of the Argentine Government of breaking down ideological barriers"—international rapprochement was clearly Lanusse's central theme in foreign policy.[181]

Documents from the Argentine foreign ministry archives provide four additional observations that support the interpretation of bureaucratic sabotage as against the dominant interpretation of presidential agency. First, documents in the months preceding the trip exhibit pessimism over Brazilian intentions and the prospects for cooperation. On February 2, the director of policy of the ministry of public works complained at length about Itamaraty's "very reticent and particularly obstructionist" attitude and its having "accentuated its traditional stall tactic."[182] He concludes with respect to the upcoming presidential visit that "apparently few possibilities exist for arriving at spectacular accords with Brazil at this moment in the area of hydro resources," although a couple of limited joint declarations reaffirming prior agreements might be possible.[183] More importantly, I did not encounter a single document that anticipated a major diplomatic breakthrough for the summit—if an unforeseen gaffe had actually torpedoed cooperation, expectations of rapprochement ought to have figured prominently in the records preceding the visit.

Second, the Argentine foreign ministry appears more pro-rivalry than other agencies. One month before the summit, the director of the National Commission on Atomic Energy (CNEA) expressed his desire for a nuclear accord with Brazil, "an interest that has been manifested for several years, but which political reasons determined by the [Foreign] Ministry has postponed to the present." What "political reasons" were these? Over 1970 and 1971, the foreign ministry had explained that an accord should be delayed "until the general conditions of our relations with that country were more favorable, reserving that accord as an element of negotiation, given the interest demonstrated by Brazil."[184]

Third, the archives reveal multiple proposals for using the trip to maintain, rather than to overcome, rivalry with Brazil. A memorandum for the foreign minister from the head of the Latin America department, Hugo Boatti Osorio, concludes:

Towards the goal of capitalizing on the favorable position that has been obtained, it seems opportune to arrive at a direct confrontation with Brazil in the area in which it is possible to obtain the greatest advantages . . . it would not be inconvenient to follow through with the upcoming meeting of the Foreign Ministers and even a Presidential visit to Brazil on the occasion of inaugurating the monument to San Martín. Such meetings should not exceed their strictly formal significance, avoiding any appearance of alliance. *If such a policy were to fail, one could always provoke a bilateral confrontation* or the dispute could be referred to the meeting of the Group of Experts scheduled for October, reserving the meeting of the Intergovernmental Coordinating Committee for later negotiations.[185]

Nor does this appear to be an isolated sentiment. Writing to at least two cabinet secretaries, Rear Admiral Carlos Francisco Peralta, subsecretary of security in the secretariat of the National Security Council, argued that the trip should be used primarily as an opportunity to outmaneuver the Brazilians and that "if the conversations do not have the result that is sought, the joint communiqué could be anodyne enough to demonstrate this. Brazil being the country that made the invitation, a show of this nature would reveal that it has been Itamaraty and not Argentina who has failed."[186] State agencies not only did not expect rapprochement to occur; they actually intended to prevent it.

Can these bureaucratic preferences be connected to the actual triggering incident, Lanusse's gaffes? Ideally, archival research would uncover a draft of the speech, with the offending textual inserts handwritten in the margin, dated and initialed. The documentary record, at least on the Argentine side, does not yet afford such a smoking gun, but it does enable us to reconstruct over the weeks and days prior to the summit Argentine diplomats' abundant awareness of Brazilian sensitivity to departures from protocol and agreed-upon texts. Osorio had reported to Foreign Minister de Pablo Pardo several of Brazilian Ambassador Azeredo da Silveira's objections to recent Argentine diplomatic gestures, including "The surprising presentation of the hydroelectricity document in the Meeting of Cuenca del Plata Experts in Brasília, when the other documents had been passed on to him," which "was seeming to depart from the manifested intention of avoiding sterile discussions in the multilateral arena and progressing toward a common accord in the development of the Multinational Program."[187]

Cables from Argentine diplomats in Brazil to Buenos Aires in the days immediately prior to the visit also reflect clear awareness of Brazilian insistence on specific textual foreknowledge. On March 11, Undersecretary José María Ruda reported on the previous night's negotiations with the Brazilian delegation, noting that "serious differences are encountered in relation to natural resources and the Environment." Ruda's further analysis bears distinct parallels with the eventual "gaffe":

> The undersigned sustained a long one-on-one conversation after the meetings, on this issue with Chancellor Gibson Barboza, who expressed to me that 'in the Abstract' there can be Brazilian opposition to mentioning 'international law', but that the question would be analyzed at the highest Brazilian level with eyes on the Water issue in the Cuenca that is to say with political criterion, in accord with the moment. In such circumstances, it is not possible—he added—to accept a primitive proposal. I manifested surprise that in the area of natural resources and the environment general international law would not govern relations between the two countries. Gibson proposed to avoid problems eliminating the whole paragraph. I answered saying that I would consult. It appears premature to present formulas with divergent positions of the two parties.[188]

Later that day, Counselor Nereo Melo Ferrer, head of the Argentine embassy's Brasília section, sent an urgent cable stating that Itamaraty requested a Portuguese version of Lanusse's speech, frankly admitting, "I will proceed to effect a translation, but given the responsibility that this implies, I ask whether there already exists a version in that language."[189] These documents do not definitively demonstrate that the gaffes were intentional, but they do raise the stakes—senior Argentine diplomats, acting in good faith, should have known exactly how Brazil would see any departure from the script and should have briefed Lanusse accordingly. Alternatively, these exchanges may indicate Brazilian diplomats preparing the groundwork for an eventual complaint: by explicitly warning the Argentines about protocol, Brazil would be able to select almost any departure as grounds to scuttle rapprochement.

History, Bureaucracy, and Peacemaking

The joint declaration signed by Lanusse and Médici emphasizes three principles: "that comprehension [and] mutual respect are the necessary bases of a firm and indissoluble friendship," that there is a "contribution that falls to Argentina and Brazil in the solution of the problems of international peace and security and, in particular, of those that affect Latin America," and "that solidarity should be the constant and permanent guide in their state-to-state relations."[190] Thin protestations of friendship, however, could not conceal the absence of any agreement on the fundamental hydroelectric dispute or the complete stall in prospects for rapprochement. The summit's breakdown is hard to reconcile with the conventional interpretation of a gaffe, whether accidental or malicious, by President Lanusse; instead, the vested interests of foreign ministries and armed forces in perpetuating rivalry, enabled by economic expansion and clearly visible in the preparations for the trip, offer a more persuasive explanation for rapprochement failure.

Bestowing a medal on his Argentine counterpart Luis Maria de Pablo Pardo the day after the gaffes, Brazilian Foreign Minister Mario Gibson Barboza cryptically proclaimed, "No man of responsibility in government can ignore the great historical and geographical affinities existing between Brazil and Argentina, under penalty of not having conditions to exercise his charge."[191] The converse may reveal a more apt lesson: leaders unable to control their administrations may be unable to achieve international cooperation and therefore might be wise to refrain from risky international overtures until they have obtained the clear support of their own governments.

Videla and Figueiredo, 1980: The Turning Point

In 1980, the governments of Argentina and Brazil finally achieved rapprochement, ending centuries of rivalry. General Jorge Rafael Videla, president of Argentina, described the moment as an inflection point in the arc of bilateral relations, announcing that "between Argentines and Brazilians something transcendent just happened."[192] After extensive negotiations, the Argentine, Brazilian, and Paraguayan governments reached a Tripartite Accord on October 19, 1979, which resolved the hydroelectric dispute that had fueled rivalry for nearly two decades: an "instrument of transcendent importance," in the Argentine foreign ministry's view.[193] During 1980, Argentina and Brazil created twenty-eight bilateral accords, not only regulating hydropower but also promoting commerce and nuclear cooperation. Equally striking were the reciprocal visits between Videla and General João Baptista Figueiredo, president of Brazil. Figueiredo's trip to Buenos Aires in May, the first by a Brazilian president since 1935, was "an exceptional accomplishment" that brought "relief at the overcoming of tensions and a hope in the potential that great things would be done for the future," according to his foreign minister, Ramiro Saraiva Guerreiro.[194] Over the following decade, authoritarian and democratic governments alike continued to build stable peace, strategic alliance, and economic integration. Thus, according to Videla's third foreign minister, Carlos Washington Pastor, the "definitive opening" of 1980 has "historic transcendence" and "is fundamentally the beginning of what would later become Mercosur."[195] What drove this diplomatic breakthrough and why did it endure? What changed after the failed summits of 1947, 1961, and 1972 that enabled the presidents to overcome rivalry?

Public statements by the two presidents suggest that security concerns and economic changes stimulated cooperation but do not clarify whether or how these factors related to one another. The *New York Times* reported that Videla, in Brasília in August 1980, called for a " 'crusade' against subversion in South America, and defended the harsh rule in his country as a 'war,' " while "the Brazilian reaction was decidedly cool" and Videla "received little support" from Figueiredo, who "devoted his remarks instead to calls for the relaxation of the longtime rivalry between the two nations and for economic aid to the area's underdeveloped countries," since in Brazil, "terrorism is a concern of the past."[196] If anti-Communism or developmental needs (ongoing concerns throughout the Cold War) drove rapprochement, then why didn't Argentina and Brazil cooperate earlier? And if the two governments had divergent interests, with Buenos Aires focused on security and Brasília on economics, then how did they achieve a diplomatic breakthrough that had eluded their predecessors?

Parochial interest offers a more cogent explanation not only of Argentine-Brazilian similarities in 1980 but also of the difference between rapprochement success and the previous failed summits. Rather than the threat of subversion, which had been annihilated in both countries well before 1980, look at the ongoing mission that countersubversion provided for state security agencies; rather than the ever-present quest for development, focus on the magnitude of economic constraints facing state decision makers. This perspective identifies two epochal shifts that drove Argentina and Brazil to overcome their rivalry. First, the emergence of guerrilla groups in 1968–1970 produced the most significant restructuring of security agencies and priorities since the formation of national states in the late nineteenth century. Second, the oil shocks beginning in October 1973 catalyzed inflation, foreign debt, and an imbalance of payments while hastening the collapse of the import-substitution model of industrialization (ISI) for the worst economic conditions since the Great Depression. Under these conditions, the armed forces and the foreign ministries ceased obstructing bilateral cooperation and gave up their old missions of interstate rivalry in order to focus on the ongoing alternative mission of countersubversion. This created political space for presidents to set aside the end runs that had characterized so many of their predecessors' failed efforts and to negotiate, with the help of state agencies in both countries, a new foundation for bilateral cooperation. In short, this is a story of the divesting of the conflict's vested interests.

This argument contrasts with two alternative explanations from existing studies of the 1980 rapprochement. The first claims that the Chilean threat, and particularly the Beagle Channel crisis in 1977–1978, pushed Argentina into the arms of Brazil.[197] The second emphasizes the role of leaders' personalities: in particular, it claims that Figueiredo's childhood experience in Argentina, during his father's exile from Brazil, imbued him with a cooperative attitude toward the bilateral relationship.[198] Neither of these arguments presents a compelling account of Argentine-Brazilian rapprochement in broader historical perspective. Personal and cultural affinities were present in some previous rapprochement failures, and Argentina had maintained rivalries with both Chile and Brazil since independence despite wars and militarized crises. If anything, the conflict with Chile temporarily worsened Argentine-Brazilian relations, since Argentina prevented Brazilian trucks from transshipping goods to Chile, and Brazil retaliated by closing its borders to Argentine commerce.[199]

Additionally, both claims have timing problems. Videla began seeking rapprochement with Brazil shortly after the March 1976 coup, well before the Beagle Channel dispute escalated (when Argentina rejected an arbitration award in January 1978), and the two countries negotiated the formula for the Tripartite Accord in late 1978, before Figueiredo's inauguration.[200] In December 1978, Brazilian Foreign Minister Azeredo da Silveira noted in an interview that although the time was not right to achieve an agreement with Argentina due to "a problem that isn't ours" (an allusion to the Beagle crisis), the negotiations were proceeding well, and the basic framework for an accord already existed.[201] Three days later, when asked whether an accord would be signed before Figueiredo took office, Silveira replied: "I will make every effort for this. If this accord cannot be signed under the current government, and I hope that it still can, I will make every effort so that the next administration receives it almost completed."[202] Similarly, Oscar Camilión, the Argentine ambassador in Brasília, recalls that in 1978 "Silveira and Itamaraty, at the end of the [Ernesto] Geisel administration, were inclined to reach an accord. Thus, we had the basic text of the tripartite treaty complete, there were few modifications that were introduced later."[203] Saraiva Guerreiro notes that he and Figueiredo were able to reach an accord with Argentina so "rapidly" because "the basic facts already existed."[204]

In successive sections, I present four interrelated arguments about the shift in Argentine-Brazilian relations from the March 1976 coup in Buenos Aires to the presidential visits of 1980, drawing on documents from the Argentine foreign ministry archives. First, anti-Communism and countersubversion provided a clear internal security mission that continued well after the threat had been annihilated (by about 1973 in Brazil and 1978 in Argentina), which provided a beneficial alternative to rivalry for these agencies but clearly coexisted with it in the mid-1970s. Relatedly, external pressure over the human rights abuses committed during this mission, particularly from the United States under Jimmy Carter, enhanced solidarity between Argentina and Brazil. Thus, threat alone did not simply displace rivalry.

Second, the timing of successful rapprochement and its acceptance by the armed forces and foreign ministries in Argentina and Brazil had a significant economic component. Stagnation and decline, catalyzed by the 1973 and 1979 oil shocks, mounting external debt, and inflation forced budgetary tradeoffs in both Argentina and Brazil, reoriented both countries' foreign policies, and induced some surprising partnerships. Third, as a parochial interest argument would expect under these conditions, diplomatic behavior shifted from obstruction and sabotage of cooperative possibilities by the bureaucracy, and attempted end runs by presidents and ambassadors around this obstacle, toward "routine diplomacy" with top agency officials' cooperative participation between 1976 and 1979. Fourth, decision makers at the time recognized factors like the Chile threat and presidential personality but saw them as marginal rather than central causes of cooperation.

Internal Missions and Human Rights Abuses

Announcing a coup in March 1976, the Argentine military vowed to "continue fighting, without quarter, all forms of subversion, both open and clandestine, and . . . eradicate all forms of demagoguery."[205] For the armed forces, the coup was a logical extension of their ongoing internal security mission, swiftly proliferating from counterinsurgency in Tucumán province in February 1974 to widespread repression.[206] The new junta, the Process of National Reorganization, installed General Jorge Videla, who led the Tucumán operations, as president. Brazil had previously escalated its own repressive operations and welcomed the junta's promise of a renewed Argentine anti-Communist commitment.[207] Argentine and Brazilian intelligence services collaborated through Operation Condor, an organization launched by Augusto Pinochet's Chile, to eliminate leftists who had fled abroad.[208]

And yet the military regimes, committed to combating a common enemy, did not easily or swiftly overcome their rivalry. Rapprochement came well after the Argentine junta liquidated the insurgent threat (though repression continued) and after the United States shifted from support under Ford to pressure under Carter. Defending national sovereignty against outside critics gave the foreign ministries a prominent mission in the countersubversive struggle, as is clear in Argentine Foreign Minister Carlos Washington Pastor's recollection that "in 1978 the military action had terminated, but the guerrillas had shifted their destructive campaign abroad," linked with human rights and media groups and the "hostility of Mr. Carter toward our country."[209]

The shared struggle against leftist subversion in the region offered the two military governments a prominent cooperation opportunity. One of the first Brazilian gestures after the Argentine coup involved defense against human rights criticism. An aide-memoire from the Brazilian ambassador sought Argentine assistance in minimizing the impact of an Inter-American Human Rights Commission report critical of Brazil, an idea the Argentines welcomed because "without affecting our interests" it "would contribute to consolidating relations with Brazil."[210] Similarly, Oscar Camilión's first move in Brasília emphasized countersubversion as the centerpiece of bilateral cooperation: "I transmitted to General Geisel the special greetings of President Videla, I made mention of the intentions of the Argentine government relative to the relations with Brazil, and I referred, succinctly, to the great national priority that in these moments the fight against subversion represents," to which Geisel "expressed his hope in a swift victory against terrorism and violence."[211] Conversely, rivalry served both regimes' enemies. Camilión reported in 1977 that the Brazilian military considered rivalry "very serious. . . . They understand that some important international economic interests, like infiltrated leftist groups, work to deepen it," and emphasized "caution to prevent an irreversible escalation."[212] Internal repression continued after the Tripartite Accord: at a regional meeting of army commanders in November 1979, Argentine General Roberto Viola, Videla's chosen successor, advocated strengthening the anti-Communist focus of Latin American militaries, a plan the other delegations "accepted with great approval."[213]

However, shared concerns about subversion coexisted with rivalry rather than displacing it. Argentine internal security policy in the northeast (near the Brazilian border) indicates concern about Brazilian sponsorship of subversion: "Although currently neither conflicts nor disputes exist with respect to the border demarcation with Brazil, the Brazilian policy of expansion of its border areas is well known," involving "the population of its borderlands and the establishment of centers of border development with the support of the Armed Forces, while the 'pioneers' penetrate in the neighboring regions."[214] Videla, however, had "reaffirmed the geopolitical importance of the Argentine Northeast" as "an important element within the ambit of the bilateral relations with Brazil, which can be seen developing in a climate of understanding and collaboration."[215] Not only the natural "demographic pressure" of Brazil but also "the political pressure that impels an expansionist tendency" was particularly dangerous given the frontier's vulnerability to "illegal activities like contraband, introduction of drugs, and entry of human and bellic materiel that would aid subversion in the rest of the country."[216] This coexistence of multiple adversaries also affected Argentine policy toward other neighboring states: in September 1977, the Argentine embassy in Bolivia's annual "Plan of Action" sought "the creation of a state of dependency of the Bolivian armed forces with respect to our armed forces," to "neutraliz[e] the expansionist actions of Brazil in the sphere of the Bolivian armed forces," while also calling for "accords and the interchange of information between the armed forces of both countries towards the goal of acting in coordination on the common border, especially in everything related to the fight against subversion," goals Brazil might support.[217]

Foreign pressures over human rights abuses and nuclear development helped tip the scales in favor of rapprochement. According to Camilión, US pressure over the nuclear program "had abundant domestic implications:" "the numerous critics . . . are silenced" while "in the Armed Forces there are no two opinions about this issue and a General as conservative as Minister Sylvio Frota does not let a day pass without proffering imprecations against the United States."[218] Although the Brazilian press had been "very optimistic" prior to First Lady Rosalynn Carter's visit to Brazil in June 1977, neither Silveira nor the State Department shared this view, according to Camilión, and "deep problems remain" in the relationship while the Carter administration "maintains offensive attitude" regarding human rights.[219] Human rights pressures were critical in Brazil's decision to break its (by then largely symbolic) postwar military accords with the United States in 1978, Camilión reported.[220] Even after the United States moderated its human rights stance, relations with Brazil remained tense. Vice President Walter Mondale's 1979 visit to Brazil, although "previously acrimonious issues in the area of human rights and political system are in practice overcome," was according to Camilión "a political act of courtesy" rather than one of cooperation.[221] A year later, Camilión reported that a State Department–Itamaraty working group finally "open[ed] the horizon of bilateral relations . . . that passed through a chilling in recent years due to the human rights policy of the Carter administration."[222]

From the Oil Shocks to the Debt Crisis

For energy-importing countries, the October 1973 global oil shock catalyzed long-term structural flaws of the import-substitution model of industrialization that had dominated Latin America for much of the twentieth century. Amid the economic problems of the 1970s—an imbalance of payments, rampant inflation, and declining growth rates—Latin American governments relied increasingly on foreign loans, leading to the debt crisis and the "lost decade" of the 1980s.[223] Economic pressures created strange bedfellows in foreign affairs: most notably, anti-Communist Argentina expanded trade with the Soviet Union.[224] The oil shock's effects on Brazil were quick, significant, and far-reaching. In March 1974, Geisel (who unlike his predecessor and successor had run Petrobás, the state oil company, not the intelligence service) backpedaled in a speech on the military regime's developmental achievements, admitting "that the drastic changes which have taken place in the world scene—such as the serious energy crisis . . . have serious repercussions on the national scene."[225] Internationally, the Geisel administration's strategy of "responsible pragmatism" included courting oil-exporting states in Africa and the Middle East (condemning the policies of their opponents in Israel and South Africa, for instance).[226] However, economic crisis is not a simple cause of rapprochement. If it were, Brazil and Argentina ought to have overcome rivalry during the depression of the 1930s, during shorter crises like in 1962–1963, right after the oil shock in 1974–1975, or perhaps later, at the peak of the debt crisis.[227] Economic decline combined with an alternative mission for the agencies that had benefited from rivalry, though, is a powerful source of rapprochement.

During 1976 and 1977, Argentine diplomats reported that the Geisel administration managed to stave off major economic sacrifices despite increasing fault lines in the Brazilian "miracle." In May 1976, Ambassador Jorge Casal noted increasing criticism within Brazil of the Itaipú project's mounting costs and speculated that such concerns might lead Brazil to renegotiate its treaty with Paraguay (a situation that Argentina might exploit).[228] In July, Casal's replacement, Oscar Camilión, observed that deficit spending on public works created "a rough patch of considerable magnitude" since "the government cannot abandon the realization of certain basic projects like the hydroelectric and the nuclear, and at the same time contain inflation. This coexistence of conflictive objectives surely has to produce fissures in the heart of the administration, but its abandonment would imply, even partially, the renunciation of the current development scheme."[229] Although the situation was worrisome, Camilión expected that "the 'Brazilian model' . . . does not have to lose dynamism."[230] In October, the Argentine consul in Foz de Iguazú (who provided regular reports on the construction progress of the nearby Itaipú dam) expected Brazilian Foreign Minister Silveira to declare "that the chronogram of the Itaipú works will not alter, notwithstanding the grave economic situation of his country."[231] And in March 1977, Camilión reported that although at present "the weak area of the Brazilian system is not so much the economic and the social as the political," looking forward, "The external financial position . . . continues to be an unprotected Achilles tendon."[232]

By 1979, however, economic contraction and the debt burden caused budgetary sacrifices that impacted the operations and missions of state security agencies. Even in Argentina, less dependent on foreign oil, Economy Minister José Martínez de Hoz emphasized to Foreign Minister Pastor in January 1979 the "importance . . . for the fulfillment of the policy of containing public expenditures" of "the reduction or postponement of expenditures that by their characteristics are not considered essential" and asked for details on proposed travel, auto maintenance, conferences, and building construction.[233] In Brazil, domestic critics assailed the nuclear program as an "enormous unproductive white elephant at the cost of hundreds of millions of dollars."[234] A report by the Argentine foreign ministry's Latin America department the week before the Tripartite Accord echoes Camilión's predictions: "the deterioration of the economic situation is destined to convert itself into the grave preoccupation of the Figueiredo government in the immediate future," particularly over escalating inflation, US interest rates, and Brazilian debt.[235] A second oil shock, in 1979, exacerbated this predicament. The Argentine foreign ministry's director-general of intelligence argued that although Brazil had resolved the initial problem of fuel supply through quick deals with Iraq and Mexico (and later Iran), rising fuel costs still posed a "red-hot economic problem" that would "impose a halt to certain imports and a deceleration of domestic industrial enterprise, establishing priorities of execution."[236]

Argentine documents indicate that Brazil's foreign policy assertiveness depended on economic prosperity, while economic weakness compelled a search for new foreign partnerships. Growth, Camilión argued, had enabled the Brazilian military regime to disagree with the US on several occasions over the direction of security policy.[237] Conversely, the 1973 oil shock sharply altered Brazil's Middle East policy, including taking a pro-Palestinian stance and exporting military vehicles to Arab states in exchange for petroleum.[238] The main driver of Brazilian foreign policy change, according to Camilión in 1979, was a Brazilian economy beset by "grave crisis," particularly in the energy sector, which "creates positive conditions for an accord" with Argentina, since "Brazil really needs to diminish the number of its problems. Even in an area as sensitive as Itaipú, where instincts operate with enormous force, the issue has lost all prominence against the magnitude of other realities."[239] Figueiredo's first trip abroad was not to Argentina but rather to Venezuela; although many observers speculated that this was an overture to the region's democracies, linked to Figueiredo's domestic opening, the Argentine embassy cautioned that the primary motivation was economic and the major goal was Venezuelan oil.[240] Meanwhile, Brazilian leaders appealed to the international financial powers for help—two and a half years before Mexico's default—especially to boost trade as the "sole alternative to control the foreign indebtedness and make viable the retaking of economic growth."[241]

From End Runs and Sabotage to the Routine
Diplomacy of Rapprochement

The changing conduct of diplomacy from end runs and sabotage in 1976 to the active cooperation of the bureaucracy by the end of 1978 shows that formerly intransigent state agencies had fallen into line behind the presidents' rapprochement agenda and strongly supports a parochial interest argument. Foreign policy was a bureaucratic and factional battleground in Argentina after the coup. The service branches took over several civilian agencies, with the navy— under Videla's chief domestic rival, Admiral Massera—acquiring the foreign ministry (the Proceso's first two foreign ministers were navy admirals with no interest in reaching out to Brazil).[242] Videla, however, was able to appoint key ambassadors, including Oscar Camilión (a known supporter of cooperation with Brazil) in Brasília.[243] This set the stage for a pattern of end runs and sabotage over the next two years. The Argentine and Brazilian foreign ministries oscillated between tactical cooperation and backsliding on hydroelectric negotiations, taking extreme positions and taking offense. Meanwhile, Camilión tried to bypass Itamaraty's obstruction and to engage Geisel and the Brazilian public.[244] In 1978, Videla, who had personally suggested the trilateral format for negotiations, installed his brother-in-law, Air Force Brigadier Carlos Washington Pastor, as foreign minister.[245] Personnel shifts did not immediately produce political breakthroughs, however. Angry notes and position-hardening continued into the early months of 1979, even though the technical formula for an accord (eighteen turbines for the Itaipú dam and a 105-meter height for Corpus) had been reached in October 1978.[246] From late 1978 through 1980, however, presidents ceased their end runs and deferred to the foreign ministries, which reached the Tripartite Accord and set the agenda for the presidential visits.

In 1976 and 1977, cooperative overtures between Argentina and Brazil involved presidential, ambassadorial, and eventually military end runs around the bureaucratic channels of the foreign ministries. After meeting with the new Argentine ambassador, Oscar Camilión, before his departure from Buenos Aires, Brazilian journalists reported that he supported rapprochement and represented Videla's thinking as against the traditional operations of the Argentine foreign ministry.[247] In his first report from Brazil, Camilión explained that his overtures had met with encouragement from Geisel but resistance from Itamaraty. Geisel "expressed in clear form his objective of strengthening relations with Argentina within the framework of the first priority of his government which is South America" and "was clear also in the mention of those who work to create obstacles in the bilateral relationship and very direct in the suggestion that he would see it directly each time that it was needed," while Silveira was "very cordial in personal terms but eluded in careful manner any reference either to issues between Brazil and Argentina or even to bilateral relations," essentially refusing to negotiate.[248] Facing obstruction, Camilión launched his own press campaign with "a positive attitude that will improve the climate, reestablish confidence, win adepts in the influential social circles and neutralize the spokesmen of extreme positions, in particular those who have access to the press."[249]

By the summer of 1977, foreign ministry recalcitrance (and Geisel's apparent unwillingness to intervene) was frustrating senior military commanders, who began opening their own back-channel communications as well as working directly with ambassadors. The heads of both countries' air forces, for instance, exchanged visits, and Itamaraty accused the armed forces of trying to intervene in foreign policy. Camilión reported to the Argentine foreign ministry that although he'd told the press that the visit "responded to a private invitation . . . and had only that character," the Brazilian air force minister had "admitted that in the course of conversations the Itaipú issue came up, as did the necessity of maintaining open routes of dialogue on the issue."[250] One of Camilión's senior military contacts conveyed "his serious preoccupation with the state of the bilateral relationship. He directly put the responsibility on Itamaraty for the state of things . . . Shortly, he added, 'heads will roll.' He continued saying that . . . there is no-one in the Armed Forces who wants anything but a good and growing positive relationship with Argentina."[251]

Meanwhile, the Argentine foreign ministry apparently spent as much energy restricting other state agencies' access to negotiations with Brazil as it did bringing the Brazilians into dialogue. Videla had created an inter-agency commission in 1976 to establish Argentina's position on the hydroelectric issue and to find a way to politically "compatibilize" the Corpus and Itaipú projects; the commission's June 1977 final report shows not only the foreign ministry's bureaucratic turf battles but also its perception of parochial factors in Brazilian foreign policymaking. The conclusion recommends a "Unity of National Action," rebukes end runs by presidents and ambassadors, and unsubtly advocates that standard bureaucratic channels (that is, the foreign ministry) continue to manage foreign policy, since without such a "unified and adjusted coordination of the internal governmental front," any deviation "tends to create a false and inconvenient image of duality with respect to the position that the Republic effectively maintains or, directly, to favor the non-negotiating model of Brazil."[252] The report also saw Silveira's hard-line position in Brazil not as reflecting animosity but rather as a way to shore up his domestic position vis-à-vis "other sources of power," to bait the Argentines into taking the "emotional challenge" of "nationalistic appeals," "to 'drive crazy' the Argentine diplomacy and . . . aid a hard-line or confrontational position, which would justify the non-realization of negotiations."[253] Camilión saw his role as trying to open the road to rapprochement, but the Argentine foreign ministry's Latin America department thought that his mission "opens a new negotiating stage."[254] Although "a policy of confrontation" was "discarded," cooperation was not the goal, but rather "strengthening [Argentina's] negotiating capacity" and "promoting the realization of specific actions that attend to the immediate objective of improving the current position of weakness . . . in which our country finds itself in relation to Brazil."[255]

End runs by Argentine junta members frustrated not only Silveira's Itamaraty, but also the Argentine Foreign Ministry, which attempted to suppress them. First, a Foreign Ministry memorandum before Admiral Massera's January 1977 trip to Brazil argued that his public communications ought to be "reinforcing our negotiating strategy with Brazil" by hewing closely to talking points taken from Argentine Foreign Minister César Guzzetti's speech in Brasília the previous month (the speech featured rhetorical flights about the contagion of confidence, but primarily sought to force Brazil to admit that it needed to negotiate over Itaipú rather than pretending that no problems existed).[256] Second, a June 1977 Foreign Ministry letter to Brigadier General Orlando Agosti, Commander in Chief of the Argentine Air Force, urged him to delay his trip to Brazil, or if for military reasons this were not desirable, he should bear in mind "the strategy that our country is developing for overcoming the dispute," since Agosti's rank and position meant that any gesture "could not avoid inserting itself within the strategy that the Republic is developing in relation to that problem."[257] Moreover, although bilateral relations had been cordial since a December 1976 regional foreign ministers' summit in Brasília, Brazil's position was "when not elusive and dilatory, frankly negative to any concrete possibility of achieving an understanding with our country," so Agosti should convey "the preoccupation of our Government with the attitude that that country maintains and the conviction that—in case the current situation is not modified—Argentina will be obliged to reconsider in a global manner its relations with Brazil."[258] Broadly, the Foreign Ministry pushed the head of the Air Force to stay out of foreign policy, or if he chose to get involved, to threaten Brazil in order to back up the Foreign Ministry's strategy.

From 1976 to 1978, rather than reciprocal, gradual movement towards a negotiated solution of the hydroelectric issue, documents reveal repeated backsliding and escalation. At the December 1976 ministerial summit, "the bases of a new understanding between Argentina and Brazil were laid," and "for the first time the acceptance that problems existed regarding the exploitation of shared rivers was achieved, and it was agreed that it was necessary to overcome these through negotiated formulas," according to a Foreign Ministry summary for Videla.[259] Videla traveled to Paraguay in April 1977 and obtained agreement to hold trilateral negotiations, but in Brazil, Silveira, apparently backtracking, "showed himself opposed to trinational negotiations and suggested that the accord should be sought through secret bilateral conversations." And yet when Camilión proposed on May 17 that bilateral talks should begin (with trilateral negotiations to come later), Silveira "responded vaguely," promising a formal response after consulting with Geisel. Even more troublesome than this tactical delay was the bombshell (also May 17) of Silveira's remarks to a secret session of the Brazilian Senate, categorically rejecting trilateral talks, blaming the ongoing hydroelectric dispute on "Argentine indecision," and claiming that "Paraguay abandoned the pendular policy to incline itself towards Brasília." The Foreign Ministry recognized that the speech might be an Itamaraty trap having "as objective 'riling up' Argentine diplomacy and encourage it to a position of hardness or confrontation, which would justify the non-realization of negotiations," and noted "the discomfort that the constructive and firm attitude maintained by Argentina creates."

As of February 1977, Argentine decision makers disagreed about whether Brazil's minimum acceptable height for Corpus would be 115 or 105 meters, and whether Itaipú would operate 18 or up to 30 turbines (the more turbines at Itaipú, and the lower the height of Corpus, the less hydropower for Argentina).[260] After tripartite negotiations began in September, "Brazil declare[d] that in Itaipú it will not install more than 18 machines," and seemed amenable to a 105 meter height for Corpus, but by November, Brazil's delegation presented an "extreme posture" that Argentina should, among other things, be content with only a 100-meter height for Corpus, thus "its previous verbal expression . . . hardens." The Brazilian position retreated even further in 1978 when an accord with Paraguay established 20 turbines for Itaipú and "brought to a new 'impasse' the trilateral efforts."[261]

Recalcitrance rather than progressive negotiation was not restricted to the Brazilian side. A 1977 memorandum from Federico Barttfeld, head of the Argentine foreign ministry's Latin America department, argued that the December 1976 meeting's promise was "gradually defrauded by a series of gestures or acts that would seem to want to bring back the relationship to levels more negative even than those reached since 1973," actions based on Itamaraty's "attitude of systematic intransigence" and "truly dilatory policy."[262] Because Brazilian obstinacy, according to Barttfeld, was sustained in part by its "security that in Argentina any "military solution" to the problem has been discarded," the memorandum proposed undermining this confidence through "a gradual hardening of the Argentine attitude, that would exhibit sufficient proofs of its firm will" to refuse cooperation without clear concessions. Additionally, Argentina should reach out to other states in the region to bring pressure on Brazil and simultaneously "Reinforce militarily the Mesopotamian region—especially the sectors bordering Brazil—as a solid base of an eventual strategy of confrontation with that country." Argentina should recall its ambassadors in Brasília and Asunción and "instruct them in accord with the present strategy. This recall will further have a symbolic value" in those countries. Moreover, "the Republic should accelerate—in quality of an unavoidable national objective—the concretion of a nuclear weapon. The simple act of a rigorous tendency towards that end, to the extent possible visualizable by Brazil, would imply an unsubstitutable element of pressure."

By the end of 1978, routine diplomacy took hold. After Videla's inter-agency commission ended, the Foreign Ministry assumed full control of the Brazil negotiations.[263] In March 1979, Figueiredo sent a note to Videla, who passed it to Foreign Minister Pastor so that "the Ministry in your charge would study the course of action to follow," rather than replying directly.[264] And shortly before both the Tripartite Accord and the first Videla-Figueiredo summit, Argentine Foreign Ministry officials traveled to Brazil rather than leaving the negotiations to Ambassador Camilión.[265] Nor did the Argentine Foreign Ministry see the

Accord as a tactical, limited agreement such as those considered in earlier years; the arc of rapprochement and the agenda of presidential meetings was clear. The treaty, according to an internal weekly summary, would "augur a new stage of dynamic realizations in the relations of our country with Brazil . . . and its political transcendence exceeds" simply resolving the hydroelectric issue.[266] Less than four weeks after the Accord, the Brazilian government announced the first presidential visit, and in December, the Argentine Foreign Ministry recognized that the impending summit would have "singular transcendence" and anticipated "diverse accords of cooperation in the scientific, technological and cultural area, and of complementation in commercial and financial matters."[267] A February 1980 draft of the Argentine-Brazilian nuclear accord indicates that the foreign ministries had hammered out major agreements before the presidential meetings.[268]

Reconsidering Alternative Interpretations

Finally, archival documents illustrate the limitations of the 'Chile threat' and 'leader personality' explanations of rapprochement. At the height of the Beagle Channel crisis, in summer 1978, a Brazilian firm sought to export 1000 trucks to Chile via Argentine territory, and Argentina forbade any transshipment of vehicles (as potential war materiel).[269] On August 18, Brazilian Ambassador Garcia de Souza requested a policy change, warning that the ban could be seen as a "blockade . . . impinging very probably on the Corpus-Itaipú negotiation."[270] Ultimately, the Argentine Foreign Ministry's Latin America department recommended upholding the ban. The department feared that backing down would embolden the Chileans, enrage Argentine nationalists, and obtain little from the Brazilians, whereas standing pat, despite angering both Brasília and Santiago, would "demonstrate that though Argentina has a firm will to negotiate, it does not cease in the defense of the rights that attend it."[271] Far from cooperating with Brazil while facing a Chilean threat, Argentina managed to inflame both rivalries simultaneously.

By the Tripartite Accord in late 1979, Argentine-Chilean relations were slowly thawing. In October, the Argentine delegation to a regional meeting was instructed to prevent further transportation flare-ups: the delegates would not propose new accords but also would not "discourage eventual proposals that could arise."[272] Three weeks later, the Latin America department recommended "reinitiation of the bilateral mechanisms of physical integration with Chile . . . in gradual form," through small steps that "despite the technical character" would provide "great political significance."[273] Argentina maintained disputes with Brazil and Chile in 1977–1978 and later improved relations with both; one conflict did not displace the other.

Camilión's predecessor, Jorge Casal, whose brief tenure began scant weeks before the Argentine coup, provides a valuable perspective regarding Brazilian personalities. Casal's initial report from Brazil in March 1976 supports Camilión's impressions that the Geisel administration refused to negotiate and specifies the absence of any personal antipathy.[274] Camilión's cables emphasized Geisel's quest for political opening and his domestic political constraints while casting Figueiredo as a hard-liner with no indication of support for cooperation with Argentina.[275] After Figueiredo's inauguration, Camilión did argue that this might help rapprochement ("Figueiredo wishes not only to end the problem of the Paraná but to maintain the best possible relations with Argentina" while "the greatest obstacle to the solution of the Paraná issue was in the person of Geisel").[276] However, this heavy revision to his tone from the Geisel years draws on talks with Garcia de Souza, whom the new administration had just sacked. Camilión may even have worried about his own job, observing, "It could be that Brazil—at least Itamaraty—sustains the expectation that the culmination of the negotiation will have totally new protagonists," in which case "it falls to Argentina to decide whom its own men will be."[277]

A briefing memorandum for President Videla from the foreign ministry on his upcoming meeting with Figueiredo profiles the Brazilian president and features his childhood experience in Argentina (along with his devotion to boxing, his fondness for tango, and his staunch anti-Communism) but concludes that personality matters at most on the margins:

> That sympathy for our country . . . functioned as an accelerator in his policy of rapprochement, just as the invincible antipathy that General Geisel professed toward us worked as a brake for an understanding that the previous president considered rationally convenient. But, naturally, what the government of Brazil does today is not explained by personal sentiments but by the conviction shared in the circles of power, particularly the Armed Forces, that Brazil has to strengthen its condition as a Latin American country.[278]

What, then, pushed Brazil into the arms of Argentina? Two forces apparently motivated Figueiredo: pressure from the Carter administration ("He considers Carter a disgrace to the West and like all Brazilian military men he has not forgiven the North American campaign against the nuclear accord with Germany and the pressures in the area of human rights") and the dire straits of the Brazilian economy ("He understands that inflation represents today the principal political threat to his program and even to his own stability").[279] Overall, archival evidence supports a parochial interest explanation of Argentine-Brazilian rapprochement.

US Foreign Policy and the Cold War in the Southern Cone

Does this account overemphasize domestic politics at the expense of international factors? Especially, to what extent did the United States influence Argentine-Brazilian relations during the Cold War? It is tempting to argue that the United States had long managed to divide and conquer its Latin American allies diplomatically and that solidarity among Latin American rivals would emerge only in opposition to the regional hegemon. Each of the three failed summits occurred when both countries' leaders had broadly positive relations with Washington and subscribed to US policy initiatives for the hemisphere, while the leaders who achieved rapprochement in 1980 vehemently disapproved of the Carter administration's stance on Latin America. And at the margins, US assistance may have exacerbated Argentine-Brazilian rivalry in the early postwar years by contributing to arms races and concerns about relative gains, and US pressure on Argentina and Brazil in the late 1970s may have aided rapprochement.

However, US foreign policy can neither be blamed for maintaining Argentine-Brazilian rivalry nor credited with its resolution. First, as the two largest countries in South America, Brazil and Argentina were relatively insulated against the distorting effects of US policies, and their governments exercised a great deal of autonomy in foreign policymaking. Not only did Argentina and Brazil sever their military assistance agreements with the United States in 1977–1978, but as far back as 1961 Jânio Quadros rejected a US offer of $100 million in economic assistance, deeming the amount too small and the conditions too onerous. From Juan Perón's call for a "third position" in foreign affairs to the "responsible pragmatism" of Brazil's military regime three decades later, Argentine and Brazilian leaders repeatedly demonstrated that their choices of foreign partners would not be dictated by Washington. As a corollary, the sources of enduring rivalry between these two powers must be sought in South, rather than North, America.

Second, during the 1947, 1961, and 1972 summits, US decision makers seemed isolated from events in Argentina and Brazil and the repercussions that US policies might have for the relationship between these allies. If US actions reinforced rivalry, this was purely accidental, since Washington's attention lay elsewhere. The Truman administration wanted a Rio Treaty, but it was primarily focused on Eurasia and seemed ready to delegate Latin American conflict resolution altogether to the Organization of American States. Perón was a war-time problem for US foreign policy, but by 1947, Argentina's international disputes were at most a minor irritant. The Kennedy administration sought Latin American support for an Alliance for Progress but increasingly viewed the entire region through the prism of Cuba. By pushing the anti-Castro agenda so heavily in 1961–1962, the United States may have exacerbated the untenability of Arturo Frondizi's presidency and contributed to the overthrow of one of the Alliance's staunchest supporters. And the Nixon administration's foreign policy, rotating between Moscow, Beijing, and Hanoi, had just enough Latin America attention to address the perceived threat of Salvador Allende in Chile. (The March 1972 Lanusse-Médici summit fell between Nixon's trip to China in February and Kissinger's secret mission to the USSR in April.) Nixon's famous remark that "we know that as Brazil goes, so will go the rest of that Latin American continent" was offered in a personal toast to Emílio Médici, and if it sowed discord in Argentina and other Latin American states, this was hardly a design of US foreign policy.[280] Henry Kissinger's *White House Years*, nearly 1,500 pages long, completely omits Brazil and mentions Argentina only briefly as a potential target of Chilean-sponsored leftist revolution.[281]

Third, Argentine-Brazilian cooperation in the late 1970s apparently emerged beneath the Carter administration's radar. Carter's primary focus in Latin America was the Panama Canal treaty renegotiation, and South American countries like Argentina only entered the US agenda when they touched the live wire of a global issue like human rights or the Soviet grain embargo over Afghanistan.[282] Carter called for Latin American conflict resolution and solidarity in three speeches at the Organization of American States, but he primarily meant territorial disputes, made no reference to Argentine-Brazilian relations, and in any case preferred that third parties other than the United States take the lead on mediation.[283] At the time of the Tripartite Accord in 1979, Carter's attention was on the primary campaign against Ted Kennedy, the unfolding Iranian revolution, the Soviet Brigade in Cuba, the Sandinista takeover of Nicaragua, and the (ultimately failed) effort to ratify SALT II.[284] During the Argentine-Brazilian presidential summits of May and August 1980, Carter was managing negotiations with Egypt and Israel, continuing the primary against Kennedy, reacting to Cuba's Mariel boatlift, and dealing with staff turnover (Secretary of State Cyrus Vance resigned in April after the failed rescue of Iran hostages, and his replacement, Ed Muskie, started off poorly in talks with the Soviet Union).[285]

Overall, the United States consistently had higher foreign-policy priorities, not only outside Latin America but even within the region, than fostering conflict resolution among its South American allies. High-level recognition that US policies might bring unintended and even unwanted consequences in Latin America is extremely rare, but Carter's national security advisor, Zbigniew Brzezinski, provides a notable exception. In his journal, Brzezinski observed in March 1977 that "our human rights concerns . . . have prompted a kind of coalition of Latin American countries against us," and in August 1978 that the US was "running the risk of having bad relations simultaneously with Brazil, Chile, and Argentina."[286] Ironically, this last observation came just two months after Carter had announced at the OAS that the Canal treaty "should be a good omen that other disputes in our hemisphere can also be settled peacefully," promised "to join in the effort to find peaceful and just solutions to other problems," and declared "an opportunity to reaffirm our commitment to harmony in this hemisphere and to avoid conflict."[287] As the Cold War relationship between Argentina and Brazil repeatedly demonstrated, such conundrums of unintended consequences pervade rivalries among allies.

Lessons from Argentine-Brazilian Relations

Anti-Communism deeply influenced security decision making in Argentina and Brazil throughout the Cold War, but the longstanding rivalry between the two countries persisted. Despite shared alignment with the United States against the Soviet Union and the rise of leftist guerrilla groups after the Cuban Revolution, from the Rio Treaty of 1947 to the "dirty wars" of the 1970s, a common enemy provided an opportunity for, but not an effective cause of, rapprochement.

This changed when postwar economic growth, always erratic, finally gave out amid the oil shocks and debt increases of the 1970s. Economic and security factors worked in tandem to reshape organizational priorities and open political space for leaders to achieve lasting diplomatic breakthroughs. Plentiful state resources enabled mission expansion: state security forces developed internal security operations beginning in the 1960s without having to sacrifice preexisting missions connected to interstate rivalry. As a result, presidential summits in 1947, 1961, and 1972, under democratic as well as authoritarian governments, that sought to deliver bilateral cooperation between these rival states foundered on organized resistance within their own governments. These obstacles and antecedents demonstrate the difficulty and impressiveness of the diplomatic achievements that undergird the present era of stable peace, strategic alliance, and economic integration.

More important than the institutions and ideology that characterize particular regime types, or the preferences and personalities of individual leaders, was the underlying and ongoing power and autonomy of state agencies, particularly the armed forces and the foreign ministries. These agencies exerted an overwhelming gravitational pull against unfavorable policy changes, using an array of tools from threats to foot-dragging to outright coups, to protect their parochial interests. Against this obstruction, presidents pursued international cooperation with an equally creative—though uniformly unsuccessful—set of maneuvers, from going public to going personal. When rapprochement succeeded in 1979–1980, presidents relied on the support of state agencies that remained powerful but whose interests had shifted towards internal rather than external missions, catalyzed by the resource constraints of the late 1970s.

The following chapters demonstrate that these dynamics operated with similar force across the rest of the region during the Cold War, from Central America to the Andes, from the Cuban Revolution to the debt crisis. As with the presidential summits between Argentina and Brazil, careful comparison of similar cases where outcomes diverge, using primary sources from multiple countries, helps explain why some allied states overcome their conflicts but others remain rivals despite clear incentives to cooperate.

CHAPTER FOUR

The 1959 Cuban Revolution and Central American Rivalries

The present world situation calls for a large measure of unity and cooperation on the part of the non-Communist nations. . . . The main goal of Soviet strategy is to break the free world apart. . . . This United States mutual security program is one of the ways to prevent the success of Soviet strategy. It helps indispensably to maintain a unity which is vital to our own security.

—*Secretary of State John Foster Dulles, 1954*

Despite the best efforts of the Inter-American Defense Board, the Rio Pact, and the OAS to forge a coalition against a foreign threat, long-standing regional animosities often had precedence over a foreign enemy. Regional "cold wars" attracted much greater attention.

—*Michael Gambone, 1997*

In Cold War Latin America, anti-Communism and the shared threat of leftist insurgency provided an important stimulus for rapprochement among interstate rivals. However, a common foe was not a sufficient cause of cooperation between Argentina and Brazil: as the previous chapter demonstrated, three presidential summits unsuccessfully attempted to overcome rivalry between 1947 and 1972. A critical difference between these events and the successful episode of 1980, which founded the current era of cooperation and regional integration, was the decline of Argentine and Brazilian economies. State resource constraints, in the context of an alternative mission for the state agencies that had sabotaged previous overtures, enabled rapprochement. Does this argument hold for other rivalries, or is it limited to the Argentine-Brazilian relationship? And can we test the effects of missions and constraints in a more controlled environment rather than tracing both of them across time in one rivalry?

This chapter analyzes relations among rival Central American states in the shadow of the Cuban Revolution of 1959, when a wave of rebellions spread across the region. Although few insurgencies were truly Cuban-sponsored, most were Cuban-inspired; while none successfully overthrew a government between Castro's victory in 1959 and the Sandinista takeover of Nicaragua in 1979, they posed a very real threat, particularly to the smaller countries of Central America and the Caribbean. I address a specific empirical puzzle: given a common foe, why did Honduras and Nicaragua shift from rivalry to rapprochement while Costa Rica and Nicaragua, and El Salvador and Honduras, did not?

Following my parochial interest theory, I argue that the critical barrier to cooperation in early Cold War Central America was the policy preference structure of the armed forces and that two variables—mission availability and state resource constraints—determined these preferences.[1] The threat of leftist subversion during the Cold War offered a new mission to Latin American militaries but only induced those forces to give up their old missions of rivalry when economic constraints (including the unavailability of foreign aid) compelled policy tradeoffs. Specifically, given a common foe, rival countries tend to maintain their conflict if their economies are prospering; alternatively, rivals are most likely to achieve rapprochement if their economies are constrained. Thus, national economic conditions affect policy responses to security threats either by enabling security agencies to maintain multiple missions or by forcing tradeoffs among those missions.

Consistent with this argument, I make three main empirical points in this chapter, each of which yields new insights on foreign relations in Cold War Latin America. First, the combination of Cuban threat and US indifference created strong incentives for subregional security cooperation. Second, presidents of threatened countries needed the support of their armed forces in order to achieve international rapprochement. Third, the armed forces only extended this support where state financial resources were constrained. Irrespective of regime type, ideology, or actual threat levels, presidents responded to the preferences of the armed forces, which were parochially self-interested and heavily affected by national economic conditions and external resource availability. Specifically, in the context of a common foe and weak US support, the least prosperous rivals (Honduras and Nicaragua) achieved rapprochement by convincing their armed forces to focus on countersubversion. In contrast, greater prosperity and stronger expectations of US assistance enabled security forces in El Salvador and Costa Rica to maintain their rivalries with Honduras and Nicaragua, respectively, in addition to addressing the subversive threat.

For data, I rely on published but rarely examined primary sources to provide a first cut at these case histories, which few scholars have yet explored. Latin American government documents served primarily to measure the degree of conflict or cooperation in a bilateral relationship; I used the Foreign Relations of the United States (FRUS) series to triangulate on the motivations and preferences within each Latin American government.[2] Particularly for the small countries of Central America, with close economic relationships with the United States, these documents offer a valuable and virtually untapped record of frequent, frank interactions between Latin American officials and US diplomats. I rely on qualitative measures of Latin American leaders' threat levels since quantitative data on political violence in Latin America are so poor and tend to understate or miss altogether the threats armed groups pose to weak regimes in small countries.[3] Data on the macroeconomic situations of these countries, however, are more reliable.[4]

The chapter proceeds in five sections. First, I assess the basic congruence of my argument and the alternative hypotheses with the Central American cases. Second, I argue that a window of opportunity existed for subregional security cooperation, by demonstrating both the emergence of transnational insurgency as a common threat to the governments of Central America and the lagged and inconsistent US responses to that threat. This section also suggests a counterfactual hypothesis: had the Dwight D. Eisenhower administration responded immediately to the Cuban Revolution with internal security assistance for beleaguered governments in the region (as Harry Truman did in Greece and Turkey, or as John F. Kennedy later did in Latin America with the Alliance for Progress), Nicaraguan-Honduran rapprochement probably would not have occurred when it did. US neglect of Latin America is hardly always benign; however, in this case, the absence of US resources created incentives for subregional cooperation.[5]

Third, I trace the path to peace between Nicaragua and Honduras, arguing that the combination of common threat and economic weakness altered the preferences of the armed forces in both countries, such that they were willing to give up the missions of rivalry in order to keep the new mission of counterinsurgency. This preference shift opened domestic political space for presidents to achieve international cooperation with their erstwhile rival country. Fourth, I examine two negative cases (El Salvador and Honduras, and Costa Rica and Nicaragua). The most important difference between these cases and the successful Nicaragua-Honduras case was the greater economic strength of El Salvador and of Costa Rica, coupled with greater expectations of US support, which mitigated the policy tradeoff pressures created by Cuban threat and the overall US ambivalence about internal security assistance. Finally, I briefly summarize the chapter's findings and revisit the issue of US foreign policy attention and objectives, identifying unintended consequences of US reactions to revolution in Cuba and across the region.

Competing Arguments on Cooperation among Rivals

The alternative hypotheses discussed in chapter one offer some plausible accounts of the positive case of rapprochement between Nicaragua and Honduras and useful perspective on the broader pattern of cooperation and conflict in Cold War Central America. However, state resource constraints provide a superior explanation of the variation in outcomes across these cases. First, a balancing argument would expect that rivalries with the highest degree of common threat would be most likely to end. Applied to Central America, the balancing expectation would be that Nicaragua and Honduras simply faced a stronger threat from Cuban-sponsored subversion. Clearly, Nicaragua faced a high threat and Costa Rica a far lower one, so Costa Rica's lack of motivation for rapprochement fits this argument. However, if the threat to Nicaragua induced territorial concessions to Honduras (by accepting the International Court of Justice decision in 1960), then Nicaragua should have been motivated to bargain with Costa Rica as well, but there is no indication of Costa Rica seeking any such negotiations. Even more importantly, balancing does not explain why Honduras and El Salvador, both of which faced moderately high threats, failed to cooperate.

Second, a bandwagoning argument would expect that an asymmetrical distribution of power between the two rivals could cause the weaker state, facing both a strong rival and a new common foe, to sue for peace. Alternatively, more evenly matched rivals would have a harder time agreeing to cooperate even with a common foe on the horizon. Bandwagoning might fit the pattern of Honduran policy outcomes, since Honduras sought cooperation with the stronger of its two rivals, Nicaragua. However, it does not explain the absence of rapprochement between the most unequal countries, Nicaragua and Costa Rica. Furthermore, bandwagoning falters over Costa Rica's insistence on maintaining only a small civil guard, having abolished its army in 1948—if the weakest country in the neighborhood feels comfortable simultaneously weakening itself further and continuing its rivalry with a stronger rival, then bandwagoning arguments seem unhelpful.

Third, although standard democratic peace arguments cannot be fairly tested in these cases since no two rival countries in Central America at this time were consolidated democracies, there is still the possibility that joint democratization itself might produce rapprochement. However, if the presidents of Nicaragua and Honduras were sufficiently liberalizing to perceive one another as like-minded and trustworthy—after all, Luis Somoza of Nicaragua and Ramón Villeda Morales of Honduras were both (indirectly) elected reformist civilians, though Villeda was installed by a preemptive military coup—then why did Nicaragua not pursue rapprochement with Costa Rica, a much more liberal state, or Honduras with El Salvador, which was arguably democratizing more than Nicaragua was?

Fourth, a counterrevolutionary concert hypothesis argues that regime security in the context of revisionist actors depends on joint defense against transnational threats. Nicaragua and Honduras appear strong candidates for partnership against subversion, particularly given close relations between the military and conservative economic elites in each country, so a counterrevolutionary argument might be made for Nicaraguan-Honduran rapprochement. This hypothesis also correctly expects Nicaragua not to look south to liberal Costa Rica for support against the common threat. However, it is unable to account for the absence of rapprochement between El Salvador and Honduras. If the Honduran military was economically and politically conservative and deeply invested in containing leftist subversion, the Salvadoran military was arguably at least as committed to this agenda.

Fifth, identity spillover focuses on the self-reinforcing character of cooperative behavior, particularly through security institutions. During the 1950s, Central American countries built a series of subregional organizations and began constructing a common defense framework. Although CONDECA (the Central American Defense Council) did not formally launch until 1963, preliminary discussions among military leaders began in 1956. The two countries not to participate fully in these early institutions—El Salvador and Costa Rica—were also the two countries not to achieve rapprochement with their respective rivals.[6] Conversely, Nicaragua and Honduras, the two states that achieved rapprochement, were among the most vigorous supporters of the new Central American institutions of the 1950s, including the Organization of Central American States (ODECA), the revived Central American Court of Justice, and the military planning sessions that led to CONDECA. However, if regional security cooperation leads to rapprochement, and if Central American security institutions contributed to Nicaraguan-Honduran peacemaking in the late 1950s, then why did a common identity not prevent the 1969 Football War between CONDECA allies El Salvador and Honduras?

Finally, norm promotion would focus on the degree to which the various Central American countries complied with the rules of the US vision of security practice for the isthmus. However, one of the largest steps toward inter-American cooperation within the postwar US-promoted hemispheric security vision—Costa Rica's progress in disarmament—failed to produce cooperation between Costa Rica and Nicaragua. Moreover, none of the Latin American rivalries ended in the fourteen years between the end of World War II and the Cuban Revolution: Latin America did not see a peace and cooperation dividend under the umbrella of US-sponsored security institutions and military-to-military contacts.

Against these alternatives, and following the parochial interest theory articulated in chapter two, I argue that the relative availability of missions and resources for a state's armed forces heavily influences policy toward the rival country. Rivalry empowered the armed forces in each of the Central American countries, creating vested interests in opposition to presidential rapprochement initiatives, despite the clear common threat of Cuban-style insurrection. The critical difference between the Nicaraguan-Honduran relationship and the other Central American rivalries was economic: resource scarcity induced armed forces in Nicaragua and Honduras to focus on the alternative mission of dealing with internal threats while giving up the external mission of rivalry, acquiescing to the presidential push for rapprochement.

A Window of Opportunity in Central America

Border disputes and rivalries have plagued Central America since independence, but the persistence of many of these conflicts after the emergence of a common threat creates a puzzle for international relations theory.[7] Why did shared anti-Communism and the prospect of leftist subversion and insurgency help some states, but not others, to achieve rapprochement in Cold War Latin America? A critical factor, I argue, was timing: the Cold War arrived in Latin America much later than in Europe or East Asia, where US leaders focused their attention. Fidel Castro's victory in Cuba quickly transformed most Latin American countries' national security policies, but the United States was slower to perceive the Castro regime and transnational subversion as a regional security threat and slower still to provide internal security assistance to anti-Communist governments.

After World War II, the inter-American system focused on "hemispheric security," emphasizing conventional military threats from the Soviet Union rather than the problem of transnational Communist subversion. Nor did anti-Communism translate automatically into collective security: Nicaragua, Honduras, and Guatemala joined the 1947 Inter-American Treaty of Reciprocal Assistance (the Rio Treaty) but recorded official reservations about ongoing territorial disputes.[8] Furthermore, the Rio Treaty provides far more detail on conflict resolution procedures among members than on measures for defending against outside attack.[9] Even when President Truman invoked the Rio Treaty based on North Korean aggression against US forces, little Latin American solidarity emerged, and only Colombia sent troops.[10] Subsequent attempts to buy support for global anti-Communism had little success and risked backfiring by spurring arms races among Latin American allies.[11] Far from aiding internal security efforts, the United States encouraged disarmament in areas that would not promote hemispheric security, and the reinvestment of those budget shares in economic development.[12]

The spread of Communism and transnational subversion became increasingly serious problems in Latin America over the 1950s, but these were usually separate issues: political violence was largely non-Communist, while Communist subversion was largely nonviolent. Internal security problems linked to permeable borders pervaded the Caribbean Basin in the 1950s, particularly in Nicaragua.[13] From the nineteenth century onward, Central American leaders often gave sanctuary to the domestic opponents of their interstate rivals, enabling disgruntled exiles to return at the head of an armed group.[14] Following World War II, a loose association of prodemocracy rebels called the Caribbean Legion staged several attempts to overthrow Caribbean Basin dictatorships, while dictators attempted to undermine democratic governments that sheltered the revolutionaries.[15] In contrast to all this agitation, Communist activity in the hemisphere hardly seemed like a serious threat. According to a May 1958 National Security Council report, Communists focused on trade relations, political parties, and propaganda rather than on inciting rebellion.[16]

Although inter-American military planners gradually reinterpreted the common foe as the threat of Communist subversion rather than Soviet armed forces, US internal security assistance was still not forthcoming.[17] The Mutual Security Program—designed to shore up US allies against the Communist foe—focused primarily on East Asia and secondarily on the Near East and the European periphery, with Central America well off the radar.[18] Besides, if an acute Communist threat arose in a Latin American country, the United States stood ready to intervene directly (albeit covertly), as by overthrowing leftist President Jacobo Arbenz in Guatemala in 1954.[19]

This all changed after the Cuban Revolution. The success of Fidel Castro's guerrillas in toppling the dictatorship of Fulgencio Batista ultimately demonstrated that transnational rebellion linked to leftist ideology was a serious threat to all.[20] The Cuban Revolution "redefined revolutionary possibilities," inspiring generations of rebel movements throughout the Americas.[21] Cuban support for revolution abroad, "an important element and a consistent defining feature of Cuban foreign policy since January 1959," began long before the schism with the United States and the receipt of Soviet sponsorship.[22] In addition to the demonstration effect of insurgent victory, the Castro regime began exporting the revolution through military advisors, training, and arms. Cuba's armed forces held, and increased, a sizable advantage over those of most of its neighbors, particularly in terms of number of personnel: in 1960, Cuba's regular armed forces numbered about 38,000, more than double the combined strength (17,400) of the five Central American republics (table 4.1).[23] Cuba was also more highly militarized than its neighbors, with two and a half times as large a portion of its population in the military as the most devoted Central American country (0.56 percent, compared with Nicaragua's 0.22 percent), and increased its advantage from there, more than doubling its forces by 1962 (to 80,000, not counting a militia of 200,000).[24]

More dangerous than the sheer number of Cuban troops was the ability of even small groups to promulgate Cuban insurgent doctrine abroad as a revolutionary "vanguard." Ernesto "Che" Guevara's *Guerrilla Warfare*, published in 1960, emphasized the ability of small, dedicated groups (*focos*) of guerrillas to energize a broader agrarian population to rise up against the ruling class. In 1959, rebels based in Cuba attempted invasions of Haiti, Panama, Nicaragua (twice), and the Dominican Republic; however, it is unclear how many of these operations reflected the official policy of the Cuban government.[25] As Secretary of State Christian Herter explained to President Eisenhower, "for the OAS [Organization of American States] to go into action, it is necessary to prove that one of the Latin American Republics is actually interfering in the internal affairs of another Latin American nation. This is not easy to do because many of the outside invaders are being given support by internal elements in Nicaragua, the Dominican Republic, and Panama."[26] The small size and cost of incursions offered Cuba plausible deniability, leaving each country in the region to interpret for itself the actual threat posed by the revolutionary regime.

US ambivalence in first co-opting, then targeting, and finally containing the Cuban regime only compounded the problem for Central American countries.

TABLE 4.1
Armed strength, 1960

	Troops	Population in thousands	Percentage of population under arms
Cuba	38,000	6,797	0.56
Costa Rica	1,200	1,171	0.10
El Salvador	3,000	2,612	0.11
Guatemala	7,500	3,765	0.20
Honduras	2,500	1,953	0.13
Nicaragua	3,200	1,477	0.22

Source: Troop and population data from *Statistical Abstract of Latin America, 1962* (Los Angeles: UCLA Center of Latin American Studies, 1962).
   Note: Costa Rica disbanded its army in 1948; the 1,200 figure reflects the Guardia Civil.

The delay between Castro's victory in 1959 and the arrival of US internal security assistance to threatened governments in 1962 forced Central American countries to provide for their own security, either individually or collectively. At first, US leaders took a sympathetic (albeit paternalistic) view of Castro. In February 1959, Director of Central Intelligence Allen Dulles worried more about Cuban instability than about Castro's leftist tendencies, arguing that "the new Cuban officials had to be treated more or less like children. They had to be led rather than rebuffed."[27] By 1960, the United States had recognized Castro's government as presenting a security threat to the region but opted to respond at the source, using armed intervention to topple the regime. This must have seemed plausible after the "successes" of similar efforts in Iran in 1953 and Guatemala in 1954, although in retrospect, the Guatemala operation was a dangerous model.[28] In March 1960, Eisenhower began plans for a covert invasion, which ultimately landed Cuban exiles at the Bay of Pigs in April 1961 after Kennedy's inauguration. The Bay of Pigs fiasco reaffirmed the Kennedy administration's determination to pursue a regional and developmental, rather than Cuba-specific and interventionist, strategy to deal with Communist subversion. Economic development and counterinsurgency would enable Latin American countries to fight their own battles if necessary but were intended to prevent those conflicts from arising in the first place.

   Under Kennedy, the Alliance for Progress transferred impressive amounts of aid to Latin America; however, security assistance to Central America was virtually nonexistent until Nicaragua and Honduras had already forged their own path to cooperation. Although the United States steadily increased military assistance to South America beginning in 1954, it essentially ignored Central America until 1962, sending only $5.5 million to the isthmus for the entire decade 1952–1961 (figure 4.1). In contrast, each of the following three years the

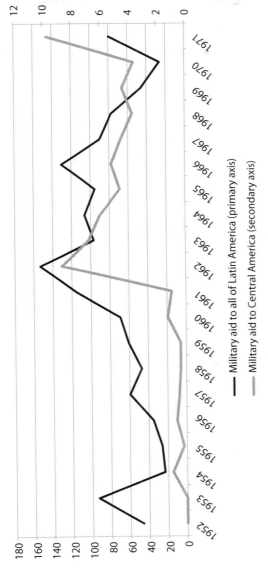

Figure 4.1. US military assistance to Latin America, 1952–1971 (in millions of historical US$).

Source: US Agency for International Development, *Greenbook* (US Overseas Loans and Grants: Obligations and Loan Authorizations, 1 July 1945–30 September 2006, http://qesdb.usaid.gov/gbk/query_historical.html, accessed in 2008; the current site is http://gbk.eads.usaidallnet.gov/data/)

United States surpassed that total: $8.7 million in 1962, $6.8 million in 1963, and $6.0 million in 1964. In 1959, Nicaragua received just $100,000, an amount National Security Advisor Gordon Gray admitted was "negligible."[29] The contrast with 1963, when Nicaragua received $1.6 million in military aid and also was allowed to purchase several jet aircraft, is stark.[30] Until the Alliance for Progress, when the United States provided not only funding for security and development but also training in counterinsurgency and civic action, Central American security forces were on their own.[31] US military assistance to Latin America, which intended to arm those countries against the shared Communist foe, unintentionally exacerbated regional tensions once it arrived.[32] Conversely, the absence of aid exacerbated the budgetary pressures faced by the region's poorest countries and—equally unintentionally—enabled rivals Honduras and Nicaragua to cooperate against the threat of Cuban-sponsored insurgency.

In the window of opportunity between the emergence of a transnational insurgent threat and the US decision to commit serious resources to combat it, rival states in Central America faced critical security policy decisions. Ultimately, only Nicaragua and Honduras opted to cooperate with one another against their common foe. The Central American states sensed the Cuba threat more quickly and felt it more deeply than the United States, but threat alone was insufficient to drive rapprochement among rival non-Communist states. Rather, the degree of economic resource constraint faced by these states, and the degree of support each leader expected from the United States to alleviate both the security threat and the economic pressures, explains why the leaders of Nicaragua and Honduras, but not of the other rivals, gained the support of their armed forces for rapprochement.

From Borders to Brotherhood: Nicaragua and Honduras

Honduras and Nicaragua both faced increasing security threats from insurgent groups and perceived Cuban sponsorship behind a facade of dissident exiles. Military leaders in both countries leveraged this threat to demand greater political authority and more armaments from their own presidents and from the United States. However, US policymakers were much more skeptical about both the degree of threat to the Central American governments and the level of Cuban involvement, and they offered little support to the worried leaders. The United States not only restricted military and economic assistance but also refrained from important symbolic gestures of support, forbidding both President Ramón Villeda Morales of Honduras and President Luis Somoza of Nicaragua from making official visits to the United States.[33]

Without new revenues or an increased US commitment to defend their regimes, Nicaraguan and Honduran leaders were forced to make their own security and to devote scarce resources toward that end. This in turn required the
armed forces to sacrifice their old mission of rivalry. Nicaragua and Honduras
saw one another as partners of last resort. Had the Eisenhower administration
offered military assistance to Central American governments fearful of Cuban-
sponsored insurgency—which Nicaragua and Honduras, and particularly their
armed forces, gladly would have accepted—those countries would have had far
lower incentives to cooperate with one another. In fact, increasing military capabilities might have increased the likelihood of war: Honduras told the United
States in December 1955 with respect to the territorial dispute that "she could
settle the matter by recourse to arms," while cross-border flows of rebels and
counterinsurgent security forces easily could have triggered escalation.[34]

At stake in Honduran-Nicaraguan rivalry was a territorial dispute dating to the
1830s breakup of the Central American Federation. Although Spain had offered
an arbitration award in 1906, it favored Honduras and thus Nicaragua rejected it;
Nicaragua maintained de facto occupation of the contested territory. The dispute,
and rebel activities on both sides of the frontier, provoked numerous clashes.
Honduran President Ramón Villeda Morales described this record in 1961 as "a
hundred years of fruitless fights, of fears and threats. . . . A hundred years of seeing the friendship between our nations torn and the trust between their governments broken."[35] In the 1950s, regime security began to trump border disputes:
among other incidents, both countries' heads of state were violently removed
from power in 1956. In Nicaragua, dictator Anastasio Somoza Sr. ("Tacho") was
assassinated (by "a group of Sandinistas—I should say Communists," according
to the memoirs of his son Anastasio Jr., or "Tachito").[36] In Honduras, a military
coup established a precedent for the armed forces to act as kingmakers, although
the junta ceded power to a civilian (Villeda Morales) the following year.[37] Following these events, Honduras and Nicaragua signed a July 1957 agreement in Washington to submit their dispute to the International Court of Justice. Nicaragua,
however, did so only grudgingly, responding to OAS pressure as well as to Honduran troops occupying the disputed zone, which had recently been incorporated
as the Department of Gracias a Dios by the Honduran military government (prior
to installing Villeda Morales as president) in a move that brought the two countries to "the verge of war."[38] There was no guarantee that either country would
respect an adverse judgment, and Honduras had little expectation that Nicaragua
would even participate in the arbitration.[39] Territorial negotiation would provide
an opportunity for rapprochement, but with no guarantees.

A string of violent overthrow attempts made Honduran and Nicaraguan leaders deeply insecure about their political survival. Castro's military progress inspired uprisings in Nicaragua beginning in October 1958 (before Batista's fall in Cuba), and the Somozas (President Luis and his brother Tachito, head of the armed forces) openly worried about invasion by exiles based in Honduras and Costa Rica.[40] Facing concrete intelligence of a forthcoming invasion, President Somoza intended to "smash it bloodily, in order to prevent the development of a situation like the one in Cuba."[41] US Ambassador Thomas Whelan observed that the Nicaraguan government felt tremendously insecure, "faced with massive threats from both north and south which GON [the government of Nicaragua] is convinced are INTL in character, and furthermore believing that US Government will do nothing to displease Nicaragua's enemies."[42]

General Somoza provided further details: Castro was spreading US$100,000 a month to allies in Central America, roughly six hundred pro-Castro rebels in Nicaragua were "coalescing" under "the flag of the late opposition leader-bandit Sandino," and the Nicaraguan government found it "about three times as difficult now to take effective action against pro-Castro opposition as in the past."[43] Also noteworthy is Somoza's presentation of the Cuba threat as "a serious matter throughout Central America," rather than solely a threat to Nicaragua: "In General Somoza's opinion Castro exercises a great influence in Central America and he must be stopped."[44] Overall, the Somozas endured twenty-three coup attempts between 1959 and 1961, exile groups launching incursions from Honduras and Costa Rica, and an increasingly leftist tenor of rebellion shown by the linking of insurgent operations to labor strikes.[45] Repressing such uprisings enhanced the Somoza family's "dependence on the National Guard"—although the Guard never obtained political autonomy, its members were handsomely rewarded with raises and nonmilitary prebends.[46] Nicaragua wanted security cooperation, and lacking US assistance, it turned to its neighbors.

Honduras, too, faced increasing subversion, some of it Communist, although a Cuban connection was far less apparent than in Nicaragua.[47] The threat facing Honduras was less ideological, at least in the short run. Despite President Ramón Villeda Morales's anti-Communism, the State Department was "deeply concerned over the outlook for continued political stability in Honduras" since Villeda had "accomplished virtually nothing, for lack of economic means," leading to popular unrest.[48] Villeda survived two coup attempts in 1959. The leader of the first revolt, former Honduran Armed Forces Chief of Staff Armando Velásquez Cerrato, took refuge in Nicaragua before launching a second rebellion, this time a "full scale revolt in Tegucigalpa with the assistance of disloyal police and military units," which was also soundly defeated.[49]

Villeda faced a difficult dilemma: he needed his military to defend him against exile groups, but the armed forces increasingly wanted to focus on fighting Communism. The military also had explicit veto power over any mission changes. The 1957 constitution declared that the president was not commander in chief, empowered the head of the armed forces to decide whether presidential instructions to the military were constitutional, and allowed the armed forces to determine—in secret—their own budget.[50] Furthermore, the revolutionary government in Cuba was targeting Honduras's rival, Nicaragua. Rafael Somarriba, a former Nicaraguan National Guard officer exiled in Cuba, claims to have acted as Che Guevara's personal emissary to Villeda, requesting Honduran permission and assistance to stage an invasion of Nicaragua.[51] Villeda could either help or hinder Cuban efforts, and in either case his military could accuse him of being soft on an important adversary. Furthermore, cooperation with Cuba could have earned Villeda the enmity of the United States, whereas opposition to Cuba did not guarantee any particular special treatment from Washington and could have added Honduras to Castro's list of governments to overthrow. Facing all of these threats, Villeda needed international cooperation to protect his administration, but US aid was not forthcoming. In foreign policy as in domestic affairs, military preferences were vital. Villeda "went out of his way to accommodate the military" and was "more concerned with the threat to hemispheric security from Castro's Cuba than with that to political freedom from reactionary despotism in the neighboring republics."[52]

The military in both Honduras and Nicaragua embraced the new mission of fighting Communism, which justified expanded resources and authority. However, this mission did not automatically imply cooperation with traditional rivals. In Nicaragua, even Anastasio Somoza Sr., longtime dictator and founder of the Guardia Nacional, worried that cooperation with Honduras would cost him domestic support.[53] The Nicaraguan military, and the Guardia Nacional in particular, had always received a large share of the national budget under the Somozas (from 1951 to 1961, official spending on defense and security always constituted between 24 percent and 31 percent of the total); retaining this parochial benefit was a chief motive behind the 1947 coup against a nominal president, Leonardo Argüello, who strayed from the official Somoza line.[54] After Somoza's assassination in 1956, his son Luis quickly moved to "[ensure] the loyalty of the National Guard," "formalized his grip on the presidency through fraudulent elections," and unleashed "considerable repression," although he moderated this substantially after taking office.[55] Border conflicts with Honduras (and Costa Rica) made "mobilization of the *Guardia* . . . an essential feature of the state's survival" and "the deployment of troops along Nicaragua's northern and southern frontiers . . . a standard part of the *Guardia's* military mission."[56]

Similar tensions pervaded Honduras, although Villeda Morales did a poorer job of ensuring military loyalty. Villeda "created a separate Civil Guard subject to presidential control" in order to achieve more reliable internal security, but this cut into military prerogatives; Villeda's party's candidate to succeed him promised further cuts to military autonomy, which directly provoked Villeda's overthrow in 1963.[57] Colonel Osvaldo López Arellano, chief of the Honduran Armed Forces (and the author of the 1963 coup, which made him president), met in Washington with State Department officials in December 1958 and railed against the "ineptitude," partisanship, corruption, and "softness towards Communism" of the Villeda administration, which he saw as simultaneously trying to "curtail the role of the military by cutting the budget" and "running the country into bankruptcy."[58] However, Colonel López agreed with the United States that the Villeda administration should be protected in power, which of course involved "the military as a guardian of Honduran democracy," so the Honduran military protected Villeda during the coup attempts of 1959.[59]

The tension between Honduran anti-Communism and rivalry with Nicaragua is evident in Rafael Somarriba's discussion of his encounters with Villeda in 1959. According to Somarriba, Villeda received warmly the Cuban proposal to overthrow Somoza (after reassurances that Nicaragua would not become a Cuban puppet) but "became disconcerted" at Somarriba's offer of additional arms for Villeda to protect himself against fallout from the Honduran military's opposition to this Cuban adventurism.[60] Villeda told Somarriba that "this is a very serious issue" and ultimately requested five thousand M1 rifles, twice as many as there were troops in the Honduran army at the time.[61] If "President Villeda knew that he could not at this moment weaken the power of the armed forces" and "opted to create a neutralising force," namely the civil guard, then he was clearly looking for policy changes that would effectively address emerging threats while minimizing opposition from the armed forces.[62] Although the civil guard move clearly backfired, his outreach to Somoza's Nicaragua should be seen as a much more successful instance of the same plan.

Although Honduran and Nicaraguan leaders felt acutely vulnerable to transnational Communist subversion, Washington remained skeptical of the threat.

Guillermo Sevilla-Sacasa, Nicaragua's ambassador to the United States (and brother-in-law of Luis and Tachito Somoza), frequently relayed intelligence on threats to Nicaragua and pushed, unsuccessfully, for US support. In 1958, Assistant Secretary of State for Inter-American Affairs Roy Rubottom repeatedly dismissed Sevilla-Sacasa's worries of "imminent" invasion, observing that "revolutionary exiles lived on such rumors and deliberately generated them without foundation in hopes of keeping governments in a state of agitation."[63] In a 1959 meeting with Rubottom, Tachito Somoza worried about Cuban sponsorship of revolution and Cuba's *foco* model of insurgency, and he appeared preoccupied with analyzing the causes of Batista's fall; in response, Rubottom argued that the Batista regime was a "house of cards" far more vulnerable than other governments in the region, including Nicaragua's.[64]

In 1959 and 1960, the United States began to recognize the threats facing Nicaragua but still did little to defend the Somoza regime. Rubottom, who had previously downplayed the exile threat, expressed in January 1959 his "uneasy feeling that Nicaragua is in for serious trouble . . . especially with more and more attention being paid the Somoza regime by the roving groups of revolutionaries who have been invited, in Castro's own words, to come to Cuba and receive haven and assistance."[65] When General Somoza met with Thomas Mann (Rubottom's successor) in Washington in October 1960 for a "courtesy call," the conversation focused solely on what Mann called the "Cuba threat;" although this indicates an increasingly militarized US assessment of Central American instability, Mann offered no concrete assistance.[66]

Contrary to the common perception of the United States as eternally coddling the Somoza family of dictators, US leaders displayed a striking ambivalence toward Nicaragua.[67] When Tachito visited the United States in 1959, the United States offered no promises of economic or military assistance; even Somoza's request for two hundred Browning automatic rifles (which had been ordered previously, but not delivered) and some training ammunition went unmet.[68] In case the message was not getting through, Assistant Secretary Rubottom underscored three points in a "private conversation" with Somoza: Nicaragua needed to "keep itself absolutely clean in dealing with its neighbors," Nicaragua ought to "desist in its efforts to purchase arms in the United States," and the Somoza name was "a serious political liability."[69] In the State Department's view, US support for Nicaragua should be contingent on Nicaraguan progress toward democracy and improved relations with the "responsible opposition," which would "thwart efforts of outside-supported groups with doubtful ideologies to make overthrow attempts."[70]

Privately, US leaders felt that Luis Somoza was making strides toward political openness, but they feared embracing the regime too strongly since "accusations" of supporting dictators "would probably be fanned by communist elements."[71]

Honduras, too, found the United States unreceptive to aid requests. As late as September 1960, State and Defense (following congressional restrictions as well as the desire to avoid "provoking immediate requests from Nicaragua and Guatemala for similar equipment") put clear limits on military assistance to Honduras, restricting "grant equipment" for 1961 to "exclusively that required by infantry battalion[s] Honduras has agreed [to] maintain for hemispheric defense" and refusing to meet requests from the embassy and the commander in chief, Caribbean, for increased army equipment.[72] Secretary Herter further admonished that "Emb and CINCARIB should not encourage Hondurans [to] anticipate [a] grant program of [the] character and dimensions recommended."[73] Although Herter acknowledged that the United States would "consider" future requests, they would only be granted if the necessary equipment did not exist in any agency of the Honduran government, if the request was absolutely "indispensable . . . for maintaining law and order against communist-Castro fomented disorders," and if the aid received presidential approval.[74] In other words, Honduras was on its own in terms of internal security, which provided a clear impetus to cooperate with Nicaragua.

Even setting aside the costly and domestically complicated issue of foreign aid, the United States refrained from cheaper symbolic support for the governments of Honduras and Nicaragua. To avoid the charge of coddling dictators, the United States declined to invite either of the Somoza brothers for an official visit (although their travel to the United States could have been disguised as medical or personal visits).[75] Additionally, the United States did not want to be seen taking sides in the Nicaraguan-Honduran border dispute and declined to extend to Villeda honors, such as a formal visit, that were denied the Somozas.[76] Villeda Morales visited Miami and New Orleans in 1960 at the request of commercial organizations, but the United States had attempted to dissuade him even from this unofficial trip and relented only after news of the invitations became public.[77] Rhetorical gestures of support for the presidents of Honduras and Nicaragua could have helped to deter their domestic and foreign opponents from launching invasions or coups; instead, US reluctance to promise political or economic support unintentionally enhanced Nicaraguan and Honduran incentives to cooperate with one another.

When the United States finally acted to defend Central America against Cuban-sponsored subversion in late 1960, it did so by deploying US forces rather than through security assistance programs, providing no organizational benefits to Central American armed forces. The United States moved the aircraft carrier USS *Shangri-La* into the coastal waters off Nicaragua and Guatemala to assist in quelling invasions should the governments of those countries request help. Although this was undoubtedly a major step, it was both temporary and offshore (lasting from November until December 7, 1960, when "the two Governments decided that the emergency had passed"), avoiding any commitment to internal security on the Central American mainland.[78] After all, planning for what became the Bay of Pigs invasion was well under way at this point—since the United States intended to resolve the Cuba problem by itself, it would have had little reason to anticipate a prolonged anti-Communist struggle in the region.

Facing the threat of Cuban-sponsored insurgency, and lacking a clear US commitment to fund their internal security so that they could avoid sacrificing other priorities, the presidents of Nicaragua and Honduras moved to overcome their traditional rivalry, and the armed forces acquiesced. In February 1959, the Nicaraguan and Honduran ambassadors to the United States signed a remarkable "Accord on Territorial Asylum."[79] The accord discussed disputed territory and citizens of third countries, seeking to prevent "clandestine activities done by nationals of the other country, be they political émigrés or not, permanent or temporary residents, transients or people of third nationalities." The accord focused on the common threat of subversion originating "within . . . jurisdiction" of either state, whether officially sanctioned or not. The ongoing territorial dispute, however, posed real obstacles to effective cooperation against subversion: while the treaty awaited ratification, Nicaraguan exiles in Honduras were preparing a new invasion of Nicaragua and planning to land in the disputed territory to thwart any cooperation with Honduras.[80]

Cooperation against subversion thus paved the way for resolving the longstanding territorial dispute. When the International Court of Justice (ICJ) announced its decision in favor of Honduras on November 18, reaffirming the 1906 Spanish award, both sides accepted it, and Villeda expressed his interest in meeting with Somoza.[81] Why did Nicaragua, which had rejected the 1906 Spanish ruling, accept the same settlement in 1960, and why did Honduras not merely accept the ruling but also actively push for deepening bilateral cooperation? Ungoverned territory was becoming less of a resource to be fought over than a source of vulnerability; more important than which side wound up with the land was the fact that someone would be in charge of policing it. Subversives had always crossed these disputed frontiers, but after the Cuban Revolution, this vulnerability became particularly acute. Given the very real threat that

Cuban-sponsored invaders would land in disputed territory to drive a wedge between non-Communist governments, Nicaragua's acceptance of territorial loss seems prudent. As Villeda Morales explained,

> Among brother nations—and of course I refer to Nicaragua and Honduras—there is no room for victors or vanquished, because in our case there is a common aspiration and a common goal: the integration of our peoples.... The zone of territory where political and administrative jurisdiction was mutually contested, from now on will be neither a source of discord nor the sower of seditious adventures, but fertile terrain to seal with a flourish the indestructible friendship between Honduras and Nicaragua.[82]

Additionally, the Honduran military could have taken the settlement and still maintained rivalry with Nicaragua, but it chose not to because its interests were better served by rapprochement and counterinsurgency. When Nicaragua worried that "Honduran students and elements of Honduran Guardia Civil would provoke an incident" by moving into the territory prior to Nicaraguan withdrawal, Villeda made it clear that the Honduran government "does not intend" to "force untimely or disorderly takeover of territory.... In answer [to the] suggestion that students or Guardia Civil might move precipitously, he pointed out students or others could not possibly arrive at [the] border without air transportation," which the Honduran military notably declined to provide.[83] Nicaragua's acceptance of a disadvantageous territorial settlement, and Honduras's restraint in implementing it, indicate how important improved bilateral relations were to the security of the two governments.

Cementing the rapprochement, Presidents Villeda and Somoza met at the border town of El Espino on January 10, 1961.[84] According to Marco Tulio Zeledón, the secretary general of the Organization of Central American States (ODECA, in Spanish), who attended the meeting, the two presidents' main goal was to "begin the negotiations" to work out an implementation plan for the border settlement, but the more important achievement was the public symbolism of the "historic meeting" itself, with the "fraternal embrace" between the two leaders, and their renaming of the town to "La Fraternidad" ("Brotherhood").[85] The meeting was a "transcendental act for the peace and harmony of the Central American family."[86] Although in the following months "differences arose" and were inflamed by "strong sectors of public opinion in both nations" concerning the implementation of The Hague's settlement, the presidents of the two countries retained a "serene and well-thought-out attitude" in policymaking, and "fortunately there no longer remains any reason for discord or difference between the two Governments."[87] Although there had been domestic pressures in both Nicaragua and Honduras against rapprochement, in 1961 these represented at most an ineffectual minority that failed to impede presidential policies. Meeting with Luis Somoza on the border, Villeda noted that "those who have been inciting you to not fulfill your promised word, are those who have always opposed the ideals of Central American unity, and, in a more limited sphere, the proposals of fraternal connections between Nicaragua and Honduras."[88]

Persistent Conflicts: Costa Rica–Nicaragua and El Salvador–Honduras

Why did the Nicaraguan-Honduran success story not hold for the other rivalries in the isthmus? What made El Salvador (rival with Honduras) and Costa Rica (rival with Nicaragua) different? El Salvador and Costa Rica had greater prosperity and greater expectations of US support to protect their governments, which increased their ability to maintain multiple security missions, incorporating anti-Communism while retaining rivalry. What made the difference was the relative inability of Honduran and Nicaraguan leaders to obtain additional resources to address the new mission of anti-Communism. In a condition of scarcity (partly due to an unsympathetic US aid policy), the Honduran and Nicaraguan armed forces made a policy tradeoff, sacrificing the old mission of rivalry for the new one of anti-Communism. In contrast, Costa Rica and El Salvador counted on better economic forecasts and a stronger expectation of US support, and presidential outreach to rival countries faced stern domestic vetoes. To support this argument, three major points need to be established: that these rivalries were comparable to Honduras-Nicaragua in terms of stakes and significance, that intra-governmental actors with missions linked to the rivalry maintained significant influence on presidential foreign policy initiatives (even if they lacked constitutional veto capacity), and that relative economic prosperity and US support enabled those actors to maintain rivalry despite available alternative missions in the late 1950s and early 1960s.

First, like the Nicaraguan-Honduran rivalry, conflicts between Honduras and El Salvador, and Nicaragua and Costa Rica, combined longstanding territorial disputes with frequent cross-border sponsorship of armed rebellion. From the 1830s through the 1950s, Central American states frequently attempted new forms of alliance or reunification, but this "history of frustration" was accompanied by "the equal persistence of bitter rivalries" and "violent clashes."[89] Honduras and El Salvador inherited multiple territorial disputes, both on land and in the Gulf of Fonseca, from the breakup of the Central American Federation, which were ultimately resolved by the International Court of Justice in 1992.[90]

During the mid-twentieth century, Salvadoran inequality and demographic expansion increasingly pushed migrants into Honduras (many of whom were deported back to El Salvador as undesirables), creating an additional source of tensions that ultimately escalated to the Football War of 1969.[91]

In contrast to common assumptions that Costa Rica has been tranquil domestically and pacific internationally (at least since its abolition of the army in 1948), inviting analogies to Switzerland, Costa Rica's rivalry with Nicaragua closely resembled other Central American conflicts.[92] This involved not only border disputes (the province of Guanacaste seceded from Nicaragua and joined Costa Rica in the nineteenth century, while disputes over control and access on the San Juan River continued into the twenty-first century, resolved by the ICJ only in 2009) but also tacit state support for subversion, immigration tensions, and multiple armed clashes, including a little-known war in 1978 and a militarized crisis in 1998.[93] Nicaraguan troops intervened in the 1948 Costa Rican Civil War, and one of the first invocations of the Rio Treaty intended to sort out mutual cross-border sponsorship of rebellion between Somoza's Nicaragua and Costa Rica under José Figueres's post–civil-war Junta.[94] Nor did Costa Rica's demobilization of the army (by executive decree in December 1948 and reaffirmed in Article 12 of the 1949 constitution) noticeably affect this conflict: the Somozas and Figueres traded sponsored invasions back and forth, including in 1953, 1955, 1958, and 1960.[95] These interventions, and the resulting increase in troop numbers (from 1,200 in 1949 to 4,500 in 1978) and military capacity of the Guardia Civil, represent a serious obstacle to any claim that Costa Rica wholeheartedly demilitarized during the early Cold War, even though defense spending fell as a percentage of GDP over the 1960s and 1970s.[96]

Second, rivalry empowered armed spoilers in each country. As Thomas Anderson explains, nationalism in Central America was "carefully fostered by politicos and militarists for their own aggrandizement," and one Salvadoran general he interviewed admitted that "all wars in Central America are essentially civil wars."[97] El Salvador may be the paradigmatic case. During the first six decades of the twentieth century, Costa Rica and Nicaragua reorganized and renamed their security forces and Honduras experienced some inter-service rivalries, but in El Salvador a relatively professionalized, autonomous army exerted a consistent and controlling influence on politics.[98] Lt. Col. Mariano Castro Morán, a member of the military government in 1961, reflected that the major political forces in the country have been "organized group[s]"—first and foremost, the army—whose goals "are legitimate: defense of their interests."[99] Army support is critical for foreign policy, in Morán's view:

A basic relationship of inseparability exists between a country's capacity to negotiate with other peoples, whatever the nature of the negotiation may be, and the existence of a National Army. And that is that notwithstanding all the institutional apparatus created by the ingenuity of peoples for the solution of international conflicts, one country is not qualified to negotiate with another, if in the discussion room its delegates are not backed up by an honest, efficient, strong apparatus, capable of guaranteeing the national security of a country as much within the internal area as in the external. That is to say, that at the discussion table, representatives of those countries that have the backing of a powerful National Army speak with a greater tone of voice.[100]

Here, the importance of the army for international negotiations is not that it represents the last argument of kings but rather that it provides or withholds the preeminent domestic stamp of approval for any foreign policy initiative.

Nor were such withdrawals of support merely hypothetical: the armed forces launched seven successful coups between 1900 and 1979.[101] In addition to outright coups, one former civilian junta member explained that "the army maintains the veto power over who can be President," not only with respect to civilian candidates but also regarding ambitious officers.[102] Morán's call in 1983 for a shift away from "border security" and toward what he calls "integral security" (an inward-focused and multidimensional concept of security blending counterinsurgency with social and economic reforms to combat poverty and inequality) necessarily implies that such a shift had not happened until that point and that external defense had been a primary mission of the Salvadoran army during the preceding decades.[103]

In Costa Rica, the relationship between border conflict and internal political struggles played out rather differently.[104] Neither Costa Rica nor Nicaragua had an army in name during the 1950s and 1960s, but each maintained an armed force with the mission of border security and national defense. In Nicaragua, this was the Guardia Nacional, formed by the senior Somoza under US military tutelage; in Costa Rica, it was the Guardia Civil, created after the army's demobilization in 1948. As Deborah Yashar explains, demobilization "did not leave Costa Rica . . . defenseless. The post-1948 Civil Guard assumed the army's responsibility, and Figueres maintained his extralegal army."[105] The army's demobilization eliminated a major rival to Figueres's Army of National Liberation, which was committed to opposing Somoza's Nicaragua. Thus, when "the first test of Costa Rican demilitarization came only ten days after the policy had been announced" with an invasion of exiles crossing from Nicaragua, "the forces from the civil war were still under arms, and as they were willing to support the junta, the military danger was small."[106] Politically, Figueres and his Army (later, Party) of National Liberation benefited from these clashes with Nicaragua, while domestic rivals such as Mario Echandi suffered. When Echandi was a congressional opposition leader during Figueres's presidency, a Somoza-backed invasion by Costa Rican exiles strengthened Figueres's hand (Echandi was falsely accused of colluding with the invasion, and the United States sold Figueres's government "three fighter planes at a dollar apiece").[107] And during Echandi's presidency, Figueres "continued to instigate and participate in conspiracies against Somoza" while Echandi "was maintaining cautiously cordial relations with the dictator."[108] Although José Figueres converted his Army of National Liberation into the Party of National Liberation and shifted the site of domestic political conflicts from the battlefield to the halls of government, parochial benefits from ongoing confrontation with Nicaragua continued.[109]

Third, how did anti-Communism and economic conditions affect these rivalries at the end of the 1950s? Costa Rica, like its neighbors, began cracking down on transnational subversion and opposed Communism, but threat perceptions and security policy played out in a unique way. Unlike his colleagues, Echandi did not worry consistently about being overthrown. He even offered to sell or give away unneeded Costa Rican arms and aircraft to the United States, but the US military was not interested; later, he proposed trading them for communications and transportation equipment (mainly radio-equipped jeeps), which the State Department advocated in order to resolve the "greatest weakness of the Public Forces."[110] However, his government did have to confront multiple rebel groups. In August 1959, the Guardia Civil apprehended a few rebels near the border, who admitted that an armed group of about a hundred intended to provoke a clash between Nicaraguan and Costa Rican forces.[111] A more serious test came in November 1960, during a series of battles between rebels and Costa Rican forces near the Nicaraguan frontier, in which the director general of the Guardia Civil, Lt. Col. Alfonso Monge, was killed.[112] The Echandi government, "alarmed by conflicting and confusing reports," was quick to perceive the violence as a Cuban-sponsored insurgency and immediately requested US military help; however, as soon as intelligence confirmed that the rebels were Nicaraguans intending to overthrow Somoza, Echandi's government withdrew its request.[113] Thus, Costa Rica, by and large, felt secure even without a traditional army: insurgent violence was anomalous, economic performance was strong, and Costa Rica sought US assistance rather than regional cooperation.[114]

Although Costa Rica arguably faced only a low level of threat from Cuba and the leftist rebels it inspired, the same cannot be said for El Salvador. When Salvadoran President José Maria Lemus (an army lieutenant colonel elected in 1956) met with the US ambassador a scant four months after Batista's fall, he worried at length about a Cuban-sponsored invasion of his country, which he and his foreign minister saw as "the number-one objective of the Communists in Central America."[115] Nor were his preoccupations unwarranted: escalating leftist agitation (backed by Cuba) ultimately made Lemus's position untenable, and a military junta replaced him in October 1960.[116] Escalating unrest seriously preoccupied the army and its rural National Guard affiliates.[117] Domestic instability in El Salvador in this period was therefore less an existential threat to state survival and more a useful new mission for the armed forces that also threatened the security of presidential administrations. During the early 1960s, political instability and popular agitation worsened, raising fears of an outright insurgency, while economic conditions remained strong—conditions under which I would expect the Salvadoran army to veto presidential rapprochement attempts.[118]

Ultimately, rapprochement between Nicaragua and Honduras was not an alliance of the most threatened, the most democratic, or the most reactionary but rather an alliance of the poorest in the context of a common threat. Although none of the Central American republics could be considered a developed country, a few key distinctions separated the more prosperous from their less fortunate counterparts (table 4.2). In 1958, Guatemala and El Salvador each registered a gross domestic product of between $600 and $650 million, while Honduras and Nicaragua both came in between $300 and $350 million. Costa Rica was in between, at $438 million. In per-capita terms, however, Costa Rica led the pack at $407, followed by El Salvador ($254), Nicaragua ($232), Honduras ($194), and Guatemala ($180). Additional figures bear this out and provide a more detailed picture of the national economies as they relate to security decision making. After all, for government leaders to fund policy priorities, they need usable resources, and GDP is only a rough indicator of these. Guatemala and El Salvador had the most gold and foreign reserves, followed by Costa Rica, with Honduras and Nicaragua lagging considerably. Total exports offer a similar profile: El Salvador and Guatemala ahead, Costa Rica in the middle, and Honduras and Nicaragua lagging. Honduras and Nicaragua faced a much tighter economic situation than their neighbors, not only domestically but also in terms of US assistance, and thus the pursuit of protection against the common threat of Communist insurgency was more likely to force them to set aside the old mission of rivalry.

TABLE 4.2
Central American economies, circa 1958

	GDP (millions of US$)	GDP per capita (US$)	Reserves (millions of US$)	Exports (millions of US$)
Guatemala	638	180	50	102.5
El Salvador	619	254	48	116.5
Costa Rica	438	407	25	96.9
Honduras	343	194	10	71.9
Nicaragua	320	232	9	71.1

Source: Statistical Abstract of Latin America, 1960 (Los Angeles: UCLA Center of Latin American Studies, 1960).

US support compounded this situation. Both economic and symbolic gestures dissuaded Salvadoran and Costa Rican leaders, but not their Nicaraguan and Honduran counterparts, from major policy changes. The presidents of El Salvador and Costa Rica made trips to the United States, enhancing their sense of security and expectations of US support, a privilege denied their colleagues in Honduras and Nicaragua. President Lemus made an official visit to the United States in March 1959; the Salvadoran government was keenly aware of the uneven treatment extended by the United States to Central American leaders in this regard and placed a high value on not being snubbed.[119] Within El Salvador, the visit was viewed as a harbinger of national prestige and development.[120] Costa Rica's Echandi visited the United States in March 1958, and although this could be only an "informal visit" since he was at that point president-elect, he did receive a "luncheon in his honor with President Eisenhower at the White House" in addition to the kinds of travel and business meetings that Villeda Morales was grudgingly permitted.[121]

Furthermore, the language used by US agents to Salvadoran and Costa Rican leaders implies a greater likelihood of financial and diplomatic support than does the language to Nicaragua and Honduras. Although Salvadoran requests for military assistance were initially rejected and an official Military Assistance Program was unlikely, a US envoy promised Lemus that "we were now exploring the feasibility of utilizing other channels through which it might be possible to provide certain types of assistance to the public security forces."[122] Specifically, Ambassador Thorsten Kalijarvi proposed that Washington "through the International Cooperation Administration [ICA], assist the government here in improving the capability of those units and organizations charged with public security and with control over the national frontiers," by sending a consultant and "a modest number of light motor vehicles and the necessary communications equipment."[123] General López Ayala, sub-secretary of defense for public security, was "warmly in accord," while the foreign minister, who brought the proposal to Lemus, claimed that Lemus "was greatly heartened by this show of interest."[124]

As with El Salvador, the United States expanded internal security assistance to the Costa Rican Guardia Civil using the ICA as an alternative channel to traditional military aid.[125] The United States also supported Costa Rica economically. Most notably, the State Department backed Echandi's quest for a reallocation of tax revenues on bananas, taking on the Treasury Department to do so.[126] Although winning such a concession was undoubtedly important for Echandi domestically, Echandi's main goal in the banana tax negotiations was to obtain greater revenues in order to improve Costa Rica's balance of payments situation. Like Nicaragua and El Salvador, Costa Rica was hurting from lower world coffee prices in the late 1950s, but unlike Nicaragua, Costa Rica was able to parlay its stability and more diversified economy into greater support from the United States to withstand such pressures.[127]

Do the Costa Rican–Nicaraguan and Salvadoran-Honduran diplomatic records bear this out? The relatively low level of internal threat may have contributed to the lack of Costa Rican–Nicaraguan rapprochement, but the prospect of internal vetoes was critical as well. Mario Echandi had met with Tachito Somoza on the border during the electoral campaign in 1958, leading some in the National Assembly to speculate about illegal campaign contributions from the Somozas.[128] As president-elect in 1959, Echandi traveled to all of the Central American countries; when Echandi met with (and hugged) President Luis Somoza, however, the National Assembly—dominated by members of José Figueres's Partido de Liberación Nacional (PLN)—censured him, declaring itself "not in agreement with his attitude regarding his meeting and fraternal embrace on the border with Peñas Blancas, with President Somoza."[129] Had Echandi sought rapprochement? This seems unlikely: the Costa Rican foreign ministry carefully reported that "in fulfillment of constitutional demands, and of natural obligations of courtesy with governments with which we maintain normal relations, President Echandi in the company of various cabinet ministers and a group of citizens, traveled first to the southern border and then to the northern one where he met with the Excellent Presidents de la Guardia of Panama and Somoza of Nicaragua."[130] If Echandi drew a censure over a strictly formal and constitutionally mandated meeting with a neighboring head of state, he must have expected that any serious rapprochement attempt with Nicaragua would draw even greater opposition from Figueres's forces, which depended on rivalry for much of their political influence. During his presidency, Echandi "tried to follow a line of neutrality" while Figueres continually provoked Somoza.[131] When Figueres, Echandi's longtime opponent, met with Tachito Somoza in 1971, Echandi wrote a bitter op-ed in *La Nación* decrying the hypocrisy of political factions that opposed his own outreach to Nicaragua while keeping silent as his successor did the same.[132]

As for El Salvador and Honduras, a series of presidential meetings provided ample opportunity for rapprochement, but a breakthrough never occurred.[133] The annual reports of the Salvadoran foreign ministry reflect increasing concerns about instability in the country and across Central America but emphasize nonintervention and regional organizations rather than bilateral cooperation with neighbors.[134] Lemus and Villeda Morales met on the border in January 1960, but this was a trilateral encounter with the president of Guatemala, General Miguel Ydígoras Fuentes, a staunchly anti-Communist dictator closely tied to the United States, and its focus was apparently strictly economic, laying the groundwork for a free trade treaty among the three countries to complement existing regional integration agreements.[135] A bilateral follow-up meeting in March to discuss migration problems (still apparently shorn of any security dimension) produced only an "interesting exchange of opinions on the practical possibilities for achieving Central American integration" and created a commission to study Salvadoran migrants in Honduras.[136] The junta that overthrew Lemus apparently made no outreach to Honduras; although subsequent Salvadoran leaders reached a few accords with Honduras during 1962 and 1963, these became dead letters after Villeda's overthrow in 1963.[137] Furthermore, despite these presidential efforts, the territorial dispute remained unresolved, and border security and migration problems actually worsened across the decade, culminating in the 1969 Football War. Two years before the war broke out, former President Villeda Morales suggested in private that "the current border squabble with El Salvador, which could have been settled very easily, is being pushed by both the military there and the military here to take people's minds off of internal affairs."[138]

Conflict Resolution among Small States
Rethinking Great Power Involvement

To what extent did US foreign policy, rather than strictly local factors of economic resources and civil-military relations, affect the pattern of cooperation and conflict in Central America? Compared to Argentina and Brazil, the Central American countries are fundamentally small states, defined not merely by population but by a low level of capabilities that creates a sense of vulnerability in economic, national security, and foreign policymaking.[139] Thus, the cases in this chapter are those ostensibly most susceptible to US influence, whether intentionally wielded, accidentally deployed, or simply withheld. US government actions or inactions regarding security threats that it perceived as minor (if it noticed them all) may have had huge consequences. And indeed a central finding of this chapter is that the dearth of US military assistance on the isthmus before 1961 reinforced other incentives for cooperation between Nicaragua and Honduras, while the influx of resources under the Alliance for Progress may have helped to stabilize rather than transform the other rivalries in the subregion.[140]

However, two factors suggest that US foreign policy did not strictly determine conflict outcomes in Central America. First, since US policy toward the subregion was broadly one of inattention, with a minimal level of support for any regimes, the minor variation in US policy across these governments cannot explain the divergent outcomes of the three rivalries addressed in this chapter. Diplomatic signals such as privately scolding the Somozas or positioning naval assets near Costa Rica surely mattered at the margins, but over the course of the Cold War, rhetorical threats and promises from Washington frequently failed to compel compliance from Central American leaders as divergent as Jacobo Arbenz, Oscar Arias, and Manuel Noriega. Although great powers can shape the incentives that face small states, domestic political considerations are often far more powerful influences on foreign policy decision making.[141]

Second, the United States was not the only outside power able to influence the behavior of vulnerable Central American governments. The absence of Soviet intrusion in Central America, at least in terms of fomenting insurgency, is particularly important, as was a postwar pullback of Mexican engagement in Central American affairs.[142] As noted above, El Salvador reached out to Guatemala (comparatively, the behemoth of Central America) for security assistance, while Cuba may have offered weapons to the Honduran government (and, elsewhere, weapons against the Nicaraguan one). The Cold War politics of patronage in Yugoslavia, Egypt, Pakistan, and elsewhere reveal that superpower influence can be offset by the presence of other suitors. Moreover, the smaller the threatened state, the greater the range of outside parties that might be able to offer it meaningful assistance.

Finally, analysts of US foreign policy might consider two counterfactual scenarios. Although Nicaragua and Honduras achieved rapprochement ten days before Kennedy's inauguration, different US choices in 1961 might have raised or lowered the odds of other leaders following in the footsteps of Luis Somoza and Ramón Villeda Morales. First, could the United States have imposed stronger aid conditionality to incentivize rapprochement? Foreign assistance through the Alliance for Progress was a centerpiece of the Kennedy administration's strategy in the Americas, and US policymakers might have opposed heavy conditionality as unnecessarily tying hands needed for the anti-Communist struggle.[143] Moreover, the Alliance responded to years of lobbying by Latin American leaders trying to shore up democratic government through economic reforms and steady growth, and Latin American nationalists likely would have decried conditionality as a new wave of North American tutelage.[144] However, the United States could have done more to draw a line between countries' domestic policies and foreign relations and to couch its foreign policy objectives in the framework of pan-American institutions. Although economic and political reforms are particularly controversial when dictated from abroad, foreign policy changes might be considered less intrusive. Had resources for internal security operations in the 1960s been linked more closely to the Rio Treaty's objectives of conflict resolution among allies, for instance, other Central American rivalries might have followed the Nicaraguan-Honduran path.

Second, what if the United States had more forcefully combated the insurgent threat "at its source," that is, in Cuba?[145] Kennedy certainly considered stronger measures than he ultimately authorized for the Bay of Pigs invasion, such as US air support. Moreover, had Nixon won the presidency in 1960 he might have been far more disposed to escalation in Cuba, because of his personal experiences with Latin American upheaval since 1958 and because preparations for a US-sponsored exile invasion of Cuba had already been initiated by Eisenhower.[146] The counterfactual effects of such escalation on Central American rivalries, however, are difficult to gauge. A more powerful invasion in 1961 might either have swiftly overthrown Castro or (more likely) produced a protracted foreign-supported insurgency, which could have removed Cuban sponsorship of subversion from the threats facing Central American leaders, contained the revolutionary threat on the island rather than the isthmus (at least for the duration of the conflict), and undermined the prospects for rapprochement. Alternatively, a pitched battle in Cuba might have emboldened prospective rebels elsewhere, while the destruction of the Castro regime could have sent veteran revolutionaries into exile and catalyzed new insurgencies, strengthening the incentives for subregional cooperation among threatened governments. Ultimately, economic and security factors combined to shape the incentives for conflict resolution among Central American rivals because of the underlying political power of the armed forces. This institutional problem, generally beyond the capacity of the United States to resolve, bedeviled aspiring peacemakers across the region and throughout the Cold War.

Resource Constraints and Rapprochement

Rivalry among allies frequently undermines effective cooperation against common threats. Rather than forming ranks behind a hegemonic ally and setting aside their internecine disputes, small states often maintain rivalries against one another and at times frustrate great power objectives. Domestic political factors, and particularly the parochial interests of state agencies such as the armed forces, heavily influence decision making in these seemingly paradoxical conflicts and contribute to rivalry persistence. In some cases, however, the state agencies that perpetuate rivalry can be persuaded to sacrifice it in favor of new missions, as in Nicaragua and Honduras after the Cuban Revolution of 1959. Thus, even major policy change does not necessarily require institutional restructuring. As Honduran President Ramón Villeda Morales explained in 1959, "The necessary thing is not to destroy the army, but to put it to work."[147]

When several rival states face a common foe, those with the most severe national resource constraints, like Honduras and Nicaragua, are most likely to achieve rapprochement. Conversely, those in situations of relative plenty, like El Salvador or Costa Rica, are most likely to maintain their rivalries. What about when several rivalries face acute economic crises? Which rivals will cooperate, and which conflicts will continue? I address just such a situation—rivalries among Andean countries during the debt crisis of the 1980s—in the following chapter.

CHAPTER FIVE

The 1980s Debt Crisis and Andean Rivalries

Let us not listen deafly to these warnings because history teaches
that economic crises constitute the breeding ground for political
tensions and international conflicts.

—*Miguel Schweitzer, Chilean foreign minister, 1983*

To the extent that democratic governments resolve international
disputes, however, they may also deprive their armed forces of
external missions that would reduce the probability of those forces
intervening in internal politics. From the standpoint of civilian
control, happy is the country with a traditional enemy.

—*Samuel Huntington, 1991*

Among states with a common adversary, with alternative missions readily available for the armed forces, the degree of state resource constraint affected leaders' ability to achieve rapprochement, as the previous chapter demonstrated in Central American rivalries facing the threat posed by the 1959 Cuban Revolution. Conversely, if several rivals faced serious resource constraints, then to what extent would the availability of alternative missions affect the prospects for rapprochement? In this chapter, I conduct a controlled comparison of relations among South American rivals given a common situation of resource constraint—the debt crisis of the 1980s. These relationships offer a specific empirical puzzle: why did Argentina and Chile achieve rapprochement while Ecuador and Peru, Colombia and Venezuela, and Bolivia and Chile did not? Each of these rivalries along the Andean mountain range had lasted for well over a century prior to the debt crisis, and each involved an ongoing territorial dispute, so what explains the variation in outcomes during a period of shared economic crisis?

Furthermore, why did a rapprochement initiative between Argentina and Chile succeed in 1984 though previous summits had failed?[1] The absence of cooperation in three of these cases, and the late arrival of cooperation in the fourth case, is doubly puzzling because all of these states shared a nominal common foe (the Communist Bloc, and more concretely, Latin American leftist insurgencies) during the Cold War.

My central argument is that the armed forces' prior mission development determined leaders' political capacity to achieve rapprochement during the crisis. In all of the countries studied here, interstate rivalry provided a core mission for the armed forces. However, the military in Argentina, Chile, Peru, and Colombia had also developed an internal security mission by combating insurgency and terrorism in the years before the debt crisis, whereas Venezuela, Bolivia, and Ecuador had not recently faced serious internal threats. In states with internal security missions, the debt crisis forced policy tradeoffs and military acceptance of international cooperation; in states without those missions, the sole mission of rivalry determined policy outcomes by preventing presidents from achieving a peace that would undercut the military's vested interests. Cold War human rights abuses and "dirty wars" had a silver lining, enabling subsequent leaders to achieve international peace, while countries that had been spared civil war found international rivalries harder to abandon despite the incentives offered by regional economic crisis. Additionally, at the level of individual government agencies or military service branches, parochial interest suggests that, ceteris paribus, those with dual missions are likely to sacrifice one in the context of recession, while those with a single mission will defend it against encroachment.

The chapter proceeds in six sections. First, I briefly assess the congruence of each of the hypotheses introduced in chapter one with the three cases of continued rivalry (Chile-Bolivia, Peru-Ecuador, and Colombia-Venezuela) and the one case of rapprochement (Argentina-Chile). Second, I describe the evolution of Argentine-Chilean relations in the late Cold War, identifying major turning points. Third, I argue that parochial interest explains the shift to rapprochement between Buenos Aires and Santiago in the early 1980s, drawing extensively on published primary sources including the memoirs, speeches, and interviews of key policymakers and the annual reports (*Memorias*) of the two countries' foreign ministries. Fourth, I test the alternative hypotheses in more detail in the Argentine-Chilean case. Fifth, I briefly summarize the main findings from this analysis. Finally, I consider possible unintended consequences of US foreign policy on the Andean rivalries.

Persistent Conflicts: Peru-Ecuador, Colombia-Venezuela, and Bolivia-Chile

Under what conditions will economic crisis produce cooperation rather than conflict, given a preexisting rivalry? Minxin Pei and Ariel David Adesnik suggest that economic crisis involves annual inflation above 15 percent or declining or flat GDP growth; given "a history of chronic high inflation—the case in several Latin American nations—a crisis must also include a significant deterioration in economic or financial circumstances as described by historians and other analysts."[2] Data on these economic factors demonstrate that all seven countries in this chapter suffered a serious and prolonged crisis. Using the growth metric, Chile experienced crisis in 1982 and 1983 and recorded the worst decline of all seven countries in 1982 with a drop of 10.3% in GDP, although it ultimately achieved the best growth rate of the group over the entire period 1981–1990.[3] Bolivia had the longest-lasting crisis, with negative or flat growth from 1979 through 1986.[4] Fully 28 of the 70 country-years (seven countries, 1981–1990) count as crises on the growth metric alone. Using the 15-percent-inflation metric, every country experienced a crisis nearly every year (the only exceptions are Venezuela 1982–1986, Bolivia 1987, and Chile 1981 and 1988).[5] Bolivia's 1985 inflation rate of 11,750 percent is one of the highest ever recorded, and while hardly representative, it indicates the magnitude of economic carnage that Latin America suffered during this period.[6] Furthermore, Pei and Adesnik do not include the specter of national debt, which was at the core of the Latin American crisis of the 1980s. As figure 5.1 shows, for the seven countries studied here, total GDP nearly tripled in nominal terms during the 1970s (before stagnating and declining in the 1980s and recovering in the 1990s), but total external debt stocks increased even faster. Debt as a percentage of GDP climbed from less than 25 percent in the 1970 to nearly 50 percent in 1983 and more than 75 percent in 1989 before declining as the economies recovered. One might hypothesize that the magnitude or duration of economic crisis would affect the probability of rapprochement. However, I suggest that the fundamental distinction is one of kind rather than degree. Countries either undergo crisis or function normally, and all seven of these South American countries were clearly in crisis for much of the 1980s, despite some variation in the timing and nature of their economic problems. Thus, the effects of crisis on rivalry behavior likely depend on some intervening variable.

Which factors interact with economic crisis to produce rapprochement? Several prominent international relations (IR) hypotheses seem initially plausible;

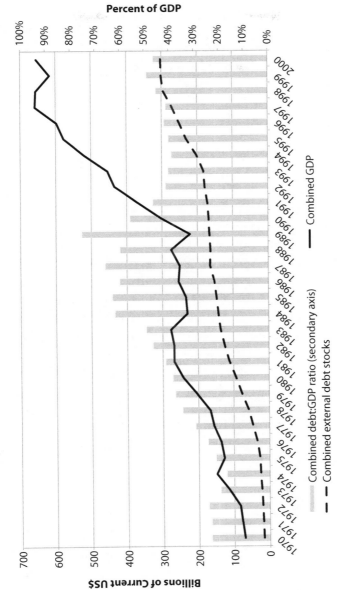

Figure 5.1. GDP and debt in seven South American countries, 1970–2000 (Argentina, Bolivia, Chile, Colombia, Ecuador, Peru, Venezuela).

Source: Calculated from World Bank, World Development Indicators

I consider liberal, realist, and constructivist arguments in turn. First, a democratic peace hypothesis suggests that consolidated democracies might be best equipped to achieve rapprochement; a related argument holds that democratization itself might induce fragile regimes to seek peace with one another. Latin America in the 1980s offers an important set of cases to test this argument given the spread of the "third wave" of democracy across the region.[7] Colombia, Venezuela, Peru (after a transition from military rule in 1980), and Ecuador (after its democratic transition in 1979), maintained democracies throughout the decade, but neither the Colombian-Venezuelan nor the Peruvian-Ecuadorean rivalry ended during the 1980s. Democratization for peace, emphasizing vulnerable leaders' cooperation, might offer some insight on the Argentine-Chilean case, since Argentina democratized in 1983 and (if one rather generously credits the Pinochet regime's official story) Chile became a "protected democracy" after a referendum in 1980; however, this hypothesis would also expect Chile to achieve rapprochement with Bolivia (which democratized in 1982). A democratic peace argument for rapprochement does not work in these cases.

Second, perhaps a shared counterrevolutionary ideology might enable rival governments to cooperate. In the context of the Cold War, staunch anti-Communism might lead to rapprochement in the face of perceived common threat. This might apply most strongly to the military dictatorships that preceded the democratic transitions mentioned above. Despite signs of nascent cooperation emerging between Chile and pre-transition Argentina, however, this outcome did not occur between Chile and the military rulers of Bolivia between 1980 and 1982.[8] If one discards Pinochet's "protected democracy" rhetoric, Chile absolutely qualifies as a counterrevolutionary regime, but this hardly explains the successful rapprochement with the newly democratic Argentine government of Raúl Alfonsín, an outspoken defender of human rights and of the non-aligned movement. Counterrevolution and authoritarian institutions do not necessarily covary, however: democratic Colombia was a staunch US ally in the midst of decades-long counterinsurgency operations against leftist groups such as the FARC (Revolutionary Armed Forces of Colombia). Arguably the most important shift toward counterrevolution in this period occurred in Peru, after its democratic transition—the Peruvian military regime actually had several progressive tendencies (inaugurating land reform and other antipoverty programs), at least in its initial phase, while over the course of the 1980s and 1990s (culminating in the 1992 *autogolpe* or self-coup of Alberto Fujimori) Peru's civilian government increasingly defined itself against the insurgent threat of the Maoist Sendero Luminoso (Shining Path). This increasing focus on counterrevolution, however, coexisted with ongoing and even escalating conflict with Ecuador.

Third, one of the most prominent realist hypotheses on rapprochement involves the need to balance against a common threat; in the developing world, the relevant threats are usually internal rebellions rather than potential invasion by a foreign state, but these threats might induce the same kind of cooperation. As figure 5.2 indicates, Chile, Peru, and Colombia faced escalating political violence in this period (Peru's Sendero Luminoso was the strongest single insurgency). For much of South America, though, insurgent threats receded as Cuba retrenched from its "export of revolution," the USSR was bogged down in Afghanistan, and democratization and economic crisis shifted both incumbents and opposition forces onto new political terrain where Communism was no longer a viable option. Although Chile's ongoing repression of leftists, and escalating armed clashes with the Movimiento Izquierdista Revolucionaria (MIR, the Leftist Revolutionary Movement) over the 1980s may well have influenced its search for rapprochement with Argentina, why did this same factor not push for cooperation with Bolivia, and why did an even higher level of threat not cause Peru (throughout the decade) and Colombia (in some years) to make peace with Ecuador and Venezuela, respectively, even at the cost of serious compromises?

Fourth, perhaps a growing asymmetry of power might cause a weaker rival to bandwagon with a stronger one. Bandwagoning might appear to explain Argentine peacemaking after its disastrous defeat by the United Kingdom in the Falklands/Malvinas War. However, data on troop strength and defense spending in South America before and after the peak years of the debt crisis enable some rough estimates of the power ratios in each rivalry, which undermine a bandwagoning thesis.[9] Argentina's decline in defense spending and troop strength was the steepest in the region, but this brought the Argentine-Chilean rivalry closer to parity, not further from it, since Argentina began the decade with a 4.7:1 advantage over Chile in defense spending and a 2:1 advantage in troops. Therefore, a bandwagoning argument cannot explain this case. A more subjective consideration of strength and weakness might imply that Argentina's decline would cause it to sue for peace even while objectively near parity with its rival. However, as Alfred Stepan points out, Argentina was not alone in revising downward its estimate of its own military capability in the wake of the Falklands War—others in the region learned the same lessons.[10] Furthermore, as I will demonstrate below, Chile was hardly extracting maximal concessions from

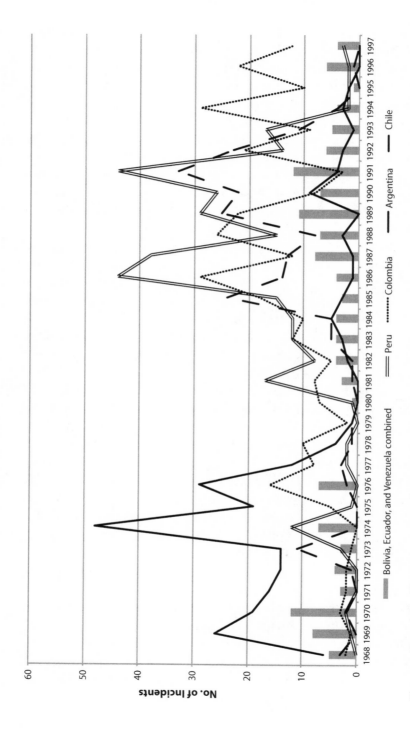

Figure 5.2. Terrorist incidents in seven South American countries, 1968–1997.
Source: Terrorism Knowledge Base (www.tkb.org), based on RAND data, accessed in 2007. Note: This site expired in 2008. See Brian Houghton, "Terrorism Knowledge Base: A Eulogy (2004–2008)," *Perspectives on Terrorism* 2, no. 7 (2008)

a humbled rival, while Argentina, albeit not exactly negotiating from strength, did not appear overawed by Chilean power. In the other cases, bandwagoning would predict rapprochement between Peru and Ecuador, and Chile and Bolivia: both of these cases had troop ratios above 3:1 and defense spending ratios that rose over time from 2.2:1 to 4.2:1 in the Peruvian-Ecuadorean case and from 4.1:1 to 5.1:1 in the Chilean-Bolivian case. Bandwagoning might correctly expect continued Colombian-Venezuelan rivalry, though: Colombia's troop advantage, only 1.7:1 at the beginning of the decade, was lost altogether as Venezuela achieved parity by 1987–1988.[11] High and increasing power imbalances failed to produce rapprochement, while cooperation emerged between a pair of countries shifting closer to power parity, seriously undermining a bandwagoning argument.

Fifth, perhaps the promotion of new norms of solidarity by a mutually respected third party could powerfully stimulate rapprochement. The United States, as the sole great power in the Americas and the leader of the Western Bloc, might be able to persuade rival anti-Communist states to set aside their disputes, for example. The Vatican might also have this sort of influence in a heavily Catholic region, and the success of papal mediation between Argentina and Chile clearly contributed to those countries' rapprochement in 1984, as will be shown below. However, cooperative norm promotion had an uneven track record in this period, especially if one includes overtures from neighboring countries—Colombia attempted to broker rapprochement between Bolivia and Chile starting in 1983, the United States attempted to convince Argentina and the United Kingdom to avoid war over the Falklands/Malvinas Islands in 1982, Argentina and the Secretary-General of the Organization of American States (OAS) pushed Colombia and Venezuela to stand down during their 1987 crisis, and Argentina, Brazil, and Chile separated Peru and Ecuador after their 1981 clash, but none of these initiatives had much success.[12]

Sixth, multilateral, and particularly subregional, cooperative endeavors might spill over into bilateral relations, constructing a new collective identity as a by-product of other activities. Mere membership in global and regional institutions such as the UN and OAS would not explain any of the variation in rivalry outcomes within the region, since all of the countries studied here were members. However, over the 1960s and 1970s, a host of new subregional organizations from trade pacts to mediation groups to intelligence-sharing arrangements provided venues for cooperative interaction among small groups of Latin American countries. Unfortunately, these organizations seemed to have little positive effect on bilateral relations among their members. The Andean Pact (formed by Bolivia, Peru, Ecuador, Chile, and Colombia in 1969 and joined by Venezuela in 1973, with Chile withdrawing in 1976) offers a good example. In the 1980s, the Andean pact comprised a club for the members of three ongoing rivalries, while the one case of rapprochement occurred between an ex-member (Chile) and the one Andean country that had never joined (Argentina). Similarly, Pinochet's Chile had launched Operation Condor to integrate the repressive activities of the Southern Cone militaries against a perceived common leftist threat starting in 1975, but enthusiastic participation by Argentina failed to prevent the two countries from marching to the brink of war in 1978.[13] Furthermore, Bolivia was a Condor participant, but a rapprochement attempt between the Chilean and Bolivian dictators of both countries in 1975 had failed, and La Paz broke off diplomatic relations in 1978.[14] Colombia and Venezuela participated in the Contadora peacemaking initiative in Central America starting in 1983, but this appears not to have spilled over into their bilateral relations. All seven of the rival countries participated in the Cartagena group to address the debt crisis, but this initiative began in 1984, after Argentine-Chilean rapprochement was already underway, and it quickly fell apart with little impact on relations among the other rivals.

I argue that the critical difference across these cases is that Venezuela, Ecuador, and Bolivia never developed the institutional mission of countersubversion by devoting scarce local resources to combat a real internal threat. As figure 5.2 shows, the most serious insurgent threat to any of these countries occurred in Argentina during the 1970s. Although the guerrillas (and thousands of civilians) had been wiped out long before the 1984 rapprochement, this repression constituted an ongoing internal mission for the Argentine armed forces, making them more amenable to accepting rapprochement with Chile (and the loss of their external mission of rivalry) when the debt crisis hit. Thinking in terms of organizational mission and parochial interest helps us understand part of the puzzle this chapter introduced at the outset—the emergence of cooperation between an authoritarian and a democratic government, against a common foe that was escalating in one country but already defeated in the other one, and in contrast to the continuation of rivalry among neighboring countries. Although the data in figure 5.2 begin in 1968, it is worth recalling that Venezuela in the early 1960s, and Bolivia later that decade, briefly faced Cuban-instigated guerrilla groups, although these were quickly suppressed with US assistance. US aid—financial or military, covert or open—undermined the institutional transformation of recipient countries' security establishments from external to internal missions and unintentionally prolonged regional rivalries.

In these negative cases, efforts by presidents and diplomats to achieve rapprochement generally foundered on opposition from the armed forces. In the wake of the 1979 Nicaraguan revolution and the "concomitant fear of a recrudescence of a Cuban-supported guerrilla insurgency in the Caribbean Basin," Colombia and Venezuela reached an accord in 1981 that would have resolved their territorial dispute, but the Venezuelan military successfully opposed it (the Colombian armed forces, while less enthusiastic than the presidents, "would not have objected strenuously").[15] A presidential summit in 1985 likewise failed to resolve their border dispute, and the two countries experienced a militarized crisis in 1987.[16] The power of the armed forces to influence foreign policy even in consolidated democracies, and the resistance by a national military against nascent international cooperation that would threaten its core mission, fits a broader regional pattern. Despite shared concerns about leftist insurgencies and economic crisis, a rapprochement effort between Bolivia and Chile failed in 1984–1986, and Ecuador and Peru actually clashed militarily along their common border in 1981 and 1991 and fought an outright war in 1995.[17] Counterfactually, if Venezuela, Ecuador, and Bolivia had devoted their armed forces to internal security and repression, and if serious guerrilla threats had emerged in those countries, they would have been far more likely to achieve rapprochement during the debt crisis of the 1980s. This argument appears more congruent than the alternative hypotheses with the pattern of rivalry and rapprochement across the four cases, but how well does it explain the actual success of conflict resolution and the emergence of cooperation between Argentina and Chile? In the next section, I briefly outline the trajectory of Argentine-Chilean relations and the emergence of rapprochement; afterward, I assess how well the relevant hypotheses explain this case.

From Crisis to Cooperation: Argentina and Chile

Argentine-Chilean relations for nearly two centuries after independence consisted of a contentious rivalry marked by numerous disputes over inhospitable terrain along their common border, from the Andean highlands to Patagonian glaciers to islands and channels near the Straits of Magellan.[18] Disagreements over a few portions of the border are still unresolved, although these primarily reflect technical problems of cartography rather than serious political conflicts.[19] This record of conflict, however, also featured recurrent presidential meetings and rapprochement efforts as well as periodic bilateral accords and waves of regional integration schemes that quickly became moribund.[20] How can we explain this dual history of rivalry and cooperation attempts? One Chilean scholar argues that it reflects a lack of coherent policy until at least the mid-1980s: although Chile's foreign policy as a whole has been "very uniform and consistent," it simply "has not designed a defined policy, of any permanence, towards the Argentine Republic" and thus operated "in an improvised manner against the circumstances that have presented themselves and without taking initiatives."[21] I suggest that a focus on intragovernmental politics offers a clearer explanation for this inconsistency: periodic presidential initiatives toward rapprochement and economic cooperation foundered on opposition from the armed forces, which had vested interests in maintaining rivalry. After all, not only did summits fail to transform the bilateral relationship, but they also proved insufficient to prevent militarized crises from breaking out. Most seriously, a crisis over the Beagle Channel brought both countries to the brink of war in 1978 despite a series of meetings between Presidents Jorge Videla of Argentina and Augusto Pinochet of Chile.[22]

A mediation offer from the Vatican led both countries to stand down and to participate in a mediation process that proceeded gradually and unevenly to a successful conclusion in 1984 with the Treaty of Peace and Friendship (henceforward, "the Treaty").[23] Rapprochement was hardly a guaranteed outcome of mediation in the early 1980s, however. Chile repeatedly condemned Argentine military incursions (by ship and plane) in its southern territory, protesting "reiterated violations of our sovereignty" and "the provocative attitude exhibited in several of these cases by the Argentine armed forces," arguing that "these deeds were seriously perturbing the process of Papal mediation."[24] Meanwhile, both countries made a series of arrests of possible spies (though releasing them as signs of good faith for the mediation, at the request of papal representatives), and Argentina closed its entire border after one such incident.[25] These tensions continued after Argentina invaded the Malvinas/Falkland Islands, triggering war with the United Kingdom. Chile maintained neutrality, abstaining from OAS resolutions that condemned the United Kingdom, and Chilean analysts worried even after the war that Argentine hardliners on the Malvinas issue would endanger Argentine-Chilean rapprochement.[26]

However, cooperation began to emerge during 1982 and 1983 even before Argentine democratization, although this mainly indicated a return to the status quo of the mid-1970s (i.e., before the Beagle Channel crisis) rather than the achievement of wholly new accords. First, regarding the papal mediation process, which was the keystone of the bilateral relationship, Argentina denounced in January 1982 a previous treaty (from 1972, on the Judicial Solution of Controversies) that had provided the juridical foundation for mediation; in September, though, Argentina retracted its denunciation, and the two countries agreed to extend the treaty to support the pope's efforts, which gave mediation a serious "push."[27] Second, in September 1983, Argentina and Chile ratified a nuclear treaty that had been signed in 1976 and drafted a new complementary accord on nuclear fuel cycles and heavy water, a symbolically important step given the security dimension of the nuclear issue.[28] Third, conversations between Argentine and Chilean diplomats revived in frequency and magnitude from 1981 to 1983, although these produced little fruit in the short run.[29] Meanwhile, Pinochet was clearly laying the domestic groundwork for a possible rapprochement, arguing in a March 1982 speech that in terms of the Argentine dispute "One should not confuse common sense with weakness, let alone cowardice."[30] Finally, the mediation process survived the death, in February 1983, of Cardinal Samoré, who had been instrumental in making and keeping the peace since the Beagle Crisis.[31]

Furthermore, although cooperation increased with Alfonsín's election and inauguration, the contribution of democratization to peacemaking is debatable.[32] Chile often lacked credible interlocutors during Argentina's dual regime change (the collapse of the Galtieri junta in the wake of the Falklands/Malvinas defeat and General Reynaldo Bignone's installation as head of a temporary military government, and the new elections that civilian Raúl Alfonsín won in October 1983), so any new leader with a mandate might have been welcomed.[33] Besides, during the campaign, Alfonsín hardly signaled major impending transformations of foreign policy, arguing that although a democratic government might "attain the respect of other democratic countries," in terms of economic relations, just like a military regime, "everyone does the business they can and obtains the prices they can."[34] After the election, Pinochet clearly preferred to focus on working with the president-elect rather than the lame-duck Bignone administration, and Alfonsín sent a personal envoy to Pinochet; at the inauguration, Chilean Foreign Minister Miguel Schweitzer met with Argentine leaders, including Dante Caputo, Alfonsín's foreign minister–designate.[35]

After a joint declaration in January 1984, Caputo and Chilean Foreign Minister Jaime del Valle signed the final Treaty of Peace and Friendship on November 29, in the presence of the Pope.[36] The Treaty offered multifaceted mechanisms of conflict resolution, which one Chilean lawyer summarized as "consultation, direct negotiations, conciliation and arbitrage," that clearly sought not only to resolve one dispute but also to prevent future ones from escalating—a serious improvement over Chilean-Argentine peace treaties of the nineteenth century.[37] Nor was peacemaking purely rhetorical: in 1984, for the first time that decade, there were no official protests over military incursions.[38] The Treaty did far more than simply resolve a specific dispute: it inaugurated bilateral cooperation in a wide array of issue areas from trade to joint border demarcation, which unfolded through new accords, visits, bilateral commissions, and other initiatives. In 1984, the two countries negotiated a bilateral economic integration accord, devoted major attention to physical integration (principally transportation and infrastructure), and even began talks on the Antarctic.[39] Over the remainder of the decade, relations gradually improved, but cooperation remained relatively shallow (though broad) until the 1990s, when Chilean democratization, a presidential summit between Chile's Patricio Aylwin and Argentina's Carlos Menem, and Chile's accession as an associate member to the Mercosur trade pact consolidated the new relationship.[40] Establishing a definitive date for rivalry termination is often difficult, but for Argentine-Chilean relations, 1984 is clearly the major inflection point in the bilateral relationship.[41] As Pinochet recalled, "we had consolidated peace in an extensive zone of conflict."[42]

Explaining Rapprochement

An onward-and-upward story of democratization, regional economic integration, and military and political cooperation fits well with several IR liberal explanations of stable peace.[43] However, these accounts are insufficient to explain the initial rapprochement between Argentina and Chile in 1984, which laid the political groundwork for integration.[44] Studies that interpret the protracted rivalry primarily in terms of territorial nationalism and socially constructed mistrust likewise have difficulty explaining the speed of rapprochement after Argentine democratization, perhaps leading them to underestimate the continued political power of the armed forces in both countries.[45] Even resolving the Beagle Channel dispute could not eliminate conflict, because other issues waited in the wings, from Antarctic claims to Patagonian migration to border demarcation in the Andes.[46] Integration and shared democracy may be vital for stable peace, but a deeply political process of conflict resolution between two very different regimes was the prerequisite for integration.[47] As Alfonsín recalled, when he took office, "the regional context was not favorable to the development of integration with neighboring countries, due to the existence of military regimes in Chile and Brazil," but he still "attempted to eliminate hypotheses of conflict with neighboring countries and transform relations of rivalry into effective, concrete, and permanent cooperation."[48]

Why did Argentina and Chile achieve rapprochement at the height of the debt crisis, while other regional rivals did not? And how did Alfonsín and Pinochet achieve rapprochement despite dramatically different political systems, while several of their predecessors had failed? To support my argument about why rapprochement succeeded when it did, I present three main empirical points. First, economic crisis provided a clear impetus for Argentine-Chilean cooperation, and this affected presidential foreign policy initiatives. Second, the preferences and behavior of the armed forces shifted decisively, from actively promoting the Beagle Channel standoff in 1978 to acquiescing to rapprochement in 1984 despite retaining tacit veto power over foreign policy. And third, the actions of individual service branches confirm the importance of prior mission development in this shift. Subsequently, I address alternative explanations for rapprochement.

The landmark achievements of the Treaty, not only in resolving a longstanding territorial dispute but also in catalyzing economic integration and new areas of bilateral cooperation, would have come to naught if either country's government had declined to ratify it. A persuasive explanation of Argentine-Chilean rapprochement thus needs to address not only the timing of the Treaty but also the domestic politics of ratification.[49] Who supported it and who opposed it? If former proponents of rivalry accepted the treaty, what changed their position? For Chile, the governing junta (the heads of the military service branches) had to approve any treaty; for newly redemocratized Argentina, the senate held that role (formally, at least; informally, the Treaty's acceptance by the armed forces remained critical). Pinochet's letter to the junta asking for ratification of the Treaty repeatedly refers to outside observers, perhaps indicating an attempt to pressure or persuade the service branches to acquiesce; after summarizing the Treaty's overall importance, Pinochet added his own "reflections," emphasizing that "for the first time in our history, a treaty is under the moral protection of the Holy See" and that "both the procedure followed during these years, and the solution achieved and that is reflected in the Treaty that I submit to your consideration, have had broad repercussion in the world as an example of good sense and political maturity."[50] In Argentina, Alfonsín called for a nonbinding public referendum on the Treaty; its tremendous support (81% of the vote) convinced enough senators from multiple parties to ratify the treaty, although the Peronists unanimously opposed it (the senate vote was 23-22 in favor of ratification, with one abstention).[51]

Randall Parish's account of Argentine-Chilean rapprochement quite correctly emphasizes the degree of presidential authority as a key factor.[52] However, this discussion of ratification leaves us with an unresolved puzzle: if Argentine military fragmentation after democratization explains the armed forces' retreat from foreign policy issues, then why didn't the armed forces (either as a whole, or as service branches or factions) take advantage of this opportunity to veto cooperation, since civilians were divided along party lines? In Chile, still an authoritarian regime in which every service branch had the constitutional right to veto a foreign treaty, Parish claims that ratification was "never in doubt," despite recounting the recalcitrance of the navy chief, Admiral José Toribio Merino.[53] Furthermore, discussing a later round of territorial dispute resolution in the 1990s after Chile had democratized and Argentina had consolidated its transition, Parish says that the Argentine military objected but lacked the political power to influence policy, while the Chilean armed forces "clearly retained the capacity to obstruct . . . if they chose."[54]

The acquiescence of the Argentine and Chilean armed forces to conflict resolution in 1984 needs to be explained. To do so, I argue that economic crisis provided tremendous incentives for rapprochement and that a prior shift in the armed forces' available missions caused them to support ratification of the Treaty in the context of that crisis. These two factors—the development of an internal security mission during the "dirty wars" of the 1970s and the policy tradeoffs resulting from economic crisis in the early 1980s—were jointly sufficient to cause rapprochement, irrespective of regime type. This is not to say that these factors were necessary for rapprochement, though: democratization, globalization, and the end of the Cold War in the early 1990s might have ended rivalry by themselves, for example.

The economic crisis clearly pushed both countries toward rapprochement. The sputtering and backsliding of the mediation process from 1980 to 1982 coincided with a domestically stable and prosperous Chile; Chilean diplomats praised the country's progress not only economically but also politically in the wake of the 1980 referendum that conferred an official presidential term on Pinochet.[55] Pinochet, reflecting on the 1981 economy, argued that it "was not yet disturbing. . . . Yes, some momentary problems existed," but "I swore categorically that in that year we would have the lowest inflation rate in the history of Chile" and "my affirmation has been absolutely correct."[56] The Chilean government remained confident of immunity from serious crisis even after the global recession began; a critical turning point came with the April 1982 sacking of Finance Minister de Castro and the currency devaluation that June.[57]

The 1982 crash produced major Chilean economic policy shifts away from the controlled orthodoxy of the "Chicago Boys," including turnover of four finance ministers by 1985, currency devaluation, some protectionism, and some debt-equity swaps.[58] By late November 1982, Foreign Minister Rojas argued at the OAS that "the global economy is crossing through its most severe crisis since the end of the Second World War," lamented the "inexplicable contradiction" that such a problem had not produced economic cooperation, and blamed this absence on "a dangerous lack of political will."[59] Pinochet summarized the Chilean economy of 1982 as "rearing up; unemployment increasing," with 1983 looking even worse.[60] Although Chile registered more than 6 percent GDP growth in 1984, copper prices fell to "the lowest rate in Chilean economic history" and this "united with the problem of indebtedness"; many predicted the fall of the regime.[61] By 1986, however, Foreign Minister del Valle was able to proclaim that "we are walking firmly on the path to economic recovery."[62] Argentine-Chilean rapprochement thus succeeded during the brief window of Chilean economic vulnerability.[63]

The economic crisis was particularly dangerous for the Chilean regime in relative terms, because Chile had performed so well over the previous decade (earning the "miracle" moniker), and because the government had pinned its legitimacy on continued economic success.[64] Decline unleashed opposition, and political violence escalated as the Chilean Communist Party declared 1983 to be the "decisive year."[65] In turn, repression provoked international condemnation over human rights violations, which isolated the regime further, limited its economic options, and exacerbated Chile's reliance on its Latin American neighbors for diplomatic support as well as economic cooperation.[66]

The Argentine economic window of opportunity for rapprochement lasted much longer than the Chilean one. Though Chile recovered swiftly from the crisis, Argentina did not (until the 1990s), which introduced tension and uncertainty into Argentine foreign policy.[67] As Jorge Lavopa et al. argued, "The critical economic situation thus provoked as well as the deteriorated image of the country in the international community, brought President Raúl Alfonsín to prioritize as immediate objectives of his government the elimination of the hypothesis of conflict and the development of the processes of regional integration."[68] For Argentina, "The problem of Latin American foreign debt was becoming the most important theme on the country's foreign policy agenda at the regional level," while domestically, in addition to the debt problem Argentina faced "runaway inflation . . . and insufficient resources for attending to society's multiple demands," but more than this, "economic problems seemed less important than political ones," particularly the tenuous authority of the civilian regime to govern and to control the old corporate interests such as the military and the unions.[69] Regional integration would be useful to improve the balance of payments, but as Alfonsín argued, "we do not believe that Latin American integration is an exclusively economic phenomenon but that it should be, above all, a political act."[70]

In 1984 Latin American leaders sought regional solidarity to deal with the debt crisis, meeting in Quito in January, Cartagena in June, and Mar del Plata in September.[71] In May 1984, Pinochet wrote to Alfonsín to express his solidarity in confronting the debt crisis, offering "my congratulations [for the] valiant initiative you have begun [in the] sense [of] denouncing the gravity of the social, economic, and political consequences that the current interest rates on foreign debt imply for the countries of the region" and "the full support for that initiative and the solidarity of my country and the Government [over which] I preside. Your Excellency can be sure of the collaboration of Chile to the end of finding new formulas to permit our peoples to rediscover the path of economic and social development that Latin America requires with such urgency."[72]

Although economic crisis beset each of the rival states in Latin America, most failed to achieve rapprochement despite these incentives. To understand why Argentina and Chile took a cooperative path in the context of economic collapse, it is essential to examine the preferences and behaviors of the two countries' armed forces. After all, the military had dominated government in the years preceding rapprochement, and the armed forces had been major proponents and beneficiaries of continued international rivalry. In Chile, the armed forces had benefited from major expansion during the prosperous early years of Pinochet's rule (the budget quintupled and the personnel doubled from 1972 to 1981).[73] Previously, economic difficulties and cutbacks in defense spending had produced military unrest against the Eduardo Frei government in the 1960s.[74] "The government's survival depended on the unity of the armed forces," argues Alan Angell, and that unity was found more in hierarchy and concern with national security (and the parochial and personal benefits of defense spending) than with agreement on clear policy choices.[75] Rivalry with Argentina was an important source of military prebends and prerogatives.[76]

Chilean anti-Communism and an internal security focus for the military began, as in much of Latin America, in the wake of the Cuban revolution; however, a shift away from the traditional mission of external defense against foreign rivals was neither immediate nor inevitable.[77] Internal security emerged as a major mission immediately following the 1973 coup, but this coexisted with rivalry for nearly a decade. In Chile, military repression under Pinochet preempted any serious armed opposition; the major armed rebel group, the MIR, had organized as early as 1965 but had not launched any major operations until after the coup

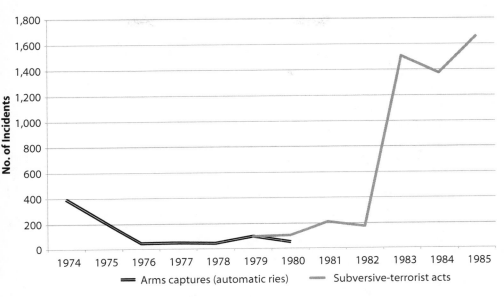

Figure 5.3. Chilean subversive threat, 1974–1985.
Source: Data compiled from Augusto Pinochet, *El Camino Recorrido*, Vols. II–III

and the ensuing crackdown.[78] Armed rebellion escalated during the early 1980s (figure 5.3), and Pinochet described the conflict not as a temporary flare-up but rather by analogy to an earlier "long war": "Irregular War was declared by the 'Moors.' What would the 'Christians' do?"[79] In terms of ratifying the Treaty, it is important to remember that Pinochet hardly had unlimited power.[80] The armed forces could have blocked ratification, and there was some resistance within Chile to the Treaty, even though it was generally favorable to Chilean interests.

In Argentina, the guerrilla threat had been even more serious. It led directly to the March 1976 coup (and the 1976–1983 military regime calling itself the "Process of National Reorganization"). Rivalry with Chile had also been an important source of the military's political power and autonomy. As Alfonsín pointed out, during a border standoff with Chile in 1965 the democratic Argentine government of Arturo Illia "employed the necessary energy, but contained the *golpista* [pro-coup] sectors that wanted to transform the episode into a pretext for a war."[81] An early wave of Argentine guerrillas in the early 1960s, inspired by the Cuban revolution, was quickly eliminated, but more serious threats came from the ERP (Ejército Revolucionario del Pueblo, or People's Revolutionary Army) and the Montoneros later that decade. Military repression was initially hesitant but escalated in late 1974 as Argentine political polarization and instability neared the level of civil war. The primary motivation for the 1976 coup was to wipe out the insurgent threat.

Although the guerrillas were fundamentally defeated by the end of 1978, and even though the Malvinas defeat in 1982 seriously weakened the political power of the military, coups were a real possibility until the end of the 1980s.[82] "As was often said at that time, in Argentina there had been no storming of the Bastille."[83] However, the military's main concerns were domestic, involving human-rights prosecutions and defense spending rather than rivalry. In foreign policy, Alfonsín worried that the restive armed forces might revive not interstate conflicts but rather the regional anti-Communist struggle that then engulfed Central America:

> I'll give you some examples of to what degree this was a vital issue. If the violence had reinstalled itself in any bordering country it could have happened that the antidemocratic sectors in Argentina would energize. As a result, the groups of the antidemocratic left . . . could have considered that they once again had an opportunity. Or on the other hand, they could have installed aid and assistance networks to the insurgents and this would bring together the potential repressors. . . . Our foreign policy with respect to Central America was very clear. We repeated, 'we don't want a war installed in the region.' And this was not only, although primarily, due to solidarity with the Central American peoples. We acted also in the service of the national interest. The installation of a war in that territory implied the regeneration, the broadening, the reinstallation of the East-West conflict after appearing to have been overcome.[84]

Alfonsín's former foreign minister, Dante Caputo, also referenced this fear: "One of the priorities of 1983 was to prevent the strategic conflict between Soviets and Americans from bringing similar consequences to those of the 1970s."[85] Particularly noteworthy in 1984 was the lack of military opposition to Alfonsín's initiatives regarding Chile. This is not to say that the military would have been able to orchestrate another Beagle encounter, but it certainly had the political power to dissuade a fragile civilian government from acting against its interests.[86]

The common threat of leftist rebellion did induce international cooperation initiatives both covertly and overtly, but these had little impact on the broader rivalry. Covertly, Argentine-Chilean intelligence services collaborated against domestic opponents through Operation Condor, but this did not prevent the 1978 militarized crisis, let alone deliver rapprochement. In the open, Chilean Foreign Minister Rojas Galdames argued at the United Nations in 1981 that "We consider of particular importance the study of the problem of terrorism, whose escalation constitutes an extremely grave threat. . . . Therefore, we have been giving a decided support to all those measures that, internationally concerted, seek to halt effectively this despicable and criminal method of political struggle."[87] Later that year, at the OAS, Rojas underscored that "the problem of collective security has acquired new relevance. Terrorism, supported from outside the region, from perfectly defined centers of power, is seriously disturbing the peace of many of our nations. . . . The inter-American system should, to survive as such, be ready to give its solidarity to the nations that require it."[88]

Further evidence for the military missions thesis comes from differentiating the behavior of the various service branches in each country rather than considering them monolithically. In both countries, the army gained more political power during the 1970s than the navy did; this both enabled and was reinforced by the army's dominance of (and the navy's marginalization from) domestic repression. Thus, when economic crisis compelled retrenchment and policy trade-offs, the army had a more viable alternative mission than the navy did, and therefore the army was more willing to support rapprochement and to ratify (whether de facto, in the Argentine case, or de jure, in the Chilean one) the Treaty than the navy was.

In Chile, Pinochet largely excluded the navy from power and from the spoils of the regime. The army gradually consolidated most of the senior government positions, especially after 1978 with the ouster of Air Force General Leigh; the navy did retain control of the foreign ministry (for a while), though. Pinochet's intelligence apparatus, the DINA, began as a separate entity from the service branches under the control of Colonel Manuel Contreras, but it increasingly came under army control. Broadly speaking, the army acquired dual internal and external missions, while the navy really only had the external one, and the navy was the only significant source of opposition within Chile to the Treaty of Peace and Friendship with Argentina.[89] This strongly supports a parochial interest argument. Moreover, the treaty reinforced longstanding Chilean claims, so the navy was clearly not operating out of territorial nationalism, and the treaty hardly betrayed Chilean national interests. Thus, we should interpret Pinochet's claims of the unity of the armed forces on the tenth anniversary of the coup (September 11, 1983) as at least partially aspirational rather than descriptive.[90]

In Argentina, the navy had promoted conflict with Chile in 1978 (sabotaging President Jorge Videla's overtures toward Pinochet) and Britain in 1982.[91] In the division of spoils among the Argentine service branches following the 1976 coup, the foreign ministry became a fiefdom of the navy, whose leader, Admiral Massera, was President Videla's archrival—the Proceso's first two foreign ministers were navy admirals.[92] As Videla explained in a later interview, "the war was a crazy idea; the Navy was the most hardline."[93] The Argentine Navy also attempted to fight above its weight class with respect to the "dirty war"; the most frequently publicized tales of horrific state-directed torture and murder concern the navy and particularly its Mechanics' School (the Escuela Superior de Mecánica de la Armada, or ESMA), a notorious torture facility.[94] A massive study of Southern Cone human rights violations, however, paints a slightly different picture: the army actually had more facilities for repression, and tortured and killed more people, than the navy did.[95] This suggests that the army obtained the bulk of the parochial benefits from the mission of countersubversion, while the navy tried to compensate by working harder with the resources it had. Additionally, it appears that Admiral Massera actually pushed (unsuccessfully) for the Proceso to declare victory in the "dirty war" in 1978, publishing a list of the fallen on both sides and ceasing further countersubversion (or at least curtailing its most repressive measures), which Videla opposed.[96] This behavior is difficult to reconcile with the image of Argentine repression as predominantly a navy affair, but once one recognizes that the parochial benefits from the countersubversion mission flowed primarily to the army, then simultaneous naval efforts to play a weak hand as strongly as possible and to unceremoniously end the game make more sense.[97]

Ultimately, rapprochement succeeded because the domestic actors in both countries that had maintained rivalry for their own interests in the past, and who retained the power to do so throughout the 1980s, acquiesced to presidential rapprochement initiatives to focus on their other major mission of internal security in the context of economic crisis. For the armed forces of Argentina and Chile, rapprochement was not a shift from hatred to brotherhood, or even from war to peace, but rather from one mission to another. As one Chilean scholar explained, although it is unlikely "that in the immediate future grave problems could arise for Chile caused by border conflicts," "The hypothesis of a territorial conflict or of other border frictions could arise, not from the nature of the remaining problems, but from the attitude that the nationalist sectors of one or the other country could adopt in this respect, or, more seriously, the military sectors, including for reasons of internal politics."[98]

Alternative Hypotheses

Realist arguments do not give much traction on the case. Argentina's search for rapprochement in the wake of the Malvinas/Falklands defeat might qualify as bandwagoning, but Argentina had already overcome its rivalry with Brazil before the war, suggesting some source of conflict resolution other than national insecurity. Additionally, Argentina's willingness to butt heads with great powers not only over the Malvinas/Falklands (even after the war) but also over economic issues indicates that material weakness hardly compelled restraint, while Chile's consistent stance favoring conflict resolution hardly seems like a posture of intimidation. A balancing logic seems to fit Chilean threat perceptions: facing a rising tide of terrorism, confronted with outside pressure and sanctions on human rights, and enmeshed in a regional economic crisis, Chile turned toward Argentina (and the rest of the region) for solidarity against common threats and problems. However, Argentine political violence had already dissipated (see figure 5.2): a true counterinsurgent coalition would have emerged in the mid- to late 1970s at the height of the "dirty war," but Operation Condor failed to translate into rapprochement. Certainly Argentina and Chile found temporary common cause in defending the region against the ravages of the economic crisis, including the Cartagena process. However, this interpretation would involve a very loose and dubious interpretation of "balancing against threat."

Constructivist approaches likewise offer less-than-compelling explanations of Argentine-Chilean relations. Regarding norm promotion, for example, Chile consistently resisted any exercise of moral authority by the UN and even the OAS. What about the influence of the United States? Actually, neither a redemocratized Argentina nor an obstinately anti-Communist Chile was particularly receptive to North American tutelage. There is some debate as to how conflictual Raúl Alfonsín was with the United States.[99] However, Alfonsín asserted in 1983, "An end must be put to the panamericanism that means nothing more than the quest to satisfy US interests through pseudo-neighborly schemes with Latin America."[100] Similarly, Pinochet recalls in 1984 "a strong reaction of rejection" against US officials who "came to stick their noses in our affairs," such as Assistant Secretary of State for Inter-American Affairs Langhorne Motley.[101] Chile and Argentina shared a Cold War vision of Communist threat, of each other as an ally against the USSR, and against leftist rebellion sponsored by Cuba but also of the United States as an increasingly unreliable leader of the Western Bloc.[102] Papal mediation seems a much more plausible source of norm promotion, though it tells us little about timing (particularly, why both countries accepted a settlement in 1984 that they had refused at the beginning of the decade). Finally, if cooperative interactions are expected to spill over into common identity, why did Operation Condor not yield rapprochement between Chile and Argentina in the mid-1970s, or at least prevent a near-war in 1978 at the height of internal repression? Other regional organizations have even less bearing on the emergence of cooperation—the Cartagena initiative on debt solidarity, for example, quickly fell apart as Chile opted by February 1985 to negotiate "in a separate form its foreign debt, and that as a private issue of the country."[103]

Liberal arguments also have difficulty explaining the rapprochement. A counterrevolutionary ideology clearly fits the Pinochet regime but hardly works for Alfonsín's civilian administration. A democratization argument works somewhat better—certainly democratization contributed to Alfonsín's policies toward cooperation with neighboring countries, but it seems excessive to credit Chilean foreign policy changes during the first half of the 1980s to Chilean democratization. Furthermore, Alfonsín supported democratization across the region,[104] which hardly explains the success of cooperation with Pinochet. Even if we accept the Pinochet government's rhetoric of "institutional consolidation" and "protected democracy" after the 1980 plebiscite, there is no indication that this purported regime change actually influenced Chile's relations with other democratic governments.[105] The tight management of debate surrounding the plebiscite and the drafting of the new constitution militate against an easy reading of this as objective "democratization."[106] Additionally, part of Michael Barletta's "diversionary peace" argument about Alfonsín and Brazil's José Sarney involved their mutual recognition of fragility and political reformism.[107] Clearly, the Argentines did not see Pinochet in this light, or a presidential visit between Alfonsín and Pinochet would have been logical.

Having evaluated the explanatory power of alternative IR theories, it is also important to assess the possible effects of the Reagan administration's foreign policy on relations among rival Andean countries. Combined with the discussion of unintended consequences of US foreign policy from Truman through Carter in the foregoing chapters, this suggests some troubling lessons for contemporary policymakers and security analysts regarding rivalries among allies.

The United States and Andean Rivalries

In some ways, the Reagan administration may have undermined incentives for rapprochement: almost immediately after taking office, Reagan asked Congress to renew small amounts of military funding for Argentina and Chile, and Secretary of State Alexander Haig declared that counterterrorism had displaced human rights as a policy priority.[108] To the extent that aid restrictions and human rights pressures under Carter had contributed to conflict resolution between Argentina and Brazil in 1979, in other words, even these marginal influences were reversed for the rivalries that persisted into the 1980s. However, a contradictory vector of US policy was arguably even more powerful: US interest rate hikes and resistance to regional debt restructuring exacerbated the economic crisis that incentivized Argentine-Chilean rapprochement in 1984. Ironically, the greatest US contribution to peacemaking in Latin American foreign policy in the first half of the decade came not from State or Defense but from the Treasury Department and the Federal Reserve.[109]

Reagan, like Carter, focused overwhelmingly on Central America and the Caribbean rather than on South America, and this too may have unintentionally reinforced opportunities for conflict resolution in the Andes.[110] Speaking at the OAS in February 1982, Reagan proposed the Caribbean Basin Initiative (CBI), a combination of foreign aid ($350 million for 1982), expanded trade (including lower US tariffs on most imports from Caribbean and Central American states), and investment incentives, to stabilize governments in the subregion against the prospects of Cuban-inspired insurgency. "If we do not act promptly and decisively in defense of freedom, new Cubas will arise from the ruins of today's conflicts," Reagan argued, which "requires us to help governments confronted with aggression from outside their borders to defend themselves. . . . Let our friends and our adversaries understand that we will do whatever is prudent and necessary to ensure the peace and security of the Caribbean area."[111] Even beyond the CBI, US foreign policy in Latin America focused on combating leftist revolution, both by aiding counterinsurgency in El Salvador (which received the lion's share of the CBI funds) and by attacking revolutionary regimes in Nicaragua (through protracted sponsorship of the Contras) and (much more briefly but with overt and overwhelming force) in Grenada. Thus, during the final stages of Argentine-Chilean rapprochement negotiations between December 1983 (Alfonsín's inauguration) and November 1984 (the Treaty of Peace and Friendship), the Reagan administration devoted its Latin American attention almost exclusively to sustaining the Contras and to combating and circumventing congressional restrictions on that assistance.

There is no indication that the Reagan administration opposed the Vatican mediation effort or the prospect for peace between Argentina and Chile, but conflict resolution in the Andes was hardly a central US policy objective. Arguably what Reagan wanted most from South America was an absence of headaches and distractions from other priorities: barring the Falklands/Malvinas War, Argentina is almost entirely absent from Reagan's memoirs and those of his secretaries of state, and Pinochet (who, unlike the Argentine junta, had refrained from invading territory claimed by other states) is not to be found except in reference to Chilean democratization at the decade's end. However, Reagan's support for counterrevolution in the Caribbean Basin suggests that had a new leftist insurgency arisen in the Andes, the United States might have either intervened or assisted the beleaguered government, mitigating the likelihood that this new threat could lead to subregional cooperation and rapprochement. However, congressional reluctance on these counts, particularly for larger countries farther away, might have tied Reagan's hands. Argentina and Chile maintained rivalry while Operation Condor received tacit approval from the Gerald Ford administration, escalated to the brink of war but also began mediation during the Carter administration's opposition, and completed the tentative process of rapprochement during the Reagan administration's inattention.

Although Reagan administration policies can neither be credited for Argentine-Chilean rapprochement nor blamed for ongoing rivalries elsewhere in South America, the legacies of previous US policy efforts continued to shape regional relationships, including in the Andes. In particular, because the prior development of alternative security missions based on the emergence of leftist insurgent groups affected the likelihood of rapprochement at the time of the debt crisis, US interventions in Latin America earlier in the Cold War may have had long-term consequences. By helping some Latin American governments eliminate nascent threats, particularly in Venezuela and Bolivia in the 1960s, the US unintentionally reduced the prospects for rapprochement later on (between Venezuela and Colombia and between Bolivia and Chile). Conversely, by supporting military coups and repressive dictatorships, particularly in Chile in the 1970s, US policy may have galvanized armed resistance that led, indirectly, to international cooperation.

And just as previous US foreign policies might have had an impact, at the margins, on South American conflict behavior during the 1980s, so might the foreign policies of other third parties. In particular, what might the successful Vatican mediation in the Beagle Channel dispute tell us about mediation's role in rapprochement? The religious dimension may indeed have bolstered the Vatican's legitimacy and success in both Argentina and Chile. However, the Catholic Church's lack of military power or tranche of foreign aid resources meant that it provided no material inducements to Argentina and Chile, thus permitting the policy tradeoffs of the debt crisis to operate undisturbed. Had the United States taken the lead in mediation—as it did between Egypt and Israel, for instance—it would likely have offered substantial military aid agreements, which, perversely, would have undermined the willingness of state agencies to sign on to full cooperation with the rival state.

In chapter four I argued that the time lag between the Cuban Revolution and the US resource commitments of the Alliance for Progress strengthened incentives for threatened, resource-deprived countries to work together, and thus that the Eisenhower administration's Latin America policy (and the presidential transition period before Kennedy launched his own agenda) may have accidentally protected rapprochement between Nicaragua and Honduras. Here, the Reagan administration's reticence to resolve the debt crisis, and its focus on Central America and the Caribbean rather than South America, likewise appears to have unintentionally reaffirmed the primarily domestic conditions that enabled Argentina and Chile to overcome their rivalry.

Alternative Missions and Conflict Resolution

Ultimately, what changed between 1982 and 1984 to push Argentina and Chile away from rivalry and into a successful rapprochement? Quite a lot of factors shifted, of course: Argentina's military loss to the United Kingdom, Argentine democratization, the onset of the Latin American debt crisis, the ongoing process of papal mediation, and the evolving US foreign policy agenda. What is the most persuasive causal story? Is there a straightforward connection between crisis and cooperation? Not likely, or else other countries in the region, similarly beset by the debt crisis, would have ended their rivalries. Furthermore, economic crisis alone would not explain why the pressure groups that had previously supported rivalry changed their policy positions—the armed forces might well cling to existing threat scenarios and missions in an economic crisis, all else being equal. Does mediation ineluctably produce rapprochement? Again, outside diplomacy should have worked with Peru and Ecuador, or Chile and Bolivia. And as we just saw, the Reagan administration's priority engagement in Central rather than South America may have unintentionally and marginally aided Argentine-Chilean rapprochement, while more direct mediation and assistance could have backfired. What about loss and democratization—would any Argentine government have sought a truce with Chile, irrespective of the economic decline and mediation? Actually, the Peronist electoral campaign of 1983, and the position of the Peronist plurality in the senate during Alfonsín's push to ratify the Treaty, hardly made rapprochement with Chile an inevitable consequence of democratic transition.

The most compelling explanation of Argentine-Chilean rapprochement in 1983–1984 involves military acquiescence to presidential cooperation initiatives, driven by the combination of an alternative mission defined by internal threats and the policy tradeoffs compelled by serious economic contraction. Additionally, this argument offers the best available explanation of the broader regional pattern of continued rivalries among the other Andean countries during the 1980s. It also suggests some important counterfactuals. First, had debt relief and foreign assistance been more quickly forthcoming in the wake of Mexico's default in October 1982, and had fewer countries retained sanctions on Chile, Argentine-Chilean rapprochement might have been delayed by several years, as the armed forces in both countries might have been emboldened to defend both their internal and external missions. Second, had Venezuela, Ecuador, or Bolivia developed serious internal security missions during the peak years of the Cold War in Latin America, the onset of economic crisis in the 1980s might have enabled presidents of those countries to gain military support for rapprochement with Colombia, Peru, or Chile, respectively.

Economic crises provide powerful incentives for rival countries to cooperate, but rapprochement remains a rare outcome because vested interests seek to retain their parochially beneficial missions rather than retrenching. During the 1980s debt crisis in Latin America, rivalry continued where at least one country's armed forces had not previously developed an alternative mission based on counterinsurgency. In the two rival countries that overcame their conflict, Argentina and Chile, the armed forces had already developed vested interests in internal security. As in previous chapters, the combination of state resource constraints and an alternative mission for government agencies offers a powerful explanation of whether, when, and which rival countries will achieve rapprochement. Do these findings hold up beyond the specific context of Cold War Latin America? In the following chapter, I suggest that parochial interest contributes significantly to explaining the difficulties of regional counterterrorism cooperation since September 11, 2001.

CHAPTER SIX

From the Cold War to the Global War on Terrorism

The United States is in the early years of a long struggle, similar to what our country faced in the early years of the Cold War. . . . A new totalitarian ideology now threatens. . . . Its content may be different from the ideologies of the last century, but its means are similar: intolerance, murder, terror, enslavement, and repression. Like those who came before us, we must lay the foundations and build the institutions that our country needs to meet the challenges we face.

—*US National Security Strategy, 2006*

For someone familiar with the history of US-Latin American relations, the new rhetoric of the war on terrorism sounds hauntingly familiar.

—*Kathryn Sikkink, 2004*

In Cold War Latin America, interstate rivalries often persisted because state agencies on both sides had vested interests in maintaining the status quo of protracted conflict. Despite Latin American armed forces' increasing attention to the threat of Communist insurgency, rapprochement between rival anti-Communist countries was a rare outcome, one that occurred only when state resource constraints forced policy tradeoffs, pressured state agencies to abandon their defense of rivalry, and opened domestic political space for leaders to achieve cooperative breakthroughs. What can these cases tell us about the prospects for overcoming contemporary international rivalries? Does parochial interest explain rivalry persistence despite common threat outside the context of Cold War Latin America, or are the guardian agencies I analyze in previous chapters unique to the civil-military politics of a particular region and age?

In this chapter I argue that the era of global counterterrorism after September 11, 2001, presents important similarities with the Cold War, and that the persistence of rivalry among countries facing a common threat from local insurgencies linked to the networks and ideology of transnational jihad is as puzzling as intrabloc rivalries were during the long struggle between the United States and the Soviet Union. Rivalry among actual or prospective counterterrorism partners vastly complicates coalition-building efforts and threatens to undermine effective regional counterterrorism initiatives, so it presents a serious policy problem as well.

The chapter proceeds in three sections. First, I compare the Cold War with the Global War on Terrorism (GWOT), with respect to the potential for a common foe to cause rapprochement. I acknowledge the inherent flaws and dangers in uncritical reliance on historical analogies (as well as the conceptual problems with the GWOT label itself), but I suggest that the two struggles have three main points in common: a protracted, global ideological struggle, a manifestation of common threat from local insurgent vanguards, and a central role for alliances and coalitions in countering that threat. Second, based on this analysis, I examine the set of rivalries as of 1999, identifying cases where insurgencies in Muslim countries might constitute common threats for rival governments.

Third, I analyze one of these most likely cases, the rivalry between Morocco and Algeria. As in Cold War Latin America, rivalry continued despite a clear common threat, and the continuation of conflict benefitted powerful security agencies in each country. Also, Moroccan and Algerian diplomatic behavior suggests that failed rapprochement initiatives in 2003 and 2005 reflected, respectively, sabotage by state agencies and end runs by national leaders King Mohammed VI and Prime Minister Abdelaziz Bouteflika. A resource curse, I suggest, is part of the problem: Algerian economic growth, fueled by oil export revenue, inhibits policy tradeoffs between internal and external security missions. In turn, this implies that US security assistance to the two countries, to subsidize counterterrorist operations in the sparsely populated deserts of the Maghreb, might unintentionally reinforce rivalry among allies.

Insurgent Vanguards and Regional Coalitions in Two Eras

No analogy in international politics should be applied uncritically, and the Cold War-GWOT comparison is no exception. However, recent efforts by the United States to assemble an effective coalition of allies against the common threat of Islamist terrorism do raise the question of whether rivalry among allies is likely to persist in the present era as it did during the Cold War. Analogical reasoning in international politics has serious consequences, as Yuen Foong Khong shows: analogies exert cognitive pressure on decision makers, limiting and directing their choice of policy options to those that fit the selected historical precedent rather than those that fit contemporary facts and analysis; thus, an analogy's usefulness for policy should be tested empirically rather than just debated rhetorically.[1] There is also the worry that leaders might cherry-pick comfortable or heroic narratives, glossing over the less sanguine aspects of the real historical episodes.[2] Thus, to determine whether theoretical and policy lessons from earlier cases are still relevant, we need to investigate to what extent and in which ways the situations are parallel.[3]

Studies of the Global War on Terrorism frequently cite the Cold War either as a model or a cautionary tale. Walter Russell Mead's *Power, Terror, Peace, and War* prominently argues that both eras reflect protracted ideological struggles that tend to inflate the security apparatus of participating states (and that concomitantly raise "moral challenges" for those states to live up to their cultural ideals) and in which a containment strategy is appropriate.[4] Official US government documents likewise bring up the Cold War analogy to guide policy in areas ranging from domestic mobilization to alliance management and from international institution-building to contesting ideologies and public diplomacy.[5] Most prominently, the *2006 National Security Strategy* employs this analogy on page one: "The United States is in the early years of a long struggle, similar to what our country faced in the early years of the Cold War . . . a new totalitarian ideology now threatens. . . . Its content may be different from the ideologies of the last century, but its means are similar."[6] Similarly, Deputy Secretary of Defense Gordon England argued when rolling out the *2006 Quadrennial Defense Review*, "Much like Korea was at the beginning of the long war against Soviet Communism, Iraq and Afghanistan are the early battles in another Long War against an extremist ideology."[7] Even critics of US counterterrorism policy see Cold War parallels, both in rhetoric and action.[8] Richard Falk, for instance, finds echoes of the Cold War in the "hunting license" that permits states to destroy their domestic opponents and in "Faustian Bargains" between the United States and oppressive regimes only too willing to link their own objectives with US policy.[9]

Three facets need analysis: the nature of the adversary, the strategic response, and the role of alliances within that strategy. First, who or what is the adversary? Even setting aside the facile criticisms that a war on terrorism, like a war on drugs or poverty, does not have an actual adversary (but rather a phenomenon, a behavior, or a set of actors so inclusive as to be misleading about the actual source of threat), US efforts to define the enemy have been unclear and uneven.[10]

The variety of labels for the adversary—including jihadi extremism, islamofascism, militant Islamic radicalism, and of course, terrorism—reflects this confusion.[11] The United States faces an organizational core defined by al-Qaeda, a network of other groups and individuals connected to that core though still very much autonomous, a figurehead in Osama bin Laden (at least until US special forces killed him in Abbottabad, Pakistan, on May 2, 2011), and an ideology with appeal in multiple regions.[12] This complexity is not terribly different from the Cold War, however—recognition of distinctions between social democracy and Communism, between nationalist and Marxist insurgencies, and of potential schisms among Communist countries was slow in coming. From Joseph McCarthy's hearings on un-American activities to Henry Kissinger's pursuit of détente with the Soviets and simultaneous normalization with China, and over the course of the Vietnam War, America's definitions of the precise boundaries of its principal adversary changed dramatically.

The most useful approach, as during the Cold War in the developing world, is to focus on the link between this transnational adversary and local insurgencies. This connection is particularly evident in Robert Pape's argument that suicide terrorism is embedded in "primarily nationalistic" terrorist "campaigns."[13] Several analysts have explicitly labeled al-Qaeda itself an insurgency, and one influential study argued, "While destroyed embassies in Africa, disemboweled tourists in Luxor, heavily listing naval combatants in Aden, and collapsed skyscrapers garner the lion's share of media coverage, the survival and, in most cases, the progress of the world's multiple ongoing Islamist insurgencies are likely the events that will have the most positive long-term effect for bin Laden's al Qaeda movement."[14] Although there are numerous differences between al-Qaeda and the Soviet Union, especially the fact that the USSR's nuclear arsenal threatened US survival while al-Qaeda is much weaker and that al-Qaeda displays a decentralized network structure while the Soviet Union ran a central state apparatus, the key point of similarity for applying the analogy is the nonmilitary, and particularly the ideological, dimension of the contest, which fuels a protracted struggle that flares up in contested parts of the developing world.[15] Thus, David Kilcullen compares al-Qaeda not to the Soviet Union itself but to the Communist Internationale (Comintern), "a holding company and clearing-house for world revolution," and Bruce Hoffman sees it as a "force multiplier" for local insurgencies.[16]

Indeed, the strongest parallel between Cold War leftist insurgency and contemporary global jihad is the organizational and ideological emphasis on a revolutionary vanguard that catalyzes low-intensity conflicts in the developing world.[17] In Che Guevara's words, "The guerrilla band is an armed nucleus, the fighting vanguard of the people."[18] The name "al-Qaeda," usually translated as "the base," is closely connected to the vanguard idea.[19] According to Gilles Kepel and Jean-Pierre Milelli, the jihadist use of "vanguard" ("*tali'a*" in Arabic) dates to Sayyid Qutb's 1964 book, *Signposts*, which "took it from Marxist discourse."[20] Abdullah Azzam, a Palestinian who preceded bin Laden in bringing Arabs to Afghanistan to fight the Soviets, wrote in his 1988 essay "The Solid Base" that "Every principle must be supported by a vanguard, which clears a path for itself toward society, at the price of vast efforts and heavy sacrifices. . . . This movement is the thunderbolt that causes the community's energy to burst forth, and triggers a long jihad in which its members take the role of leaders, pioneers, imams, and spiritual guides."[21] Prior to merging with bin Laden's organization, Ayman al-Zawahiri ran an Egyptian militant group called "Vanguards of Conquest"; his 2001 polemic *Knights under the Prophet's Banner* argued that the goal of a fundamentalist Islamic state in the Arab heartland could not be achieved unless the jihadists inspired mass support, without which they ran "the risk of seeing the Muslim vanguard killed in silence in a battle waged by the elite against the authorities."[22] Osama bin Laden, though not one of the leading jihadi thinkers, also discussed the vanguard model in his "Message to the American People": "All we have to do is send two mujahedeen to the Far East to wave a banner proclaiming 'Al Qaeda,' and the generals run . . . we have experience in using guerrilla warfare and attrition to fight tyrannical superpowers, as we, alongside the mujahedeen, bled Russia for ten years, until it went bankrupt and was forced to withdraw in defeat."[23]

Bringing the train of jihadi strategy full circle, a prominent recent manual for al-Qaeda followers, Abu Musab al-Suri's *Global Islamic Resistance Call*, cites Mao Zedong and Che Guevara, among others, on the dangers of engaging the enemy too soon, too conventionally, in fixed positions, and the manual argues that future operations should involve a combination of small-cell terrorism and "light guerrilla warfare" until political and military space opens up to fight more "Open Front" wars.[24] From Qutb's proposals to seize national power through coups, to Azzam's globalized struggle to achieve a territorial base as a springboard for future jihad, to bin Laden and Zawahiri's partially deterritorialized strikes at the "far enemy," to Al-Suri's suggested military responses to worldwide US counterterrorism since September 11, the central recurring thread is the necessity of a hardened cadre of ideologically and militarily trained operatives to ignite broader struggles and catalyze political change in the Islamic world, a model that Che Guevara would instantly have recognized. However, it is critical not to overstate the connections among insurgent groups across the Muslim world, or between any of them and al-Qaeda.[25] Again, this is not so different from earlier eras: a standard criticism of Cold War US policy toward conflicts in the developing world is that of a Procrustean tendency to see all wars of libera-tion, nationalism, or ethnicity as driven by Communist ideology and to suspect the hidden hand of Soviet (or Cuban, or Chinese) sponsorship.[26]

What is the appropriate strategy to deal with this adversary? Analogical rea-soning produces a clear policy recommendation: adopt a strategy of contain-ment and encourage embattled allies in the developing world to pursue counter-insurgency. Thus, Marc Sageman argues that al-Qaeda is like the Soviet Union in that its ideology is unattractive, its global ambitions are unattainable, and its cause is "self-limiting," so "the logical strategy is one of containment while wait-ing for the threat to disintegrate for internal reasons."[27] Similarly, Ian Shapiro proposes that containment would "ensure that we do not become entangled in the next Iraq—be this in Iran, Syria, North Korea, or elsewhere," instead allow-ing schisms to emerge within the adversary's ranks by avoiding Manichean lan-guage such as "clash of civilizations" or "Axis of Evil," and by encouraging some Islamist groups to struggle with the obligations of governance that could put them at odds with al-Qaeda.[28] The early post–September 11 period of unilateral-ism, neoconservatism, and direct US military action is thus likened to John Foster Dulles's proposed "rollback" strategy—ultimately a losing contender to George Kennan's containment recommendations—for dealing with the Soviet Union.[29] Similarly, Bruce Hoffman proposes replacing the GWOT construct, so closely associated with unilateralism and rollback, with a new model of Global Counterinsurgency (GCOIN).[30]

The value to the United States of committed allies may be even higher for global counterterrorism than it was during the Cold War, for at least three rea-sons. First, instead of balancing power to deter conventional or nuclear attack, the military dimension of contestation involves special operations, stabilization efforts, and reconstruction programs in several locations at once. Second, in the intelligence realm, the adversary is both more dispersed and (where concen-trated) more difficult to interpret and to infiltrate, due to remote locations, low numbers of enemy operatives, and US foreign language unpreparedness. Third, to the extent that counterterrorism or counterinsurgency needs to address root causes rather than simply killing enemy combatants, "the most practical way to proceed would be to form a new or expanded system of alliances and relation-ships," particularly in the Middle East.[31]

An astute study published in early 2001 frankly details the extent to which the United States is "dependent on foreign partners" for effective counterterrorism: "Foreign help is critical because of the transnational nature of the threat and because the United States simply does not have the information, resources, access, or authority to do by itself what needs done," from intelligence to renditions to "maintaining a consistent diplomatic stance towards a state sponsor."[32] Foreign partners are particularly critical for successful offensive military operations against terrorist groups.[33] The contemporary challenges of weak states—including their propensity to feed insurgency—only heighten the importance of regional allies for intelligence, border security, and spoiler management.[34] As one counterinsurgency analyst bluntly argues, "leveraging partners and local forces to fight a protracted conflict is a *sine qua non* for ultimate success."[35]

Several analysts' proposals for enhanced US counterterrorism alliances and partnerships draw on the lessons of the Cold War. The Cold War appears to remain the yardstick for measuring alliance effectiveness in Afghanistan and Iraq: European "frustrations resulted from the fact that the military campaign did not fit the model all had come to expect during the Cold War" in which allies would "join together and defeat a common enemy."[36] Thus, new alliances and global and regional organizations are needed to provide an "axis of stability in the battle against extremism" and help "to contain the most dangerous crises points—India-Pakistan, Israel, the Korean Peninsula, and the Taiwan Straits."[37] Although some argue that the United States will need to rely on flexible and thinly institutionalized arrangements for counterterrorism cooperation, rather than rigid alliance structures like NATO, this is still compatible with a containment strategy.[38] Ian Shapiro notes that George Kennan "had little time" for "international instruments" of foreign policy, including law, institutions, and "collective defense arrangements like NATO" but argues that these are critical for bolstering legitimacy and democracy in the current struggle; furthermore, the United States needs allies for providing human intelligence, cutting off financial flows to terrorist groups, and preventing territorial sanctuary and popular support for those groups.[39]

Key US government strategy documents also show the emphasis placed on the Cold War model for alliance management. Especially, the 2006 *National Strategy for Combating Terrorism* makes numerous references to the importance of allies and coalition partners to the success of US counterterrorism efforts.[40] Most prominently, the document draws on the Cold War analogy both in analysis and prescription, emphasizing that the GWOT "will be a long war. Yet we have mobilized to win other long wars" and noting, "During the Cold War we

created an array of domestic and international institutions and enduring partnerships to defeat the threat of communism. Today we require similar trans-
formational structures."[41] The *2006 NSCT* frankly claims that "most of our
important successes" in the GWOT "have been made possible through effective
partnerships," while "Continued success depends on the actions of a powerful
coalition of nations maintaining a united front against terror," with multilateral
and regional organizations playing an "essential" role.[42] The *2006 NSCT* concludes that "it will be essential for our partners to come together to facilitate
appropriate international, regional, and local solutions to the challenges of terrorism."[43] This final point makes the lessons of Cold War Latin American rivalries particularly important—the *2006 NSCT* goes beyond the need for partners
to work directly with the United States, noting that partners need to "come together" with one another, yet as the previous chapters demonstrate, this cooperation is rare and difficult to achieve.

How much of this approach has changed under the administration of President Barack Obama? Although analysts will debate the national security and
foreign policy consequences of the transition from Bush to Obama for years to
come, an examination of some initial strategy documents suggests that despite
some changes of language and focus from the Bush years, the emphasis on
counterinsurgent alliances has redoubled. In his preface to the *2010 National
Security Strategy*, President Obama recalled that "we were part of the most powerful wartime coalition in human history through World War II, and stitched
together a community of free nations and institutions to endure a Cold War";
going forward, "we will be steadfast in strengthening those old alliances that
have served us so well, while modernizing them to meet the challenges of a
new century," including "countering violent extremism and insurgency."[44] The
2010 NSS's insistence that "this is not a global war against a tactic—terrorism or
a religion—Islam," and that instead "We are at war with a specific network, al-
Qa'ida, and its terrorist affiliates," fits a containment strategy rather than one of
rollback.[45] The *2010 Quadrennial Defense Review*, while eliminating the "long
war" language of its predecessor, implicitly recognizes the protracted nature of
the struggle against al-Qaeda by emphasizing the fiscal and personnel strain
the United States has faced from years of war, by focusing on sustainability, and
by underscoring the importance of allies.[46] Finally, the *2011 National Strategy for
Counterterrorism* identifies al-Qaeda "and its affiliates and adherents" as the
"paramount threat" and argues on page one that "the source of the threat to the
United States and its allies has shifted in part toward the periphery—to groups
affiliated with but separate from the core of the group in Pakistan and

Afghanistan," so the 2011 NSC "maintains our focus on pressuring al-Qaʻida's core while emphasizing the need to build foreign partnerships and capacity and to strengthen our resilience" and "augments our focus on confronting the al-Qaʻida-linked threats that continue to emerge from beyond its core safehaven in South Asia."[47] Because of this continuing emphasis on regional counterinsurgent alliances, and because intrabloc rivalries have undermined previous efforts against common adversaries, we need to understand the relationship between the common struggle against terrorism and the persistence of regional rivalries in the Islamic world.

Rivalries and Counterterrorism since 2001

What are the prospects for continued rivalry among allies, and are these likely to hinder US counterterrorism efforts? In this section, I apply the lessons of the preceding chapters to the contemporary period, evaluating the effects of counterterrorism on relations among rival countries in the post–September 11 era. My parochial interest theory predicts at least three things for international counterterrorism cooperation, all else being equal. First, regional rivalries will tend to make counterterrorism cooperation less likely and less effective even when there is a pressing common threat. Second, resource constraints will affect security agencies' willingness to sacrifice existing missions to focus on new threats, and thus enhanced foreign and military assistance by the United States is likely to exacerbate rivals' intransigence rather than to coax them into sustained partnership. Third, US efforts to define its coalitions along democratic lines are likely to underestimate the potential for cooperation among authoritarian regimes and overestimate the ability of democratic leaders to deliver cooperation when opposed by vested bureaucratic interests.

Even a cursory examination of world reactions to US policy since September 11 demonstrates the difficulty of achieving and sustaining effective cooperation against a common foe. First of all, the countries most eager to join a counterterrorism bandwagon after September 11 were not traditional allies of the United States but rather regional powers like China and Russia seeking to tar their own internal enemies with the brush of global terrorism.[48] Second, as Sageman points out, existing US allies were "initially lackluster," and the Muslim world "offered only minimal protest" to the US invasion of Afghanistan (hardly a commendation of solidarity after the September 11 attacks); eventually, terror attacks in Bali, London, Casablanca, and elsewhere forced a majority of countries "to realize that this was not just an American problem, but a global concern with domestic consequences for them as well."[49] Unfortunately, the simultaneous

US war in Iraq reversed this progress, not only exacerbating terrorist enlistment that previously "was in the process of being extinguished" but also angering the broader Muslim community that had at the very least remained "mute" when the US invaded Afghanistan.[50]

As discussed in previous chapters, rivalries are the least-likely cases for security cooperation—if even the venerable Atlantic alliance has trouble presenting a united front, what chance do rival countries have to make collective action work? Replicating as closely as possible my research strategy from earlier chapters, I focus on rivalries among governments facing the prospect of al-Qaeda–linked insurgency, which primarily means Islamic countries. No Muslim country since the fall of the Taliban has had a fundamentalist Islamist government (though Iran may be a possible exception), so transnational jihad presents a potential common foe for all these governments, particularly since the senior al-Qaeda leadership only targeted the "faraway enemy" of the United States after giving up on their ability to topple the "near enemy" of secular nationalist regimes and traditional monarchies in the Middle East.[51] Furthermore, as David Kilcullen observes, there are distinct overlaps between the pattern of contemporary Islamist insurgencies and the areas of historical Islamic caliphates and the proposed future caliphate called for by al-Qaeda.[52] Even if one does not entirely accept former National Security Council Counterterrorism Coordinator Richard Clarke's "concentric circles" model as a description of the jihadist threat rippling outward from the hard core of al-Qaeda to the entire Islamic world, the goal of a vanguard insurgency as opposed to terrorism is to draw support from the general population to redress shared grievances.[53]

Where could affiliates of al-Qaeda wage insurgency, particularly with any chance of success? Only in Islamic societies (or places with substantial and geographically concentrated Muslim minorities, such as India, Israel, and the Philippines). Daniel Byman lists nine countries battling "al-Qaida linked insurgencies" after 2001, all of which are Islamic-majority countries except India.[54] Certainly there are important counterterrorism roles for alliances with Europe and Japan, such as in police work and financial operations, and with states in all continents on intelligence matters; as Nora Bensahel observes, the United States correctly relies on an overlapping "coalition of coalitions" in which different combinations of states tackle different functional areas.[55] Additionally, the United States can undertake several important counterterrorism policies on its own, particularly within the purview of homeland security. However, given the increasing importance of partnerships with counterinsurgent governments in the Islamic world, I restrict my focus to the prospects for alliance effectiveness against terrorism with those countries and to the role that rivalries might play in disrupting the counterterror coalition.

The prospect of al-Qaeda–connected insurgency varies widely across the Islamic world. Abu Mus'ab al-Suri, in his 2004 instruction manual for jihadists, concludes that "the great majority of Islamic states and entities, which comprise more than 55 states, are not at all suitable for open confrontation."[56] Al-Suri's "most suitable" candidates are "Afghanistan . . . Central Asia . . . Yemen and the Arab Peninsula . . . Morocco and North Africa . . . The Levant and Iraq," and he also lists Turkey, Pakistan, and parts of Africa.[57] This may reflect a shift from the focus of Islamist insurgencies prior to September 11—Afghanistan, Kashmir, Chechnya, the Philippines, Algeria, and Indonesia—in that Southeast Asia no longer seems as prominent.[58] In response, the United States is promoting regional cooperation in the Maghreb, South Asia, and elsewhere, in order to counter the jihadi threat.[59]

Is regional rivalry likely to prevent or disrupt cooperation against the common threat of Islamist insurgency? Alternatively, might the imperatives of counterterrorism cooperation induce rapprochement among erstwhile rivals, and if so, which are the most likely cases to examine? Table 6.1 lists thirty-eight active rivalries as of 1999, ten of which involved two states simultaneously facing internal conflicts; in six of those ten rivalries, both states faced a primarily Muslim (though not necessarily Islamist, let alone al-Qaeda–affiliated) rebellion.[60] These are some of the most likely cases for rapprochement caused by a common foe—though as the previous chapters suggest, the hurdles to cooperation are quite high even with such strong incentives. We should also consider cases where a common threat might emerge in the future, by examining the latent potential for insurgency—and, thus, for rivalry to disrupt international counterterrorism cooperation. Rivalries in which one country meets the above criteria, while the rival is an Islamic-majority state without an active internal conflict, and those where both countries are Islamic-majority, neither of which has an active insurgency, comprise another fourteen likely cases out of the thirty-eight total rivalries. Again, I in no way want to overstate the degree of common identity among governments of Islamic states, among rebel groups, or even among Islamist insurgencies—cleavages between Sunni and Shia, for example, may trump all others, and in any event I do not want to stretch the assumptions of the Cold War–GWOT analogy past the breaking point. An additional complication for case selection arises from states participating in more than one rivalry. Of the six rivalries where both states face Muslim rebel groups, Iraq, Egypt, India, and Israel each participate in two. The only rivalry of the six

TABLE 6.1

Rivalries, internal conflicts, and religious affiliation, circa 1999

		Country A				Country B			
Region	Begin	Name	Internal conflict	Muslim insurgency	Muslim majority	Name	Internal conflict	Muslim insurgency	Muslim majority
MENA	1962	Algeria	Y	Y	Y	Morocco	Y	Y	Y
MENA	1945	Egypt	Y	Y	Y	Iraq	Y	Y	Y
Asia	1947	India	Y	Y		Pakistan	Y	Y	Y
MENA	1948	Iraq	Y	Y	Y	Israel	Y	Y	
MENA	1948	Egypt	Y	Y	Y	Israel	Y	Y	
Asia	1948	China	Y	Y		India	Y	Y	
MENA	1991	Egypt	Y	Y	Y	Sudan	Y		Y
Africa	1965	Ethiopia	Y			Sudan	Y		Y
Africa	1994	Sudan	Y	Y		Uganda	Y		
Europe	1992	Bosnia	Y		Y	Croatia	Y		
Asia	1996	Afghanistan	Y	Y	Y	Iran			Y
MENA	1979	Egypt	Y	Y	Y	Iran			Y
MENA	1968	Iraq	Y	Y	Y	Saudi Arabia			Y
MENA	1946	Iraq	Y	Y	Y	Syria			Y
MENA	1961	Iraq	Y	Y	Y	Kuwait			Y
MENA	1986	Bahrain	Y	Y	Y	Qatar			Y
MENA	1948	Israel	Y	Y		Syria			Y
Asia	1973	China	Y	Y		Vietnam			
Asia	1949	China	Y	Y		Taiwan			

Americas	1831	Colombia		Venezuela	Y
Europe	1992	Bosnia		Serbia	Y
Europe	1991	Croatia		Serbia	Y
MENA	1958	Iran	Y	Iraq	Y
MENA	1990	Saudi Arabia	Y	Yemen	Y
Asia	1991	Kazakhstan		Uzbekistan	Y
Africa	1975	Cameroon		Nigeria	Y
Europe	1955	Greece		Turkey	Y
MENA	1979	Iran	Y	Israel	Y
Africa	1993	Eritrea	Y	Sudan	Y
Europe	1998	Eritrea	Y	Ethiopia	Y
Americas	1965	Argentina		Britain	Y
MENA	1968	Iran	Y	Saudi Arabia	Y
MENA	1946	Jordan	Y	Syria	Y
Asia	1991	Armenia		Azerbaijan	Y
Americas	1966	Guyana		Venezuela	
Americas	1959	Cuba		USA	
Asia	1948	North Korea		South Korea	
Americas	1836	Bolivia		Chile	

Source: List of rivalries, participants, and dates adapted from Colaresi, Rasler, and Thompson, *Strategic Rivalries*, 38–50; data on religious affiliation drawn from CIA *World Factbook* online, www.cia.gov/library/publications/the-world-factbook/fields/2122.html, accessed in 2008; list of rebellions as of 1999 from Heidelberg Institute on International Conflict Research, *Heidelberg Konfliktbarometer 2000*, www.hiik.de/de/konfliktbarometer/pdf/Konfliktbarometer_2000.pdf.

that does not involve at least one of these countries, and thus arguably the most straightforward case, is that of Morocco and Algeria. Thus, if the common foe of Islamist insurgency is ever going to produce rapprochement, the Maghreb is where we should look first.

Algeria and Morocco: Protracted Rivalry in the Maghreb

Morocco and Algeria in many ways present the most likely case among contemporary rivalries for cooperation against a common foe. Both are Sunni Muslim countries with mostly secular (or at least, Islamic without being Islamist) governments struggling to control popular demands for political opening and reform; both face longstanding insurgencies and have recently experienced vicious terrorist attacks linked to al-Qaeda, and both are members of the United States' Trans-Sahara Counter-Terrorism Initiative as well as NATO's Mediterranean Dialogue.[61] Furthermore, calls for regional unity in the Maghreb have longstanding political resonance, dating back to Morocco's support for Algeria's independence struggle in the late 1950s (and given new life with the Arab Maghreb Union, founded in 1989); given the "common language, religion, and history of colonization" in the region, "it is surprising that relations have been so bad."[62] Certainly there are important divisions as well, which underpin rivalry: Algerian support for the Polisario guerrillas in the Moroccan-held territory of Western Sahara, the Tindouf territorial dispute, and incompatibility between Algeria's nationalist military-dominated regime and Morocco's traditional monarchy. Given the prominence of common threat, however, both IR scholars and US policymakers ought to ask, why has counterterrorism not displaced rivalry, and what can be done to remedy this?

Rivalry between Morocco and Algeria is longstanding, sporadically violent, and expensive. Conflict began with Algerian independence from France in 1962 and led to a border war in 1963.[63] Beyond any specific territorial dispute, Morocco and Algeria are "inherent rivals, neighboring states of the same size with differing histories, state systems, ideologies, and external allies," and they "have been vying with each other for regional dominance since their independence."[64] Spain's withdrawal from its colonial territories in Western Sahara (which bordered both Algeria and Morocco) in 1975 created a power vacuum that escalated the rivalry.[65] Morocco claimed the territory but faced an insurgent threat from the Polisario (an abbreviation of "Popular Front for the Liberation of Saguía el Hamra and Río de Oro," the names of the former Spanish territories), which in turn received aid from Algeria. In November 1975, King Hassan II led 350,000 Moroccan civilians on the Green March into the northern section of

Western Sahara (Mauritania had annexed the southern half); the following year, Algeria officially recognized an independent Sahrawi Arab Democratic Republic (declared by the Polisario), and Morocco and Algeria broke diplomatic relations. After a military coup in 1978 supported by the Polisario, Mauritania withdrew from the Western Sahara, the Moroccan military occupied the evacuated territory (thus staking its claim to the entire Western Sahara), and the Polisario fled to refugee camps across the Algerian border, in the Tindouf region.[66] The Sahara dispute has been at a standstill ever since, despite attempts at mediation. Meanwhile, Moroccan counterinsurgency, Algerian support for a proxy war in the contested territory, and both sides' preparations for a possible escalation to interstate war have been costly.[67] One analyst estimates that the Sahara war absorbed 25 percent to 40 percent of the Moroccan budget beginning in 1976, although Morocco also received foreign aid from Gulf Arab monarchies, especially Saudi Arabia, and the United States up through the mid-1980s.[68] The Western Sahara dispute is thus deeply entwined with Algerian-Moroccan rivalry, and neither is likely to be resolved without a lasting solution to the other.[69]

Failed attempts at reconciliation by heads of state have punctuated the course of this rivalry. Morocco's King Hassan II and Algeria's Chadli Benjedid met in February 1983, May 1987, and May 1991. Although the two countries restored diplomatic relations in May 1988 as part of this process and King Hassan traveled to Algiers for a Maghreb summit that year, they were unable to resolve the Sahara dispute or put an end to bilateral rivalry.[70] These summits were driven by a combination of economic imperatives (both incentives to integrate and the need to cut security budgets related to the Sahara conflict), outside mediation (particularly by France in 1983, Saudi Arabia in 1988, and the United Nations in 1991), and domestic political vulnerability.[71]

The 1991 summit in particular illustrates the domestic obstacles facing would-be peacemakers. After UN Secretary General Javier Pérez de Cuéllar had met separately with King Hassan II and Algerian President Chadli Benjedid in their respective capitals, the two leaders held a three-day summit in the Algerian border city of Oran in May, with particular focus on Western Sahara.[72] At the time, King Hassan supported the US-led Gulf War to oust Saddam Hussein from Kuwait, and Moroccan Islamic fundamentalists and nationalists portrayed him as insufficiently Muslim and insufficiently Arab, respectively, for doing so.[73] In Algeria, Benjedid faced massive demonstrations by fundamentalist supporters of the Islamic Salvation Front (FIS, in its French acronym), which was poised to win upcoming parliamentary elections.[74] That December, the FIS won the first round of parliamentary elections, and the Algerian military prevented the second round of elections with a coup against Benjedid.[75] Neither the military nor the president it installed to replace Benjedid, Mohammed Boudiaf, restarted the rapprochement process with Morocco, and with the coup and Boudiaf's assassination in June 1992 (by a member of the Algerian special forces), Algeria fell into civil war.[76]

Perhaps the stalled Western Sahara dispute, the failure of rapprochement initiatives by Algerian and Moroccan heads of state, and the persistence of rivalry were unsurprising when North African governments seemed relatively unthreatened. The rise of Islamist insurgency and terrorism in both countries in the 1990s and 2000s, and the shift in US policy after September 11, however, make the lack of cooperation much more surprising. Both Moroccans and Algerians have been active in al-Qaeda's networks, for instance.[77] In Algeria, the main Islamist militant organization renamed itself in 2006 from the Salafist Group for Preaching and Combat (GSPC) to Al-Qaeda in the Islamic Maghreb (AQIM) and appears to be increasingly applying al-Qaeda's rhetoric and tactics, including the April 2007 attacks in Algiers; however, these trends also meet resistance from the GSPC's "traditional leaders" since "Algerian terrorist groups have always been fiercely independent."[78] It is important to recognize, however, that violence in Algeria had substantially reduced from the height of the civil war in the early 1990s: the GSPC merged with al-Qaeda in part out of desperation, although the merger seems to have revived it.

Morocco has also faced an escalation of terrorism and repression, though it started at a lower level than Algeria. The 2003 bombings in Casablanca and the 2004 bombings in Madrid (also perpetrated by Moroccans) appear to have placed Islamist terrorist groups, rather than the longstanding Sahrawi separatists of the Polisario, at center stage for Moroccan internal security. One analyst argues that the Casablanca bombings served as Morocco's September 11, shattering the commonly held notion of "Moroccan exceptionalism" from the regional pattern of Islamist political violence.[79] Islamist militant groups in Morocco, principally the GICM (Moroccan Islamic Combatant Group) and SJ (Salafiya Jihadia), emerged in the 1990s. Although some of their leaders participated in the Afghan war in the 1980s and the groups display some operational hallmarks of al-Qaeda, such as simultaneous attacks, evidence of explicit collusion between the groups and al-Qaeda remains anecdotal.[80] Morocco still lacks a true al-Qaeda–linked insurgency, with "lone wolf" attacks linked to al-Qaeda much more common, although AQIM remains a serious threat in the eyes of the Moroccan government, which sees its handiwork in recent plots.[81] Any operational link between the Polisario and an al-Qaeda affiliate like AQIM would heighten the prospect of serious insurgent violence in Morocco and would underscore the common threat to both Rabat and Algiers, but such connections remain hypothetical.[82]

Testimony at a US House Committee on Foreign Affairs hearing in 2007 underscores the importance of the common threat and its potential—as yet unrealized—to produce security cooperation in the Maghreb. C. David Welch, assistant secretary of State for Near Eastern Affairs, starkly described the threat of jihadi terrorism in North Africa: "The number of spectacular terrorist attacks in the region has risen, terrorist groups are using tactics and attacking targets that they had previously avoided, and terror cells have been discovered in places where they had not been seen before. We also are seeing evidence that the region's terrorist groups are increasingly attempting to build ties with each other and with the global jihadist network."[83] This creates a possible stimulus for regional cooperation, as the Kingdom of Morocco explained in a written statement to the Committee: "we believe it is essential to resolve these issues without further delay so that, as a region, we can advance the interests of our own people while protecting them from extremist influences that seek to take advantage of our differences and undermine the stability of both our individual nations and our region as a whole."[84] And yet rivalry has persisted despite these incentives. Congressman Tom Lantos, the committee chairman, observed that "given the tensions among the countries of North Africa, my impression is that the cooperation is minimal, and in some cases barely existing."[85]

Parochial Interest, Sabotage, and End Runs in Algerian-Moroccan Relations

Parochial interest helps to explain the persistence of Algerian-Moroccan rivalry in the face of common threat, since rivalry is defended in both countries by the state agencies whose interests it serves. In Algeria, Steven Cook demonstrates that the military has vetoed any cooperation with Morocco: Presidents Chadli Benjedid and Abdelaziz Bouteflika (elected in 1999 and re-elected in 2004 and 2009) have pushed for rapprochement, and the proscribed Islamist opposition has also called for it, but the military holds final authority and brooks no change of policy.[86] Although Bouteflika has managed to replace some high military officers with those more loyal to him, "the military continues to be the critical power-broker in the political system"; one of the generals he ousted from the capital was made ambassador to Morocco, a posting that "betrays the continuing influence of the military."[87] As President Bouteflika has tried to push forward with political reforms, he has had to pay off the armed forces, authorizing, for example, $6.3 billion of arms purchases from Russia; it is unclear to what extent the need for parity with rival Morocco was the main cause, or mostly a rhetorical justification, for this buildup.[88]

In Morocco, King Mohammed VI (who took the throne after his father, Hassan II, died in 1999) may have much more authority than his Algerian counterpart; however, the *makhzen,* or state apparatus, wields tremendous influence over policy behind the scenes, and the security forces are key players in the *makhzen.*[89] Historically, the armed forces had less political prominence in Morocco than Algeria, due to their lesser role in the independence struggles, although they were still strong enough in the 1970s that they attempted two coups. Since then, the monarchy has combined direct control of the armed forces (eliminating the Ministry of Defense and imprisoning officers involved in coup attempts) with significant side payments including tacit acceptance of military corruption and, using the rivalry with Algeria as a central rationale, steadily upgrading military equipment, including a major purchase of French Rafale fighter jets.[90] Even the Green March, after the purges of coup-prone officers, may demonstrate not the monarchy's power but rather its reactivity: one analyst argues that in 1975 "it is quite likely that if Hassan had not acted decisively, the Moroccan Army would have moved into the Sahara without him. . . . King Hassan has been a follower and rallier, rather than a leader, of public opinion on the Sahara issue . . . the King has exercised a restraining influence—not only on the Istiqlal party, which still espouses Morocco's irridentist claims to territories in western Algeria, but also on military commanders who want to attack Polisario sanctuaries across the border in the Tindouf region of southwest Algeria. In the midst of a war he cannot afford to lose, Hassan is like a man obliged to ride on the back of a tiger."[91]

Those surprised by the lack of cooperation between Morocco and Algeria despite the pressing common threat of jihadist insurgency and terrorism should consider the lessons of international rivalries in Cold War Latin America. In particular, these conflicts suggest the absence of serious resource constraints has enabled state agencies to sustain both internal and external security missions. From 1981 to 2010, Morocco's GDP grew at an average of 3.81 percent and Algeria's at 2.74 percent; in the 2001–2010 decade, the rates were even higher, with Algeria at 3.7 percent and Morocco at 4.95 percent.[92] Equally impressive, both countries have paid down (and grown out of) their foreign debt: Morocco declined from a high debt burden of 131 percent of GNI in 1985 to a low of 24 percent in 2008, and Algeria from a high of 83.5 percent in 1995 to a mere 3.5 percent in 2008.[93] Figure 6.1 illustrates these impressive achievements. Fur-

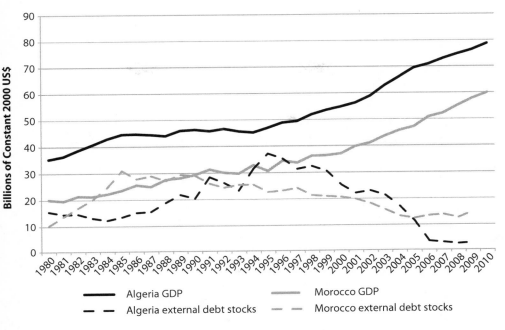

Figure 6.1. GDP and foreign debt in Algeria and Morocco, 1980–2010.
Source: World Bank, World Development Indicators

thermore, both countries have weathered the global economic crisis of the late 2000s admirably. In Algeria, growth has been sustained primarily by oil and natural gas exports; in Morocco, by foreign trade (particularly fishing and agriculture, though increasingly in energy), remittances, and tourism.[94]

All of this enabled a prolonged, if uneven, expansion of defense spending and manpower (figure 6.2). Between the late 1980s and the late 2000s, the two countries' combined defense expenditures have more than doubled in constant dollar terms, and their combined troop strength has nearly doubled. Additionally, the two countries have generally kept pace with one another's buildup. In most years neither country has outspent the other by more than 50 percent (i.e., the spending ratio stays between 0.67 and 1.5), and the main outliers represent temporary retrenchment by one country rather than a dramatic increase by the other. Morocco outspent Algeria by two to one in 1991 during Algeria's abortive democratic opening (a ratio the Algerian military quickly rectified), and Algeria did the same in 2000 after Moroccan defense cuts in the relatively threat-free period of the late 1990s (Morocco swiftly reversed course in 2001 due to increased

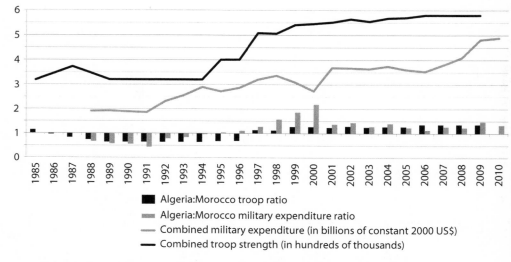

Figure 6.2. Defense spending and manpower in the Algerian-Moroccan rivalry, 1985–2010.
Source: Calculated from World Bank, World Development Indicators Online, except troop data for 1987 from Institute for International and Strategic Studies, *The Military Balance, 1987–1988* (London: IISS, 1988); troop data for 1986 and 1988 are averages of the IISS 1987 figure with the World Bank figures for 1985 and 1989, respectively

security concerns). In terms of troops, Morocco held about a 50-percent advantage from 1988 to 1994, and although Algeria gained numerical superiority in 1997 it has yet to reach a 50-percent advantage. These data suggest that security forces in Algeria and Morocco have expanded to meet their internal security threats while maintaining their external missions associated with rivalry.

In this situation, a parochial interest argument would expect the state apparatus to defend both missions against encroachment and rapprochement initiatives by national leaders to involve diplomatic end runs. As anticipated, Moroccan and Algerian heads of state have employed such maneuvers, including private personal meetings, letters, and envoys, to seek rapprochement, though without success. King Mohammed and Abdelaziz Bouteflika met privately for two hours after a summit of Arab leaders in Algiers on March 24, 2005.[95] The meeting was particularly important because it was the first visit by a Moroccan head of state to Algeria since 1991 (by King Hassan II, King Mohammed's father); Bouteflika had visited Morocco in 1999 for King Hassan's funeral, and Bouteflika and Mohammed had also met at other regional meetings.[96] After a 2007 al-Qaeda suicide bombing in Algeria, King Mohammed sent a letter to

President Bouteflika offering "total commitment to defeat the criminal terrorism gangs" and seeking "solid bilateral cooperation, to mobilise all our energy and unite our efforts to eradicate terrorism in our region," noting that Algeria's internal security is also "an integral part of Morocco's security."[97] In 2010, the leaders exchanged letters: Bouteflika declared to King Mohammed that the "two brother countries" were "united by their historic links and challenges of the future,"[98] while King Mohammed, after sending a delegation to the funeral of Bouteflika's brother, wrote to Bouteflika on Algeria's independence day (July 5) that he wanted to achieve "reconciliation and solidarity between the two countries."[99] In April 2011, President Bouteflika visited Tlemcen, a city on the border with Morocco, and declared that "Morocco is a neighbor and brother. We must cooperate."[100] In a speech on November 7, 2011, King Mohammed similarly called for cooperation "with sister Algeria, to achieve a new Maghreb order."[101]

Meanwhile, the foreign ministers of both countries have repeatedly articulated incompatible positions and mutual recriminations, interspersed with occasional platitudes on regional unity. An interview with Mohammed Benaissa, the Moroccan foreign minister, on Al Jazeera TV in August 2003 illustrates the divergence:

> Benaissa: Algeria always says that [the Western Sahara] file is now at the United Nations and concerns the separatist Saharans, who live in Tindouf, and Morocco. We, on the other hand, say that this is a regional geo-political problem, basically between Algeria and Morocco. . . .
>
> [The interviewer]: Several days ago, Abdelaziz Bouteflika also made an appeal to restore relations between Morocco and Algeria. It seems that Algeria has the same desire?
>
> Benaissa: But the brothers in Algeria say let us leave the Sahara file aside and focus on other files, both bilateral and within the AMU. Could they cite an example of any country in the world that asks its neighbour to normalize matters while keeping a problem, an armed group that is supplied with weapons by Algeria, as if nothing has happened. This is not possible. If the Polisario were on Mars, then we would accept this. But they are on Morocco's borders, inside Algeria, and armed inside Algeria. Algeria and its diplomacy are mobilizing all resources against Morocco as regards this file. Therefore, we say, let us sit together—with the Algerian brothers and the others—and let us start a frank and direct constructive dialogue to arrive at a political solution, which we all can agree on.[102]

Confirming the difference in perspectives, Algerian Foreign Minister Belkhadem declared in October 2004 that "no crisis nor tension between Algeria and

Morocco" existed; although "there is a divergence" regarding Western Sahara, "in other fields, notably bilateral cooperation, there is no divergence between us, but rather a joint approach."[103] As with the Brazilian position vis-à-vis Argentina in the mid-1970s, Algeria in 2004 denied the existence of a negotiable dispute.

In 2009, Moroccan Foreign Minister Taieb Fassi Fihri, at a meeting of the Arab Maghreb Union, voiced Morocco's desire to restore normal relations with Algeria, but he appeared to undermine this by telling the Moroccan House of Representatives that Morocco "cannot tolerate provocative maneuvers by the enemies of its territorial integrity, both inside and outside of the kingdom" and that "Algeria has set up a strategy aimed at annihilating Morocco's achievements in the defense of territorial integrity."[104] In turn, Belkhadem (at that point secretary-general of the FLN, though apparently angling for an official position as the government's minister on relations with Morocco) dismissed the allegations, arguing that Moroccan leaders "do not know exactly what they want," since Morocco was simultaneously negotiating with the Polisario and making accusations against Algeria.[105]

Mutual recriminations continued in 2011. After series of meetings between high-level officials in both governments generated public speculation that the two countries would open their borders (which had been closed since 1994), Algerian Prime Minister Ahmed Ouyahia dismissed the rumors, declaring that the border with Morocco would remain closed given the absence of a "good climate for re-establishing trust" based on Moroccan accusations that Algeria had aided Libya's mercenaries.[106] Fassi Fihri responded that that Morocco "regretted" Ouyahia's assertions and denied that Morocco had made such accusations in the first place.[107]

A new opening appears to be underway. However, the lessons of Cold War Latin America suggest several reasons to doubt its prospects: the litany of previous diplomatic failures, the continued strength of the Algerian economy, the prospects for increasing US assistance, and the possibility of uncontrolled popular unrest in both countries. Fassi Fihri and Algerian Foreign Minister Mourad Medelci met at the Arab-Turkish Cooperation Forum on November 16, 2011, after which Medelci declared, "Very soon, we will find the path that leads us to something we all dream of, not only bilateral relations between Algeria and Morocco, but also this ambition we have for the Maghreb."[108] In January 2012, Saad Eddine Othmani (who replaced Fassi Fihri as Morocco's foreign minister) visited Algiers, again discussing the improvement of relations.[109] Also in January, Algeria briefly opened one border crossing for a bicycle race, at Morocco's request.[110] In February, the Arab Maghreb Union foreign ministers met (in Morocco) for the first time in eighteen years.[111] While there, Algerian Foreign Minister Medelci signed a memorandum of understanding with Othmani, setting up ongoing consultation mechanisms between the two countries' foreign ministries.[112] This is an important achievement, though it resolves no fundamental issues and does not constitute rapprochement in itself.

Alternative Arguments and Testable Predictions

What are we to make of these openings and closings? What are the prospects for rapprochement in the near future? The evolving relationship between Algeria and Morocco offers a valuable case in which to test the predictions of several theories of international rapprochement. A balancing argument has trouble explaining the lack of rapprochement during the past decade of serious common threat from insurgent and terrorist groups, but a resurgence of al-Qaeda in the Islamic Maghreb could create a path to cooperation between the two countries. A bandwagoning hypothesis is consistent with the existing lack of cooperation, since Algeria and Morocco have been relatively evenly matched for decades, and neither country seems able to completely outpace the other in terms of defense buildup; if the Moroccan economy and defense spending collapse, however, this might induce rapprochement on Algerian terms, including concessions to Polisario. Norm promotion has difficulty accounting for the lack of rapprochement and subregional security cooperation after a decade of US counterterrorism coordination in North Africa; however, perhaps both countries simply need more time to become convinced of their common interests. Alternatively, identity spillover might suggest that the revived Arab Maghreb Union could deliver concrete cooperation and eventual rapprochement (although it would have to explain why this international forum failed to do so in the 1980s and 1990s). Next, if the Arab Spring leads to full democratization in Algeria and Morocco (perhaps along Tunisia's lines), including civilian dominance over the armed forces, democratic peace arguments would expect this to lead to rapprochement. Alternatively, a conservative crackdown against these nascent popular uprisings (Bahrain might offer a model here) could produce a common counterrevolutionary ideology for both governments and lay the groundwork for rapprochement.

Fundamentally, parochial interest suggests that rapprochement between Algeria and Morocco is likely to require either the political marginalization of the security forces (perhaps through true democratic transitions) or the redirection of their interests toward the alternative mission of counterterrorism (which requires state resource constraints). Economic factors that could stimulate rapprochement in the next few years include a steep fall in oil prices, the withholding of foreign aid by the United States, France, and the Gulf states, a renewed global recession, and an unsustainable fiscal burden from social spending to stave off popular protests. The current dialogue between Algeria and Morocco, however, seems catalyzed not by democratization, by an escalation of internal threat, or by economic imperatives but rather by acute political vulnerability during the Arab Spring. As such, it resembles the failed rapprochement attempt of 1991. In fact, prospects for rapprochement are in some ways lower now than in 1991, when UN mediation of the Western Sahara dispute still seemed promising.[113] Although Algerian-Moroccan rapprochement might precede and facilitate a final resolution of the Western Sahara issue, rapprochement is unlikely to occur without a shift in at least one party's position, and such a shift has not occurred. Negotiations have been stalled since James Baker's resignation in 2004 after Morocco's rejection of his settlement proposal.[114] According to the UN secretary general's report in 2009, "the positions of the parties . . . remained far apart on ways to achieve a just, lasting and mutually acceptable political solution."[115]

As in Cold War Latin America, regional rivalries are undermining contemporary coalition-building efforts against the common threat of terrorism and insurgency in the Islamic world. Once again, a parochial interest argument resolves this puzzle by identifying and explaining a pattern of policy obstruction within rival states. The leaders of Algeria and Morocco are constrained from effective peacemaking primarily because their security forces maintain powerful vested interests in rivalry and because economic conditions including foreign aid, resource exports, and overall growth permit state agencies to avoid difficult tradeoffs among missions. For rival countries like these, aligned in the global counterterrorism effort but facing internal opposition and minimal resource constraints, the prospects for rapprochement appear bleak.

CHAPTER SEVEN

The Organizational Politics of Conflict Resolution

No monarch or dictator or group of oligarchs is ever absolute.
They rule not only subject to the data of the national situation but
also subject to the necessity of acting with some people, of getting
along with others, of neutralizing still others and of subduing the
rest. And this may be done in an almost infinite variety of ways
each of which will determine what a given formal arrangement
really means either for the nation in which it obtains or for the
scientific observer; to speak of monarchy as if it meant a definite
thing spells dilettantism.

—*Joseph Schumpeter*

The administrative staff, which externally represents the
organization of political domination, is, of course, like any other
organization, bound by obedience to the power-holder and not
alone by the concept of legitimacy. . . . There are two other means,
both of which appeal to personal interests: material reward and
social honor. The fief of vassals, the prebends of patrimonial
officials, the salaries of modern civil servants, the honor of
knights, the privileges of estates, and the honor of the civil
servant comprise their respective wages. The fear of losing them
is the final and decisive basis for solidarity between the executive
staff and the power-holder.

—*Max Weber*

Why do many rival governments fail to cooperate when facing parallel internal
security threats and sharing the same great power allies, while a few succeed?
Under what conditions are diplomatic efforts by heads of state likely to achieve

rapprochement instead of collapsing into discord and recrimination? Why did rivalries among anti-Communist governments so frequently mar the unity of the Western Bloc during the Cold War, particularly in Latin America, and what are the consequences of contemporary rivalries in the Islamic world for US counterterrorism coalitions? Studies of international relations, whether emphasizing disparities of power, regime type, or identity, tend to argue that rivalries persist despite incentives to cooperate because of a combination of fear and mistrust, a situation in which each state sees the other as the paramount threat to national security. In turn, such perspectives highlight the power of leaders to transform conflicts through diplomatic engagement, costly signals, political will, and emotional creativity. However, the experiences of Cold War Latin America reveal that rivalries often persist for reasons having more to do with domestic politics than with foreign threats, that the interests determining policy are often parochial rather than national, and that peacemaking overtures often founder on organized internal opposition rather than the other side's intransigence. This yields important lessons for scholars and practitioners of international conflict resolution, particularly in the era of global counterterrorism.

What drives internal opposition to rapprochement, and under what conditions can leaders overcome or circumvent it? The parochial interest argument in this book, detailed in chapter two, explains that the agencies of the state are likely to act primarily to protect their organizational benefits, which derive from existing missions, and are therefore likely to defend the policy status quo and to maintain rivalry. In this situation, agencies tend to sabotage initiatives that threaten their parochial interests, so the head of state is likely to explore alternative methods of policy implementation to achieve rapprochement, including the use of personal envoys and public diplomacy as end runs around the obstructionist bureaucracy. Parochial interest also expects that the emergence of a common foe is most likely to cause rapprochement between international rivals in the context of state resource constraints, when budgetary tradeoffs force government agencies to give up their vested interests in rivalry in order to focus on the new mission offered by the common foe.[1]

In this concluding chapter, I address four questions. First, what are the primary findings from the case studies? Second, what is the significance of the argument and evidence for the study of international relations? Third, what policy recommendations follow for would-be peacemakers, including leaders of rival countries and third parties interested in mediation? Finally, what ethical implications arise from this research, particularly regarding the role of leadership in conflict resolution?

Comparative Lessons

The Cold War, due to its global scope and bipolar structure, provides an ideal setting in which to evaluate the effects of a common foe on relations between rivals. The abundance and persistence of rivalries among Western Bloc allies (two-thirds of which occurred in Latin America) is an important puzzle that deserves explanation. As chapter one showed, rivalry among allies was a persistent problem in Cold War Latin America. Despite near-unanimous hemispheric anti-Communism, and despite an increasing threat of Communist insurgency in the wake of the Cuban Revolution, only three pairs of Latin American rivals achieved rapprochement during the Cold War (Nicaragua and Honduras, Argentina and Brazil, and Argentina and Chile). Although a mixture of conflict and cooperation is common in all international relationships and particularly prevalent in the history of relations among Latin American countries, the frequent failure of intra-bloc rivals to effect cooperation against their common threat by overcoming their regional disputes seems deeply surprising.[2] A parochial interest explanation, tested against several alternative arguments, helps to resolve this puzzle and to account for the variation in cooperation and conflict among rival countries in Cold War Latin America.

Comparative analysis of the three cases of successful rapprochement in Cold War Latin America (Argentina-Brazil 1980, Nicaragua-Honduras 1961, and Argentina-Chile 1984) against prior cooperative overtures and ongoing neighboring rivalries strongly support a parochial interest theory. It also provides uncomfortable evidence against several prominent alternative arguments from realist, liberal, and constructivist schools of thought in international relations (table 7.1). Examination of Argentine-Brazilian presidential summits in chapter three, Central American rivalries in the shadow of the Cuban revolution in chapter four, Andean rivalries during the debt crisis in chapter five, and Moroccan-Algerian relations since 2001 (extending the argument beyond Latin America and after the Cold War, to the Islamic world in the era of global counterterrorism) in chapter six yields seven main empirical conclusions corresponding to each of the tested hypotheses introduced in chapter one.

First and foremost, as predicted by my parochial interest theory, rival countries achieved rapprochement when facing the combination of an alternative security mission and macroeconomic duress. Neither of these factors was sufficient in isolation. El Salvador increasingly focused on the threat of leftist insurgency after the Cuban Revolution but failed to overcome rivalry with Honduras due to a lack of resource constraints. Conversely, Bolivia was battered by

TABLE 7.1
Hypotheses and case predictions in Cold War Latin America

	Argentina-Brazil (Chapter 3)				Central America, 1959–1961 (Chapter 4)				The Andes, 1980s (Chapter 5)		
	1947	1961	1972	1980	El Salvador–Honduras	Costa Rica–Nicaragua	Nicaragua–Honduras	Argentina-Chile	Bolivia-Chile	Colombia-Venezuela	Ecuador-Peru
Balancing	–	–	+	–	+	–	+	–	–	–	–
Bandwagoning	–	–	+	+	–	+	+	–	+	–	+
Democratic peace	+	+	–	+	+	+	+	–	–	+	+
Counter-revolutionary Ideology	+	–	+	+	+	–	+	–	+	–	–
Norm promotion	+	+	+	–	–	+	–	+	+	+	+
Identity spillover	–	+	+	+	–	–	+	+	+	+	+
Parochial interest	–	–	–	+	–	–	+	+	–	–	–
Actual outcome	–	–	–	+	–	–	+	+	–	–	–

Note: + signifies rapprochement, – signifies rivalry.

the debt crisis of the 1980s, but because its armed forces lacked an alternative mission, it failed to resolve its conflict with Chile. Argentina faced mounting public insecurity in 1972, but a stable economy removed any incentives to cooperate with Brazil, which likewise experienced urban insurgency and an economic "miracle." Argentine-Brazilian rapprochement occurred in 1980 because countering leftist insurgency (and international human rights pressure) provided an alternative security mission for the armed forces (and the foreign ministries) and because mounting economic difficulties in the wake of the oil shocks forced tradeoffs among policy priorities. The successful rapprochement initiatives between Honduras and Nicaragua in 1961, and Chile and Argentina in 1984, depended on a similar conjunction of economic and security factors that altered the interests of powerful state agencies.

Second, rapprochement is not simply a function of threat level, as some realists might have expected. Argentina and Brazil failed to overcome rivalry in the early and middle 1970s, when the common threat of insurgency was highest, and achieved rapprochement in 1980 after the threat had been repressed. Nor were Argentina in 1984 and Honduras in 1961, when they achieved rapprochement with Chile and Nicaragua, respectively, much more threatened than their neighbors. Common threat failed not only to induce rapprochement and stable peace in many Latin American rivalries but also to prevent those rivalries from escalating to war (as Honduras and El Salvador did in 1969 and Chile and Argentina nearly did in 1978) and thus even to keep a negative peace.

Third, bandwagoning (another realist hypothesis) likewise fails to explain these cases of rapprochement. For Argentina and Brazil, rapprochement attempts during periods of power preponderance by Argentina (1947) and Brazil (1972) failed, while the failed effort that broke the most cooperative ground (1961) occurred in a situation of relative parity. Furthermore, although Argentina was certainly declining in the years before the 1980 rapprochement, Brazil was suffering, too: mutual weakness and mounting debt after the global oil shocks, not growing asymmetry, contributed to cooperation. Nor can Argentine decline in the early 1980s explain its cooperation with Chile, since Argentina was the stronger state at the beginning of the decade and its collapse brought the rivals closer to parity, and since other Andean rivalries with similarly unbalanced power ratios (in terms of defense spending and number of troops) of three, four, or even five to one failed to resolve their conflicts. In Central America, as of 1960, Nicaragua only held a 1.3-to-1 advantage (hardly preponderant) in troop strength over Honduras, while in the rivalries that continued, El Salvador's

1.2-to-1 ratio over Honduras was about the same, while Nicaragua's 2.7-to-1 lead over Costa Rica (a nation without a formal army) was far larger.

Fourth, subregional security institutions did not have the spillover effect of boosting cooperative identities that some constructivists might expect. The two main subregional security creations in Cold War Latin America, Operation Condor in South America (created in 1975) and CONDECA in Central America (the Central American Defense Council, created in 1963), did boast as members rivals that attained rapprochement. However, participation in these institutions did not cause rapprochement. Nicaraguan-Honduran rapprochement emerged before CONDECA and Argentine-Brazilian rapprochement occurred independent of Operation Condor. Furthermore, CONDECA members Honduras and El Salvador went to war with one another in 1969, and enthusiastic Condor participants Argentina and Chile escalated a longstanding territorial dispute into a militarized crisis in 1978 that nearly resulted in war. Neither can other subregional institutions such as the Central American integration accords (1951–1952, 1956, 1960), the Andean Pact (1969), the Plata Basin Treaty (1969), or the Amazon Treaty (1978) explain the variation in rivalry outcomes.

Fifth, a constructivist argument about norm promotion also falls short. First of all, US-sponsored institution-building and socialization in Latin America during and after World War Two had minimal effects on regional rivalries. In fact, US aid and arms sales exacerbated rivalry between Argentina and Brazil and sparked naval arms races among the Pacific Coast states of South America in the postwar period. Additionally, when the United States, after years of trying to build hemispheric solidarity beginning with World War II and the Chapultepec Conference of 1945, invoked the Rio Treaty to summon Latin American assistance for the Korean War, the results were frustrating: only Colombia sent any troops. Between Chapultepec and the Cuban Revolution, there were no cases of rapprochement in Latin America, and the rapprochement between Nicaragua and Honduras unfolded before the United States developed or promoted the new concepts of internal security and limited war. The promotion of "national security doctrine" by the United States in Latin America during the 1960s and 1970s had equally dim results in terms of cooperation among rivals. Argentina and Brazil achieved rapprochement not when the United States was promulgating internal warfare but rather when the Carter administration was pressuring both countries about their human rights violations. And although Augusto Pinochet in Chile subscribed to the Reagan administration's vision of a renewed counterinsurgent approach to the Cold War in Latin America, his partner in the 1984 rapprochement, Argentina's Raúl Alfonsín, surely did not.

National security decisions by Latin American governments about regional rivalries and domestic insurgent threats ultimately reflected the preferences of Latin American leaders and state agencies much more than the dictates of the United States.

Sixth, a liberal argument about counterrevolutionary regimes does not hold up. If fear of leftist insurrection caused cooperation in Central America, then why did Nicaragua and Honduras, but not El Salvador (headed by a succession of military commanders and juntas) and Honduras, overcome their rivalry in the 1960s? In the Southern Cone, why did a rapprochement attempt under Argentine and Brazilian military regimes in 1972 fail, while a subsequent effort succeeded in 1980? And in the Andes, why did the repressive military rulers of Bolivia not overcome their conflict with Augusto Pinochet's Chile, while newly democratic Argentina did? Part of the problem with regime-based arguments is that Latin American leaders often perceive significant differences between their own national systems and those of their colleagues, differences that do not correspond closely with the concepts of democracy and authoritarianism commonly employed in political science. Self-identified distinctions between relatively open, liberalizing regimes and more repressive ones, for instance, were clearly visible in both the 1972 and 1980 Argentine-Brazilian summits, even though in both instances, both countries had military governments headed by Army generals.

Seventh, although liberal democracy may contribute to the development and persistence of stable peace, the effects of democratic transitions and institutions on rapprochement in Latin America are frequently overstated. Democracy did not deliver lasting rapprochement between Argentina and Brazil under Arturo Frondizi and Jânio Quadros in 1961. More than two decades later, democratization in the 1980s did spur integration and cooperation on the road to Mercosur, but it postdated rapprochement and cannot explain the acquiescence of military actors, who remained powerful throughout the decade. Although Nicaragua and Honduras were both ruled by civilians at the time of rapprochement in 1961, this is hardly a case of liberal peace: Nicaragua's Luis Somoza was highly authoritarian (not to mention the son and elder brother of uniformed dictators), and Honduras's Ramón Villeda Morales had little control over the military that ultimately overthrew him. In the other cases of rapprochement (Argentina-Brazil 1980 and Argentina-Chile 1984), one or both of the participating governments was an authoritarian military regime rather than a democracy. Meanwhile, rivalries between Colombia and Venezuela, and Peru and Ecuador, persisted under democratic governments.

However, parochial interest does not contradict the democratic peace proposition but rather complements it. Whereas democratic peace outlines a path to cooperation involving the political defeat of military and bureaucratic actors through their complete subordination to elected civilians, parochial interest explains how cooperation can evolve even when those state actors retain their power and influence, a situation all too common in the fragile democracies and liberalizing autocracies of the developing world. To the extent that transitions from authoritarianism frequently produce stable outcomes far short of liberal democracy, the democratic peace is an unlikely source of rapprochement in the developing world, and the path of redirected parochial interests becomes particularly important.

Directions for International Relations Research

This study's intended contributions, and its limitations, suggest four places to refocus and recalibrate international relations scholarship on security decision making: the state, the economic context, the region, and the sources. First, a parochial interest perspective calls attention to the role of the state as a collection of largely autonomous actors influencing foreign policy. This contrasts not only with the oft-critiqued unitary rational actor assumption in international relations scholarship but also with much recent work on the domestic politics of international relations that has focused on the democratic politics of pluralist societies.[3] Although this is a useful correction, it is necessarily an oversimplification. Even in democracies, the effects of majority opinion on foreign policy behavior are distorted by the partially autonomous actions of the state bureaucracy, while even under authoritarian regimes, government action is partly shaped by societal pressures. States and their bureaucratic agencies come in different forms and interact with their societies in complex ways, and this variation may have powerful effects on foreign relations that scholars have yet to identify.[4]

For the most part, this book has addressed Latin American states and their agencies as though these were closely comparable. Though useful for testing a range of hypotheses, this approach minimized important distinctions that other scholarship could put in the foreground. Some state agencies may be unique, such as Costa Rica's Civil Guard (after the disbanding of the army), Brazil's foreign ministry (with its imperial inheritance of autonomy and organizational culture), and the navy of presently landlocked Bolivia.[5] In 1980 in Argentina and 1961 in Nicaragua, presidents counted on senior diplomats (a foreign minister and an ambassador in Washington, respectively) who were family members by marriage; the policy outcomes of these relationships, however, surely varied as a result of the institutional context of both countries' foreign ministries.

Second, parochial interest highlights the macroeconomic context of security policy, showing that fiscal constraints intervene between threat perceptions and policy responses by changing the incentives of state actors whose support is essential for major policy change. Recent work at the intersection of political economy and national security has tended to emphasize material incentives either at the state level or at the level of societal groups, rather than within the state apparatus itself. Scholars have addressed how the expansion of international commerce and the globalization of production affects national incentives with regard to international conflict, how free trade agreements with hard legal standards and material consequences can induce human rights compliance, and how pressure groups can distort the national interest to suit their parochial ends (often with unintended consequences).[6] The collapse of the Soviet Union in particular highlights economic factors in rapprochement. The burdens of defense spending and foreign aid to Eastern European allies in the context of autarkic industrial production accelerated the Soviet economy's inexorable decline and induced Moscow to sue for peace with the United States.[7]

Future research could address important economic variation beyond the blunt factor of resource constraints emphasized in this book, focusing particularly on the level and strategy of development.[8] Most of the Cold War Latin American governments examined here headed developing nations (part of the Third World, as it was then called) and employed some form of import-substitution industrialization (ISI) as a growth strategy, but the exceptions and different configurations surely matter. For instance, scholars have argued that the turn toward open markets, including the privatization of state assets, systematically affected state security behavior in and beyond Latin America during the peak years of globalization and neoliberalism at the end of the Cold War.[9] If this is true, then we might examine the foreign policy consequences of similar economic policy changes in the 1970s by Augusto Pinochet in Chile and Economy Minister José Martínez de Hoz in Argentina, as well as earlier experiences with austerity measures and structural adjustment, as in Argentina under Arturo Frondizi. Variations within ISI, from the mobilizing populism of Juan Perón (1946–1955) to the more technocratic approach of Brazil's military government after 1964, likely affected the power and preferences of domestic stakeholders regarding foreign policy. Similarly, with the resurgence and diversity of state involvement in the Latin American economies after more than a decade of frustration over neoliberalism, to what extent and in what ways do these "left turns" catalyze regional solidarity?

Third, and connected to the previous points about the diversity of political and economic systems within Latin America, a major goal of this project has been to advance the systematic study of Latin American international relations, and the foreign relations of other developing regions, rather than to reduce these to the effects of great powers' foreign policy on those countries.[10] It would be extremely misleading to suggest that US hegemony in the Americas elimi- nates the potential for meaningful autonomous action by other states, or that the relative absence of major interstate war indicates a region free from conflict—both across countries and over time, Latin America is a region of tremendous variation in foreign affairs.[11] These diverse cases should be used to test prominent arguments from other areas of international relations, as this book has sought to do. Unfortunately, engagement between international rela- tions theories of conflict and cooperation, and studies of regional politics and foreign policy in the Americas, is still underdeveloped.[12] The deepening of cooperation between Argentina and its neighbors Brazil and Chile in the 1980s and 1990s is rapidly becoming a critical case in international relations scholarship—a welcome development, but one that will hopefully inspire fur- ther analysis of the region's rich international political history.[13]

However, a satisfying account of regional foreign relations should do more than mechanically pit North American hypotheses against Latin American data: it should also address analyses from historians, political scientists, policy analysts, and journalists in the countries under study. Although these accounts may seem less accessible or intrinsically interesting to some international rela- tions scholars than to area studies experts, they offer profound correctives to an otherwise distorted set of theoretical lenses. As Victoria Hui explained with reference to the ancient Chinese states system, there is an important difference between asking why the balance of power "failed" in China and asking what caused imperial domination to succeed there but not in Europe: the second per- spective takes Chinese cases and scholarly analyses on their own terms and as a source of otherwise-overlooked alternative arguments rather than merely as data to refute pre-existing hypotheses.[14] The Latin American analyses cited in the preceding chapters suggest a number of critical foreign policy concepts and debates without clear equivalents in North American international relations the- ories or exact definitional matches in English. In particular, studies of Perón's Third Position in Argentina, the independent foreign policy of Jânio Quadros and João Goulart, and the pragmatism (responsible or otherwise) of some of their successors in Brazil reveal that governments do not merely opt for align- ment or neutrality but rather design foreign policy strategies on a vast land- scape marked by autonomy and sovereignty, insertion and projection, neutral- ism and nonintervention.[15] In addition to their value for understanding the historical episodes for which they were developed, these ideas could profitably be re-exported to analyze European or Asian cases.

Finally, major changes in foreign policy need to be analyzed comparatively, not only with other instances of change but also with unsuccessful reform attempts and with situations where policy reform seemed to have clear incentives.[16] To explain rapprochement, we need to explain why conflict resolution efforts often fail and to identify the processes that reinforce enduring rivalries. Qualitative research has much to contribute to these tasks.[17] Especially, exploring negative cases requires grappling with primary sources and adopting the research tools of historians, including archival work, not only because scholars have often overlooked these episodes but also because the accounts we do have (including the memoirs of decision makers) are partial, scattered, and frequently conflicting.[18]

Although primary documents can help us support or overturn major arguments about the causes of international conflict and cooperation, they also suggest the limits of our hypotheses and research designs, indicating new lines of inquiry. For instance, leaders' awareness of their predecessors' records, and their simultaneous negotiation with multiple foreign counterparts, might indicate a problematic interconnectedness of cases.[19] Do failed attempts at conflict resolution enhance the likelihood of future peacemaking by creating an ongoing dialogue, reduce the odds of cooperation by confirming mistrust and strengthening hardliners, or have little effect on subsequent relations (making such overtures less risky than we might assume)?[20] The answers connect to broader issues in security studies, such as whether and how crises and military mobilizations affect the subsequent likelihood of conflict. Additionally, archival records indicate a long tail of negative cases, including presidential summits that were proposed but rejected (or pledged but obviated by coup or death) and less formal meetings that occurred in the course of other diplomatic travel, which, if analyzed in comparison to more prominent cases, might alter our findings about the conditions that favor or oppose conflict resolution. Scholars of terrorism and insurgency should address these challenges as well: in between peace and civil war, the archival records of national security will likely reveal a host of groups that formed but did not arm, armed but never attacked, or were repressed quickly and covertly, to say nothing of groups that remained latent through successful deterrence by the state.

Recommendations for Aspiring Peacemakers
In Great Powers

How can the United States and other great powers most effectively manage alliances against terrorist and insurgent threats, given the persistent problems of intrabloc rivalry and parochial interest? The experiences of Cold War Latin America explored throughout this book suggest three major recommendations to make allies' policy tradeoff between rivalry and counterterrorism more acute: restrict military aid, promote human rights, and minimize troop presence abroad.

Limiting military assistance might seem counterintuitive given that developing partner capabilities has anchored US strategy after September 11, 2001, just as it did during the Cold War.[21] Furthermore, many US partners—governments in the Islamic world fighting actual or latent rebellions linked to al-Qaeda—woefully lack basic organizational capacities for counterinsurgency.[22] In Pakistan, for instance, Christine Fair observes that US military aid and training buys influence, goodwill, and leverage, while aid reductions exacerbate security concerns vis-à-vis India.[23] More generally, Daniel Byman argues that "The United States should greatly expand the scope and scale of security assistance programs," as it did in the early decades of the Cold War.[24] Others even advocate a new Marshall Plan for allies in the global counterterrorist campaign.[25]

However, such aid programs in the context of regional rivalries are likely to undermine partner states' incentives to focus on the common foe of terrorist or insurgent groups. Expanding capabilities should require American allies to bear serious costs, rather than simply creating units armed, funded, and trained (or even led) by the United States. The United States should not enable allies to dodge difficult tradeoffs—instead, it should encourage them to commit to new missions by sacrificing obsolete ones and especially to set aside rivalries with other US partner states. To the extent that resources such as dollars, arms, and manpower are fungible across missions, US military assistance might directly support the common objective of counterterrorism but also indirectly enable US allies to divert their own resources toward other security priorities such as regional rivalries that ultimately undermine coalition effectiveness.

There are additional reasons to be pessimistic about the effects of security assistance. One RAND project concludes that internal security aid historically has not improved democracy or human rights, and other studies show that aid is more usually an indicator than a cause of alignment.[26] Additionally, US military aid to counterinsurgent regimes often does little to professionalize those countries' security forces and ironically may undermine prospects for reform by offering the symbolic stamp of US approval for the status quo.[27] Further-more, unintended consequences of aid include incentives for allies to overstate their internal security threats, a sense of dependence and humiliation in the recipient country, and increased corruption and inequality. In the first scenario, US aid is merely maldistributed, but in the latter two, it could actually enhance popular grievances and strengthen the prospects for insurgency.[28] Paul Pillar's 2001 recommendations on alliances against terrorism are worth revisiting: pro-vide "assistance to the other government in developing its counterterrorist capa-bilities," but emphasize training rather than an influx of foreign aid, and employ oversight to ensure that aid "does not get siphoned off into other activities."[29]

Human rights promotion, too, faces the objection that many of America's staunchest allies against Islamist terrorism have dubious track records on civil and political liberties but nonetheless deserve support.[30] As Jeane Kirkpatrick famously argued during the Cold War, the United States should not equate the authoritarianism of friendly governments with the totalitarianism of hostile re-gimes.[31] However, arguments in favor of human rights range from the purely moral to more instrumental claims that supporting unsavory governments "fos-ters breeding grounds and safe havens for extreme forms of terrorism" and "erodes American legitimacy."[32]

The logic of parochial interest lends further credence to human rights pro-motion. As with restrictions on military aid, the US objective for allies should be mission constraint. By helping restrain allies from the harshest measures of internal security, the United States can improve their prospects for successful counterinsurgency and counterterrorism and, conversely, enhance its own public diplomacy by retaining the moral high ground.[33] Additionally, careful counterin-surgency takes heavy commitments of manpower and time, increasing countries' need for foreign cooperation and assistance and making the policy tradeoff be-tween rivalry and counterterrorism even more acute. Furthermore, human rights standards provide a domestic political justification in the United States to cut military aid even to allies, where recipient countries are engaged in repressive antiterrorist operations. Finally, shared resentment among rival countries over US human rights pressures might in itself contribute to rapprochement.

However, advancing human rights does not mean promoting democratic transitions, particularly by force. For one thing, democratic transitions in the context of institutional underdevelopment can actually increase the prospects of international and civil war.[34] These risks might be particularly acute in the con-text of rivalry. For another, while international factors can sometimes tip the balance of political transitions in favor of democracy, research on democracy

promotion cautions against expecting interventions to force successful democratic transitions, particularly without massive resource commitments or in heavily militarized countries.[35] Furthermore, democratization in many cases would
be a deal breaker for the security agencies of US allies.[36] Improved treatment of
human rights may be as much of a concession as the US can push for, but it is a
valuable one nonetheless.

The third pillar of mission constraint involves restrictions on the deployment
of US combat forces and military advisory missions. Essentially, the United
States should not fight other countries' battles for them on their territory, even
if they are American battles too. Cold War containment offers several reasons
for this, including an asymmetry of interest between great powers and local forces
in peripheral conflicts that makes great powers' victory less likely and a global
perception of illegitimacy and imperialism in great powers' launch of preventive
wars that undermines future alliance support and victory in the world ideological
battle.[37] Additionally, as Byman argues, "The risk of being 'chain-ganged' into a
conflict is immense, as every government has an incentive to tie its local struggle to the US effort against Al Qaeda."[38] The United States should provide operational space for other countries to develop new missions in response to
common threats, rather than simply eliminating those threats. The extended
deployment of US forces in Afghanistan (and, until recently, in Iraq) undermines the credibility of US threats or promises to intervene elsewhere. Although
this might harm American deterrence of adversaries, it has the silver lining of
temporarily forcing other allies to fend for themselves, contributing to subregional cooperation and the transcendence of rivalry.

However, the United States should shift—and convince its allies that it
shifted—from a temporary incapacity to rescue embattled regimes elsewhere to
a principled refusal to send US troops to ensure the security of governments
that could be doing more to defend themselves. Ultimately, a containment strategy requires drawing down US forces in the Islamic world and relying on allied
front-line states for the actual counterinsurgency operations. This burden-
shifting may be precisely what al-Qaeda wants to prevent: Ayman al-Zawahiri
argued that "Our Islamic movement and its jihadi vanguard . . . must bring the
major criminals—the United States, Russia, and Israel—into the battle, rather
than allowing them to guide the battle between the jihadist movement and our
governments from afar and in safety."[39]

Broadly, these recommendations conform with the widely discussed grand
strategy of offshore balancing, which in Stephen Walt's view involves "playing
hard to get" with actual and prospective allies and regional powers, letting them

shoulder more of the burden for local security and stepping in directly "only when absolutely necessary."[40] Not only would the reduction of US troop presence in Europe and the Middle East reduce anti-Americanism, Walt argues, but it would also entice US allies to earn rather than to expect American assistance.[41] Similarly, Christopher Layne recommends passing the buck of stopping regional threats to "those whose security would be most immediately jeopardized," letting the United States "stand aloof from others' security competitions."[42]

Proponents of offshore balancing are less clear on their prescriptions with respect to foreign aid and human rights than on their recommendations for US troop deployments, but restricting foreign military assistance seems compatible with this approach. As Layne argues, offshore balancers approaching the Middle East should refrain not only from democracy promotion but also from "propping up reactionary regimes" regarding whose fates balancers should "be prepared to 'let nature take its course,'" while with regard to Europe and East Asia, they should remember that "offshore balancing is a strategy of burden *shifting*, not burden sharing" and should "devolve to other states the costs and risks of their defense."[43] Aid restrictions raise their own risks and difficulties, though. Too much support could make allies complacent, demanding, or provocative of insurgents, but too little support might make them neutral, hostile, or vulnerable to revolution.

Human rights promotion deserves more emphasis in the offshore balancing conversation, which is dominated by political realists, than it has received. Human rights (and, more broadly, the application of moral standards in foreign policy) have a venerable role in the realist tradition, after all.[44] Although Jeane Kirkpatrick argued that promoting human rights in allied countries hamstrings their security policymaking so severely that friendly governments would fall to revolution, I suggest that a limited amount of constraint can actually improve those countries' security situations relative to insurgent and terrorist threats as well as their treatment of human rights.[45]

In Rival Countries

Lessons from successful and failed rapprochement attempts in Cold War Latin America suggest three recommendations for the leaders of countries embroiled in rivalry and facing a common foe. First, when dealing with foreign patrons such as the United States, military aid may be a poisoned gift, since it can embolden domestic defenders of rivalry. Secretly convincing patrons to withhold such aid, or at least to make it conditional on rapprochement and respect for human rights, might provide a politically useful constraint, especially when combined with publicly denouncing the aid constraints in nationalist, developmentalist language, thus reaping benefits and shifting blame at the same time. If a great power is truly concerned for the political survival and international cooperation of its ally and is willing to bear the economic costs of foreign aid, then it should be willing to bear the political costs of aid denial or conditionality.

Second, the rival country's leadership vulnerability, in addition to one's own, suggests that rapprochement initiatives should be strategically timed to maximize the chances of success: peacemaking may be virtuous, but so is patience. In particular, if the domestic proponents of rivalry in the other country lack an alternative mission, or if that country's resources are plentiful, then politically risky summits or major diplomatic overtures should be postponed. Conversely, when erstwhile opponents of cooperation are preoccupied with new missions, and when economic downturns, aid cutoffs, or other crises appear to heighten policy tradeoffs, a ripe moment for rapprochement should be exploited. This may involve postponing regional economic integration—which would spur growth and thus mitigate the financial pressures on the bureaucracy to accept cooperation—until the diplomatic breakthroughs of rapprochement have been consolidated.

Third, regarding one's own bureaucracy and survival in office, grand foreign policy gestures that lack state support should be meticulously avoided. Failure to deliver on foreign policy promises, particularly if the rival country spurns one's advances, is likely to earn domestic political punishment.[46] Moreover, even cooperative gestures that are reciprocated can threaten the interests of state actors with the ability to sabotage rapprochement or to remove from power the leaders that pursue it (witness the assassination of Anwar Sadat), unless those actors have been expressly coopted or defeated. In the long run, the democratic peace may offer a model for rapprochement involving the political subordination of these state actors. However, for leaders of rival countries who must make security decisions without the luxury of waiting for the consolidation of liberal democracy, the cooption of state agencies through the mission of counterinsurgency in times of resource constraint may provide a more practical path to peace.

Conflict Resolution Dilemmas

Ultimately, Cold War Latin America reveals that protracted conflicts and their resolution are not easily explained in terms of heroes and villains. Defenders of rivalry do not necessarily promote escalation and war, while advocates of cooperation are not necessarily altruists. Officers and diplomats frequently obstruct national leaders' rapprochement efforts, but they are generally patriotic and professional, and their support is essential for cooperation. Presidents and ambassadors can spark cooperative overtures, but they frequently miscalculate, provoke, and offend both at home and abroad. Superpowers sometimes encourage conflict resolution among their smaller allies, but they often overlook, overreact, and blunder. And rival states are usually both responsible for perpetuating conflict between them.

The rapprochement efforts analyzed in this book, both failures and successes, offer some encouragement to researchers and decision makers facing international rivalries. Too often, it appears that structural forces beyond immediate control, like the similarity of rival countries' political regimes, economies, or cultures, determine conflict outcomes.[47] Alternatively, it frequently seems that peacemaking depends on the political will and creative diplomacy of national leaders.[48] Neither set of factors authoritatively explains the pattern of rivalry and rapprochement, and exceptions—especially conflicts that should have been resolved, but persisted—are readily blamed on the variables emphasized by the other perspective. If structural incentives for peacemaking are in place but conflict continues, the decision makers made tactical errors: their efforts were too bold or too timid, too legalistic and comprehensive or too informal and piecemeal. Or if leaders act correctly but fail nonetheless, then they faced (and maybe misperceived) an impossible task, and peace awaits regime change, cultural or ideological transformation, or outside mediation. If several structural conditions have to align and leaders must still navigate additional challenges astutely, then the prospects for rapprochement seem remote.[49]

Instead, prospective peacemakers should worry less about calibrating their signals to foreign counterparts or interpreting the auguries of the international system and more about ensuring domestic support for conflict resolution. Peace can be achieved under a range of conditions, and a common foe is just one possible stimulus for cooperation. Rival leaders with a bountiful environment of democracy and integration, common culture and ideology, and supportive outside mediators may not need this book's advice unless cooperation surprisingly fails. However, protracted conflicts among developing countries usually lack such advantages. This book identifies a counterintuitive but pragmatic roadmap to cooperation based on parochial interest, one that leverages some conflicts to resolve others, exploits internal opposition rather than ignoring or surrendering to it, and uses crisis rather than prosperity as an opportunity for conflict resolution.

However, rapprochement involves a larger ethical dilemma. Stable peace is a costly objective, risky to attempt and difficult to attain. What are we willing to sacrifice or overlook in order to resolve international conflicts?[50] In the rivalries addressed in this book, the shared adversary of parallel insurgent groups was a vital ingredient for states to achieve rapprochement. However, a common foe might just replace one protracted conflict with another, and internal wars between states and insurgents are often much bloodier than interstate rivalries, particularly when non-combatant casualties are included. Furthermore, my parochial interest argument indicates that even these conflicts are most likely to induce international cooperation among rivals in the context of state resource constraint—itself a situation that can bring misery for those at the bottom rungs of society, as the debt crisis did in Latin America in the 1980s. Foreign aid to embattled states could mitigate some of these problems, but the fungibility of aid resources could reduce or eliminate the incentives those states face to overcome their traditional rivalries. If human security trumps national security, then ongoing international rivalry with constraints on violence might be preferable to international cooperation and the escalation of internal conflicts.

Other paths to peace also involve difficult tradeoffs. For instance, the disquieting evidence that democratization can provoke nationalist rhetoric and even war in the context of institutional weakness, despite the general finding that liberal democracies tend to refrain from fighting one another, should raise the question of whether the human costs of democratization always outweigh the continuation of authoritarian regimes. Such costs might be even higher when a country attempts to impose its form of government on others. A democratic Iraq might eventually have more pacific relations with the United States and with its neighbors than Saddam Hussein's regime did, but what is the net consequence—particularly in human lives—of Operation Iraqi Freedom as opposed to not having invaded? These calculations may be complex and clinical, but the interconnectedness of domestic and foreign conflicts compels their serious consideration in order to determine which international rivalries are worth ending and when outside powers such as the United States should encourage their resolution.

Chapter 1 · Explaining Rivalry and Rapprochement in Cold War Latin America

1. See, e.g., Thucydides, *History of the Peloponnesian War*, trans. Rex Warner (New York: Penguin, 1972), 45–46; Stephen Walt, *The Origins of Alliances* (Ithaca, NY: Cornell University Press, 1987); Stephen Rock, *Why Peace Breaks Out: Great Power Rapprochement in Historical Perspective* (Chapel Hill: University of North Carolina Press, 1989), 6; Deborah Larson, *Anatomy of Mistrust: US-Soviet Relations during the Cold War* (Ithaca, NY: Cornell University Press, 1997), 6, 36; Alexander Wendt, *Social Theory of International Politics* (New York: Cambridge University Press, 1999), 349–352; John Owen, "Pieces of Maximal Peace: Common Identities, Common Enemies," in *Stable Peace among Nations*, ed. Arie Kacowicz et al. (Lanham, MD: Rowman & Littlefield, 2000), 75, 81, 89; Charles Kupchan, *How Enemies Become Friends: The Sources of Stable Peace* (Princeton: Princeton University Press, 2010), 2, 33–37. Epigraph citations, respectively, are to Heinrich von Treitschke, *Politics*, ed. Blanche Dugdale and Torben de Bille, trans. Hans Kohn (New York: Harcourt, Brace, and World, 1963 [1916]), 13; and Norman Angell, *The Great Illusion: A Study of the Relation of Military Power in Nations to Their Economic and Social Advantage*, 3rd ed. (New York: G. P. Putnam's Sons, 1911), 312.

2. See Miroslav Nincic, *The Logic of Positive Engagement* (Ithaca, NY: Cornell University Press, 2011); Jennifer Lind, *Sorry States: Apologies in International Politics* (Ithaca, NY: Cornell University Press, 2008); Andrew Kydd, *Trust and Mistrust in International Relations* (Princeton: Princeton University Press, 2005), 184–244; William Long and Peter Brecke, *War and Reconciliation: Reason and Emotion in Conflict Resolution* (Cambridge, MA: MIT Press, 2003); Stephen Rock, *Appeasement in International Politics* (Lexington: University Press of Kentucky, 2000), esp. 10–15; Tony Armstrong, *Breaking the Ice: Rapprochement between East and West Germany, the United States and China, and Israel and Egypt* (Washington, DC: United States Institute of Peace, 1993).

3. Kupchan, *How Enemies*, especially 390–399. Kupchan also identifies several structural factors, such as the compatibility of social orders, similarity of cultures, and the openness and power diffusion of domestic political institutions, that can induce or impede rapprochement. Rock, *Why Peace Breaks Out*, maintains that structure routinely trumps leadership.

4. Valuable introductions include Janice Gross Stein, "Image, Identity, and the Resolution of Violent Conflict," in *Turbulent Peace: The Challenges of Managing International*

Conflict, ed. Chester Crocker, Fen Osler Hampson, and Pamela Aall (Washington, DC: United States Institute of Peace, 2001), 189–208; Herbert Kelman, "Social-Psychological Dimensions of International Conflict," in *Peacemaking in International Conflict: Methods and Techniques*, 2nd ed., ed. I. William Zartman (Washington, DC: United States Institute of Peace, 2007), 61–107.

5. See, e.g., Arie Kacowicz, *Zones of Peace: South America and West Africa in Comparative Perspective* (Albany: State University of New York Press, 1998); Etel Solingen, *Regional Orders at Century's Dawn: Global and Domestic Influences on Grand Strategy* (Princeton: Princeton University Press, 1998).

6. William Thompson, "Identifying Rivals and Rivalries in World Politics," *International Studies Quarterly* 45, no. 4 (Dec. 2001): 557–586; see Wendt, *Social Theory*, 258.

7. On escalation, see Russell Leng, *Bargaining and Learning in Recurring Crises: The Soviet-American, Egyptian-Israeli, and Indo-Pakistani Rivalries* (Ann Arbor: University of Michigan Press, 2000); John Vasquez and Christopher Leskiw, "The Origins and War Proneness of Interstate Rivalries," *Annual Review of Political Science* 4, no. 1 (2001): 295–316; on proliferation, Sonali Singh and Christopher Way, "The Correlates of Nuclear Proliferation: A Quantitative Test," *Journal of Conflict Resolution* 48, no. 6 (Dec. 2004): 859–885. I address alternative definitions of rivalry below.

8. Thompson, "Identifying," 560; see also Michael Colaresi, Karen Rasler, and William Thompson, *Strategic Rivalries in World Politics: Position, Space, and Conflict Escalation* (Cambridge: Cambridge University Press, 2007). I discuss alternative rivalry concepts in the research design section, below.

9. Richard Haass, *Conflicts Unending: the United States and Regional Disputes* (New Haven: Yale University Press, 1990); I. William Zartman, "Analyzing Intractability," in *Grasping the Nettle: Analyzing Cases of Intractable Conflict*, ed. Chester Crocker, Fen Osler Hampson, and Pamela Aall (Washington, DC: United States Institute of Peace, 2005).

10. See G. R. Berridge and Alan James, *A Dictionary of Diplomacy* (New York: Palgrave, 2001), 200; Kupchan, *How Enemies*, 8–9, 30–31; Gordon Craig and Alexander George, *Force and Statecraft: Diplomatic Problems of Our Time*, 2nd ed. (New York: Oxford University Press, 1990), 248–255.

11. Berridge and James, *A Dictionary*, 62; Craig and George, *Force and Statecraft*, 248–255. See *The Cold War as Cooperation*, ed. Roger Kanet and Edward Kolodziej (Baltimore: Johns Hopkins University Press, 1991). Armstrong, *Breaking the Ice*, uses normalization as a proxy for rapprochement; however, rivalries often persist despite mutual diplomatic recognition (e.g., India-Pakistan, US-USSR).

12. As I explain below, I consider conflict resolution efforts not leading to rivalry termination as failed rapprochement initiatives, and even successful rapprochement often predates rivalry termination by one or more years.

13. On stages of peacemaking, see Kupchan, *How Enemies*; Thompson, "Identifying," 559–562; Arie Kacowicz and Yaacov Bar-Siman-Tov, "Stable Peace: A Conceptual Framework," in *Stable Peace*, ed. Kacowicz et al. On peaceful relationships, see Emanuel Adler and Michael Barnett, eds., *Security Communities* (New York: Cambridge University Press, 1998); Kacowicz, *Zones of Peace*; Karl Deutsch et al., *Political Community and the North Atlantic Area: International Organization in the Light of Historical Experience* (Princeton: Princeton University Press, 1957). On cooperation theories, see Kenneth Schultz,

"The Politics of Risking Peace: Do Hawks or Doves Deliver the Olive Branch?" *International Organization* 59, no. 1 (Winter 2005): 2; Virginia Page Fortna, *Peace Time: Cease-Fire Agreements and the Durability of Peace* (Princeton: Princeton University Press, 2004), 1–6; Larson, *Anatomy of Mistrust*, 36; Stephen Brooks, *Producing Security: Multinational Corporations, Globalization, and the Changing Calculus of Conflict* (Princeton: Princeton University Press, 2005), 7; Armstrong, *Breaking the Ice*, 20–21.

14. Overviews of hypotheses include Karen Rasler, "Political Shocks," in *Evolutionary Interpretations of World Politics,* ed. William Thompson (New York: Routledge, 2001), 241; Kacowicz and Bar-Siman-Tov, "Stable Peace," in *Stable Peace,* ed. Kacowicz et al., 28–30; Bruce Russett and Harvey Starr, *World Politics: The Menu for Choice,* 4th ed. (New York: W. H. Freeman, 1992), Chapter 14; Richard Ned Lebow, "Transitions and Transformations: Building International Cooperation," *Security Studies* 6, no. 3 (Spring 1997): 154–179. Quantitative studies include D. Scott Bennett, "Measuring Rivalry Termination, 1816–1992," *Journal of Conflict Resolution* 41, no. 2 (Apr. 1997): 227–254; Gary Goertz and Paul Diehl, "The Initiation and Termination of Enduring Rivalries: The Impact of Political Shocks," *American Journal of Political Science* 39, no. 1 (Feb. 1995): 30–52; works on individual rivalries include Kydd, *Trust and Mistrust*; and Evelyn Goh, *Constructing the U.S. Rapprochement with China, 1961–1974: From "Red Menace" to "Tacit Ally"* (New York: Cambridge University Press, 2005); comparative monographs include Kupchan, *How Enemies*; Eric Cox, *Why Enduring Rivalries Do—Or Don't—End* (Boulder, CO: First Forum Press, 2010); John David Orme, *The Paradox of Peace: Leaders, Decisions, and Conflict Resolution* (New York: Palgrave MacMillan, 2004); Armstrong, *Breaking the Ice*; and Rock, *Why Peace*.

15. Long and Brecke, *War and Reconciliation*, presents a valuable effort to overcome the domestic-international divide.

16. Lebow, "Transitions," 165, 174; Zartman, "Analyzing Intractability," in *Grasping the Nettle*, ed. Crocker et al., 47; Alexander George and Andrew Bennett, *Case Studies and Theory Development in the Social Sciences* (Cambridge, MA: MIT Press, 2005), 159–162.

17. See, e.g., Rock, *Why Peace*, 11–12; Wendt, *Social Theory*, 342–343. Kupchan, *How Enemies*, Kacowicz, *Zones of Peace*, and Armstrong, *Breaking the Ice*, are surely correct that factors like restraint and satisfaction instead of aggression and revisionism are vital to peacemaking, but if cooperative behavior and preferences lead to cooperative outcomes, what causes those preferences and behaviors?

18. D. Scott Bennett and Allan Stam, *The Behavioral Origins of War* (Ann Arbor: University of Michigan Press, 2004), 4, 8–10, 17.

19. Rock, *Why Peace*, 1; Fortna, *Peace Time*, 95.

20. Leng, *Bargaining*; Gary Goertz and Paul Diehl, "Enduring Rivalries: Theoretical Constructs and Empirical Patterns," *International Studies Quarterly* 37, no. 2 (Jun. 1993): 147–171; Paul Hensel, "One Thing Leads to Another: Recurrent Militarized Disputes in Latin America, 1816–1986," *Journal of Peace Research* 31, no. 3 (Aug. 1994): 281–297.

21. Erik Gartzke and Michael Simon, "'Hot Hand': A Critical Analysis of Enduring Rivalries," *The Journal of Politics* 61, no. 3 (Aug. 1999): 777–798.

22. Zeev Maoz and Ben Mor, *Bound by Struggle: The Strategic Evolution of Enduring International Rivalries* (Ann Arbor: University of Michigan Press, 2002); Michael Colaresi and William Thompson, "Hot Spots or Hot Hands? Serial Crisis Behavior, Escalating

Risks, and Rivalry," *The Journal of Politics* 64, no. 4 (Nov. 2002): 1175–1198; Douglas Stinnett and Paul Diehl, "The Path(s) to Rivalry: Behavioral and Structural Explanations of Rivalry Development," *The Journal of Politics* 63, no. 3 (Aug. 2001): 717–740.

23. Paul Pierson, *Politics in Time: History, Institutions, and Social Analysis* (Princeton: Princeton University Press, 2004), 49–52.

24. Ibid.

25. Goertz and Diehl, "The Initiation"; Cameron Thies, "A Social Psychological Approach to Enduring Rivalries," *Political Psychology* 22, no. 4 (Dec. 2001): 721; Armstrong, *Breaking the Ice*, 66. For example, will the shock of a militarized crisis between the rivals contribute to peacemaking (Richard Ned Lebow, *Between Peace and War: The Nature of International Crises* [Baltimore: Johns Hopkins University Press, 1981]; Rock, *Why Peace*; Armstrong, *Breaking the Ice*), or is it more likely to entrench and escalate rivalry (Leng, *Bargaining*; Wendt, *Social Theory*; Hensel, "One Thing Leads to Another")?

26. See, e.g., Kupchan, *How Enemies*, 3, 6, 25, 35; Cox, *Why Enduring Rivalries*, 25–27; Orme, *The Paradox*, 150; Rock, *Why Peace*, 6; Larson, *Anatomy of Mistrust*, 6, 36; John Owen, "Pieces of Maximal Peace" in *Stable Peace*, ed. Kacowicz et al., 75, 81, 89; Wendt, *Social Theory*, 349–352; D. Scott Bennett, "Security, Bargaining, and the End of Interstate Rivalry," *International Studies Quarterly* 40 (1996): 157–183.

27. Sebastian Rosato, *Europe United: Power Politics and the Making of the European Community* (Ithaca, NY: Cornell University Press, 2011); Andrew Moravcsik, *The Choice for Europe: Social Purpose and State Power from Messina to Maastricht* (Ithaca, NY: Cornell University Press, 1998).

28. See Randall Schweller, *Unanswered Threats: Political Constraints on the Balance of Power* (Princeton: Princeton University Press, 2006).

29. Russett and Starr, *World Politics*, 375.

30. Thomas Christensen, *Worse than a Monolith: Alliance Politics and Problems of Coercive Diplomacy in Asia* (Princeton: Princeton University Press, 2011).

31. Patricia Weitsman, *Dangerous Alliances: Proponents of Peace, Weapons of War* (Stanford, CA: Stanford University Press, 2004).

32. Timothy Crawford, *Pivotal Deterrence: Third-Party Statecraft and the Pursuit of Peace* (Ithaca, NY: Cornell University Press, 2003).

33. Weitsman, *Dangerous Alliances*, 21–24; Randall Schweller, "Bandwagoning for Profit: Bringing the Revisionist State Back In," *International Security* 19, no. 1 (1994): 88–93; Jeremy Pressman, *Warring Friends: Alliance Restraint in International Politics* (Ithaca, NY: Cornell University Press, 2008), 19–21.

34. Paul Schroeder, "Alliances, 1815–1945," in *Historical Dimensions of National Security Problems*, ed. Klaus Knorr (Lawrence: University Press of Kansas, 1976), 227. See also Glenn Snyder, *Alliance Politics* (Ithaca, NY: Cornell University Press, 1997).

35. The persistence of intra-Arab rivalries despite consensus on the Israeli threat, as depicted in Walt, *The Origins of Alliances*, 203–214, 267–268, is especially provocative here.

36. Formally, the Inter-American Treaty of Reciprocal Assistance. I consider the Rio Treaty an alliance and focus on the puzzle of rivalry among treaty members, though of course it produced far less organizational development than NATO, the primary Western alliance. See John Child, *Unequal Alliance: The Inter-American Military System, 1938–1978* (Boulder, CO: Westview, 1980). I explain the research design in more detail below.

37. On Latin American conflicts, see Miguel Angel Centeno, *Blood and Debt: War and the Nation-State in Latin America* (University Park: Pennsylvania State University Press, 2002); João Resende-Santos, *Neorealism, States, and the Modern Mass Army* (New York: Cambridge University Press, 2007); and David Mares, *Violent Peace: Militarized Interstate Bargaining in Latin America* (New York: Columbia University Press, 2001). On the Cold War beyond US and Soviet perspectives, see Odd Arne Westad, *The Global Cold War: Third World Interventions and the Making of Our Times* (New York: Cambridge University Press, 2005) and Tony Smith, "New Bottles for New Wine: A Pericentric Framework for the Study of the Cold War," *Diplomatic History* 24, no. 4 (Fall 2000): 567–591.

38. Stephen Stedman, "Spoiler Problems in Peace Processes," *International Security* 22, no. 2 (Fall 1997): 53, emphasis in original.

39. Domestic political factors feature in Cox, *Why Enduring Rivalries*; Yinan He, *The Search for Reconciliation: Sino-Japanese and German-Polish Relations since World War II* (New York: Cambridge University Press, 2009); and (more skeptically) Orme, *The Paradox*. Tantalizing references to state actors include Thompson, "Identifying Rivals," 562; Wendt, *Social Theory*, 275. Expansions on these points to explore the fits and starts of Soviet-US cooperation during the Cold War include James Richter, "Perpetuating the Cold War: Domestic Sources of International Patterns of Behavior," *Political Science Quarterly* 107, no. 2 (Summer 1992): 271–301; and Lebow, "Transitions," especially 164.

40. See, e.g., Stedman, "Spoiler Problems"; Jack Snyder, *Myths of Empire: Domestic Politics and International Ambition* (Ithaca, NY: Cornell University Press, 1991); Hendrik Spruyt, *Ending Empire: Contested Sovereignty and Territorial Partition* (Ithaca, NY: Cornell University Press, 2005); Paul Pierson, *Dismantling the Welfare State? Reagan, Thatcher, and the Politics of Retrenchment* (New York: Cambridge University Press, 1994); John Brehm and Scott Gates, *Working, Shirking, and Sabotage: Bureaucratic Response to a Democratic Public* (Ann Arbor: University of Michigan Press, 1997).

41. See, e.g., Peter Feaver, *Armed Servants: Agency, Oversight, and Civil-Military Relations* (Cambridge, MA: Harvard University Press, 2003); Amy Zegart, *Flawed By Design: The Evolution of the CIA, JCS, and NSC* (Stanford, CA: Stanford University Press, 1999); George Tsebelis, *Veto Players: How Political Institutions Work* (Princeton: Princeton University Press, 2002); Graham Allison, *Essence of Decision: Explaining the Cuban Missile Crisis* (Boston: Little, Brown, and Company, 1971).

42. Daniel Carpenter, *The Forging of Bureaucratic Autonomy: Reputations, Networks, and Policy Innovation in Executive Agencies, 1862–1928* (Princeton: Princeton University Press, 2001); Lisa Miller, "Rethinking Bureaucrats in the Policy Process: Criminal Justice Agents and the National Crime Agenda," *The Policy Studies Journal* 32, no. 4 (2004): 569–588; Zegart, *Flawed by Design*; Robert Jervis, *Perception and Misperception in International Politics* (Princeton: Princeton University Press, 1976), 418–423; Leon Sigal, *Fighting to a Finish: The Politics of War Termination in the United States and Japan, 1945* (Ithaca, NY: Cornell University Press, 1988).

43. On "normal resistance," see Charles Hermann, "Changing Course: When Governments Choose to Redirect Foreign Policy," *International Studies Quarterly* 34, no. 1 (Mar. 1990): 8–12; on benefits, Zegart, *Flawed by Design*.

44. Aaron Friedberg, *In the Shadow of the Garrison State: America's Anti-Statism and Its Cold War Grand Strategy* (Princeton: Princeton University Press, 2000); Cameron Thies, "War, Rivalry, and State-Building in Latin America," *American Journal of Political*

Science 49, no. 3 (Jul. 2005): 451–465; Mary Kaldor, *The Imaginary War: Understanding the East-West Conflict* (Cambridge, MA: Blackwell, 1990); John Mueller, *Overblown: How Politicians and the Terrorism Industry Inflate National Security Threats, and Why We Believe Them* (New York: The Free Press, 2006).

45. As Snyder, *Myths of Empire,* observes, although no single domestic group prefers imperial overstretch, logrolling and rhetoric in a cartelized government can push national policy further than any one group desires.

46. Similarly, William Dixon's "weakest link principle" holds that the least democratic country in a dyad affects the likely level of bilateral cooperation. William Dixon, "Democracy and the Management of International Conflict," *Journal of Conflict Resolution* 37, no. 1 (Mar. 1993): 51.

47. Helen Milner, *Interests, Institutions, and Information: Domestic Politics and International Relations* (Princeton: Princeton University Press, 1997), 251.

48. Thompson, "Identifying."

49. This parallels the "going public" strategy by which American presidents reach for popular support, bypassing an obstinate congress, and the "boomerang" model by which some activist groups in repressive countries outflank the government to seek foreign help. Samuel Kernell, *Going Public: New Strategies of Presidential Leadership,* 4th ed. (Washington, DC: CQ Press, 2007); Margaret Keck and Kathryn Sikkink, *Activists beyond Borders: Advocacy Networks in International Politics* (Ithaca, NY: Cornell University Press, 1998).

50. See Michael Colaresi, "When Doves Cry: International Rivalry, Unreciprocated Cooperation, and Leadership Turnover," *American Journal of Political Science* 48, no. 3 (Jul. 2004): 555–570, for this point, and Kydd, *Trust and Mistrust,* for the clearest example of rapprochement as the dilemma of inter-state reassurance. Rock, *Why Peace,* 2–18, Armstrong, *Breaking the Ice,* 20–21, and Bennett, "Security, Bargaining," 159, 180, bracket domestic politics.

51. Orme, *The Paradox;* Cox, *Why Enduring Rivalries;* Paul Hensel, "Evolution in Domestic Politics and the Development of Rivalry: The Bolivia-Paraguay Case," in *Evolutionary World Politics,* ed. Thompson, 176–217; Schultz, "The Politics of Risking Peace"; and Colaresi, "When Doves Cry." On two-level games, see Robert Putnam, "Diplomacy and Domestic Politics: The Logic of Two-Level Games," *International Organization* 42, no. 3 (Summer 1988): 427–460; Milner, *Interests, Institutions.*

52. Colaresi, "When Doves Cry," 555–558.

53. Schultz, "The Politics of Risking Peace."

54. See James Mahoney and Gary Goertz, "The Possibility Principle: Choosing Negative Cases in Qualitative Research," *American Political Science Review* 98, no. 4 (Nov. 2004): 653–669.

55. William H. Mott IV, *Soviet Military Assistance: An Empirical Perspective* (Westport, CT: Greenwood Press, 2001), 6.

56. I chose 1955 for this tabulation since the Warsaw Pact formed in that year as a response to West Germany's rearmament and inclusion in NATO; two Western alliances (SEATO and CENTO) also formed in 1954 and 1955, respectively. Colaresi et al., *Strategic Rivalries,* provided the list of rivalries and their beginning and ending dates. For alliance membership, I drew on the lists of international organizations at www.worldstatesmen .org as well as the Organization of American States (OAS) list of signatories to the Rio

Treaty (www.oas.org/juridico/English/sigs/b-29.html). For states listed as direct allies of the United States, I used the list of recipients of US military assistance in the US Agency for International Development (USAID) *Greenbook* (qesdb.usaid.gov/gbk/query_historical.html). Although Yugoslavia received almost as much US aid as South Korea, I coded Yugoslavia as neutral; although Marshal Josip Broz Tito broke with Joseph Stalin's USSR in 1948, Yugoslavia remained a Communist country rather than shifting toward the Western Bloc, and it became a leader in the non-aligned movement by 1961. I coded South Vietnam, Israel, and Saudi Arabia as US allies in 1955 even though according to the *Greenbook* military assistance arrived in these countries only in 1956, 1959, and 1957, respectively, for the following reasons. In 1955, the United States sent aid to "Indochina," which presumably included South Vietnam. The United States began a military training assistance mission in Saudi Arabia in 1953 (see www.state.gov/r/pa/ei/bgn/3584.htm). As for Israel, the State Department claims (www.state.gov/r/pa/ei/bgn/3581.htm) that "Commitment to Israel's security and well being has been a cornerstone of US policy in the Middle East since Israel's founding in 1948, in which the United States played a key supporting role." On the Soviet side, I relied on Mott, *Soviet Military Assistance*, to code North Vietnam and Syria as dependent on Soviet military aid in 1955 and on the Sino-Soviet Treaty of Friendship, Alliance, and Mutual Assistance to code China as a Soviet ally (Chinese Foreign Ministry, www.fmprc.gov.cn/eng/ziliao/3602/3604/t18011.htm). Finally, I listed North Korea as a Soviet ally due to World War II Soviet occupation and postwar backing of Kim Il-Sung (www.state.gov/r/pa/ei/bgn/2792.htm).

57. The absence of Eastern rivalries in 1955 does not hold across the entire Cold War period (as the Sino-Soviet split makes clear), but they are few and far between, compared with Western ones. To what extent did shared Soviet alignment contribute to conflict resolution in the immediate postwar period, such as between Bulgaria and Romania in 1945 and Hungary and Romania in 1947? Relatedly, why did Yugoslavia's rivalries with Soviet allies Hungary and Bulgaria end after Tito's break with the Soviet Union rather than before (in 1955 and 1954, respectively; Yugoslavia realigned in 1948)? Most importantly, are we overlooking additional rivalries between Soviet allies?

58. Only 4 of the 12 Western Bloc rivalries in table 1.2 (33 percent) had ended by 1990 (though two more ended in the early 1990s), compared with 7 of 11 cross-bloc (64 percent) and 8 of 14 mixed-bloc rivalries (57 percent).

59. G. Pope Atkins, *Handbook of Research on the International Relations of Latin America and the Caribbean* (Boulder, CO: Westview Press, 2001), is a useful overview. On Southern Cone cooperation since 1980, see Brooks, *Producing Security*, Chapter 5; Kacowicz, *Zones of Peace*, Chapter 3; Solingen, *Regional Orders*, Chapter 5.

60. E.g., James Klein, Gary Goertz, and Paul Diehl, "The New Rivalry Dataset: Procedures and Patterns," *Journal of Peace Research* 43, no. 3 (May 2006): 331–348; Bennett, "Security, Bargaining"; see Colaresi et al., *Strategic Rivalries*, 36–72.

61. Thompson, "Identifying," 569, 573, 577, 583. Relatedly, see Vasquez and Leskiw, "The Origins," and Bennett, "Measuring."

62. On contested issues, see Bennett, "Measuring"; Bennett, "Security, Bargaining"; John Vasquez, *The War Puzzle* (Cambridge: Cambridge University Press, 1993).

63. See James Fearon, "Rationalist Explanations for War," *International Organization* 49, no. 3 (Summer 1995): 379–414; Ron Hassner, *The Path to Indivisibility: The Role of*

Ideas in the Resolution of Intractable Territorial Disputes (PhD diss., Stanford University, 2003); Fortna, *Peace Time*, 95–96.

64. See I. William Zartman, *Ripe for Resolution: Conflict and Intervention in Africa* (New York: Oxford University Press, 1985).

65. Haass, *Conflicts Unending.*

66. Centeno, *Blood and Debt.*

67. Cox, *Why Enduring Rivalries*, 3–4, takes a similar approach. Contrast Kupchan, *How Enemies*, 9; and Rock, *Why Peace*, 21, where the universe of cases is unspecified.

68. Thompson, "Identifying," 565–569; Colaresi et al., *Strategic Rivalries*, 286–287.

69. Valuable articulations of intra-paradigm competition include Stephen Brooks, "Dueling Realisms," *International Organization* 51, no. 3 (Summer 1997): 445–477; Andrew Moravcsik, "Taking Preferences Seriously: A Liberal Theory of International Politics," *International Organization* 51, no. 4 (Autumn 1997): 513–553; Ted Hopf, "The Promise of Constructivism in International Relations Theory," *International Security* 23, no. 1 (Summer 1998): 171–200.

70. Hans Morgenthau, *Politics among Nations: The Struggle for Power and Peace*, 2nd ed. (New York: Knopf, 1954), 186–190; Walt, *Origins of Alliances*, 18, 22; Steven David, *Choosing Sides: Alignment and Realignment in the Third World* (Baltimore: Johns Hopkins University Press, 1991), 4.

71. Morgenthau, *Politics among Nations*, 161–162.

72. Robert Jervis, "Cooperation under the Security Dilemma," *World Politics* 30, no. 2 (Jan. 1978): 167–214; Barbara Walter, *Committing to Peace: The Successful Settlement of Civil Wars* (Princeton: Princeton University Press, 2002).

73. Fearon, "Rationalist Explanations," 380; Hein Goemans, *War and Punishment: The Causes of War Termination and the First World War* (Princeton: Princeton University Press, 2000); Stephen Van Evera, *Causes of War: Power and the Roots of Conflict* (Ithaca, NY: Cornell University Press, 1999), 34.

74. See Jervis, *Perception*, Chapter 3; Lebow, "Transitions," 164; Daryl Press, *Calculating Credibility: How Leaders Assess Military Threats* (Ithaca, NY: Cornell University Press, 2005); Van Evera, *Causes of War*, 104.

75. Robert Jervis, *System Effects: Complexity in Political and Social Life* (Princeton: Princeton University Press, 1997), 222–226; Walt, *The Origins of Alliances*, 285 n. 53; Kenneth Waltz, "Structural Realism after the Cold War," in *Realism and International Politics*, ed. Kenneth Waltz (New York: Routledge, 2008), 211; Hans Morgenthau, "Alliances in Theory and Practice," in *Alliance Policy in the Cold War*, ed. Arnold Wolfers (Baltimore: Johns Hopkins University Press, 1959), 186, 197, 212.

76. See James Morrow, "Arms versus Allies: Trade-Offs in the Search for Security," *International Organization* 47, no. 2 (Spring 1993): 213–216, 232. Morgenthau, *Politics among Nations*, 166–171, observes two additional balancing methods: dividing the stronger side's alliance, rather than building up the weaker side, and territorial "compensations" (particularly, imperial acquisitions) to expand one's pool of resources.

77. Bennett, "Security, Bargaining."

78. See especially David, *Choosing Sides*; Centeno, *Blood and Debt*; *Asian Security Practice: Material and Ideational Influences*, ed. Muthiah Alagappa (Stanford, CA: Stanford University Press, 1998); Mohammed Ayoob, *The Third World Security Predicament: State Making, Regional Conflict, and the International System* (Boulder, CO: Lynne Rienner, 1995).

79. The major comparative work is Timothy Wickham-Crowley, *Guerrillas and Revolution in Latin America: A Comparative Study of Insurgents and Regimes Since 1956* (Princeton: Princeton University Press, 1992).

80. Kenneth Waltz, *Theory of International Politics* (Reading, MA: Addison-Wesley, 1979); Schweller, "Bandwagoning"; Walt, *Origins of Alliances.*

81. On windows, see Van Evera, *Causes of* War, 73–86; on power transitions, A. F. K. Organski and Jacek Kugler, *The War Ledger* (Chicago: University of Chicago Press, 1980).

82. Stephen Brooks and William Wohlforth, *World Out of Balance: International Relations and the Challenge of American Primacy* (Princeton: Princeton University Press, 2008).

83. Of course, as Organski and Kugler, *The War Ledger,* argue, there is also a possibility that the moments of power transition, before preponderance is achieved, will have a high probability of war for precisely these reasons.

84. Walter, *Committing to Peace.*

85. Ibid.

86. See Brooks and Wohlforth, *World Out of Balance*; G. John Ikenberry, *After Victory: Institutions, Strategic Restraint, and the Rebuilding of Order After Major Wars* (Princeton: Princeton University Press, 2001); Wendt, *Social Theory.*

87. See Schweller, "Bandwagoning;" George Liska, *Nations in Alliance: The Limits of Interdependence* (Baltimore: Johns Hopkins University Press, 1962), 57; David Lake, *Hierarchy in International Relations* (Ithaca, NY: Cornell University Press, 2009), Chapter 5. The counterintuitive argument that weak allies have significant bargaining power over their stronger partners comes from Snyder, *Alliance Politics.*

88. Measuring power, and even the more limited issue of military capabilities, is the subject of heated debate, although most of this focuses on relations among great powers in order to assess power transitions and the likelihood of war. Not all countries' troops are of equal battlefield potential due to variation in training and motivation; weapon counts say little about deployments or combat effectiveness; and differing levels of technology make conversations about missiles or planes across countries not readily comparable. In Cold War Latin America, though, these issues are much less pronounced. Even the most advanced countries never developed nuclear weapons (although Argentina and Brazil had nuclear programs), foreign aid and training concentrated on counterinsurgency capabilities rather than conventional warfare, and major equipment purchases (e.g., Brazil's purchase of a used aircraft carrier) were often symbolic. All else being equal, I assume that a country with more troops, a larger economy, and a higher level of defense spending is more powerful than another country with fewer resources and that leaders in both countries would concur.

89. Examples include Thies, "A Social Psychological Approach"; Ron Hassner, "The Path to Intractability: Time and the Entrenchment of Territorial Disputes," *International Security* 31, no. 3 (Winter 2006–2007): 107–138; Larson, *Anatomy of Mistrust*; Leng, *Bargaining*; Armstrong, *Breaking the Ice.*

90. Stein, "Image," in *Turbulent Peace,* ed. Crocker et al.; Larson, *Anatomy of Mistrust*; see Ziva Kunda, *Social Cognition: Making Sense of People* (Cambridge, MA: MIT Press, 1999), especially 211.

91. Wendt, *Social Theory,* 25–26, 44, 101, 108.

92. Ibid., 263, 272, 283.

93. Larson, *Anatomy of Mistrust*, 22–23; on learning, see also Dan Reiter, *Crucible of Beliefs: Learning, Alliances, and World Wars* (Ithaca, NY: Cornell University Press, 1996); Elizabeth Kier, *Imagining War: French and British Military Doctrine between the Wars* (Princeton: Princeton University Press, 1997), 41–46.

94. See, e.g., Ted Robert Gurr, "Minorities, Nationalists, and Islamists: Managing Communal Conflict in the Twenty-First Century," in *Leashing the Dogs of War: Conflict Management in a Divided World*, ed. Chester Crocker, Fen Osler Hampson, and Pamela Aall (Washington, DC: United States Institute of Peace, 2007), 131–160.

95. Alexander Wendt, "Anarchy Is What States Make of It: The Social Construction of Power Politics," *International Organization* 46, no. 2 (Spring 1992): 391–425.

96. See Nicholas Onuf, *World of Our Making: Rules and Rule in Social Theory and International Relations* (Columbia: University of South Carolina Press, 1989).

97. Wendt, *Social Theory*, 349–358. Although Wendt employs fate rather than foe, he recognizes, 349, that common fate has to be an "objective" condition to produce collective identity and that this condition is "typically . . . constituted by an external threat." Explaining ideological labor, see Larson, *Anatomy of Mistrust*, 10, 240; defending self-restraint, Ikenberry, *After Victory*; critiquing "persuasion," Ronald Krebs and Patrick Thaddeus Jackson, "Twisting Tongues and Twisting Arms: The Power of Political Rhetoric," *European Journal of International Relations* 13, no. 1 (Mar. 2007): 35–66.

98. Muzafer Sherif, O. J. Harvey, B. Jack White, William R. Hood, and Carolyn W. Sherif, *Intergroup Conflict and Cooperation: The Robbers Cave Experiment* (Norman: The University Book Exchange and Institute of Group Relations, University of Oklahoma, 1961), 202–210; Muzafer Sherif, *In Common Predicament: Social Psychology of Intergroup Conflict and Cooperation* (Boston, MA: Houghton Mifflin, 1966), 159–160; Henri Tajfel and John Turner, "An Integrative Theory of Intergroup Conflict," in *The Social Psychology of Intergroup Relations*, ed. William Austin and Stephen Worchel (Monterey, CA: Brooks-Cole, 1979), 33–47; Miles Hewstone and Katy Greenland, "Intergroup Conflict," *International Journal of Psychology* 35, no. 2 (Apr. 2000): 136–144; Samuel Gaertner et al., "Reducing Intergroup Bias: Elements of Intergroup Cooperation," *Journal of Personality and Social Psychology* 76, no. 3 (Mar. 1999): 388–402. In international relations see Wendt, "Anarchy"; Jonathan Mercer, "Anarchy and Identity," *International Organization* 49, no. 2 (Spring 1995): 229–252.

99. Morton Deutsch, *The Resolution of Conflict: Constructive and Destructive Processes* (New Haven: Yale University Press, 1973), 29–30, 351–376, 202.

100. Prominent examples include the Andean Pact (1969), the Organization of Central American States (1956), the Central American Defense Council (1963), and (covertly) Operation Condor (1975).

101. See Keck and Sikkink, *Activists beyond Borders*; *The Power of Human Rights: International Norms and Domestic Change*, ed. Thomas Risse, Stephen Ropp, and Kathryn Sikkink (New York: Cambridge University Press, 1999); on sources of norm creation beyond entrepreneurship, Martha Finnemore, *The Purpose of Intervention: Changing Beliefs about the Use of Force* (Ithaca, NY: Cornell University Press, 2003), Chapter 5; Arie Kacowicz, *The Impact of Norms in International Society: The Latin American Experience, 1881–2001* (Notre Dame, IN: University of Notre Dame Press, 2005), 28–30.

102. Richard Price and Nina Tannenwald, "Norms and Deterrence: The Nuclear and Chemical Weapons Taboo," in *The Culture of National Security: Norms and Identity in World Politics*, ed. Peter Katzenstein (New York: Columbia University Press, 1996), 114–152; Keck and Sikkink, *Activists*; Finnemore, *The Purpose*.

103. Thomas Risse, "'Let's Argue!' Communicative Action in World Politics," *International Organization* 54, no. 1 (Winter 2000): 1–39; Hopf, "The Promise," 179.

104. Finnemore, *The Purpose*, 146–147; Krebs and Jackson, "Twisting Tongues"; G. John Ikenberry and Charles Kupchan, "Socialization and Hegemonic Power," *International Organization* 44, no. 3 (Summer 1990): 285.

105. Peter Smith, *Talons of the Eagle: Latin America, the United States, and the World*, 3rd ed. (New York: Oxford University Press, 2008); Robert Pastor, *Exiting the Whirlpool: US Foreign Policy toward Latin America and the Caribbean* (Boulder, CO: Westview Press, 2001); Greg Grandin, *Empire's Workshop: Latin America, the United States, and the Rise of the New Imperialism* (New York: Metropolitan Books, 2006).

106. Moravcsik, "Taking Preferences Seriously," though see Brian Rathbun, "Is Anybody Not an (International Relations) Liberal?" *Security Studies* 19, no. 1 (Jan. 2010): 2–25.

107. See Kupchan, *How Enemies*; Rock, *Why Peace*; Kacowicz, *Zones of Peace*.

108. Bruce Russett and John Oneal, *Triangulating Peace: Democracy, Interdependence, and International Organizations* (New York: W. W. Norton, 2001), 35.

109. See Kacowicz, *Zones of Peace*, 42.

110. Russett and Oneal, *Triangulating Peace*, 198–200.

111. See Michael Doyle, "Kant, Liberal Legacies, and Foreign Affairs," reprinted in *Debating the Democratic Peace*, ed. Michael Brown, Sean Lynn-Jones, and Steven Miller (Cambridge, MA: MIT Press, 1996).

112. Walt, *Origins of Alliances*; David, *Choosing Sides*, 5; Rock, *Why Peace*.

113. John Owen, *Liberal Peace, Liberal War: American Politics and International Security* (Ithaca, NY: Cornell University Press, 1997), 16, emphasis in original.

114. Kydd, *Trust and Mistrust*; Kenneth Schultz, *Democracy and Coercive Diplomacy* (New York: Cambridge University Press, 2001); and Fearon, "Domestic Political Audiences," make similar claims about signaling resolve.

115. Michael Barletta, "Argentine and Brazilian Nonproliferation: A Democratic Peace?" in *Twenty-First Century Weapons Proliferation: Are We Ready?* ed. Henry Sokolski and James Ludes (Portland, OR: Frank Cass, 2001): 148–167; Kristian Skrede Gleditsch and Michael Ward, "Democratizing for Peace," *American Political Science Review* 92, no. 1 (Mar. 1998): 51–61; though see Edward Mansfield and Jack Snyder, *Electing to Fight: Why Emerging Democracies Go to War* (Cambridge, MA: MIT Press, 2005).

116. See Tad Szulc, *Twilight of the Tyrants* (New York: Holt, 1959); Samuel Huntington, *The Third Wave: Democratization in the Late Twentieth Century* (Norman: University of Oklahoma Press, 1991).

117. Mark Haas, *The Ideological Origins of Great Power Politics, 1789–1989* (Ithaca, NY: Cornell University Press, 2005), 4, emphasis in original.

118. Ibid., 6–18.

119. Stanislav Andreski, "On the Peaceful Disposition of Military Dictatorships," *Journal of Strategic Studies* 3, no. 3 (Mar. 1980): 3–10; Mark Peceny and Caroline Beer, with

Shannon Sanchez-Terry, "Dictatorial Peace?" *American Political Science Review* 96, no. 1 (Mar. 2002): 15–26.

120. Owen, *Liberal Peace*, 22–32, refers to this as the principle of "favoritism," which also applies among authoritarian regimes, but which he expects should be insufficient for them to form "zones of peace."

121. Daniel Byman, Peter Chalk, Bruce Hoffman, William Rosenau, and David Brannan, *Trends in Outside Support for Insurgent Movements* (Santa Monica, CA: RAND, 2001); Kristian Gleditsch, Idean Salehyan, and Kenneth Schultz, "Fighting at Home, Fighting Abroad: How Civil Wars Lead to International Disputes," *Journal of Conflict Resolution* 52, no. 4 (Aug. 2008): 479–506.

122. On these regimes, consult Guillermo O'Donnell, *Modernization and Bureaucratic-Authoritarianism: Studies in South American Politics*, 2nd ed. (Berkeley: University of California Press, 1979); Peter Kornbluh, *The Pinochet File: A Declassified Dossier on Atrocity and Accountability* (New York: The New Press, 2004); Alfred Stepan, *The Military in Politics: Changing Patterns in Brazil* (Princeton: Princeton University Press, 1971).

123. Juan José Arévalo, *The Shark and the Sardines* (New York: L. Stewart, 1961). Similarly, see Smith, *Talons*; Cole Blasier, *The Hovering Giant: US Responses to Revolutionary Change in Latin America, 1910–1985*, rev. ed. (Pittsburgh: University of Pittsburgh Press, 1986).

Chapter 2 · Parochial Interest and Policy Change

1. Thorstein Veblen, *The Vested Interests and the Common Man ("The Modern Point of View and the New Order")* (New York: B. W. Huebsch, 1919), 100, defines a vested interest as "a marketable right to get something for nothing. . . . Vested interests are immaterial wealth, intangible assets." Epigraph citations, respectively, are to V. O. Key, *Politics, Parties, and Pressure Groups*, 5th ed. (New York: Crowell, 1964), 691; and William Niskanen, *Bureaucracy and Representative Government* (Chicago: Aldine-Atherton, 1971), vi.

2. On domestic policy, see Mark Daniels, *Terminating Public Programs: An American Political Paradox* (Armonk, NY: M. E. Sharpe, 1997), 16, 26–27, 71–73; Michael Hayes, *The Limits of Policy Change: Incrementalism, Worldview, and the Rule of Law* (Washington, DC: Georgetown University Press, 2001), 51–71, 162–168; James Anderson, *Public Policymaking: An Introduction*, 5th ed. (Boston: Houghton Mifflin, 2003), 274–276; for foreign policy, see Jerel Rosati, *The Politics of United States Foreign Policy*, 2nd ed. (Fort Worth, TX: Harcourt Brace, 1999), 570–572; Morton Halperin and Priscilla Clapp, with Arnold Kanter, *Bureaucratic Politics and Foreign Policy*, 2nd ed. (Washington, DC: Brookings Institution Press, 2006), esp. Chapter 3.

3. The phrase comes from Graham Allison, *Essence of Decision: Explaining the Cuban Missile Crisis* (Boston: Little, Brown, and Company, 1971), 266.

4. Richard Ned Lebow, "Transitions and Transformations: Building International Cooperation," *Security Studies* 6, no. 3 (Spring 1997): 154–179; Michael Colaresi, Karen Rasler, and William Thompson, *Strategic Rivalries in World Politics: Position, Space, and Conflict Escalation* (Cambridge: Cambridge University Press, 2007), 4, 12.

5. On leadership in rapprochement, see Charles Kupchan, *How Enemies Become Friends: The Sources of Stable Peace* (Princeton: Princeton University Press, 2010); Tony Armstrong, *Breaking the Ice: Rapprochement between East and West Germany, the United States and China, and Israel and Egypt* (Washington, DC: United States Institute of Peace,

1993); on domestic constraints, James Richter, "Perpetuating the Cold War: Domestic Sources of International Patterns of Behavior," *Political Science Quarterly* 107, no. 2 (Summer 1992): 271–301.

6. Stephen Stedman, "Spoiler Problems in Peace Processes," *International Security* 22, no. 2 (Fall 1997): 5–53; Barbara Walter, *Committing to Peace: The Successful Settlement of Civil Wars* (Princeton: Princeton University Press, 2002).

7. I. William Zartman, *Ripe for Resolution: Conflict and Intervention in Africa* (New York: Oxford University Press, 1985); Richard Haass, *Conflicts Unending: The United States and Regional Disputes* (New Haven: Yale University Press, 1990).

8. This presumes that one does not define cases of rivalry solely in terms of conflict frequency. See Colaresi et al., *Strategic Rivalries*. On collusion, see C. Wright Mills, *The Causes of World War Three* (New York: Simon and Schuster, 1958); Mary Kaldor, *The Imaginary War: Understanding the East-West Conflict* (Cambridge, MA: Blackwell, 1990), especially 4–6, 108–114, 182–187.

9. Harold Lasswell, "The Garrison State," *The American Journal of Sociology* 46, no. 4 (Jan. 1941), 466.

10. I take up these related issues of equifinality and scope conditions in the final section of this chapter.

11. Allison, *Essence of Decision*, 96, 174, 274–275; Emily Goldman, "Mission Possible: Organizational Learning in Peacetime," and Edward Rhodes, "Constructing Power: Cultural Transformation and Strategic Adjustment in the 1890s," both in *The Politics of Strategic Adjustment: Ideas, Institutions, and Interests*, ed. Peter Trubowitz, Emily Goldman, and Edward Rhodes (New York: Columbia University Press, 1999); Stephen Krasner, "Are Bureaucracies Important? (Or Allison Wonderland)," *Foreign Policy* 7 (Summer 1972): 160–164.

12. In American politics, see, e.g., Daniels, *Terminating*; John Brehm and Scott Gates, *Working, Shirking, and Sabotage: Bureaucratic Response to a Democratic Public* (Ann Arbor: University of Michigan Press, 1997); Michael Hayes, *The Limits of Policy Change: Incrementalism, Worldview, and the Rule of Law* (Washington, DC: Georgetown University Press, 2001); Thomas Birkland, *After Disaster: Agenda Setting, Public Policy, and Focusing Events* (Washington, DC: Georgetown University Press, 1997). In comparative politics, see George Tsebelis, *Veto Players: How Political Institutions Work* (Princeton: Princeton University Press, 2002); *Bureaucrats and Policy Making: A Comparative Overview*, ed. Ezra Suleiman (New York: Holmes and Meier, 1984); Peter Evans, *Dependent Development: The Alliance of Multinational, State, and Local Capital in Brazil* (Princeton: Princeton University Press, 1979). In international relations, see particularly Charles Hermann, "Changing Course: When Governments Choose to Redirect Foreign Policy," *International Studies Quarterly* 34, no. 1 (Mar. 1990): 3–21; K. J. Holsti, *Why Nations Realign: Foreign Policy Restructuring in the Postwar World* (London: George Allen & Unwyn, 1982); Steven David, *Choosing Sides: Alignment and Realignment in the Third World* (Baltimore: Johns Hopkins University Press, 1991); *The Politics of Strategic Adjustment*, ed. Trubowitz et al.; Deborah Avant, *Political Institutions and Military Change: Lessons from Peripheral Wars* (Ithaca, NY: Cornell University Press, 1994); Elizabeth Kier, *Imagining War: French and British Military Doctrine between the Wars* (Princeton: Princeton University Press, 1997); Amy Zegart, *Flawed By Design: The Evolution of the CIA, JCS, and NSC* (Stanford, CA: Stanford University Press, 1999).

13. Stedman, "Spoiler Problems"; Walter, *Committing*; Hendrik Spruyt, *Ending Empire: Contested Sovereignty and Territorial Partition* (Ithaca, NY: Cornell University Press, 2005); Jack Snyder, *Myths of Empire: Domestic Politics and International Ambition* (Ithaca, NY: Cornell University Press, 1991); John Atkinson Hobson, *Imperialism, a Study* (New York: J. Pott and Company, 1902).

14. Conspiracy theorizing has always hovered near the investigation of parochial interests in foreign policy and is particularly prominent in studies of imperialism, but does not have to drive such analysis. On private interests and empire, see Hobson, *Imperialism*; Charles Beard, *The Devil Theory of War: An Inquiry into the Nature of History and the Possibility of Keeping Out of War* (New York: The Vanguard Press, 1936), 18–23, 116–124; William Robinson, *A Theory of Global Capitalism: Production, Class, and State in a Transnational World* (Baltimore: Johns Hopkins University Press, 2004); for critiques, Hans Morgenthau, *Politics among Nations: The Struggle for Power and Peace*, 2nd ed. (New York: Knopf, 1954), 29–34; Michael Doyle, *Empires* (Ithaca, NY: Cornell University Press, 1986); Allison, *Essence of Decision*, 37.

15. See Daniel Wirls, *Irrational Security: The Politics of Defense from Reagan to Obama* (Baltimore: Johns Hopkins University Press, 2010), 7–10.

16. Alfred Vagts, *A History of Militarism* (New York: W. W. Norton, 1937), 11–15; Kjell Skjelsbaek, "Militarism, Its Dimensions and Corollaries: An Attempt at Conceptual Clarification," *Journal of Peace Research* 16, no. 3 (1979): 215–216.

17. Dwight Eisenhower, "Farewell Address," www.eisenhower.archives.gov/speeches /farewell_address.html, accessed May 8, 2008 (emphasis added).

18. Alex Roland, "The Military-Industrial Complex: Lobby and Trope," in *The Long War: A New History of US National Security Policy since World War II*, ed. Andrew Bacevich (New York: Columbia University Press, 2007); Volker R. Berghan, *Militarism: The History of an International Debate, 1861–1979* (New York: Cambridge University Press, 1984 [1981]), 86–87.

19. James Donovan, *Militarism, USA* (New York: Charles Scribner's Sons, 1970), 2; Chalmers Johnson, *The Sorrows of Empire: Militarism, Secrecy, and the End of the Republic* (New York: Metropolitan Books, 2004), 58–64.

20. On political constraints, see Aaron Friedberg, *In the Shadow of the Garrison State: America's Anti-Statism and its Cold War Grand Strategy* (Princeton: Princeton University Press, 2000), 40–61, 292–295, 340–345; Jeremi Suri, "The Limits of American Empire: Democracy and Militarism in the Twentieth and Twenty-First Centuries," in *Colonial Crucible: Empire in the Making of the Modern American State*, ed. Alfred McCoy and Francisco Scarano (Madison, WI: University of Wisconsin Press, 2009). Contrast Anna Kasten Nelson, "The Evolution of the National Security State: Ubiquitous and Endless," in *The Long War*, ed. Bacevich. On the lack of economic ones, see Benjamin O. Fordham, "Paying for Global Power: Assessing the Costs and Benefits of Postwar US Military Spending," in the same volume.

21. See, e.g., Michael Mann, *Incoherent Empire* (New York: Verso, 2003), 9, 252; Andrew Bacevich, *Washington Rules: America's Path to Permanent War* (New York: Henry Holt, 2010), 241–244.

22. John Kingdon, *Agendas, Alternatives, and Public Policies*, 2nd ed. (New York: HarperCollins, 1995), Chapter 8; Michael Cohen, James March, and Johan Olsen, "A

Garbage Can Model of Organizational Choice," *Administrative Science Quarterly* 17, no. 1 (Mar. 1972): 1–25; Herbert Simon, *Models of Man: Mathematical Essays on Rational Human Behavior in a Social Setting* (New York: John Wiley and Sons, 1957), Chapter 14; Charles Lindblom, "The Science of 'Muddling Through,'" *Public Administration Review* 19, no. 2 (Spring 1959): 79–88.

23. John Huber and Charles Shipan, *Deliberate Discretion? The Institutional Foundations of Bureaucratic Autonomy* (New York: Cambridge University Press, 2002), 90.

24. Robert Jervis, *Perception and Misperception in International Politics* (Princeton: Princeton University Press, 1976), 415–418; Rose McDermott, *Political Psychology in International Relations* (Ann Arbor: University of Michigan Press, 2004), 249–255.

25. John Kenneth Galbraith, *How to Control the Military* (New York: Doubleday, 1969), 19–24; Donovan, *Militarism*, xix–xx, 214–215.

26. Halperin and Clapp, *Bureaucratic Politics*, 9, 24; Allison, *Essence of Decision*, 166–168.

27. Risa Brooks, "Militaries and Political Activity in Democracies," in *American Civil-Military Relations: The Soldier and the State in a New Era*, ed. Suzanne Nielsen and Don Snider (Baltimore: Johns Hopkins University Press, 2009), 215, 225–229; Michael Desch, *Civilian Control of the Military: The Changing Security Environment* (Baltimore: Johns Hopkins University Press, 1999), 4.

28. See Bacevich, *Washington Rules*, 30–32.

29. See Allison, *Essence of Decision*, 79, 87–98; Halperin and Clapp, *Bureaucratic Politics*, 99; I. M. Destler, *Presidents, Bureaucrats, and Foreign Policy: The Politics of Organizational Reform* (Princeton: Princeton University Press, 1972). My main departure from Allison's Model II is to emphasize the intentional efforts of state agencies to maintain policies that benefit them parochially, rather than to chalk up policy consistency across time to inertia or momentum.

30. See David Sylvan and Stephen Majeski, *US Foreign Policy in Perspective: Clients, Enemies, and Empire* (New York: Routledge, 2009); Andrew Bacevich, *American Empire: The Realities and Consequences of US Diplomacy* (Cambridge, MA: Harvard University Press, 2002), 57, 69–72; Roland, "The Military-Industrial Complex," in *The Long War*, ed. Bacevich, 340, 363.

31. Dan Smith and Ron Smith, *The Economics of Militarism* (London: Pluto Press, 1983), 12, 62–71.

32. Allison, *Essence of Decision*, 7. Snyder, *Myths of Empire*, notes that logrolling in cartelized systems often produces more imperial expansion than desired by any one group, implying that the opposite outcome—insufficient imperialism to satisfy the interests of those groups—is unlikely. The persistence of international rivalries may be the result of coalitions like those described by Snyder getting it exactly right—enough saber-rattling, arms construction, and diplomatic wrangling to satisfy the parochial groups, but not enough to cause war or other disaster.

33. Snyder, *Myths of Empire*, 14–16.

34. Paul Hensel, "One Thing Leads to Another: Recurrent Militarized Disputes in Latin America, 1816–1986," *Journal of Peace Research* 31, no. 3 (Aug. 1994): 281–297; Paul Pierson, *Politics in Time: History, Institutions, and Social Analysis* (Princeton: Princeton University Press, 2004), 49–52.

35. The arrow at the far left in figure 2.1 indicates that the original source of conflict is external to my theory. A theory of rivalry origins (as opposed to rivalry maintenance and rapprochement) is outside the scope of this book.

36. See Galbraith, *How to Control*, 33–35.

37. Allison, *Essence of Decision*, 80, 145.

38. See Roland, "The Military-Industrial Complex," in *The Long War*, ed. Bacevich, 356. Nor is the creation of new agencies or programs a solution, since powerful existing agencies will influence or dominate these new entities and policies. See Zegart, *Flawed by Design*; Niskanen, *Bureaucracy*, 195; Allison, *Essence of Decision*, 93, 145.

39. Tsebelis, *Veto Players*; Spruyt, *Ending Empire*.

40. Allison, *Essence of Decision*, 83–84, 96, 168–170.

41. See Niskanen, *Bureaucracy*, 189.

42. Mills, *The Causes of World War Three*; see also Snyder, *Myths of Empire*.

43. Allison, *Essence of Decision*, 82.

44. On alternative benefits and their tradeoffs, see Goldman, "Mission Possible," in *The Politics of Strategic Adjustment*, ed. Trubowitz et al., 258 n. 18; Halperin and Clapp, *Bureaucratic Politics*, 61; James Q. Wilson, *Bureaucracy: What Government Agencies Do and Why They Do It* (New York: Basic Books, 1989), 179–195; Bacevich, *Washington Rules*, 228; Snyder, *Myths of Empire*, 31–33.

45. Daniel Carpenter, *The Forging of Bureaucratic Autonomy: Reputations, Networks, and Policy Innovation in Executive Agencies, 1862–1928* (Princeton: Princeton University Press, 2001); Samuel Huntington, *The Soldier and the State: The Theory and Politics of Civil-Military Relations* (Cambridge, MA: Harvard University Press, 1957); Lasswell, "The Garrison State," 457–458.

46. See Huber and Shipan, *Deliberate Discretion?*, 78–83.

47. Niskanen, *Bureaucracy*, 38, emphasis in original.

48. As Paul Pierson argues in *Dismantling the Welfare State? Reagan, Thatcher, and the Politics of Retrenchment* (New York: Cambridge University Press, 1994), 2–6, organized groups with vested interests in the continuation of a welfare policy can successfully resist conservatives' drive to retrench government programs.

49. Common interests in themselves are frequently insufficient to cause cooperation, though. See Robert Keohane, *After Hegemony: Cooperation and Discord in the World Political Economy* (Princeton: Princeton University Press, 1984); Mancur Olson, *The Logic of Collective Action: Public Goods and the Theory of Groups* (Cambridge, MA: Harvard University Press, 1971). Resistance to international cooperation often comes from interest groups whose policy preferences diverge from those articulated by the president (Helen Milner, *Interests, Institutions, and Information: Domestic Politics and International Relations* [Princeton: Princeton University Press, 1997], esp. 60–65).

50. Allison, *Essence of Decision*, 93, 271.

51. Allison, *Essence of Decision*, 176 n. 71, attributes this line to Don Price.

52. See Anderson, *Public Policymaking*, 274.

53. Olson, *The Logic*, 33–36, 43–65, 126–131, 141–148.

54. Snyder, *Myths of Empire*, 34–35.

55. See Gideon Rose, "Neoclassical Realism and Theories of Foreign Policy," *World Politics* 51, no. 1 (Oct. 1998): 144–172.

56. Michael Colaresi, "When Doves Cry: International Rivalry, Unreciprocated Cooperation, and Leadership Turnover," *American Journal of Political Science* 48, no. 3 (Jul. 2004): 555–570; Kenneth Schultz, "The Politics of Risking Peace: Do Hawks or Doves Deliver the Olive Branch?" *International Organization* 59, no. 1 (Winter 2005): 1–38; Paul Hensel, "Evolution in Domestic Politics and the Development of Rivalry: The Bolivia-Paraguay Case," in *Evolutionary World Politics*, ed. William Thompson (New York: Routledge, 2001), 176–217; John David Orme, *The Paradox of Peace: Leaders, Decisions, and Conflict Resolution* (New York: Palgrave MacMillan, 2004).

57. Zegart, *Flawed by Design*; Peter Feaver, *Armed Servants: Agency, Oversight, and Civil-Military Relations* (Cambridge, MA: Harvard University Press, 2003); Avant, *Political Institutions*.

58. Huber and Shipan, *Deliberate Discretion?*, 96–97; Brehm and Gates, *Working, Shirking*.

59. Brehm and Gates, *Working, Shirking*.

60. James Burk, "Responsible Obedience by Military Professionals: The Discretion to Do What Is Wrong," in *American Civil-Military Relations*, ed. Nielsen and Snider, 151, 158, 160–162, 168.

61. Allison, *Essence of Decision*, 90, 79; Halperin and Clapp, *Bureaucratic Politics*, 139–180; Kingdon, *Agendas, Alternatives*, 197–201.

62. See Brooks, "Militaries," in *American Civil-Military Relations*, ed. Nielsen and Snider; Donovan, *Militarism*, 232–233.

63. Thorstein Veblen, *The Engineers and the Price System* (New York: B. W. Huebsch, 1921), 1, attributes the "conscientious withdrawal" phrase to the IWW (the Industrial Workers of the World, or "Wobblies").

64. Veblen, *The Engineers*, 7, 20.

65. Geoff Brown, *Sabotage: A Study in Industrial Conflict* (Nottingham, UK: Bertrand Russell Peace Foundation / Spokesman Books, 1977), xii, 13–19.

66. Thus, Brehm and Gates, *Working, Shirking*, 30, portray bureaucratic sabotage as "negative output." See also Allison, *Essence of Decision*, 172–178, 267–268.

67. James C. Scott, *Weapons of the Weak: Everyday Forms of Peasant Resistance* (New Haven, CT: Yale University Press, 1985), 29–34, 290–296, describes a litany of tactics ("foot dragging, dissimulation, false compliance, pilfering, feigned ignorance, slander, arson, sabotage, and so forth") used by peasants to resist being squeezed by landlords and other authority figures without incurring acute repression.

68. See Halperin and Clapp, *Bureaucratic Politics*, 254–272.

69. Feaver, *Armed Servants*, 287–292 (although Feaver refers to shirking rather than sabotage); Brooks, "Militaries," in *American Civil-Military Relations*, ed. Nielsen and Snider, 218–224.

70. Burk, "Responsible Obedience," in *American Civil-Military Relations*, ed. Nielsen and Snider, 163–168.

71. David Dunn, "How Useful is Summitry?" in *Diplomacy at the Highest Level: The Evolution of International Summitry*, ed. David Dunn (New York: St. Martin's Press / MacMillan, 1996), 251, 265.

72. Chas. W. Freeman Jr., *Arts of Power: Statecraft and Diplomacy* (Washington, DC: United States Institute of Peace Press, 1997), 96.

73. Erik Goldstein, "The Origins of Summit Diplomacy," in *Diplomacy at the Highest Level*, ed. Dunn, 34. Raymond Cohen, *Theatre of Power: The Art of Diplomatic Signalling* (New York: Longman, 1987), similarly castigates Carter's trip to Iran and mismanagement of the "hotline" to the Soviet Union.

74. Andrew Gillett, *Envoys and Political Communication in the Late Antique West, 411–533* (New York: Cambridge University Press, 2003); Goldstein, "The Origins," in *Diplomacy at the Highest Level*, ed. Dunn, 25; John W. Foster, *The Practice of Diplomacy* (Boston: Houghton Mifflin, 1906), 21.

75. Freeman, *Arts of Power*, 102.

76. Margaret Keck and Kathryn Sikkink, *Activists beyond Borders: Advocacy Networks in International Politics* (Ithaca, NY: Cornell University Press, 1998).

77. Cohen, *Theatre of Power*, 154–160.

78. Sir Harold Nicolson, *Diplomacy* (New York: Oxford University Press, 1942 [1939]), 91–93, 144–145.

79. As this chapter's epigraph from Niskanen's *Bureaucracy* indicates, this is an oversimplification, since agencies often assume tasks themselves without waiting for assignments.

80. Snyder, *Myths of Empire*, 56, notes that "external threats" can increase cartelization, particularly in late developing states (these threats seem largely economic, when protectionism or depression threatens a state's ability to secure resources needed to develop), augmenting "the domestic political hand of military and autarkic cartels."

81. André Blais and Stéphane Dion, "Conclusion," in *The Budget-Maximizing Bureaucrat: Appraisals and Evidence*, ed. André Blais and Stéphane Dion (Pittsburgh: University of Pittsburgh Press, 1991), 360: agencies generally follow "a budget-boosting rather than a budget-maximizing strategy."

82. Agencies may face trade-offs among these benefits. See Halperin and Clapp, *Bureaucratic Politics*, 51; William Niskanen, "A Reflection," in *The Budget-Maximizing Bureaucrat*, ed. Blais and Dion, 18–19.

83. Halperin and Clapp, *Bureaucratic Politics*, 38–39, 49, 57.

84. Allison, *Essence of Decision*, 76, 82.

85. See Niskanen, *Bureaucracy*, especially 38–42.

86. Pakistan's support for some of the Kashmiri guerrilla groups in Indian territory is a clear but hardly isolated example. See Daniel Byman, Peter Chalk, Bruce Hoffman, William Rosenau, and David Brannan, *Trends in Outside Support for Insurgent Movements* (Santa Monica, CA: RAND, 2001).

87. See, e.g., Alexander Wendt, *Social Theory of International Politics* (New York: Cambridge University Press, 1999), 349–358; Richard Ned Lebow, *Between Peace and War: The Nature of International Crises* (Baltimore: Johns Hopkins University Press, 1981), 268–271, 336.

88. Thomas Homer-Dixon, "On the Threshold: Environmental Changes as Causes of Acute Conflict," *International Security* 16, no. 2 (Fall 1991): 76–116; Jessica Mathews, "Redefining Security," *Foreign Affairs* 68, no. 2 (Spring 1989): 162–177; Michael Brown, "New Global Dangers," in *Leashing the Dogs of War: Conflict Management in a Divided World*, ed. Chester Crocker, Fen Osler Hampson, and Pamela Aall (Washington, DC: United States Institute of Peace, 2007), 39–51.

89. See Richard Shultz, Douglas Farah, and Itamara Lochard, *Armed Groups: A Tier-One Security Priority* (Colorado Springs, CO: US Air Force Institute for National Security Studies, INSS Occasional Paper 57, 2004).

90. This suggests that the destruction of the power of vested interests might be an alternative path to policy change and peacemaking, as international relations liberals have long argued; I address this in more detail in the final section of this chapter.

91. Allison, *Essence of Decision*, 92.

92. See David Welch, *Painful Choices: A Theory of Foreign Policy Change* (Princeton: Princeton University Press, 2005); Kier, *Imagining War*, 41–46; Snyder, *Myths of Empire*, 316; Dan Reiter, *Crucible of Beliefs: Learning, Alliances, and World Wars* (Ithaca, NY: Cornell University Press, 1996); for an overview, see Hermann, "Changing Course."

93. Lebow, *Between Peace and War*, Chapter 9; Stephen Rock, *Why Peace Breaks Out: Great Power Rapprochement in Historical Perspective* (Chapel Hill: University of North Carolina Press, 1989).

94. Lebow, "Transitions."

95. Stanley Hoffman, *Gulliver's Troubles, Or the Setting of American Foreign Policy* (New York: Council on Foreign Relations / McGraw-Hill, 1968), 277; Allison, *Essence of Decision*, 68, 85, 98.

96. The overall size of the budgetary pie depends on several factors including the size of the economy and its growth rate, the rate of inflation, and the ability of the government to raise revenue through customs and taxation, while the share of the pie ultimately available for agencies is reduced by mandatory government spending on debt service and critical imports. Dennis Ippolito, *Why Budgets Matter: Budget Policy and American Politics* (University Park: Pennsylvania State University Press, 2003), 295–297, notes that these factors are difficult to forecast.

97. See Wirls, *Irrational Security*; *Restoring Fiscal Sanity: How to Balance the Budget*, ed. Alice Rivlin and Isabel Sawhill (Washington, DC: Brookings Institution Press, 2004), 2, 13, 24–28.

98. Ippolito, *Why Budgets Matter*, 4–15, 208–239.

99. Quotation from Allison, *Essence of Decision*, 85. Johan Olsen and B. Guy Peters, "Learning from Experience?" in *Lessons from Experience: Experiential Learning in Administrative Reforms in Eight Democracies*, ed. Johan Olsen and B. Guy Peters (Oslo: Scandinavian University Press, 1996), 29–30; Anderson, *Public Policymaking*, 273–276.

100. Domestic policy termination studies likewise indicate that economic downturn, while important, is often insufficient to cause major change. Daniels, *Terminating*, 40, 70–71; Strobe Talbott, "Foreword," in *Restoring Fiscal Sanity*, ed. Rivlin and Sawhill, viii.

101. See Jack Levy, "The Diversionary Theory of War: A Critique," in *Handbook of War Studies*, ed. Manus Midlarsky (Boston: Unwin Hyman, 1989), 259–288.

102. Daniels, *Terminating*, 66–74; Wilson, *Bureaucracy*, 214–215.

103. These are issues of equifinality (alternative causal paths to an outcome) and scope conditions (the historical, geographical, and institutional settings in which an argument should apply). See Alexander George and Andrew Bennett, *Case Studies and Theory Development in the Social Sciences* (Cambridge, MA: MIT Press, 2005), 159–162; Stephen Van Evera, *Guide to Methods for Students of Political Science* (Ithaca, NY: Cornell University Press, 1997), 41; and Gerardo Munck, "Tools for Qualitative Research," 105–121, and Charles Ragin, "Turning the Tables: How Case-Oriented Research Challenges

Variable-Oriented Research," 123–138, both in *Rethinking Social Inquiry: Diverse Tools, Shared Standards*, ed. Henry Brady and David Collier (Lanham, MD: Rowman & Little-field, 2004).

104. See Lebow, "Transitions and Transformations," 165, 174; Arie Kacowicz et al., eds., *Stable Peace among Nations* (Lanham, MD: Rowman & Littlefield, 2000); Mark Peceny and Caroline Beer, with Shannon Sanchez-Terry, "Dictatorial Peace?" *American Political Science Review* 96, no. 1 (Mar. 2002): 15–26; Stephen Van Evera, *Causes of War: Power and the Roots of Conflict* (Ithaca, NY: Cornell University Press, 1999); D. Scott Bennett and Allan Stam, *The Behavioral Origins of War* (Ann Arbor: University of Michigan Press, 2004).

105. See Colaresi et al., *Strategic Rivalries*, 75.

106. Stephen Brooks and William Wohlforth, "Power, Globalization, and the End of the Cold War: Reevaluating a Landmark Case for Ideas," *International Security* 25, no. 3 (Winter 2000–2001): 5–53; Andrew Bennett, "The Guns That Didn't Smoke: Ideas and the Soviet Non-Use of Force in 1989," *Journal of Cold War Studies* 7, no. 2 (Spring 2005): 81–109; Robert English, *Russia and the Idea of the West: Gorbachev, Intellectuals, and the End of the Cold War* (New York: Columbia University Press, 2000).

107. See Michael Brown, Sean Lynn-Jones, and Steven Miller, eds., *Debating the Democratic Peace* (Cambridge, MA: MIT Press, 1996); Bruce Russett and John Oneal, *Triangulating Peace: Democracy, Interdependence, and International Organizations* (New York: W. W. Norton, 2001); *Paths to Peace: Is Democracy the Answer?*, ed. Miriam Fendius Elman (Cambridge, MA: MIT Press, 1997).

108. Suggestions of democracy as a remedy for vested interests' pursuit of militarism and empire include Hobson, *Imperialism*, and Snyder, *Myths of Empire* (although Snyder also recognizes that increasing centralized, authoritarian control can have the same effect).

109. To the extent that liberalism, rather than democracy, underpins this commonly posited path to peace (see John Mueller, *The Remnants of War* [Ithaca, NY: Cornell University Press, 2004], 167–169; John Mueller, *Retreat from Doomsday: The Obsolescence of Major War* [New York: Basic Books, 1989], 23–24; John Owen, *Liberal Peace, Liberal War: American Politics and International Security* [Ithaca, NY: Cornell University Press, 1997], 13–17), my alternative pathway to rapprochement should be increasingly valuable.

110. See, for example, Matthew Evangelista, "Domestic Structure and International Change," in *New Thinking in International Relations Theory*, ed. Michael Doyle and G. John Ikenberry (Boulder, CO: Westview Press, 1997), 202–228.

111. See Snyder, *Myths of Empire*, and Friedberg, *In the Shadow*.

112. Samuel Huntington, *Political Order in Changing Societies* (New Haven, CT: Yale University Press, 1968), 7; Louis Fisher, *The Politics of Shared Power: Congress and the Executive*, 4th ed. (College Station, TX: Texas A&M University Press, 1998), 132–140; Zegart, *Flawed by Design*, 224–227; Friedberg, *In the Shadow*.

113. See Charles Tilly, *Coercion, Capital, and European States, AD 990–1990* (Cambridge, MA: Blackwell, 1990); Hendrik Spruyt, *The Sovereign State and Its Competitors: An Analysis of Systems Change* (Princeton: Princeton University Press, 1994).

114. See William Thompson, ed., *Great Power Rivalries* (Columbia: University of South Carolina Press, 1999).

115. However, by the same token, my theory might apply to supranational organizations such as the European Union—the more organizational cohesion Brussels acquires for defense planning and the conduct of a unified foreign policy, the more I would expect

to see the parochial interest of the organs of the European Union enforce the continuation of policies that are no longer desired by the total public or the member states.

116. Conversely, parochial interest might shed light on civil wars in which both sides possess elements of bureaucratic statehood. On variations in stateness during the twentieth century, particularly in the developing world, consult Robert Jackson, *Quasi-States: Sovereignty, International Relations, and the Third World* (New York: Cambridge University Press, 1990); Jeffrey Herbst, *States and Power in Africa: Comparative Lessons in Authority and Control* (Princeton: Princeton University Press, 2000); Tanisha Fazal, *State Death: The Politics and Geography of Conquest, Occupation, and Annexation* (Princeton: Princeton University Press, 2007).

117. Alain Rouquié, *The Military and the State in Latin America*, trans. Paul Sigmund (Berkeley: University of California Press, 1987) and Frederick Nunn, *The Time of The Generals: Latin American Professional Militarism in World Perspective* (Lincoln: University of Nebraska Press, 1992) provide evenhanded accounts of Latin American militarism, emphasizing variation within the region and over time.

118. Stanley Stein and Barbara Stein, *The Colonial Heritage of Latin America: Essays on Economic Dependence in Perspective* (New York: Oxford University Press, 1970).

119. See particularly Edward Lieuwen, *Generals vs. Presidents: Neomilitarism in Latin America* (New York: Praeger, 1964); see also Abraham F. Lowenthal, "Armies and Politics in Latin America," *World Politics* 27, no. 1 (Oct. 1974): 111, 120. The organizational and societal distinctions between different Latin American armed forces affect the likelihood of coups in their respective countries, but I suggest that for the more limited question of defense of organizational interests by obstructing particular policy changes, these militaries have much in common.

120. Evans, *Dependent Development*; Alfred Stepan, *The Military in Politics: Changing Patterns in Brazil* (Princeton: Princeton University Press, 1971); Fernando López-Alves, *State Formation and Democracy in Latin America, 1810–1900* (Durham, NC: Duke University Press, 2000), 36–48.

121. See Miguel Angel Centeno, *Blood and Debt: War and the Nation-State in Latin America* (University Park: Pennsylvania State University Press, 2002).

122. Brian Loveman, *For La Patria: Politics and the Armed Forces in Latin America* (Wilmington, DE: Scholarly Resources, 1999), Chapter 3; João Resende-Santos, *Neorealism, States, and the Modern Mass Army* (New York: Cambridge University Press, 2007).

Chapter 3 · Antagonism and Anti-Communism in Argentine-Brazilian Relations

1. Arie Kacowicz, *Zones of Peace: South America and West Africa in Comparative Perspective* (Albany: State University of New York Press, 1998), 84, argues that "among the South American international disputes the Argentine-Brazilian rivalry was the longest and most deeply rooted, and the one most influenced by geopolitical factors." Valuable introductions to Argentine-Brazilian rivalry include Léon Pomer, *Conflictos en la Cuenca del Plata en el Siglo XIX* (Buenos Aires: Riesa, 1984); Luiz Alberto Moniz Bandeira, *Conflito e Integração na América do Sul: Brasil, Argentina, e Estados Unidos da Tríplice Aliança ao Mercosul, 1870–2003*, 2nd ed. (Rio de Janeiro: Editora Revan, 2003); Miguel Ángel Scenna, *Argentina-Brasil: Cuatro Siglos de Rivalidad* (Buenos Aires: Ediciones la Bastilla, 1975); in English, see Stanley Hilton, "The Argentine Factor in Twentieth-Century Brazilian Foreign

Policy Strategy," *Political Science Quarterly* 100, no. 1 (Spring 1985): 27–51; Jack Child, *Geopolitics and Conflict in South America: Quarrels among Neighbors* (New York: Praeger, 1985), 98–105; and Andrew Hurrell, "An Emerging Security Community in South America?" in *Security Communities*, ed. Emanuel Adler and Michael Barnett (New York: Cambridge University Press, 1998), 228–264. Epigraph citations, respectively, are to João Neves da Fontoura, *Depoimentos de um Ex-Ministro: Peronismo, Minerais Atómicos, Política Externa* (Rio de Janeiro: Organização Simões Editora, 1957), 14; and Hurrell, "An Emerging," in *Security Communities*, ed. Adler and Barnett, 238. Translations from all sources in Spanish and Portuguese are mine unless otherwise noted.

2. Data compiled from the Argentine ministry of foreign relations' list of accords: www.mrecic.gov.ar/portal/seree/ditra/br2.html, accessed September 23, 2006.

3. Kacowicz, *Zones of Peace*; Stephen Brooks, *Producing Security: Multinational Corporations, Globalization, and the Changing Calculus of Conflict* (Princeton: Princeton University Press, 2005); Etel Solingen, *Regional Orders at Century's Dawn: Global and Domestic Influences on Grand Strategy* (Princeton: Princeton University Press, 1998); Andrea Oelsner, *International Relations in Latin America: Peace and Security in the Southern Cone* (New York: Routledge, 2005); Hurrell, "An Emerging," in *Security Communities*, ed. Adler and Barnett.

4. See João Resende-Santos, "The Origins of Security Cooperation in the Southern Cone," *Latin American Politics and Society* 44, no. 4 (Winter 2002): 89–126; Charles Kupchan, *How Enemies Become Friends: The Sources of Stable Peace* (Princeton: Princeton University Press, 2010).

5. This translation preserves the rhyme structure and syllable count of the original. A literal translation of the last three lines would read, "and there is in this actuality / '*mate*' that is not of chess / but '*mate*' of friendship." *El Diario*, Montevideo, Uruguay, August 20, 1980, 4.

6. Brazil sent an army to help Argentine federalists overthrow Juan Manuel de Rosas, the Buenos Aires dictator, in 1851; previously, governments based in Buenos Aires and Rio de Janeiro had fought from 1825 to 1828 over the territory that became (after stalemate and British intervention) an independent country, Uruguay. Brazil and Argentina came close to war on other occasions, including over the division of spoils from the War of the Triple Alliance in the 1870s, over potential intervention in the Chaco War between Paraguay and Bolivia in the 1930s, and during the Second World War. US President Grover Cleveland mediated the last Argentine-Brazilian territorial dispute, in 1895.

7. On hypotheses, see Rosendo Fraga, "El Concepto de las Hipótesis de Conflicto," in *Política Exterior Argentina, 1989–1999: Historia de un Éxito*, ed. Andrés Cisneros (Buenos Aires: Consejo Argentino para las Relaciones Internacionales and Grupo Editor Latinoamericano, 1998); Kacowicz, *Zones of Peace*, 80–85. On influence, see Felipe A. M. de la Balze, "Política Exterior," in *Argentina y Estados Unidos: Fundamentos de una Nueva Alianza*, ed. Felipe A. M. de la Balze and Eduardo A. Roca (Buenos Aires: Asociación de Bancos de la República Argentina / Consejo Argentino para las Relaciones Internacionales, 1997), 23, 31, 45, 63–64; Moniz Bandeira, *Conflito*, 419–421.

8. Robert Potash, *The Army and Politics in Argentina, 1928–1945: Yrigoyen to Perón* (Stanford, CA: Stanford University Press, 1969), 100–102; Stanley Hilton, *Brazil and the Great Powers, 1930–1939: The Politics of Trade Rivalry* (Austin: University of Texas Press, 1975), 9, 111–131, 186.

9. See, e.g., Rosendo Fraga, "Roca Visits Brazil," and Luiz Felipe de Seixas Corrêa, "Campos Salles Visits Argentina," both in *Missões de Paz: a Diplomacia Brasileira nos Conflitos Internacionais*, ed. Raul Mendes Silva (Rio de Janeiro: Log On Editora Multimídia, 2003), 297–305 and 306–318; Nilson Cezar Mariano, *Operación Cóndor: Terrorismo de Estado en el Cono Sur* (Buenos Aires: Lohlé-Lumen, 1998), 15; Francisco Rojas Aravena, "Presentación," in *Argentina, Brasil y Chile: Integración y Seguridad*, ed. Francisco Rojas Aravena (Caracas, Venezuela: FLACSO–Chile / Editorial Nueva Sociedad, 1999), 9–10; Andrés Cisneros and Carlos Piñeiro Iñíguez, *Del ABC al MERCOSUR: La Integración Latinoamericana en la Doctrina y Praxis del Peronismo* (Buenos Aires: Instituto del Servicio Exterior de la Nación / Nuevohacer / Grupo Editor Latinoamericano, 2002), 333–334; Oelsner, *International Relations*, 161.

10. On negative cases, see James Mahoney and Gary Goertz, "The Possibility Principle: Choosing Negative Cases in Qualitative Research," *American Political Science Review* 98, no. 4 (Nov. 2004): 653–669. Inter alia, Deborah Larson, *Anatomy of Mistrust: US-Soviet Relations during the Cold War* (Ithaca, NY: Cornell University Press, 1997), takes a similar approach.

11. The list omits bilateral travel by presidents-elect (e.g., Arturo Frondizi to Brazil, 1958) and ex-presidents (e.g., Juan Perón, detained in Brazil while attempting to return to Argentina from his exile in Spain, 1964), presidential visits that occurred en route to other destinations (Pedro Aramburu stopped in Rio en route from Panama to Argentina in 1956 but saw Juscelino Kubitschek, whose own return from Panama was delayed, only briefly at a reception; Arturo Frondizi met João Goulart at Galeão Airport in Rio on his way to the United States, 1961), and visits that were proposed but not consummated (most prominently, Perón and Getúlio Vargas, 1950–1954). The four presidential summits addressed in this chapter are those of Eurico Dutra and Juna Perón, May 1947; Jânio Quadros and Arturo Frondizi, April 1961; Emílio Médici and Alejandro Lanusse, March 1972; and João Figueiredo and Jorge Videla, May (and August) 1980.

12. A major cooperative escalation occurred in 1986, well after the initial rapprochement, marked by the meeting of Presidents Raúl Alfonsín and José Sarney.

13. Specifically, for the 1947 and 1961 summits, I draw on documents from the Brazilian foreign ministry archive (Arquivo Histórico do Itamaraty, cited as AHI) in Brasília, and for the 1972 and 1980 episodes, I employ documents from the Argentine foreign ministry archives (Archivo Histórico de la Cancillería Argentina, cited as AHCA) in Buenos Aires. Security classification prevented access to Secret-level Brazilian materials after 1970; in Argentina, my search was restricted to Series 47, América Latina, 1950–1985 (some material in this series predated this period, but documents regarding Brazil seemed too sparse to support a case study for 1947 or 1961). Thus, for each case in this chapter, I rely on the archive that offered the most comprehensive set of available documents. For AHI documents, I cite a folder (*maço*) or a bound volume title, in addition to noting (where available and relevant) the document's author, recipient, type and title, number, date, length, and level of classification. For AHCA documents, given the present disorganization of the archive, citations are necessarily more extensive; I provide the series number (47) followed by the number of the *bulto* (i.e., pair of boxes stored together), the label from the specific box, and the container information within that box (sometimes a folder, sometimes a binder, occasionally a stack of unbound pages), in addition to the same document-specific information supplied for AHI sources.

14. See Amado Luiz Cervo, *Relações Internacionais da América Latina: Velhos e Novos Paradigmas* (Brasília: Universidade Nacional de Brasília, Instituto Brasileiro de Relações Internacionais, 2001), 157, 173, 175–176, 178–179, 193; Moniz Bandeira, *Conflito*, 241. Hence my reference to US Admiral David Farragut's 1864 exclamation, "Damn the torpedoes!" (Loyall Farragut, *The Life of David Glasgow Farragut, First Admiral of the United States Navy, Embodying His Journal and Letters* (New York: D. Appleton and Company, 1879), 416–417.

15. *Historia General de las Relaciones Exteriores de la República Argentina*, ed. Andrés Cisneros and Carlos Escudé, vol. 13, Chapter 61 (Buenos Aires: CARI / Grupo Editor Latinoamericano, 1998).

16. "The Hemisphere: Orations at the Bridge," *Time* magazine 49, no. 22, June 2, 1947, 42; "Peron and Dutra Dedicate Bridge: Argentine, Brazilian Presidents Reported Planning Move to End Paraguayan War," *New York Times*, May 22, 1947, 13.

17. Juan Archibaldo Lanús, *De Chapultepec al Beagle: Política Exterior Argentina, 1945–1980*, vol. II (Buenos Aires: Hyspamérica, 1986 [1984]) 8; Mariano Bartolomé, "Las Relaciones Argentina-Brasil: Del Conflicto a la Cooperación," *Geopolítica: Hacia una Doctrina Nacional* 15, no. 39 (1989): 31.

18. The most extensive scholarly accounts, drawing on archival research, are Moniz Bandeira, *Conflito*, 235–249; Cervo, *Relações Internacionais*, 147–179; and Iuri Cavlak, *A Política Externa Brasileira e a Argentina Peronista (1946–1955)* (São Paulo: Annablume, 2008), especially 54–60, 105–119.

19. See, e.g., Moniz Bandeira, *Conflito*, 238–240; Félix Luna, *Argentina de Perón a Lanusse, 1943–1973* (Buenos Aires: Editorial Planeta, 1972), 61–62.

20. Gerson Moura, *O Alinhamento sem Recompensa: A Política Externa do Governo Dutra* (Rio de Janeiro: Fundação Getúlio Vargas, 1990), 53–56, 66–67.

21. Mônica Hirst, *O Pragmatismo Impossível: A Política Externa do Segundo Governo Vargas (1951–1954)* (Rio de Janeiro: Fundação Getúlio Vargas, 1990), 25–28.

22. Cavlak, *A Política Externa*, 13–14, 199–202.

23. Lanús, *De Chapultepec*, vol. II, 8.

24. Scenna, *Argentina-Brasil*, 329.

25. See, e.g., Gabriel Porcile, "The Challenge of Cooperation: Argentina and Brazil, 1939–1955," *Journal of Latin American Studies* 27, no. 1 (Feb. 1995): 129–159, especially 150.

26. Moniz Bandeira, *Conflito*, 240–241.

27. On the importance of the change in ambassadors, see Cavlak, *A Política Externa*, 56–60.

28. Moniz Bandeira, *Conflito*, 240–241.

29. Dean Acheson, *Present at the Creation: My Years in the State Department* (New York: W. W. Norton, 1969), 187–190; Lanús, *De Chapultepec*, vol. I, 30–36.

30. Stephen Rabe, *Eisenhower and Latin America: The Foreign Policy of Anticommunism* (Chapel Hill: University of North Carolina Press, 1988), 14.

31. Acheson, *Present at the Creation*, 219–233; George Kennan, *Memoirs, 1925–1950* (Boston: Little, Brown, 1967), 322–375. See Rabe, *Eisenhower*, 13–24. Truman signed the aid bill for Greece and Turkey on May 22, the day after the Dutra-Perón meeting.

32. See John Child, *Unequal Alliance: The Inter-American Military System, 1938–1978* (Boulder, CO: Westview Press, 1980). Subsequent meetings included Bogotá, Colombia, in 1948, and Caracas, Venezuela, in 1954.

33. See Lanús, *De Chapultepec*, vol. I, 43–48, and vol. II, 7–9; Tad Szulc, *Twilight of the Tyrants* (New York: Holt, 1959), 137; Cisneros and Iñiguez, *Del ABC al MERCOSUR*, Chapter 6.

34. Lanús, *De Chapultepec*, vol. I, 132–138.

35. "Peron-Dutra Meeting: Presidents May Discuss Date for Foreign Ministers' Parley," *New York Times*, May 19, 1947, 13.

36. "Peron and Dutra Dedicate Bridge," *New York Times*.

37. "The Hemisphere," *Time* magazine.

38. "Mediation is Hinted in Paraguayan War," *New York Times*, May 23, 1947, 13; "Civil War Believed Discussed," *New York Times*, May 21, 1947, 13.

39. "Civil War Believed Discussed," *New York Times*.

40. Ibid.; "The Hemisphere," *Time* magazine.

41. "The Hemisphere," *Time* magazine.

42. Frank M. Garcia, "Grip on Paraguay Charged to Peron: Argentine Accused in Brazil Congress of Aiding Morinigo With 'Imperialistic' Aim," *New York Times*, June 11, 1947, 16; "'Imperialistic' Policy Charged," *New York Times*, June 11, 1947, 16; "Peron Arms Paraguay, Brazil Hears," *Washington Post*, June 11, 1947, 1, 3.

43. See Glauco Carneiro, *Lusardo: O Último Caudilho* (Rio de Janeiro: Editora Nova Fronteira, 1977), vol. I, 25–32, 72–74, 80–92, vol. II, 567.

44. Juan Perón, *Perón Expone Su Doctrina* (Buenos Aires: Presidencia de la Nación, Subsecretaría de Informaciones, 1951), 372–373.

45. AHI, Maço 920 (42) (41) Confidencial "Relações Políticas e Diplomáticas. Brasil-Argentina," Ambassador Baptista Lusardo to Itamaraty, Telegrama No. 133, "Audiência promovida pelo General Nicolás Accame na qual tomaram parte o Embaixador do Brasil e o Presidente e Vice-Presidente da República Argentina," June 10, 1945, 2 pp.

46. Ibid.

47. AHI, Maço 920 (42) (41) Confidencial "Relações Políticas e Diplomáticas. Brasil-Argentina," Exteriores to Embassy in Buenos Aires, Telegrama (Number illegible), "Audiência promovida pelo General Nicolás Accame na qual tomaram parte o Embaixador do Brasil e o Presidente e Vice-Presidente da República Argentina," June 12, 1945, 1 p. The use of the first person in this telegram (and others like it) requires some clarification: messages from Itamaraty to embassies were usually not signed by individuals but rather bore the subscript "Exteriores" for the ministry of foreign relations, though the author was assumed to be either the foreign minister or the general secretary (the number-two post).

48. AHI, Maço 920 (42) (41) Confidencial "Relações Políticas e Diplomáticas. Brasil-Argentina," Exteriores to Ambassador Lusardo, Buenos Aires, Telegrama No. 219, "Econtro do Presidente Dutra com o Presidente Perón," October 24, 1946, 1 p.

49. Ibid.

50. Ibid.

51. AHI, Maço 920 (42) (41) Confidencial "Relações Políticas e Diplomáticas. Brasil-Argentina," João Baptista Lusardo to Raul Fernandes, January 20, 1947, 3 pp.

52. On ABC, see, e.g., Ana Luiza Gobbi Setti Reckziegel, *O Pacto ABC: As Relações Brasil-Argentina na Década de 1950* (Passo Fundo, RS, Brazil: Editora Universidade de Passo Fundo, 1996); Paulo Renan de Almeida, *Perón-Vargas-Ibáñez: Pacto ABC: Raízes do Mercosul* (Porto Alegre, Brazil: Editora Pontifícia Universidade Católica do Rio Grande

do Sul, 1998); Alberto Methol Ferré, *Perón y la Alianza Argentino-Brasileña* (Córdoba, Argentina: Ediciones del Corredor Austral, 2000); Hirst, *O Pragmatismo Impossível*; Cavlak, *A Política Externa.*

53. AHI, Maço 920 (42) (41) Confidencial "Relações Políticas e Diplomáticas. Brasil-Argentina," João Baptista Lusardo to Raul Fernandes, January 20, 1947, 3 pp.

54. Ibid.

55. Ibid.

56. AHI, Maço 920 (42) (41) Confidencial "Relações Políticas e Diplomáticas. Brasil-Argentina," Freitas-Valle to Itamaraty, Telegrama No. 451, November 6, 1947, "Presença em Buenos Aires do Senhor J. Baptista Lusardo," 1 p.

57. AHI, Maço 920 (42) (41) Confidencial "Relações Políticas e Diplomáticas. Brasil-Argentina," Freitas-Valle to Fernandes, No. 543, "Opinião no Brasil sôbre a Argentina," December 1, 1947, 2 pp.

58. AHI, Maço 920 (42) (41) Confidencial "Relações Políticas e Diplomáticas. Brasil-Argentina," Lieutenant Colonel Mario Gomes da Silva, Vice-President of the CCP, Ministry of Labor, Industry, and Commerce, to President Dutra, December 3, 1947 (also sent to Minister of Foreign Relations Raul Fernandes, December 20), 4 pp.

59. Ibid.

60. Ibid.

61. On the US point, see José Paradiso, *Debates y Trayectoria de la Política Argentina* (Buenos Aires: Grupo Editor Latinoamericano, 1993), 129.

62. AHI, Maço 920 (42) (41) Confidencial "Relações Políticas e Diplomáticas. Brasil-Argentina," Carlos Celso de Ouro Preto, Embassy in Santiago, to Itamaraty, No. 81, "Visita do Presidente Peron a Bolivia. Relações políticas Brasil-Chile-Argentina," October 20, 1947, 1 p.

63. Accioly, the general secretary, was interim foreign minister because Raul Fernandes was abroad—after the summit with Perón, Dutra and Fernandes traveled to Uruguay to meet with their counterparts in that country.

64. AHI, Maço 920 (42) (41) Confidencial "Relações Políticas e Diplomáticas. Brasil-Argentina," Freitas Valle to Interim Minister of Foreign Relations Hildebrando Accioly, Ofício No. 207, "Relações Brasil-Argentina," May 24, 1947, 6 pp. All quotations in the remainder of this section are from this document.

65. Emphasis in original.

66. Freitas notes that this plan seemed to have Perón's support.

67. Lanús, *De Chaptultepec*, vol. II, 14. Spanish-language sources render the Brazilian town "Uruguayana;" I use the Brazilian spelling throughout, including in translations from Spanish, for consistency.

68. See Christopher Darnton, "Asymmetry and Agenda-Setting in Inter-American Relations: Rethinking the Origins of the Alliance for Progress," *Journal of Cold War Studies* 14, no. 4 (Fall 2012): 120–143; Cervo, *Relações Internacionais*, 106–107. Moniz Bandeira, *Conflito*, 275–309, concurs but includes balancing US influence in the region as an objective.

69. Scenna, *Argentina-Brasil*, 357; Afonso Arinos de Melo Franco, *A Alma do Tempo: Memórias de Afonso Arinos de Melo Franco* (São Paulo: Livraria José Olympio Editora, 1979), 966.

70. See Gian Luca Gardini, *The Origins of Mercosur: Democracy and Regionalization in South America* (New York: Palgrave MacMillan, 2010), 28; Roberto Russell and Juan Gabriél Tokatlian, *El Lugar de Brasil en la Política Exterior Argentina* (Buenos Aires: Fondo de Cultura Económica, 2003); Félix Peña, "Perspectivas Futuras de las Relaciones Brasil-Argentina," *Revista Brasileira de Política Internacional* 24, no. 93–96 (1981): 144–151.

71. See, e.g., Arinos, *A Alma*, 965, 848–853; Alessandro Warley Candeas, *A Integração Brasil-Argentina: História de uma Idea na 'Visão do Outro'* (Brasília: Fundação Alexandre de Gusmão, 2010), 191; Cervo, *Relações Internacionais*, 219–221, argues that at least in the area of physical integration, not only Illia (1963–1966) but also Onganía (1966–1970) continued Frondizi's approach to Brazil. See Guillermo O'Donnell, *Modernization and Bureaucratic-Authoritarianism: Studies in South American Politics*, 2nd ed. (Berkeley: University of California Press, 1979).

72. On the resignation's Argentine impact, see Afonso Arinos Filho, *Diplomacia Independente: um Legado de Afonso Arinos* (São Paulo: Paz e Terra, 2001), 217.

73. The Galeão meeting took place when Frondizi was en route to New York to visit the United Nations and meet with Kennedy, in September 1961. "Frondizi Off to Talk with Kennedy," *Washington Post*, September 25, 1961, A10.

74. See, e.g., Moniz Bandeira, *Conflito*, 306–308.

75. Roberto Russell and Juan Gabriel Tokatlian, "El Lugar del Brasil en la Politica Exterior de la Argentina: La Vision del Otro," *Desarrollo Económico* 42, no. 167 (Oct.–Dec. 2002): 405–428; Roberto Campos, *A Lanterna na Popa* (Rio de Janeiro: Topbooks, 1994), 434.

76. Lanús, *De Chapultepec*, vol. II, 18; see Bartolomé, "Las Relaciones," 32; Scenna, *Argentina-Brasil*, 362–363.

77. Félix Luna, *Diálogos con Frondizi* (Buenos Aires: Editorial Desarrollo, 1963), 205–206; see also Luna, *Argentina*, 133.

78. Amado Luiz Cervo and Clodoaldo Bueno, *História da Política Exterior do Brasil*, 2nd ed. (Brasília: Editora Universidade de Brasília, 2002), 322, 331; Luiz Alberto Moniz Bandeira, "Brazil as a Regional Power and Its Relations with the United States," *Latin American Perspectives* 33, no. 3 (May 2006), 15–16.

79. Scenna, *Argentina-Brasil*, 351.

80. See Joseph Tulchin, "The United States and Latin America in the 1960s," *Journal of Interamerican Studies and World Affairs* 30, no. 1 (Spring 1988), 22–23.

81. "Plan to Form Bloc Denied by Frondizi," *New York Times*, May 4, 1961, 13; "Quadros Hails Trend: Says Closer Argentine Ties Bring Balance to Region," *New York Times*, July 11, 1961, 17.

82. Luna, *Diálogos*, 76, 90, 97–98. Arinos, *A Alma*, 912–914, looks equally wistfully at Mexico.

83. Gregorio Selser, "Quadros-Frondizi: Gambito de Izquierda," *Marcha* (Montevideo, Uruguay), March 24, 1961. Reprinted in Gregorio Selser, *Argentina a Precio de Costo: El Gobierno de Frondizi* (Buenos Aires: Ediciones Iguazú, 1965), 259–263.

84. Arinos, *A Alma*, 910–911, quotes the actual memorandum from his private archive.

85. From the Embassy in Brazil to the Department of State, Telegram 1384, "For the President from Secretary Dillon," Rio de Janeiro, April 12, 1961, *FRUS 1961–1963*, vol. XII, doc. 207, 429.

86. Ibid.

87. Deputy Assistant Secretary of State for Inter-American Affairs Coerr to Acting Secretary of State Bowles, May 14, 1961, "President Quadros' Attitude on Neutralism and Cuba," *FRUS 1961–1963*, vol. XII, doc. 208.

88. Luna, *Diálogos*, 37; Robert Potash, *The Army and Politics in Argentina, 1945–1962: Perón to Frondizi* (Stanford, CA: Stanford University Press, 1980), 275.

89. Luna, *Diálogos*, 120–122.

90. Moniz Bandeira, *Conflito*, 306–307.

91. Lanús, *De Chapultepec*, vol. II, 13. Lanús quotes from the original memo but without citation information.

92. Argentine historians debate the exact number of Frondizi's military crises, but estimates are in the twenties and thirties. See Rosendo Fraga, *El Ejército y Frondizi* (Buenos Aires: Emecé Editores, 1992).

93. Scenna, *Argentina-Brasil*, 353–357.

94. Luna, *Argentina*, 134.

95. Cervo, *Relações Internacionais*, 216; Moniz Bandeira, *Conflito*, 307; Candeas, *A Integração*, 187, 191.

96. Arinos, *A Alma*, 875–882, 912–914, 964–965.

97. Arinos, *A Alma*, 965–967.

98. Ibid.

99. Alberto Conil Paz and Gustavo Ferrari, *Argentina's Foreign Policy, 1930–1962*, trans. John J. Kennedy (Notre Dame, IN: University of Notre Dame Press, 1966), 203, criticize this "questionable method."

100. Luna, *Diálogos*, 89–90; Oscar Camilión, *Memorias Políticas: De Frondizi a Menem (1956–1996)* (Buenos Aires: Editorial Planeta / Todo es Historia, 2000), 96–101.

101. Thomas Skidmore, *Politics in Brazil, 1930–1964: An Experiment in Democracy* (New York: Oxford University Press, 1967), 199–203.

102. Telegram from the Department of State to the Embassy in Argentina, February 10, 1962, *FRUS 1961–1963*, vol. XII, doc. 175. An editorial footnote confirms that by "foreign policy" Rusk meant the break with Cuba.

103. Luna, *Diálogos*, 89–90, 105. Arinos, *A Alma*, 898–899, similarly argues that Brazil engaged with Cuba for regional prestige and development—and for mass popularity at home.

104. The Brazilian parliamentary constitution took effect September 2, 1961; a January 6, 1963, plebiscite restored Goulart's presidential powers, but military opposition to his policies had already escalated.

105. Memorandum of Conversation, September 25, 1961, "Situation in Brazil and Brazilian Attitude toward Cuban Problem," *FRUS 1961–1963*, vol. XII, doc. 116. Contrast Arinos's estimation, *A Alma*, 978–979, of Quadros's "habitual interest in the march of administration and of foreign policy" even "on the eve of his resignation."

106. See, e.g., Jorge Luis Romero, *A History of Argentina in the Twentieth Century*, trans. James Brennan (University Park: The Pennsylvania State University Press, 2004), 142–146; Boris Fausto, *A Concise History of Brazil*, trans. Arthur Brakel (New York: Cambridge University Press, 1999), 262–264.

107. Luna, *Diálogos*, 86–87, 125; David Rock, *Authoritarian Argentina: the Nationalist Movement, Its History, and Its Impact* (Berkeley: University of California Press, 1993), 196.

108. "The Outlook for Brazil," Washington, August 8, 1961, *FRUS 1961–1963*, vol. XII, doc. 212, NIE 93–61.

109. Ibid.

110. Letter from the Ambassador to Argentina (McClintock) to the Assistant Secretary of State for Inter-American Affairs (Martin), Buenos Aires, May 31, 1962, *FRUS 1961–1963*, vol. XII, doc. 188, 385.

111. See Skidmore, *Politics in Brazil*, 192–197.

112. "Voz do Brasil: Historia," stream.agenciabrasil.gov.br/estatico/radio_voz_do_brasil_historia.htm, accessed July 5, 2012; "Bilhetes do presidente Jânio Quadros ao Ministério das Relações Exteriores," *Cadernos do CHDD* 8 (Rio de Janeiro, 2006), 326.

113. Mauricio Joppert da Silva, "Os bilhetes do Presidente," *Jornal do Brasil*, February 26–27, 1961, 3.

114. "Bilhetes do presidente Jânio Quadros," 326.

115. Quadros to MRE, March 1, 1961, in ibid., 327.

116. Quadros to MRE, March 14, 1961, in ibid.

117. Quadros to MRE and Minister of Industry, August 22, 1961, in ibid., 480.

118. Arinos, *A Alma*, 917–919.

119. See Kathryn Sikkink, *Ideas and Institutions: Developmentalism in Brazil and Argentina* (Ithaca, NY: Cornell University Press, 1991); Celia Szusterman, *Frondizi and the Politics of Developmentalism in Argentina, 1955–1962* (Pittsburgh: University of Pittsburgh Press, 1993).

120. Luna, *Diálogos*, 45.

121. Telegram, Embassy in Brazil to State, January 4, 1962 *FRUS 1961–1963*, vol. XII, doc. 130.

122. See Edward Burks, "Visit by Frondizi Aids Ties to Chile: Disputes Remain Unsettled but Talks are Cordial," *New York Times*, September 17, 1961, 40.

123. Lanús, *De Chapultepec*, vol. II, 11–12.

124. Arinos, *A Alma*, 967.

125. See Potash, *Army and Politics in Argentina, 1945–1962*, 338–341; Fraga, *El Ejército*, 211–215.

126. Arturo Frondizi, "Mensaje al Pueblo Argentino a Raíz de la Crisis Militar Suscitada por la Entrevista con el Ministro de Industria de Cuba," in Arturo Frondizi, *La Política Exterior Argentina*, 2nd ed. (Buenos Aires: Transición, 1963), 151–156.

127. Arturo Frondizi, "Mensaje al Pueblo Argentino a Raíz de la Crisis Militar Suscitada por la Posición Argentina en Punta del Este," in ibid., 186–193.

128. See Fraga, *El Ejército*, 225, 231, 301–302.

129. AHI, Maço 920 (42) (41) Confidencial "Relações Políticas e Diplomáticas. Brasil-Argentina," Telegrama Confidencial 61, Exteriores to Santiago (Chile), "Encontro de Uruguaiana. Relações Brasil-Chile," May 5, 1961, 2 pp.

130. AHI, Telegramas-CTs Recebidas e Expedidas 1960–61 Secreto A–K, Telegrama Secreto 140, Aguinaldo Boulitreau Fragoso, Buenos Aires, to Itamaraty, "Política Interna da Argentina," April 6, 1961, 1 p.

131. AHI, Telegramas-CTs Recebidas e Expedidas 1960–61 Secreto A–K, Telegrama Secreto 130, Aguinaldo Boulitreau Fragoso, Buenos Aires, to Itamaraty, "Relações Políticas Brasil-Argentina. Entrevista dos Presidentes," March 29, 1961, 2 pp.

132. Ibid.

133. AHI, Maço Confidencial 900.1 (41) "Política Interna Argentina 1954/1961," Carta-Telegrama Confidencial 344, Hélio Antônio Scarabòtolo, Buenos Aires, to Itamaraty, "Reunião do Presidente Frondizi com o Gabinete Militar," September 28, 1961, 2 pp.

134. AHI, Maço Confidencial 900.1 (41) "Política Interna Argentina 1954/1961," Ofício Confidencial 540, Embassy in Buenos Aires to Itamaraty, October 11, 1961, 1 p., with attached *Més Político* no. 9, September 1961, 10 pp.

135. AHI, Maço 920 (42) (41) Confidencial "Relações Políticas e Diplomáticas. Brasil-Argentina," "Resumo da Conversa com o Embaixador Argentino," February 17, 1961, 2 pp. The document is unsigned and unaddressed but notes that "your excellency" had been governor of São Paulo and that "my father" had worked with Argentina.

136. Ibid.

137. AHI, Telegramas-CTs Recebidas e Expedidas 1960–61 Secreto A–K, Telegrama Secreto 6, Aguinaldo Boulitreau Fragoso, Buenos Aires, to Itamaraty, "Visita do Vice-Presidente João Goulart à Argentina," January 3, 1961, 1 p. Kubitschek ceded the presidency to Quadros on January 7; Goulart served under both.

138. AHI, Maço Confidencial 900.1 (41) "Política Interna Argentina 1954/1961," Ofício Confidencial 245, Buenos Aires to Itamaraty, "Mês politico correspondente a maio de 1961," June 13, 1961, cover note plus 10 pp. annex. Emphasis in original.

139. AHI, Maço Confidencial 900.1 (41) "Política Interna Argentina 1954/1961," Ofício Confidencial 540, Buenos Aires to Itamaraty, October 11, 1961, 1 p., with attached *Més Político* no. 9, September 1961, 10 pp.

140. Ibid.

141. Ibid.

142. AHI, Maço Confidencial 900.1 (41) "Política Interna Argentina 1954/1961," Ofício Confidencial 450, Buenos Aires to Itamaraty, September 11, 1961, 1 p., with attached *Més Político* no. 8, August 1961, 10 pp. Goulart held court for three hours at Ezeiza Airport on August 31.

143. Ibid.

144. Ibid. Mugica's argument about precedent was that Richard Goodwin had met with Guevara at Punta del Este.

145. AHI, CTs-Telegramas Recebidas e Expedidas 1962–63 Secreto Bucareste-Haia, Telegrama Secreto 222, Aguinaldo Boulitreau Fragoso, Buenos Aires, to Itamaraty, "Golpe militar na Argentina. Deposição do Presidente Frondizi," March 29, 1962, 4 pp.

146. AHI, CTs-Telegramas Recebidas e Expedidas 1962–63 Secreto Bucareste-Haia, Telegrama Secreto 119, Exteriores to Buenos Aires, "Situação política na Argentina," April 2, 1962, 1 p.

147. Ibid.

148. AHI, Ofícios 1960–62 Secreto A–L, Ofício Secreto 257, Aguinaldo Boulitreau Fragoso, Buenos Aires, to Foreign Minister San Tiago Dantas, "Reconhecimento do Govêrno argentino pelo Brasil," April 30, 1962, 6 pp.

149. AHI, Maço Confidencial 900.1 (41) "Política Interna Argentina 1954/1961," Telegrama Confidencial 342, Aguinaldo Boulitreau Fragoso, Buenos Aires, to Itamaraty, "Política exterior da Argentina. Declaração do Chanceler Bonifacio del Carril à imprensa," May 5, 1962, 1 p.

150. The first departure called for "the regularization of the use of natural resources to avoid prejudice to other States"; the second claimed that "In our Latin America, where

we all are and feel like equals, we understand that we cannot accept eventual oases of prosperity in marginalized zones, be they in national or continental ambit" (". . . e tudo acabou bem," *Veja* 185, March 22, 1972, 14).

151. "Carta ao Leitor," *Veja* 184, March 15, 1972, 17.

152. "O Acôrdo Acima de Tudo," *Veja* 184, March 15, 1972, 27.

153. ". . . e tudo acabou bem," *Veja*, 19.

154. See Romero, *A History*, 189–190; Thomas Skidmore, *The Politics of Military Rule in Brazil, 1964–1985* (New York: Oxford University Press, 1988), 117–129; Maria Helena Moreira Alves, *State and Opposition in Military Brazil* (Austin: University of Texas Press, 1985), 103–131; Alfred Stepan, *Rethinking Military Politics: Brazil and the Southern Cone* (Princeton: Princeton University Press, 1988). This is not to say that repression was solely reactive—rather, it emerged in many areas before or even without guerrilla activity.

155. Fausto, *A Concise*, 289–292; Luna, *Argentina*, 200–206; Camilión, *Memorias*, 155–156; Romero, *A History*, 192–194.

156. Guillermo O'Donnell, *Bureaucratic Authoritarianism: Argentina, 1966–1973, in Comparative Perspective*, trans. James McGuire (Berkeley: University of California Press, 1988).

157. Alves, *State and Opposition*, 121; R. S. Rose, *The Unpast: Elite Violence and Social Control in Brazil, 1954–2000* (Athens, OH: Ohio University Press, 2005), 179; Elio Gaspari, *A Ditadura Escancarada* (São Paulo: Companhia das Letras, 2002).

158. See, e.g., Telegram 0769 from the Embassy in Brazil to the Department of State, March 7, 1972, 1345Z, "Subj: Brazilian Aid to Uruguay and Bolivia Ref: A) State 031018 B) Montevideo 0408 C) State 032741 D La Paz 1159 F) USDAO Brasilia 0088," *FRUS 1969–1976*, vol. E-10, doc. 147.

159. The economic "miracle" should not be overstated: the northeast was left out of industrial expansion, workers faced wage suppression as well as crackdowns on union activism and political participation, and income inequality actually worsened over the course of the 1960s (Skidmore, *The Politics*, 143; Alves, *State and Opposition*, 106–114).

160. *FRUS 1969–1976*, vol. E-10, doc. 147; Arthur Whitaker, *The United States and the Southern Cone: Argentina, Chile, and Uruguay* (Cambridge, MA: Harvard University Press, 1976), 254.

161. Robert Kaufman, "Industrial Change and Authoritarian Rule in Latin America: A Concrete Review of the Bureaucratic-Authoritarian Model," in *The New Authoritarianism in Latin America*, ed. David Collier (Princeton: Princeton University Press, 1979), 240; Romero, *A History*, 198–199. O'Donnell, *Bureaucratic Authoritarianism*, 264–296, characterizes 1971–1972 as a period of economic crisis, including a decrease in central government tax revenue and increased spending in the interior provinces. However, the major damage, as in Brazil, was suffered by the lower classes, as real wages fell and the price of food and other staple goods rose. And as O'Donnell notes, US loans cushioned the blow to the state. I suggest that the Lanusse government anticipated that it could ride out a short period of deficit spending given the underlying economic expansion.

162. Kaufman, "Industrial Change," in *The New Authoritarianism*, ed. Collier, 244.

163. Lanús, *De Chapultepec*, vol. II, 33.

164. Russell and Tokatlian, *El Lugar de Brasil*, 38–42.

165. Fernando de Mello Barreto, *Os Sucessores do Barão: Relações Exteriores do Brasil*, vol. 2: *1964–1985* (São Paulo: Paz e Terra, 2006), 165; Moniz Bandeira, *Conflito*, 415–416.

166. *Historia General*, ed. Cisneros and Escudé, vol. XIV, Chapter 66.

167. Alejandro Agustín Lanusse, *Mi Testimonio* (Buenos Aires: Laserre Editores, 1977), 240. *Historia General*, ed. Cisneros and Escudé, vol. XIV, Chapter 66, cites this passage but without the context—namely, this short excerpt is essentially Lanusse's only reflection on his foreign policy.

168. Contrast Lanusse, *Mi Testimonio*, 240, and Mario Gibson Barboza, *Na Diplomacia, O Traço Todo da Vida* (Rio de Janeiro: Editora Record, 1992), 113–114.

169. Gibson Barboza, *Na Diplomacia*, 110–111.

170. Ibid., 112–113.

171. Ibid., 113–114.

172. Gibson Barboza (ibid., 116), claims that Lanusse blamed the gaffe on his own ignorance of "these diplomatic things" and that Gibson responded, "Some things are not about diplomacy. They are about ethics."

173. Moniz Bandeira, *Conflito*, 416; de Mello Barreto, *Os Sucessores*, vol. 2, 166.

174. Gibson Barboza, *Na Diplomacia*, 113–115.

175. *Entrevista de los Presidentes de la Argentina y Brasil* (Buenos Aires, Argentina: Argentina, Presidencia de la Nación, Secretaria de Prensa y Difusión, Dirección General de Difusión, 1972), 17.

176. Ibid., 19.

177. *Entrevista*, 18–19. Rather diplomatically for someone who (according to Gibson Barboza, *Na Diplomacia*, 116) had pled ignorance of things diplomatic, Lanusse declined to answer this question as "not pertinent."

178. Andrew Moravcsik, *The Choice for Europe: Social Purpose and State Power from Messina to Maastricht* (Ithaca, NY: Cornell University Press, 1998), 81–82.

179. *FRUS 1969–1976*, vol. E-10, doc. 147.

180. Memorandum for the President's File, Washington, December 9, 1971, "SUBJECT: Meeting with President Emílio Garrastazu Médici of Brazil on Thursday, December 9, 1971, at 10:00 a.m., in the President's Office, the White House," *FRUS 1969–1976*, vol. E-10, doc. 143.

181. Memorandum for the President's File, Washington, February 7, 1972, "SUBJECT: Telephone Conversation with President Alejandro Lanusse of Argentina on Monday, February 7, 1972 at 11:15 a.m.," *FRUS 1969–1976*, vol. E-10, doc. 74.

182. AHCA 47:91, "Brasil Parte No. 1," Black binder, "Viaje Presidencial Lanusse," Pink folder (untitled), Ing. Luis Perez Aguirre, Director Nacional de Política y Asuntos Técnicos [illegible], Ministerio de Obras y Servicios Públicos, Al Sr. Director del Departamento America Latina, Ministerio de Relaciones Exteriores y Culto, Ministro D. Enrique Ros, Expediente 12372/71-T, Nota No. 325 (cover letter and attached memorandum), February 2, 1972, 11 pp.

183. Ibid.

184. AHCA 47:91, "Brasil Parte No. 1," Black binder, "Viaje Presidencial Lanusse," Pink folder (untitled), Oscar Quihillalt, Presidente, Comisión Nacional de Energia Atómica, al Ministerio de Relaciones Exteriores y Culto, February 16, 1972, 2 pp.

185. AHCA 47:52, "Brasil Notas 1980 Nicanor Costa Mendez 1982," Black binder (untitled), "Relaciones Con Brasil: Estrategia a Corto Plazo," Hugo Boatti Osorio, Jefe, Departamento América Latina, to S. E. el Canciller, July 15, 1971, 18 pp., 17–18, emphasis added.

186. AHCA 47:91, "Brasil Parte No. 1," Black binder, "Viaje Presidencial Lanusse," Pink folder (untitled), "Informe de la Subsecretaria de Seguridad: Objetivo, Políticas y Estrategia Para la Visita del Primer Magistrado a Brasil." Sent with first cover letter to S. E. el Señor Secretario de Planeamiento y Acción de Gobierno Brigadier Mayor D. Ezequiel Alfredo Martinez on February 2, and with second cover letter to S. E. El Señor Ministro de Relaciones Exteriores y Culto Doctor D. Luis Maria de Pablo Pardo, February 3, 1972, including cover letters, 9 pp.

187. AHCA 47:52, "Brasil Notas 1980 Nicanor Costa Mendez 1982," Black binder (untitled), Hugo Boatti Osorio to S. E. el Canciller, July 26, "Conversación con el Embajador Azeredo da Silveira," 4 pp.

188. AHCA 47:44, "Colombia 1963 Brasil 1972 Notas," Binder "Año 1972. Brasil Cables," Cable No. 7-8-9-10-11-12-13 from Argentine Embassy Section in Brasília, sent by Nereo Melo Ferrer (signed by José María Ruda) to Argentine Foreign Ministry, March 11, 3 pp.

189. (Same binder as ibid.), Cable No. 17 from Brasília, March 11.

190. *Entrevista*, 25–26.

191. ". . . e tudo acabou bem," *Veja*, 19.

192. Brazil, Ministerio de Relaçoes Exteriores, *Resenha de Política Exterior Brasileira* (henceforth *Resenha*) 25:26. See also Argentina, Ministerio de Relaciones Exteriores y Culto, *Memoria de la Cancillería Argentina*, 1980, 93; Camilión, *Memorias*, 221.

193. *Memoria de la Cancillería Argentina*, 1979, 69–70, 74.

194. Ramiro Saraiva Guerreiro, *Lembranças de um Empregado do Itamaraty* (Rio de Janeiro: Editora Siciliano, 1992), 98.

195. Carlos Washington Pastor, "Chile: La Guerra o la Paz, 1978–1981," in *La Política Exterior Argentina y Sus Protagonistas, 1880–1995*, ed. Silvia Ruth Jalabe (Buenos Aires: Centro Argentino para las Relaciones Internacionales / Nuevohacer / Grupo Editor Latinoamericano, 1996), 288.

196. Warren Hoge, "Argentina's Leader Defends Harsh Rule," *The New York Times*, August 22, 1980, Late City Final Edition, A5.

197. See, e.g., Hurrell, "An Emerging" in *Security Communities*, ed. Adler and Barnett, 236; Moniz Bandeira, *Conflito*, 434; Rosendo Fraga, "A Experiência Histórica no Brasil e na Argentina de 1966 a 1983: Começo de Convergência," in *Perspectivas: Brasil e Argentina*, vol. I, ed. José María Lladós and Samuel Pinheiro Guimarães (Brasília: Instituto de Pesquisa de Relações Internacionais / Fundação Alexandre de Gusmão, 1997), 505, 511; Resende-Santos, "The Origins."

198. See *Argentina, Brasil: Perspectivas Comparativas y Ejes de Integración*, ed. Mônica Hirst (Buenos Aires: FLACSO / Editorial Tesis, 1990); Oelsner, *International Relations*, 70–71.

199. See de Mello Barreto, *Os Sucessores*, vol. 2, 249.

200. On Chilean timing, see Camilión, *Memorias*, 188–189; Lanús, *De Chapultepec*, vol. II, 236–242; on policy and personnel continuities from Geisel to Figueiredo, see Guerreiro, *Lembranças*, 94; João Clemente Baena Soares, *Sem Medo da Diplomacia* (Rio de Janeiro: Editora FGV, 2006), 46; Camilión, *Memorias*, 215; Fausto, *A Concise*, 304.

201. *Resenha* 19:94. See also Brazil's "vehement appeal" to Argentina and Chile for peace (*Resenha* 19:119–120).

202. *Resenha* 19:90.

203. Camilión, *Memorias*, 213.

204. Guerreiro, *Lembranças*, 96.

205. See translated excerpts in *The Politics of Antipolitics: The Military in Latin America*, ed. Brian Loveman and Thomas Davies (Lincoln: University of Nebraska Press, 1978), 176–178.

206. Romero, *A History*, 213.

207. Camilión, *Memorias*, 187, argues that the coup produced a "great relief" in Brazil.

208. See Peter Kornbluh, *The Pinochet File: A Declassified Dossier on Atrocity and Accountability* (New York: The New Press, 2004); J. Patrice McSherry, *Predatory States: Operation Condor and Covert War in Latin America* (Lanham, MD: Rowman & Littlefield, 2005); John Dinges, *The Condor Years: How Pinochet and His Allies Brought Terrorism to Three Continents* (New York: W. W. Norton, 2004).

209. Pastor, in *La Política Exterior*, ed. Jalabe, 290–291. Moreover, recent archival work suggests far more civilian and diplomatic involvement in repression than had been commonly assumed. See Samantha Quadrat, "Muito Alem das Fronteiras," in *O Golpe e a Ditadura Militar: Quarenta Anos Depois (1964–2004)*, ed. Daniel Aarão Reis, Marcelo Ridenti, and Rodrigo Patto Sá Motta (Bauru, São Paulo, Brazil: Editora da Universidade do Sagrado Coração, 2004); McSherry, *Predatory States*, 189.

210. AHCA 47:64, "Brasil 1975–77," Binder "1976 Brasil Providencias," Tab DGPE, Nota DAL No. 1095, Melo Ferrer to DGPE, "Corresponde: Nota de la Comisión Interamericana de Derechos Humanos," April 13, 1976, 1 p.

211. AHCA 47:65, "Brasil 1975–77," Binder "1975/76/77 Brasil Relación Política con Argentina I," Nota S 691, Camilión to Guzzetti, July 13, 1976, 12 pp.

212. AHCA 47:64, "Brasil 1975–77," Nota S 652, Camilión to Montes, July 7, 1977, 4 pp.

213. AHCA 47:37, "Colombia 1979," Binder "Colombia Pases Internos (A) Expedidos (B) Recibidos Memoranda, 1979," Nota 808, Embassy in Bogotá to Dirección General de Organismos Internacionales, "Objeto: Repercusión del Plan del General Viola," November 30, 1979, 3 pp.

214. AHCA [says 74, really 47]:82, "Brasil Parte Cvo. 8," bound coverless stack of documents on border security, "Situación Fronteriza con Brasil," [undated, but prior to June 9, 1976], 3 pp.

215. (Same stack as ibid.), "Apuntes para un Memo s/ Política de Fronteras con el Brasil," January 13, 1977, 2 pp.

216. AHCA 47:145 "Notas 1983 Cables DAS," Binder "Superinten. Nac. De Fronteras. Notas. Políticas," Blue-tabbed report, "Política de Fronteras 1977," signed by Federico Barttfeld, Jefe Dto. America Latina, August 10, 1977.

217. AHCA 47:96, "Chile 1978 Bolivia 1978," Nota S 686, Ambassador Aly Luis Ipres Corbat to Foreign Minister Oscar Montes, "Objeto: Elevar un Plan de Acción para Bolivia," September 13, 1977, 10 pp. including cover letter.

218. AHCA 47:63, "Bolivia 1968 Brasil 1977 DAS," Binder "1977 Brasil Correlativas I, desde No. 1 Hasta 339," Nota S 109, Camilión to Foreign Minister Guzzetti, February 15, 1977, 17 pp.

219. AHCA 47:104, "Brasil 1978–1981 Política Exterior," Binder "1978–9 Brasil Política Exterior Estados Unidos Europa 1980–1, 406," Cable S 568, June 6, 1977, from Brasília.

220. (Same box as ibid.), Cable S 305/78, Embassy in Brazil (Camilión) to MRE, August 15, 1978, "Sobre la Denuncia de los Acuerdos Militares con Estados Unidos," 13 pp.

221. (Same box as ibid.), Binder "1978–9 Brasil Política Exterior Estados Unidos Europa 1980–1, 406," Cable S 342 from Brasília, March 20, 1979, 1 p.

222. (Same binder as ibid.), Cable 257, March 31/April 1 [1980], from Brasília, 1 p.

223. See de Mello Barreto, *Os Sucessores*, vol. 2, 322–323; Fausto, *A Concise*, 299; Romero, *A History*, 206–209.

224. See *Historia General*, ed. Cisneros and Escudé, vol. 14, Chapter 68.

225. See translated excerpts in *The Politics of Antipolitics*, ed. Loveman and Davies, 193–195.

226. *Resenha* 4:8–10.

227. Oelsner, *International Relations*, usefully connects economic difficulties in the 1970s to rapprochement.

228. AHCA 47:144, "Brasil 1977 Santa Cruz de la Sierra 1975," Nota 511 S from Embassy in Brasília to MRE, Departamento America Latina, May 21, 1976, 1 p., cover letter with attached report "Inteligencia Política, Económica y Social," 15 pp., signed by Ambassador Jorge Casal.

229. (Same box as ibid.), Nota 768, Camilión to MRE, "Asunto: Recientes Medidas Adoptadas por el Consejo Monetario Nacional," July 27, 1976, 5 pp.

230. (Same box as ibid.), Nota 690, Camilión to MRE, "Brasil: Discurso de Reis Velloso y M. Simonsen en la Escuela Superior de Guerra," July 13, 1976, 5 pp.

231. AHCA 47:95, "Brasil 1976 Uruguay 1964," Nota S 113, Adolfo Gonzalez Alemán to Guzzetti, "Objeto: Entrevista Cancilleres Brasil-Paraguay," October 18, 1976, 1 p.

232. (Same binder as ibid.), Nota S 289, Camilión to Guzzetti, March 29, 1977, 9 pp.

233. AHCA 47:6, "Presidencia Varios 1980 Bolivia 1979," Binder "Presidencia de la Nación, Ministerios, Organismos Nacionales, Varios," Martínez de Hoz to Pastor, Nota No [35/1 (illegible)], January 31, 1979.

234. AHCA 47:64, "Brasil 1975–77," Binder "1975/76/77 Brasil Relación Política con Argentina I," Nota S 597/79, Camilión to Pastor, undated, 13 pp. Unfortunately, the follow-up binder, "1977 Brasil Relación Política con Argentina II," had suffered major water damage and was completely unusable for research.

235. AHCA 47:148 "America Latina Memos 1979 Brasil Economía 1979," Binder "1979 Año 1979 de 197 hasta 360 Memos (69)," Memorandum 284 from Departmento America Latina (Hector Subiza) to Dirección General de Política, "Asunto: Resumen Político Semanal," October 16, 1979, 6 pp.

236. (Same box as ibid.), Binder "1979 Brasil Economía," Memorandum 1050 S, Dirección General de Informaciones (Juan Carlos Cuadrado) to Departamento America Latina, "Asunto: Brasil: Crisis Petrolera Internacional," May 3, 1979, 3 pp. including cover letter.

237. AHCA 47:104, "Brasil 1978–1981 Política Exterior," Binder "1978–9 Brasil Política Exterior Estados Unidos Europa 1980–1, 406," Cable S 305/78 Camilión to MRE, August 15, 1978, "Sobre la Denuncia de los Acuerdos Militares con Estados Unidos," 13 pp.

238. AHCA 47:63, "Bolivia 1968 Brasil 1977 DAS," Binder "1977 Brasil Correlativas I, Desde No. 1 Hasta 339," Memorandum "Producción de Armas Para Exportación por Parte de Brasil," March 4, 1977, 1 p.

239. AHCA 47:64, "Brasil 1975–77," Binder "1975/76/77 Brasil Relación Política con Argentina I," Nota S 597/79, Camilión to Pastor, undated, 13 pp.

240. AHCA 47:12, "Venezuela 1979 Notas," Binder "Venezuela, Notas de la Embajada," Nota R 693/79 from Caracas, "Aspectos Políticos de la Visita del Presidente del Brasil a Venezuela," November 8, 1979, 3 pp.

241. AHCA 47:148, "America Latina Memos 1979 Brasil Economía 1979," Binder "1979 Brasil Economía," Nota 166, Camilión to Foreign Ministry, "Asunto: Brasil: Gira del Ministro Delfim Netto," March 5, 1980, 7 pp.

242. See Camilión, *Memorias*, 216.

243. María Seoane and Vicente Muleiro, *El Dictador: La Historia Secreta y Pública de Jorge Rafael Videla*, 3rd ed. (Buenos Aires: Editorial Sudamericana, 2001), 242; see Camilión, *Memorias*. Camilión served in the Argentine embassy in Rio de Janeiro, and subsequently as undersecretary of foreign relations, during the Frondizi administration.

244. *Historia General*, ed. Cisneros and Escudé, vol. 14, Chapter 68; Guerreiro, *Lembranças*, 93–95; Pastor, "Chile," in *La Política Exterior*, ed. Jalabe, 282–284; Moniz Bandeira, *Conflito*, 423–424; Camilión, *Memorias*.

245. Saraiva Guerreiro, *Lembranças*, 93. Videla and Pastor had married sisters.

246. *Resenha* 20:99–105.

247. AHCA 47:144, "Brasil 1977 Santa Cruz de la Sierra 1975," Nota 756 Embassy in Brasília to MRE Departamento America Latina, July 23, 1976, 1 p. plus 1 p. attachment; Nota 688 R, Camilión to MRE, "Asunto: Brasil-Uruguay: Visita del Canciller Uruguayo Juan Carlos Blanco," July 12, 1976, 8 pp.

248. AHCA 47:65, "Brasil 1975–77," Binder "1975/76/77 Brasil Relación Política con Argentina I," Nota S 691, Camilión to Guzzetti, July 13, 1976, 12 pp. See also Camilión, *Memorias*. Camilión arrived July 3; the previous ambassador, Jorge Casal, had left Brazil on June 27. Consejero Rafael González acted as Chargé in the interim.

249. Ibid.

250. AHCA 47:64, "Brasil 1975–77," Cable S 671, Camilión to MRE, July 5 [1977], 1 p.

251. AHCA 47:64, "Brasil 1975–77," Nota S 652, Camilión to Montes, July 7, 1977, 4 pp.

252. AHCA 47:9, "Bolivia La Paz Parte 1," folder "Comisión R1.30/76 Reseña y Evaluación al PEN 9.6.77. y demás Notas a la Presidencia 14-1-77. (Compatibilización Obras Corpus e Itaipú)," "Reseña del Cumplimiento de la Directiva Presidencial R.I. 30/76 Referente a la Compatibilización de las Obras de Corpus e Itaipú," Montes to Videla, S, June 9, 1977, 15 pp.

253. Ibid.

254. AHCA 47:64, "Brasil 1975–77," Binder "1976 Brasil Providencias," Tab DGPE, Nota DAL No. 1752, Melo Ferrer to Dirección General de Política, "Corresponde: Memo no. 64 de la SREI de Fecha 7.5.76. REF: Alalc en el Contexto de la Posición frente a Brasil," 1 p.

255. Ibid.

256. AHCA 47:65, "Brasil 1975–77," Binder "1975/76/77 Brasil Relación Política con Argentina I," Memorandum 228, Ministro Enrique Vieyra, Jefe, Grupo de Trabajo Cuenca del Plata, to Departamento América Latina, "Asunto: Temas Que Podrían Ser Considerados por el Almirante Massera con Periodistas Brasileños (Requerimiento del Departamento América Latina)," January 26, 1977, 2 pp.

257. AHCA 47:65, "Brasil 1975–77," Binder "1975/76/77 Brasil Relación Política con Argentina I," Letter to Agosti, initialed "MOA," June 28, 1977, 5 pp.

258. Ibid.

259. AHCA 47:9, "Bolivia La Paz Parte 1," Pink folder, "Reseña del Cumplimiento de la Directiva Presidencial R.I. 30/76 Referente a la Compatibilización de las Obras de Corpus e Itaipú," S, June 7, 1977, 15 pp. plus 1 p. cover letter (Nota 105 S, Montes to Videla, June 9, 1977). All citations in this paragraph are to this document.

260. AHCA 47:64, "Brasil 1975–77," Binder "1975/76/77 Brasil Relación Política con Argentina I," S "Sintesis Sobre las Negociaciones Corpus-Itaipú," 10 pp. [unsigned, undated; handwritten cover note dated November 20, 1977].

261. AHCA 47:148, "America Latina Memos 1979 Brasil Economía 1979," Binder "1979 Año 1979 de 197 hasta 360 Memos (69)," Memorandum 255 S, "Asunto: Requerimiento de la Central Nacional de Inteligencia," Hector Alberto Subiza, Departamento America Latina, to Dirección General de Informaciones, September 19, 1979, 13 pp. The rationale of the twenty-turbine proposal is still debated. See Pastor, "Chile," in *La Política*, ed. Jalabe, 282; Rubens Ricupero, "Prefácio," in de Mello Barreto, *Os Sucessores*, vol. 2, 20; Camilión, *Memorias*, 207–208; Saraiva Guerreiro, *Lembranças*, 93–95.

262. (Same binder as ibid.), Tab "Trabajo S/ Brasil, Emb. Barttfeld, Sec. López Pellegri, Sec. J. Faurie," S, undated [between May and October 1977], signed by Barttfeld, 15 pp. All citations in this paragraph are to this document.

263. See a swath of documents in AHCA 47:140, "La Paz 1981 Bolivia," Binder "Notas GTPLA."

264. AHCA 47:108, "Brasil 1977 Chile 1979," Unlabeled binder, Note 44831/79, Brigadier General Eduardo Alberto Crespi, Secretario General, to Carlos Washington Pastor, April 25, 1979, 1 p.

265. AHCA 47:148, "America Latina Memos 1979 Brasil Economía 1979," Binder "1979 Año 1979 de 197 hasta 360 Memos (69)," Memorandum 267 Departamento America Latina (Subiza) to Subsecretary General, October 1, 1979, 1 p.; AHCA 47:9, "Bolivia La Paz Parte 1," Folder "CEBAC Papeles Varios," Tab "Parte General," Cable 293 S Cancillería (SREI/DREB) to Embargentina/Brasilia, April 25, 1980, 1 p.

266. AHCA 47:148, "America Latina Memos 1979 Brasil Economía 1979," Binder "1979 Año 1979 de 197 hasta 360 Memos (69)," Departamento America Latina to Dirección General de Política, "Asunto: Resumen Político Semanal," October 23, 1979, 4 pp.

267. (Same binder as ibid.), Two memoranda from Departamento America Latina to Dirección General de Política: No. 307, "Asunto: Resumen Político Semanal," November 13, 1979, 8 pp.; and No. 357, "Asunto: Reseña Annual Sobre Paises del Área," December 21, 1979, 18 pp.

268. AHCA 47:9, "Bolivia La Paz Parte 1," Folder "CEBAC Papeles Varios," Tab "Projectos Acuerdos," "Anexo 3: Acuerdo de Cooperación entre el Gobierno de la República Argentina y el Gobierno de la República Federativa del Brasil, para el Desarrollo y la Aplicación de los Usos Pacíficos de la Energía Nuclear," February 11, 1980, 4 pp.

269. (Same box as ibid.), Folder "Transito de Automotores Brasileños a Chile. Carpeta para Señor Subsecretario," Memorandum 142 S, Raúl Medina Muñoz, Jefe, Departamento America Latina, to Subsecretaría de Relaciones Exteriores, July 14, 1978, 5 pp. A similar crisis arose in 1977 when Argentina closed a tunnel to Chile.

270. (Same folder as ibid.), Memorandum 169 S from Departamento America Latina to Subsecretaría de Relaciones Exteriores, "Venta de Camiones Brasileños a Chile," August 23, 1978, 9 pp. plus annexes.

271. Ibid. In fact, Brazil did retaliate, blocking all cross-border commerce by trucks without special permits.

272. AHCA 47:148, "America Latina Memos 1979 Brasil Economía 1979," Binder "1979 Año 1979 de 197 hasta 360 Memos (69)," Memorandum 281 S Departamento America Latina to Dirección General de Política, "Asunto: Instrucciones para la IVa. Reunión del Grupo de Trabajo del Area Básica 1—Transportes en Sus Distintos Medios y Modos—de la Cuenca del Plata," October 25, 1979, 3 pp. including cover letter.

273. (Same binder as ibid.), Memorandum S 308, Departamento America Latina (Hector Subiza) to Dirección General de Política—GTAE, "Asunto: Responder Memorandum No. 174 de GTAE," November 12, 1979, 2 pp.

274. AHCA 47:64, "Brasil 1975–77," Binder "1975/76/77 Brasil Relación Política con Argentina I," Nota S 230, Casal to MRE, "Asunto: Presentación de Credenciales. Primeras Entrevistas e Impresiones," March 3, 1976, 6 pp.

275. AHCA 47:63, "Bolivia 1968 Brasil 1977 DAS," Binder "1977 Brasil Correlativas I, desde No. 1 Hasta 339," Nota 330, Camilión to MRE, "Asunto: Las Reformas Inminentes," April 12, 1977, 6 pp.; (same folder), Nota S 315, Camilión to MRE, "Asunto: En Regimen de Excepción," April 5, 1977, 9 pp.

276. AHCA 47:64, "Brasil 1975–77," Binder "1975/76/77 Brasil Relación Política con Argentina I," Nota S 597/79, Camilión to Pastor, undated, 13 pp.

277. Ibid.

278. AHCA 47:9, "Bolivia La Paz Parte 1," folder "C.E.B.A.C. Papeles Varios," "Notas para Diálogo Señor Presidente Videla con Señor Presidente Figueiredo," undated [after October 1979, before May 1980], 6 pp.

279. Ibid.

280. Richard Nixon, "Toasts of the President and President Medici of Brazil," December 7, 1971, online by Gerhard Peters and John T. Woolley, *The American Presidency Project*, www.presidency.ucsb.edu/ws/?pid=3247.

281. Henry Kissinger, *White House Years* (Boston: Little, Brown, 1979), Chapter 17. Richard Nixon, *RN: The Memoirs of Richard Nixon* (New York: Grosset & Dunlap, 1978), 490, considered Brazil a potential target as well, but his brief discussion encapsulates the attention problem: Allende's campaign drew US concern and intervention, but Allende's death moved Chile (and the region) out of the picture.

282. Jimmy Carter, *White House Diary* (New York: Farrar, Straus, Giroux, 2010), 181–182, 308; Jimmy Carter, *Keeping Faith: Memoirs of a President* (New York: Bantam Books, 1982), 145–150, 474–477; Cyrus Vance, *Hard Choices: Critical Years in America's Foreign Policy* (New York: Simon and Schuster, 1983), 33; Zbigniew Brzezinski, *Power and Principle: Memoirs of the National Security Advisor, 1977–1981* (New York: Farrar, Straus, Giroux, 1983), 134, 431–433. See Robert Pastor, "The Carter Administration and Latin America: A Test of Principle," The Carter Center, July 1992, www.cartercenter.org/documents /1243.pdf, 3.

283. Jimmy Carter, "Organization of American States Address Before the Permanent Council," April 14, 1977, www.presidency.ucsb.edu/ws/?pid=7347; Jimmy Carter, "Organization of American States Remarks at the Opening Session of the Eighth General Assembly," June 21, 1978, www.presidency.ucsb.edu/ws/?pid=30981; and Jimmy Carter, "Organization of American States Remarks at the 10th Regular Session of the General Assembly," November 19, 1980, www.presidency.ucsb.edu/ws/?pid=45506, all

online by Gerhard Peters and John T. Woolley, *The American Presidency Project*. See also Pastor, "The Carter Administration," 29.

284. Carter, *White House Diary*, 354–366.

285. Ibid., 421–433, 453–461.

286. Quoted in Brzezinski, *Power and Principle*, 128.

287. Carter, "Organization of American States Remarks," June 21, 1978.

Chapter 4 · The 1959 Cuban Revolution and Central American Rivalries

1. In Central American states, smaller and less developed than Argentina and Brazil, foreign ministries had less prominent influence as autonomous policymaking organizations during the Cold War. Foreign ministers functioned more as personal advisors to presidents than as heads of agencies, and the role of ambassadors to rival countries (though not to Washington) appears to have been minimal. The key veto players in this chapter are the armed forces. Epigraph citations, respectively, are to "Not One of Us Alone: A Mutual Security Program," Statement by John Foster Dulles, Secretary of State, before the House Foreign Affairs Committee, April 5, 1954 (Department of State Publication 5433, General Foreign Policy Series 89, April 1954), and Michael Gambone, *Eisenhower, Somoza, and the Cold War in Nicaragua, 1953–1961* (Westport, CT: Praeger, 1997), 190–191.

2. The *Foreign Relations of the United States* (*FRUS*) documents on Central America during these years appear only as microfiche addenda and are not available in the standard bound volumes.

3. See Manuel Moreno Ibáñez, "On Measuring Political Conflict in Latin America, 1948–1967," in *Statistical Abstract of Latin America*, vol. 20 (Los Angeles: Center of Latin American Studies, University of California Los Angeles, 1980), 548–560; Timothy Wickham-Crowley, *Guerrillas and Revolution in Latin America: A Comparative Study of Insurgents and Regimes since 1956* (Princeton: Princeton University Press, 1992).

4. See particularly UCLA's *Statistical Abstract of Latin America* annual volumes from 1955 onward.

5. Similarly, see Victor Cha, *Alignment despite Antagonism: The US-Korea-Japan Security Triangle* (Stanford, CA: Stanford University Press, 1999).

6. Laun C. Smith Jr., "Central American Defense Council: Some Problems and Achievements," *Air University Review* (Mar.–Apr. 1969), www.airpower.maxwell.af.mil /airchronicles/aureview/1969/mar-apr/smithl.html, argues that "Costa Rica and Panama had been present in an observer capacity only, while El Salvador had presented an attitude of reserve."

7. See Jorge Domínguez et al., "Boundary Disputes in Latin America," *Peaceworks* no. 50 (Washington, DC: United States Institute of Peace, September 2003); and Manuel Orozco, "Boundary Disputes in Central America: Past Trends and Present Developments," *Pensamiento Propio* 14 (Jul.–Dec. 2001): 99–134.

8. Organization of American States (OAS), Department of International Law, Inter-American Treaty of Reciprocal Assistance (Rio Treaty), Signatories and Ratifications, www.oas.org/juridico/English/sigs/b-29.html.

9. Ibid. Articles 2, 7, and 18 refer solely to inter-American conflicts. Article 1, which states that the parties reject aggressive behavior such as the threat and use of force, can be read either as a further provision to prevent inter-American conflict (since most Latin

American countries would have been incapable of conflict outside the region) or as a pledge by the United States not to drag its Latin American allies into an extrahemispheric conflict of its own making.

10. John Child, *Unequal Alliance: The Inter-American Military System, 1938–1978* (Boulder, CO: Westview, 1980), 115–129.

11. See *FRUS 1958–1960*, vol. V, doc. 28, 172–173.

12. "Objectives of US Foreign Policy in Latin America," Department of State Publication 6131, Inter-American Series 51, November 1955, 10.

13. Gambone, *Eisenhower, Somoza*, 118–120.

14. See James Dunkerley, *Power in the Isthmus: A Political History of Modern Central America* (New York: Verso, 1988); and *Central America since Independence*, ed. Leslie Bethell (New York: Cambridge University Press, 1991).

15. Charles Ameringer, *The Caribbean Legion: Patriots, Politicians, Soldiers of Fortune, 1946–1950* (University Park: Pennsylvania State University Press, 1996).

16. Report from the Operations Coordinating Board to the National Security Council, May 21, 1958, *FRUS 1958–1960*, vol. V, doc. 2, 2–19.

17. The 1954 Caracas resolutions followed up on the Rio Treaty to specify further the common threat, confirming (in John Foster Dulles's words) that a Communist takeover of a Latin American country "would constitute a threat to the sovereignty and political independence of all the American states, endangering the peace of America." "Not One of Us Alone," statement by John Foster Dulles.

18. Message of President Eisenhower to the Congress, April 20, 1955, "A Program for Mutual Security," Department of State Publication 5859, General Foreign Policy Series 100, June 1955.

19. The CIA's declassified, albeit redacted, internal history of Operation PBSUCCESS has been published as Nick Cullather, *Secret History: The CIA's Classified Account of Its Operations in Guatemala, 1952–1954* (Stanford, CA: Stanford University Press, 1999).

20. Ameringer, *The Caribbean Legion*, 137, describes Castro's insurgency, launched from Mexico, as "the only successful filibustering expedition of the 1950s" and Castro as "the new patron of exile revolutionary movements."

21. Timothy Wickham-Crowley, "Winners, Losers, and Also-Rans: Toward a Comparative Sociology of Latin American Guerrilla Movements," in *Power and Popular Protest: Latin American Social Movements*, 2nd ed., ed. Susan Eckstein (Berkeley: University of California Press, 2001), 139.

22. Jorge Domínguez, *To Make a World Safe for Revolution: Cuba's Foreign Policy* (Cambridge, MA: Harvard University Press, 1989), 113–117, 143–145.

23. By "armed strength," I mean the number of soldiers or guardsmen in the principal state security forces responsible for national defense. Some countries have additional police forces (sometimes under military control) or official militia units, but counting the Cuban militia or the Costa Rican Guardia Fiscal as first-line defensive or offensive units would be misleading. Troop counts are undoubtedly a poor approximation of battle capabilities for advanced militaries, but for Central America, the figures in table 4.1 are a reasonable measure of relative strength.

24. *The Communist Bloc and the Western Alliances: the Military Balance, 1962–1963* (London: International Institute for Strategic Studies [IISS], 1963).

25. Pamela Falk, *Cuban Foreign Policy: Caribbean Tempest* (Lexington, MA: Lexington Books, 1986), 25; Domínguez, *To Make A World*, 117–118; and H. Michael Erisman, *Cuba's International Relations: The Anatomy of a Nationalistic Foreign Policy* (Boulder, CO: Westview Press, 1985), 19.

26. Memorandum of Discussion, NSC, June 25, 1959, *FRUS 1958–1960*, vol. VI, doc. 325, 541–543.

27. Memorandum of Discussion, NSC, February 12, 1959, *FRUS 1958–1960*, vol. V, doc. 10, 80.

28. Tim Weiner, *Legacy of Ashes: The History of the CIA* (New York: Doubleday, 2007); Cullather, *Secret History*.

29. Memorandum of Discussion, NSC, February 12, 1959, *FRUS 1958–1960*, vol. V, doc. 10, 89. Honduras received the same; El Salvador and Costa Rica got nothing. Guatemala was the subregional winner with $200,000. See United States Agency for International Development, USAID *Greenbook*, US Overseas Loans and Grants: Obligations and Loan Authorizations, 1 July 1945–30 September 2006, qesdb.usaid.gov/gbk/query _historical.html, accessed in 2008 (the current site for *Greenbook* data is gbk.eads .usaidallnet.gov/data/).

30. Richard Millett, *Guardians of the Dynasty* (Maryknoll, NY: Orbis Books, 1977), 226–227; this gave Nicaragua "the largest force of jet aircraft in Latin America" and the "eleventh highest" aid package in the region.

31. Under Kennedy, Internal Defense and Development (IDAD) displaced Eisenhower's model of Hemispheric Security. Child, *Unequal Alliance*, 145–155.

32. Gambone, *Eisenhower, Somoza*, 203.

33. I interpret these symbolic gestures primarily as affecting expectations of future economic and internal-security assistance. Thus, they are partially substitutable for actual resource flows, in the short run. Central American leaders and their armed forces would, I expect, have taken US pledges of future support—or promises to withhold such assistance—seriously. However, unfulfilled expectations might degrade over the longer term.

34. Citing a memorandum from the Honduran foreign minister to the State Department on December 19, 1955, International Court of Justice, *Case Concerning Military and Paramilitary Activities in and against Nicaragua (Nicaragua v. United States of America)*, vol. III, 193.

35. Ramón Villeda Morales, "Problema Fronterizo Hondureño-Nicaragüense," in *Ramón Villeda Morales: Ciudadano de América*, ed. Stefan Baciu (San José, Costa Rica: Antonio Lehmann, 1970), 177.

36. Anastasio Somoza Jr., *Nicaragua Betrayed*, as told to Jack Cox (Boston: Western Islands, 1980), 28.

37. *Honduras: A Country Study*, ed. Tim Merrill (Washington, DC: Federal Research Division, Library of Congress, 1993), also available at http://lcweb2.loc.gov/frd/cs/hntoc .html; and Darío Euraque, *Reinterpreting the Banana Republic: Region and State in Honduras, 1870–1972* (Chapel Hill: University of North Carolina Press, 1996), 68.

38. See Wayne Earl Johnson, *The Honduras-Nicaragua Boundary Dispute, 1957–1963: The Peaceful Settlement of an International Conflict* (PhD diss., University of Denver, 1964), vi; see also Bernard Diederich, *Somoza and the Legacy of US Involvement in Central*

America (New York: E. P. Dutton, 1981), 53–54. For the text of the accord—signed July 21, 1957—see www.cancilleria.gob.ni/docs/files/hn_limite57.pdf.

39. Honduras had been pushing for arbitration since 1955, but Nicaragua refused until US diplomats and OAS representatives intervened; even so, when Honduras officially filed its case, it doubted that a Nicaraguan delegation would even show up. International Court of Justice, *Case Concerning Military and Paramilitary Activities in and against Nicaragua (Nicaragua v. United States of America)*, vol. III, 193–198.

40. James Cockcroft, *Latin America: History, Politics, and US Policy*, 2nd ed. (Chicago: Nelson-Hall, 1996), 210; Thomas Whelan (ambassador to Nicaragua) to Taylor (State Department officer in charge of Nicaraguan affairs), February 11, 1958, *FRUS 1958–1960*, vol. V, Nicaragua fiche, doc. HU-1, 1,242–1,243.

41. Whelan to State (signed by Counselor William Hudson for the ambassador), 15 March 1958, *FRUS 1958–1960*, vol. V, Nicaragua fiche, doc. HU-3, 1,246.

42. Whelan to State, June 1959, *FRUS 1958–1960*, vol. V, Nicaragua fiche, doc. HU-16, 1,274–1,275.

43. *FRUS 1958–1960*, vol. V, Nicaragua fiche, doc. HU-23, 1,291–1,292.

44. Ibid.

45. Gambone, *Eisenhower, Somoza*, 163; and Millett, *Guardians*, 225. Diederich, *Somoza*, 69, notes that "1959 had marked a resurgence of the Nicaraguan guerrilla movement," in which "small bands carried out forays into the country from the Honduran and Costa Rican borders."

46. Millett, *Guardians*, 254–257; Dunkerley, *Power in the Isthmus*, 232–233; and James Mahoney, *The Legacies of Liberalism: Path Dependence and Political Regimes in Central America* (Baltimore: Johns Hopkins University Press, 2001), 252–255. All three authors characterize the overall state of Somoza-Guard relations as fundamentally corrupt.

47. Harvey Meyer, *Historical Dictionary of Honduras* (Metuchen, NJ: Scarecrow Press, 1976), 213, 371.

48. Director of Middle American Affairs William Wieland to William Snow, March 26, 1958, *FRUS 1958–1960*, vol. V, Honduras fiche, doc. HO-2, 1,196–1,197. The Honduran military sent Villeda Morales as ambassador to the United States between the 1956 coup and his presidential election by constituent assembly in 1957, precisely to reassure Washington of his anti-Communism. See Euraque, *Reinterpreting*, 72–73.

49. Editorial note, March 2, 1959, *FRUS 1958–1960*, vol. V, Honduras fiche, doc. HO-5, 1,203; *FRUS 1958–1960*, vol. V, Honduras fiche, doc. HO-6, 1,205; and editorial note, *FRUS 1958–1960*, vol. V, Honduras fiche, doc. HO-9, 1,210. See also Kirk Bowman, "The Public Battles over Militarisation and Democracy in Honduras, 1954–1963," *Journal of Latin American Studies* 33, no. 3 (Aug. 2001): 556.

50. Bowman, "The Public Battles"; and *Honduras*, ed. Merrill. Bowman observes that militarism in Honduras had been weak to nonexistent at the beginning of the Cold War and that US training shifted the Honduran armed forces' preferences toward greater activity, both military and political.

51. Excerpts from Rafael Somarriba's unpublished memoirs were brought to light in a two-part article in a Nicaraguan newspaper. "El Che y la Guerrilla Nicaragüense," *El Nuevo Diario* (Managua, Nicaragua), August 4, 2007, impreso.elnuevodiario.com.ni/2007/08/04/especiales/62583; and October 7, 2007, impreso.elnuevodiario.com.ni/2007/10/07/especiales/63067. These memoirs indicate that Che Guevara intended

to lead the revolution in Nicaragua personally (to follow in the footsteps of the earlier Nicaraguan guerrilla leader Sandino) and that Raúl Castro handed Somarriba two thousand dollars to aid the operation. See also Che Guevara, *Guerrilla Warfare*, with an Introduction and Case Studies by Brian Loveman and Thomas Davies (Lincoln: University of Nebraska Press, 1985), 363.

52. Victor Bulmer-Thomas, "Honduras since 1930," in *Central America since Independence*, ed. Bethell, 208.

53. "Letter from Esteban Mendoza to Manley O. Hudson of 2 May 1956," in International Court of Justice, *Case Concerning Military and Paramilitary Activities in and against Nicaragua (Nicaragua vs. United States of America)*, vol. III, 354. Mendoza, the Honduran foreign minister, wrote that according to a "reliable source," "due to reasons of internal politics, as President Somoza, now in power, wishes to be re-elected, the Nicaraguan Government would like to have Honduras postpone filing Court proceedings until after February 3, 1957, date on which elections will be held in that country." Since the election itself was a carefully orchestrated sham, Somoza's insecurity must have come from some other source, and the group with the most to lose from cooperation with Honduras would have been the National Guard.

54. Gambone, *Eisenhower, Somoza*, 116. Millett, *Guardians of the Dynasty*, 213, adds that guard budgets in absolute terms doubled between 1949 and 1953, backed by flows of arms from the United States.

55. Victor Bulmer-Thomas, "Nicaragua since 1930," in *Central America since Independence*, ed. Bethell, 254; see Diederich, *Somoza*, 51.

56. Gambone, *Eisenhower, Somoza*, 120.

57. Bulmer-Thomas, "Honduras," in *Central America since Independence*, ed. Bethell, 210; Meyer, *Historical Dictionary of Honduras*, 370; and Bowman, "The Public Battles." Villeda disbanded the Guardia Civil (which comprised 2,500 troops) late in 1963, but this was too little too late for the military; after the 1963 coup, the armed forces replaced the Guardia with a Cuerpo Especial de Seguridad ("El CES"), which was "virtually a branch of the armed forces, though legally separate." Meyer, *Historical Dictionary of Honduras*, 18, 109.

58. Memorandum of conversation by John Gawf, Honduran desk officer, December (date illegible) 1958, *FRUS 1958–1960*, vol. V, Honduras fiche, doc. HO-4, 1,201.

59. *FRUS 1958–1960*, vol. V, Honduras fiche, doc. HO-4, 1,201–1,202.

60. Somarriba claims that this additional support for Villeda was his own idea, having persuaded Che Guevara that "we should arm Villeda so that he can defend himself against the Army," landing weapons for both purposes simultaneously at an airstrip in Honduras. "El Che y la Guerrilla Nicaragüense," *El Nuevo Diario*. For troop levels see table 4.1.

61. Ibid.

62. Bowman, "The Public Battles," 557. Bowman notes that the Honduran public largely supported Villeda's initiatives to restrict military autonomy.

63. Whelan to State (signed by Counselor Hudson for the ambassador), March 15, 1958, *FRUS 1958–1960*, vol. V, Nicaragua fiche, doc. HU-3, 1,246; memorandum of conversation, drafted by Taylor, April 8, 1958, *FRUS 1958–1960*, vol. V, Nicaragua fiche, doc. HU-5, 1,250–1,251; and memorandum of conversation drafted by Taylor, February 21, 1958, *FRUS 1958–1960*, vol. V, Nicaragua fiche 1958–1960, doc. HU-2, 1,244–1,245.

64. Memorandum of conversation, drafted by Taylor, March 30, 1959, *FRUS 1958–1960*, vol. V, Nicaragua fiche, 1958–1960, doc. HU-12, 1,266–1,269.

65. Roy Rubottom to Whelan, January 31, 1959, *FRUS 1958–1960*, vol. V, Nicaragua fiche, doc. HU-11, 1,263–1,265.

66. *FRUS 1958–1960*, vol. V, Nicaragua fiche, doc. HU-23, 1,291–1,292.

67. Arguments of consistent US support for the Somozas from World War II to the peak of the Sandinista rebellion include Millett, *Guardians of the Dynasty*, 252, and Diederich, *Somoza*. Robert Pastor, *Not Condemned to Repetition: The United States and Nicaragua*, 2nd ed. (Boulder, CO: Westview, 2002), 289, notes variation in US attitudes over time but still considers the late 1950s and early 1960s a period of close support for the dynasty, under US ambassador Thomas Whelan.

68. Memorandum of conversation, drafted by Taylor, March 30, 1959, *FRUS 1958–1960*, vol. V, Nicaragua fiche, doc. HU-12, 1,266–1,269.

69. Memorandum of conversation, by Rubottom, April 4, 1959, *FRUS 1958–1960*, vol. V, Nicaragua fiche, doc. HU-13, 1,270.

70. Christian Herter to Whelan, June 15, 1959, *FRUS 1958–1960*, vol. V, Nicaragua fiche, doc. HU-15, 1,272–1,273. Dissenting, Whelan argued that the Somozas faced a serious threat (and that little of the opposition in Nicaragua qualified as "responsible") and that they would best be protected not by democratization but by a US security guarantee. Whelan to State, June (date illegible), 1959, *FRUS 1958–1960*, vol. V, Nicaragua fiche, doc. HU-16, 1,274–1,275; Whelan to State, August 18, 1959, *FRUS 1958–1960*, vol. V, Nicaragua fiche, doc. HU-17, 1,276–1,278.

71. C. Allan Stewart to Rubottom, drafted by Taylor, November 26, 1958, *FRUS 1958–1960*, vol. V, Nicaragua fiche, doc. HU-10, 1,261–1,262.

72. Airgram from acting secretary of state to embassy in Honduras, September 2, 1960, *FRUS 1958–1960*, vol. V, Honduras fiche, doc. HO-14.

73. Ibid.

74. Ibid.

75. Stewart to Rubottom, drafted by Taylor, November 26, 1958, *FRUS 1958–1960*, vol. V, Nicaragua fiche, doc. HU-10, 1,261–1,262.

76. Rubottom to Whelan, April 7, 1958, *FRUS 1958–1960*, vol. V, Nicaragua fiche, doc. HU-4, 1,247–1,249.

77. Acting Secretary of State C. Douglas Dillon to Eisenhower, *FRUS 1958–1960*, May 13, 1960, vol. V, Honduras fiche, doc. HO-13, 1,221.

78. Editorial note, *FRUS 1958–1960*, vol. V, Nicaragua fiche, doc. HU-26, 1,297. Protecting Guatemala appears to have been the primary objective, with Nicaragua's security seen as incidental. See Brian Loveman, *For la Patria: Politics and the Armed Forces in Latin America* (Wilmington, DE: Scholarly Resources, 1999), 161.

79. See www.cancilleria.gob.ni/docs/files/hn_asilo59.pdf.

80. Acting Secretary of State Dillon to embassy in Honduras, May 16, 1959, *FRUS 1958–1960*, vol. V, Honduras fiche, doc. HO-7, 1,206.

81. Editorial note, *FRUS 1958–1960*, vol. V, doc. 310, 820; and *FRUS 1958–1960*, vol. V, Honduras fiche, doc. HO-19, 1,234, n. 2–3.

82. "Discurso del Ciudadano Presidente de Honduras, Doctor Ramón Villeda Morales Respondiendo al Presidente de la República de Nicaragua, Ing. Luis Somoza De-

bayle en la Reunion de 'El Espino,' el 10 de enero de 1961," in *Ramón Villeda Morales*, ed. Baciu, 178.

83. *FRUS 1958–1960*, vol. V, Honduras fiche, doc. HO-18, 1,230–1,231.

84. *FRUS 1958–1960*, vol. V, Honduras fiche, doc. HO-19, 1,234, n. 4. Honduran-Nicaraguan cooperation endured well after Villeda's overthrow but broke down after Nicaragua's 1979 socialist revolution.

85. Marco Tulio Zeledón, *Un Año en la ODECA, 1960–1961* (San Salvador: Organización de Estados Centroamericanos, 1961), 346, also available at www.sica.int/cdoc /publicaciones/mem_odeca/sg2/1_odeca_1960_61.pdf.

86. Zeledón, *Un Año*, 24, 26.

87. Ibid. See Johnson, *The Honduras-Nicaragua Boundary*, 116–133 on the technical dilemmas of territorial handover.

88. Villeda later also alluded to "the reluctance of certain sectors that advise the non-execution of an international promise." "Discurso del Ciudadano Presidente," in *Ramón Villeda Morales*, ed. Baciu, 178–180.

89. Thomas Anderson, *The War of the Dispossessed: Honduras and El Salvador, 1969* (Lincoln: University of Nebraska Press, 1981), 3–10.

90. International Court of Justice, Press Release, no. 92/22, September 11, 1992, "Land, Island and Maritime Frontier Dispute (El Salvador/Honduras; Nicaragua Intervening)—Judgment of the Chamber," www.icj-cij.org/docket/files/75/10277.pdf.

91. See William Durham, *Scarcity and Survival in Central America: Ecological Origins of the Soccer War* (Stanford, CA: Stanford University Press, 1979); Anderson, *War of the Dispossessed*; Knut Walter and Philip Williams, "The Military and Democratization in El Salvador," *Journal of Interamerican Studies and World Affairs* 35, no. 1 (Spring 1993): 39–88, esp. 51–52. Switzerland references include Ana Arana, "The New Battle for Central America," *Foreign Affairs* 80, no. 6 (Nov.–Dec. 2001): 88–101; and Christopher Dickey, "Central America: From Quagmire to Cauldron?" *Foreign Affairs* 62, no. 3 (1983): 659–694.

92. See Carlos Sandoval García, *Threatening Others: Nicaraguans and the Formation of National Identities in Costa Rica* (Athens, OH: Ohio University Center for International Studies, 2004), Chapter 3.

93. Theodore Creedman, *Historical Dictionary of Costa Rica*, 2nd ed. (Metuchen, NJ: Scarecrow Press, 1991), 112–113. On 1978, see the Costa Rican public security minister's memoirs: Juan José Echeverría Brealey, *La Guerra No Declarada* (San José, Costa Rica: Editorial Universidad Estatal Distancia, 2006).

94. Millett, *Guardians*, 212–214; and Tord Høivik and Solveig Aas, "Demilitarization in Costa Rica: A Farewell to Arms?" *Journal of Peace Research* 18, no. 4 (Dec. 1981): 339.

95. Høivik and Aas, "Demilitarization," 344. For the abolition dates, see the Costa Rican Ministry of Governance, Police, and Public Security's official history at www.msp .go.cr/sobre_ministerio/historia.html.

96. Høivik and Aas, "Demilitarization," 347–349.

97. Anderson, *War of the Dispossessed*, 2, 167.

98. Alain Rouquié, *The Military and the State in Latin America*, trans. Paul Sigmund (Berkeley: University of California Press, 1987), 354; and Walter and Williams, "The Military," 42–43. As Castro Morán put it, "Political power resides in the Salvadoran Army."

Mariano Castro Morán, *Función Política del Ejército Salvadoreño en el Presente Siglo* (San Salvador: UCA Editores, 1983), 228.

99. Castro Morán, *Función Política*, 24.

100. Ibid., 24–25.

101. Ibid., 26.

102. "Conversation with Reynaldo Galindo Pohl in San Salvador, El Salvador, June 20, 1967," in Robert J. Alexander, *Presidents of Central America, Mexico, Cuba, and Hispaniola: Conversations and Correspondence* (Westport, CT: Praeger, 1995), 137–138. Galindo Pohl was a member of the 1948–1950 junta.

103. Castro Morán, *Función Política*, 351. "For the last several decades, to speak of national defense was to speak of military security, of military power; in consequence, this corresponded exclusively to the area of the armed forces."

104. Demobilization of the Costa Rican army does not necessarily disprove my hypothesis, but it does underscore the limitations of my assumptions, which reflect an ideal-typical developing country's institutions. The Costa Rican case is noteworthy because even in a nominally demilitarized country, official and quasi-official armed groups built political capital by maintaining interstate rivalry against presidential efforts toward rapprochement.

105. Deborah Yashar, *Demanding Democracy: Reform and Reaction in Costa Rica and Guatemala, 1870s–1950s* (Stanford, CA: Stanford University Press, 1997), 189. See also Høivik and Aas, "Demilitarization," 343–348. Similarly, Costa Rica's Ministry of Governance, Police, and Public Security notes that the constitutional prohibition of a standing army caused "the armed forces to come to be called the Guardia Civil," www.msp.go.cr/sobre_ministerio/historia.html.

106. Høivik and Aas, "Demilitarization," 338.

107. Rodolfo Cerdas Cruz, "Costa Rica since 1930," in *Central America since Independence*, ed. Bethell, 305–308.

108. Ibid.

109. On the shifting organizational structure of National Liberation, see the PLN's official history at www.pln.or.cr/dokuwiki/doku.php?id=start.

110. Briefing paper for March 26–29, 1958, visit of Costa Rican President-Elect Mario Echandi, undated, *FRUS 1958–1960*, vol. V, Costa Rica fiche, doc. CR-3, 841–842; and summary of discussions in Costa Rica during Milton Eisenhower's trip, July 18–21, 1958, *FRUS 1958–1960*, vol. V, Costa Rica fiche, doc. CR-9, 858.

111. "Orden de Disparar contra Guardia Civil," *La Nación* (Costa Rica), August 7, 1959.

112. See, for example, Diederich, *Somoza*, 57–61.

113. Briefing paper prepared by the officer in charge of Costa Rican Affairs, Feldman, November 21, 1960, *FRUS 1958–1960*, vol. V, Costa Rica fiche, doc. CR-29.

114. Chargé in Costa Rica Roy Kimmel to State, November 15, 1960, *FRUS 1958–1960*, vol. V, Costa Rica fiche, doc. CR-28, 918–920.

115. Lemus had the blessing of outgoing president Colonel Osorio, and his election was neither clean nor indicative of further Salvadoran democratization. The coup against Lemus on October 26, 1960, also had Osorio's blessing and established a junta run by left-leaning officers. A counter-coup on January 25, 1961, established a five-member civil-military directorate, which then held (and won) elections on December 17 and turned over power to a civilian (Rodolfo Eusebio Cardón) on January 25, 1962; however, one of

the directorate members (Col. Julio Adalberto Rivera) took power on July 1 and held it for five years. See Enrique Baloyra, *El Salvador in Transition* (Chapel Hill: University of North Carolina Press, 1982), 38–42; Castro Morán, *Función Política*; Rouquié, *The Military*, 336. Quotation from *FRUS 1958–1960*, vol. V, El Salvador fiche, doc. ES-8, May 5, 1959, 950–953.

116. Thorsten Kalijarvi to State, April 8, 1960, doc. ES-13; Kalijarvi to State, September 27, 1960, doc. ES-23, 995; and editorial note, October 26, 1960, doc. ES-25, 1,005; all in *FRUS 1958–1960*, vol. V, El Salvador fiche. Assistant Secretary Thomas Mann later explained to the secretary of state that one of the main coup motivations was Lemus's "vacillation in controlling the increasing activities of pro-Castro and pro-communist agitators, first by failure to act and later through strong-arm suppression." Mann to Herter, October 31, 1960, *FRUS 1958–1960*, vol. V, El Salvador fiche, doc. ES-27, 1,010.

117. Walter and Williams, "The Military and Democratization," 47–48.

118. The official proclamation of the 1961 regime argued that the security situation actually worsened after Lemus left office. "Proclama de la Fuerza Armada al Pueblo Salvadoreño," February 6, 1961 (reprinted as Annex II of Castro Morán, *Función Política*, 397–399).

119. Ambassador Kalijarvi to State, doc. ES-1, March 6, 1958, 925–931; and Kalijarvi to State, editorial note, doc. ES-4, 938; both in *FRUS 1958–1960*, vol. V, El Salvador fiche.

120. See El Salvador, Ministerio de Relaciones Exteriores, *Informe Anual*, 1958–1959, 5.

121. Editorial note, *FRUS 1958–1960*, vol. V, Costa Rica fiche, doc. CR-2.

122. Memorandum of conversation by OIC El Salvadoran affairs, Ross, April 1, 1959, *FRUS 1958–1960*, vol. V, El Salvador fiche, doc. ES-7, 948–949, and doc. ES-16, 971–973.

123. Kalijarvi to State, July 26, 1960, *FRUS 1958–1960*, vol. V, El Salvador fiche, doc. ES-17, 974.

124. Ibid., 974.

125. Editorial note, October–November 1958, doc. CR-13, 871; and Stewart to Deputy Assistant Secretary for Inter-American Affairs Lester D. Mallory, December 11, 1959, doc. CR-19, 883–884; both in *FRUS 1958–1960*, vol. V, Costa Rica fiche.

126. This wrangling over banana taxation was a major issue. See *FRUS 1958–1960*, vol. V, Costa Rica fiche, docs. CR-6, CR-7, CR-8, CR-11, CR-15, CR-16, and CR-18; Rubottom to Acting Secretary Dillon, May 15, 1959, *FRUS 1958–1960*, vol. V, Costa Rica fiche, doc. CR-15, 873–877.

127. Summary of discussions in Costa Rica during Milton Eisenhower's trip, July 18–21, 1958, *FRUS 1958–1960*, vol. V, Costa Rica fiche, doc. CR-9, 854–855.

128. "Las Dictaduras, la Oligarquía y los Trusts. Según Decires de la Calle Ayudaron a Financiar la Campaña del Partido Unión Nal," *La Nación* (Costa Rica), April 29, 1958.

129. The censure occurred on March 10, 1959, through legislative accord number 254. Four years later, the legislature debated revoking the censure (after then-President Orlich had met with Somoza), but the measure failed. "Revocar Voto de Censura a Echandi," *La Nación* (Costa Rica), March 27, 1963.

130. Costa Rica, Ministerio de Relaciones Exteriores, *Memoria de Ministerio de Relaciones Exteriores y Culto Presentada a la Asamblea Legislativa, 1958–1959* (San José, Costa Rica, 1959).

131. Høivik and Aas, "Demilitarization," 344. As Figueres explained in 1986, "For 35 years I fought against the Somoza dictatorship in Nicaragua because it was trying to extend its power south." Andrew Reding et al., "Voices from Costa Rica," *World Policy Journal* 3, no. 2 (Spring 1986), 318.

132. Mario Echandi, "Las Visitas a Somoza," *La Nación* (Costa Rica), June 4, 1971.

133. According to Honduran President Ramón Villeda Morales, he met four times with "six of the eleven rulers that El Salvador had" during his three years in office: José María Lemus on January 9, 1960; three members of the civil-military directorate on May 21, 1961; Rodolfo Cordón on July 24, 1962; and Julio Rivera on September 27, 1963. Ramón Villeda Morales, "Crisis Hondureño-Salvadoreña," in *Ramón Villeda Morales*, ed. Baciu, 185.

134. El Salvador, Ministerio de Relaciones Exteriores, *Informe Anual*, 1959–1960, 2–3.

135. See ibid., 12–18.

136. Ibid., 21–23.

137. The Salvadoran foreign ministry's *Informe* of 1966–1967 casts most of the blame on the Honduran side for troop incursions and foot-dragging on the creation of appropriate binational commissions; it also argues that the overthrow of Villeda set relations back. El Salvador, Ministerio de Relaciones Exteriores, *Informe Anual*, 1966–1967. At the same time, Ramón Villeda Morales argued that the coup that brought López Arellano to power "was made in the name of revindicating the international prestige of Honduras, but it is obvious from the current border troubles with El Salvador, where the Salvadorean Army came into Honduran territory, that El Salvador did not have any respect for the prestige of the Honduran government, or for the country." "Conversation with Ramón Villeda Morales in Tegucigalpa, Honduras, June 23, 1967," in Alexander, *Presidents*, 131.

138. "Conversation with Ramón Villeda Morales," in Alexander, *Presidents*, 131.

139. See Peter Katzenstein, *Small States in World Markets: Industrial Policy in Europe* (Ithaca, NY: Cornell University Press, 1985).

140. This does not mean that the transition from Eisenhower to Kennedy involved a 180-degree shift in Latin America policy: as I have argued elsewhere, the Alliance for Progress built on a foundation established at the 1960 Treaty of Bogotá. Christopher Darnton, "Asymmetry and Agenda-Setting in Inter-American Relations: Rethinking the Origins of the Alliance for Progress," *Journal of Cold War Studies* 14, no. 4 (Fall 2012): 120–143.

141. See, e.g., Miriam Fendius Elman, "The Foreign Policies of Small States: Challenging Neorealism in Its Own Backyard," *British Journal of Political Science* 25, no. 2 (Apr. 1995): 171–217.

142. See Wayne Smith, "Introduction: An Overview of Soviet Policy in Latin America," in *The Russians Aren't Coming: New Soviet Policy in Latin America*, ed. Wayne Smith (Boulder, CO: Lynne Rienner, 1992); Jürgen Buchenau, *In the Shadow of the Giant: The Making of Mexico's Central America Policy, 1876–1930* (Tuscaloosa: University of Alabama Press, 1996), 193–199.

143. See Jeffrey Taffet, *Foreign Aid as Foreign Policy: The Alliance for Progress in Latin America* (New York: Routledge, 2007).

144. Stephen Rabe, *The Most Dangerous Area in the World: John F. Kennedy Confronts Communist Revolution in Latin America* (Chapel Hill: University of North Carolina Press, 1999), Chapters 1 and 7.

145. These memorable (though here rather anachronistic) words come from Reagan's first secretary of state. Alexander Haig, *Caveat: Realism, Reagan, and Foreign Policy* (New York: Macmillan, 1984), 129.

146. Eisenhower's and Nixon's reactions to the botched invasion in 1961 indicate a preference for a more significant use of US force than Kennedy employed. Dwight Eisenhower, *The Eisenhower Diaries*, ed. Robert Ferrell (New York: Norton, 1981), 379–391; Dwight Eisenhower, *White House Years*, vol. 2: *Waging Peace, 1956–1961* (Garden City, NY: Doubleday, 1965), 613–614; Richard Nixon, *Six Crises* (Garden City, NY: Doubleday, 1962), 351–355; Richard Nixon, *RN: The Memoirs of Richard Nixon* (New York: Grosset and Dunlap, 1978), 232–235, 256.

147. "Conversation with Ramón Villeda Morales in Tegucigalpa, Honduras, September 9, 1959," in Alexander, *Presidents*, 129.

Chapter 5 · The 1980s Debt Crisis and Andean Rivalries

1. Note that Michael Colaresi, Karen Rasler, and William Thompson, *Strategic Rivalries in World Politics: Position, Space, and Conflict Escalation* (Cambridge: Cambridge University Press, 2007), date full rivalry termination at 1991. Epigraph citations, respectively, are to Chile, Ministerio de Relaciones Exteriores, *Memoria* (Henceforward, CMREM), 1983, 420, and Samuel Huntington, *The Third Wave: Democratization in the Late Twentieth Century* (Norman: University of Oklahoma Press, 1991), 247–248.

2. Minxin Pei and Ariel David Adesnik, "Why Recessions Don't Start Revolutions," *Foreign Policy* 118 (Spring 2000), 139.

3. Data from World Bank, World Development Indicators Online, www.worldbank .org/data.

4. Ibid.

5. Ibid. The World Bank does not provide Chile inflation data; I consulted data at www.inflation.eu/inflation-rates/chile/historic-inflation/cpi-inflation-chile.aspx, drawn from Chile's National Statistics Institute.

6. Ibid.

7. Huntington, *The Third Wave*. Democratization for peace arguments in the context of 1980s Latin America include Michael Barletta, "Argentine and Brazilian Nonproliferation: A Democratic Peace?," in *Twenty-First Century Weapons Proliferation: Are We Ready?*, ed. Henry Sokolski and James Ludes (Portland, OR: Frank Cass, 2001): 148–167; Arie Kacowicz, *Zones of Peace: South America and West Africa in Comparative Perspective* (Albany: State University of New York Press, 1998); Andrew Hurrell, "An Emerging Security Community in South America?" in *Security Communities*, ed. Emanuel Adler and Michael Barnett (New York: Cambridge University Press, 1998), 228–264.

8. Bolivia underwent a series of coups in this period. General Luís García Meza overthrew an interim civilian president in July 1980, General Celso Torrelio overthrew García Meza in August 1981, and General Guido Vildoso replaced him in July 1982 and in October turned power over to the newly elected Hernán Siles Suazo.

9. Ratios calculated from data in International Institute for Strategic Studies, *The Military Balance* (London: ISSS), volumes for 1981–1982 and 1987–1988. Two caveats are important. First, "bean counting" is generally a poor approximation of battlefield capacity. Second, as the IISS notes, inflation and fluctuation in exchange rates make the spending figures difficult to assess.

10. Alfred Stepan, *Rethinking Military Politics: Brazil and the Southern Cone* (Princeton: Princeton University Press, 1998).

11. The 1981–1982 defense spending ratio of nearly 36:1 in Venezuela's favor is surely misleading, perhaps driven by inflation or exchange rates; the 1987–1988 figure is 2.9:1 (see note 9).

12. Carlos Bustos, "Dos Siglos de Relaciones Chileno-Bolivianas," in *Nuestros Vecinos*, ed. Mario Artaza Rouxel and Paz Milet García (Santiago, Chile: RiL Editores, 2007), 220–222; John Martz, "National Security and Politics: The Colombian-Venezuelan Border," *Journal of Interamerican Studies and World Affairs* 30, no. 4 (Winter 1988–1989): 117–138; Mónica Herz and João Pontes Nogueira, *Ecuador vs. Peru: Peacemaking amid Rivalry* (Boulder, CO: Lynne Rienner, 2002), 36.

13. On Operation Condor, see Peter Kornbluh, *The Pinochet File: A Declassified Dossier on Atrocity and Accountability* (New York: The New Press, 2004); J. Patrice McSherry, *Predatory States: Operation Condor and Covert War in Latin America* (Lanham, MD: Rowman & Littlefield, 2005). Nilson Cezar Mariano, *Operación Cóndor: Terrorismo de Estado en el Cono Sur* (Buenos Aires: Lohlé-Lumen, 1998), 18, notes that rivalries failed to prevent Condor's emergence in the first place. However, Condor not only failed to resolve conflict between Chile and Argentina but was in fact undermined by it. See, e.g., John Dinges, *The Condor Years: How Pinochet and His Allies Brought Terrorism to Three Continents* (New York: W. W. Norton, 2004), 228. A similar situation unfolded in the other subregional security institution in Cold War Latin America: the Central American Defense Council (CONDECA) collapsed in 1969 when two members, El Salvador and Honduras, went to war against one another.

14. See, e.g., Bustos, "Dos Siglos," in *Nuestros Vecinos*, ed. Rouxel and Milet, 215–219.

15. Martz, "National Security," 121–122.

16. Ibid., 129.

17. Herz and Pontes Nogueira, *Ecuador vs. Peru*, 56; CMREM 1986.

18. Miguel Ángel Scenna, *Argentina-Chile: Una Frontera Caliente* (Buenos Aires: Editorial de Belgrano, 1981), is an excellent introduction.

19. Chilean President Sebastián Piñera in May 2010 stated his "concern" over an ongoing demarcation process, but both the Chilean and Argentine governments downplayed the significance of the comment and of the disagreement. "Minimizan el Diferendo con Chile por los Hielos," *La Nación* (Argentina), May 20, 2010, www.lanacion .com.ar/1266546-minimizan-el-diferendo-con-chile-por-los-hielos. See also Cristián Faundes Sánchez, "Reseña Histórica de los Conflictos por el Agua entre Chile y Argentina. Causas y Mecanismos de Resolución," in *Nuestros Vecinos*, ed. Rouxel and Milet, 108–109.

20. See Carolina Barros, Rosendo Fraga, and Eduardo Rodríguez Guarachi, eds., *Argentina-Chile: 100 Años de Encuentros Presidenciales* (Chile: Editorial Centro de Estudios Unión Para la Nueva Mayoría / Morgan International, 1999); Oscar Fuentes Lazo, "Chile y la Argentina: Una Relación Especial . . ." in *Nuestros Vecinos*, ed. Rouxel and Milet; Carlos Martínez Sotomayor, "El Marco del Acercamiento Politico entre Chile y Argentina," in *Chile y Argentina: Nuevos Enfoques para una Relación Constructiva*, ed. Francisco Orrego Vicuña and Pilar Armanet (Santiago, Chile: Pehuén, 1989), 12–14; Randall R. Parish Jr., "Democrats, Dictators, and Cooperation: The Transformation of

Argentine-Chilean Relations," *Latin American Politics and Society* 48, no. 1 (Spring 2006), 149–150.

21. Ramón Huidobro, "Las Alternativas de una Concertación Diplomática entre Chile y Argentina," in *Chile y Argentina*, ed. Orrego and Armanet, 18.

22. Andrés Cisneros and Carlos Escudé, *Historia General de las Relaciones Exteriores de la República Argentina*, vol. XIV (Buenos Aires: Grupo Editor Latinoamericano, 1998), www.argentina-rree.com/historia.htm, Chapter 68.

23. Thomas Princen, *Intermediary Intervention: A Model of Intervention and a Study of the Beagle Channel Case* (PhD diss., Harvard University, 1988), offers a detailed examination from the standpoint of negotiation theories.

24. CMREM 1980, 15–16; 1981, 11–12; 1982, 11–25; 1983, 12–27. Argentina also lodged at least one complaint against a Chilean warship.

25. CMREM 1981, 10; Augusto Pinochet Ugarte, *Camino Recorrido: Memorias de un Soldado*, book 3, vol. 1 (Santiago, Chile: Tall. Gráf. del Instituto Geográfico Militar de Chile, 1990–1994) 48, 52 [Henceforward cited as PCR *book:volume, page*].

26. CMREM 1982, 10; PCR 3:1, 87; Magnet, "Las Condicionantes," in *Chile y Argentina*, ed. Orrego and Armanet, 31–33.

27. CMREM 1982, 11, 584–585, 729–734.

28. CMREM 1983, 10.

29. CMREM 1981, 249; 1982, 26; 1983, 10. Unlike Chile, Argentina's 1981 *Memoria* does not even mention that the two foreign ministers met at the UN. The Chilean foreign ministry's 1982 *Memoria* was hard-pressed to note any achievements beyond "a broad and clear exchange of ideas" and "accord to maintain permanent consultations" and the "intention" of both sides to work on integration (CMREM 1982, 26).

30. PCR 3:1, 72.

31. PCR 3:1, 107–108.

32. As the Chilean foreign ministry's border division reported, "the favorable effects of the internal Argentine evolution" were "motivated as much by the results of the Malvinas conflict, as by the same process of political opening that brought about the installation of a new Government in that country"(CMREM 1983, 670).

33. Parish, "Democrats, Dictators," 151.

34. Raúl Alfonsín, *¿Qué Es el Radicalismo?* (Buenos Aires: Editorial Sudamericana, 1983), 245.

35. CMREM 1983, 11–12. These observations offer a partial correction to the argument in Parish, "Democrats, Dictators," 160, that the push for rapprochement came from President Alfonsín.

36. CMREM 1984, 23–29 (554–573 reproduces the treaty); Cisneros and Escudé, eds., *Historia General*, vol. XIV, Chapter 69. Pinochet's memoirs conflict with most of these dates: PCR 3:1, 176.

37. Guillermo Lagos Carmona, *La Delimitación Marítima Austral y el Tratado de Paz y Amistad entre Chile y Argentina* (Santiago, Chile: Editorial Jurídica de Chile, 1985), 32–36.

38. There was apparently one incident (on October 18, the day the accord was signed, although it hadn't been publicized yet) of an Argentine battery firing at a Chilean lighthouse, with rounds falling into the bay, but the two foreign ministries shut down any controversy swiftly and firmly, without recrimination (CMREM 1984, 27–29).

39. CMREM 1984, 137, 683, 789.

40. Huidobro, "Las Alternativas," 20, and Magnet, "Las Condicionantes," 36–37, both in *Chile y Argentina*, ed. Orrego and Armanet; Andrea Oelsner, *International Relations in Latin America: Peace and Security in the Southern Cone* (New York: Routledge, 2005); Claudio Fuentes and Carlos Martín, *La Nueva Agenda Argentino-Chilena* (Santiago, Chile: FLACSO-Chile, 1998).

41. Lagos Carmona, *La Delimitación Marítima*, 9; Francisco Orrego Vicuña, "Necesidad de una Política Chileno-Argentina: Una Introducción," in *Chile y Argentina*, ed. Orrego and Armanet, 7.

42. PCR 3:1, 232.

43. See, e.g., Charles Kupchan, *How Enemies Become Friends: The Sources of Stable Peace* (Princeton: Princeton University Press, 2010); Stephen Brooks, *Producing Security: Multinational Corporations, Globalization, and the Changing Calculus of Conflict* (Princeton: Princeton University Press, 2005), Chapter 5; Etel Solingen, *Regional Orders at Century's Dawn: Global and Domestic Influences on Grand Strategy* (Princeton: Princeton University Press, 1998), Chapter 5; and Kacowicz, *Zones of Peace*. In contrast, see Andrew Hurrell, "Security in Latin America," *International Affairs* 74, no. 3 (July 1998): 529–546.

44. By the same token, I would not expect a theory of rapprochement (including my own) to fully explain regional integration. For emphasis on 1984 as turning point in the relationship, see Raúl Bernal Meza, "Política Exterior Regional y las Relaciones con Argentina," in *Nuestros Vecinos*, ed. Rouxel and Milet, 25. On different IR theories better explaining different phases of improved relations, see Kupchan, *How Enemies*.

45. Such arguments include Parish, "Democrats, Dictators," 153–170; Oelsner, *International Relations*.

46. Scenna, *Argentina-Chile*, 319.

47. Martínez Sotomayor, "El Marco," in *Chile y Argentina*, ed. Orrego and Armanet, 11–15.

48. Raúl Alfonsín, in *Presidentes e o Mercosul: Reflexões Sobre a Integração*, ed. Fábio Magalhães (São Paulo, Brazil: Fundação Memorial da América Latina, 2002), 108.

49. See Parish, "Democrats, Dictators," 160–162, for an overview.

50. Reprinted in Lagos Carmona, *La Delimitación Marítima*, 95–97.

51. Cisneros and Escudé, *Historia General*.

52. Parish, "Democrats, Dictators."

53. Ibid., 161–162.

54. Ibid., 166–167.

55. CMREM 1981, 414.

56. PCR 3:1, 55.

57. Pamela Constable and Arturo Valenzuela, *A Nation of Enemies: Chile under Pinochet* (New York: W. W. Norton, 1991), 194–195; PCR 3:1, 83.

58. Simon Collier and William Sater, *A History of Chile, 1808–1994* (New York: Cambridge University Press, 1996), 370–372.

59. CMREM 1982, 481.

60. PCR 3:1, 106–107. Literally, Pinochet refers to the economy as *"encabritada,"* a word used to describe a bucking horse.

61. PCR 3:1, 179.

62. CMREM 1986, 71.

63. Alan Angell, "Chile since 1958," in *Chile since Independence*, ed. Leslie Bethell (Cambridge: Cambridge University Press, 1993), 193, characterizes Chile's recovery as "steady and sustained"; such comments are rarely applied to Argentina's economic performance.

64. Mark Ensalaco, *Chile under Pinochet: Recovering the Truth* (Philadelphia: University of Pennsylvania Press, 2000), 135; PCR 3:1, 32–36.

65. Kornbluh, *The Pinochet File*, 423–425; Collier and Sater, *A History of Chile*, 376–377; PCR 3:1, 117, 141–159. Carlos Huneeus, *The Pinochet Regime*, trans. Lake Sagaris (Boulder, CO: Lynne Rienner, 2007), Chapter 10, provides an excellent discussion of the political fallout from the economic crisis.

66. CMREM 1981, 231–235, 314–315, 387–393, 434–435; 1982, 432–444.

67. Magnet, "Las Condicionantes," in *Chile y Argentina*, ed. Orrego and Armanet, 28–29.

68. *Las Relaciones Argentino-Chilenas: Política Economica, Exterior y de Defensa: La Influencia de los Grupos de Presión, desde el Tratado de Paz y Amistad de 1984*, ed. Jorge Lavopa et al. (Buenos Aires: Consejo Argentino para las Relaciones Internacionales, 1995), 29–30.

69. Mario Rapoport, *Historia Económica, Política y Social de la Argentina, 1880–2003* (Buenos Aires: Grupo Editorial Planeta / Ariel, 2006), 733; Jorge Luis Romero, *A History of Argentina in the Twentieth Century*, trans. James Brennan (University Park: The Pennsylvania State University Press, 2004), 254–257.

70. Alfonsín, *¿Qué Es el Radicalismo?*, 238.

71. CMREM 1984, 138–144.

72. Ibid., 26.

73. Heraldo Muñoz, "Chile's External Relations under the Military Government," in *Military Rule in Chile*, ed. J. Samuel Valenzuela and Arturo Valenzuela (Baltimore: Johns Hopkins University Press, 1986), 310.

74. Constable and Valenzuela, *A Nation of Enemies*, 49; Huneeus, *The Pinochet Regime*, 112.

75. Angell, "Chile since 1958," in *Chile since Independence*, ed. Bethell, 179–192; Constable and Valenzuela, *A Nation of Enemies*, 59–60.

76. Constable and Valenzuela, *A Nation of Enemies*, 60.

77. Ibid., 46–47: Chile's transition unfolded "gradually" across the Cold War from the early 1950s.

78. Angell, "Chile since 1958," in *Chile since Independence*, ed. Bethell, 178; Constable and Valenzuela, *A Nation of Enemies*, 36–37; Huneeus, *The Pinochet Regime*, 43.

79. Data for figure 5.3 come from Pinochet's own memoirs (PCR), which, remarkably, contain statistical and qualitative appendices discussing the Communist and insurgent threat in Chile, year by year. However, some of the categories reported shift over time; the two series shown in this chart allow me to cover simply the whole period Pinochet reported, but they should not necessarily be interpreted as splicing into one series. Quotations from PCR 3:1, 133.

80. Huneeus, *The Pinochet Regime*, 78–80.

81. Alfonsín, *¿Qué Es el Radicalismo?*, 215. Nor, 223, was there a direct tradeoff between international and domestic threats: Illia sought to defuse nascent guerrilla groups, while the armed forces under Onganía wanted a frontal assault.

82. Argentine army officers staged a rebellion in 1987 and two others in 1988, despite popular opposition to their demands; although the post-Malvinas military held no interest in governing, the military as an institution continued to demand and exercise political power in policy areas directly affecting its core interests (Romero, *A History*, 261–265, 279–280). Additionally, Alfonsín was surely cognizant that an institutional reluctance to govern on the part of the military failed to prevent most of Argentina's coups—the armed forces usually would replace the sitting president with another civilian. In this respect, the 1966 and 1976 coups were aberrant, with the military seeing no alternative but to hold on to power.

83. Romero, *A History*, 261.

84. Raúl Alfonsín, *Alfonsín Responde* (Buenos Aires: Tiempo de Ideas, Grupo Editor, 1992), 26.

85. Dante Caputo, "Fundaciones sin Crítica (Notas para un Debate Elemental)," in *La Política Exterior Argentina en el Nuevo Orden Mundial*, ed. Roberto Russell (Buenos Aires: FLACSO / Grupo Editor Latinoamericano, 1992).

86. On the high level of Argentine military prerogatives after the transition, see Stepan, *Rethinking Military Politics*.

87. CMREM 1981, 247.

88. CMREM 1981, 416–417. According to Chile's one-paragraph summary of the Argentine position at the OAS, Argentine Foreign Minister Camilión echoed many of these points, linking the threat of terrorism to a call for regional cooperation.

89. See the account of the lead Chilean negotiator on the navy's recalcitrance after the Treaty was signed and before Argentina ratified it: Ernesto Videla Cifuentes, *La Desconocida Historia de la Mediación Papal: Diferendo Austral Chile-Argentina, 1977–1985* (Santiago, Chile: Universidad Católica de Chile, 2007), 640–652.

90. PCR 2, 164–166.

91. On the Beagle escalation in 1978 and the Argentine Navy's role, see María Seoane and Vicente Muleiro, *El Dictador: La Historia Secreta y Pública de Jorge Rafael Videla*, 3rd ed. (Buenos Aires: Editorial Sudamericana, 2001), 356–392; Videla Cifuentes, *La Desconocida Historia*, 140–227.

92. The first of these, Admiral Guzzetti, was seriously injured in an assassination attempt by guerrillas.

93. Seoane and Muleiro, *El Dictador*, 390.

94. In particular, see Horacio Verbitsky, *El Vuelo: "Una Forma Cristiana de Muerte": Confesiones de un Oficial de la Armada* (Buenos Aires: Editorial Sudamericana, 2004). Also, one of the two Argentine perpetrators profiled in McSherry, *Predatory States*, is a naval officer.

95. Wolfgang Heinz and Hugo Frühling, *Determinants of Gross Human Rights Violations by State and State-Sponsored Actors in Brazil, Uruguay, Chile, and Argentina, 1960–1990* (Boston: M. Nijhoff, 1999).

96. Seoane and Muleiro, *El Dictador*, 366–367. Nor can this be satisfactorily explained with reference to personal ideology, such as that Videla was a reactionary extremist favoring repressive violence while Massera was a moderate—notably, Massera seemed as staunch a supporter of repression as anyone in the junta in its early days, while Videla appears far less "hawkish" on internal security than some other top army generals such as Suárez Masón. While Massera made a point of coming up with omi-

nous *noms de guerre* for himself, Videla scrupulously avoided visiting torture facilities or adopting a nocturnal schedule, preferring to delegate such tasks, leading Massera to dismiss him as a mere "theoretician of dirty war" (Seoane and Muleiro, *El Dictador*, 239–241).

97. I in no way dismiss the repression as a "game." My point is that interservice rivalries and factional power struggles can be usefully analyzed this way irrespective of the content of those groups' policy portfolios and power bases.

98. Magnet, "Las Condicionantes," in *Chile y Argentina*, ed. Orrego and Armanet, 31–32.

99. See Cisneros and Escudé, *Historia General*, vol. XIV.

100. Raúl Alfonsín, *Ahora, Mi Propuesta Política* (Buenos Aires: Editorial Sudamericana/Planeta, 1983), 69.

101. PCR 3:1, 175.

102. Pilar Armanet, "La Política de Seguridad en Chile y Argentina desde una Perspectiva Militar," in *Chile y Argentina*, ed. Orrego and Armanet, 40–43; PCR 3:1, 20, 233–235.

103. PCR 3:1, 180.

104. Ana Margheritis, *Argentina's Foreign Policy: Domestic Politics and Democracy Promotion in the Americas* (Boulder, CO: Lynne Rienner / FirstForum Press, 2010).

105. CMREM 1983, 425–432.

106. Collier and Sater, *A History of Chile*, 364.

107. Barletta, "Argentine and Brazilian Nonproliferation" in *Twenty-First Century Weapons Proliferation*, ed. Sokolski and Ludes.

108. Mark Falcoff, *A Tale of Two Policies: US Relations with the Argentine Junta, 1976–1983* (Philadelphia: Foreign Policy Research Institute, 1989), 28–30.

109. See Riordan Roett, "The Debt Crisis and Economic Development," in *United States Policy in Latin America: A Decade of Crisis and Challenge*, ed. John Martz (Lincoln: University of Nebraska Press, 1995), 249–258.

110. On subregional focus, see Ronald Reagan, *An American Life* (New York: Simon and Schuster, 1990), 238–239, 474–487; Alexander Haig, *Caveat: Realism, Reagan, and Foreign Policy* (New York: Macmillan, 1984), 130–131; George Shultz, *Turmoil and Triumph: My Years as Secretary of State* (New York: Charles Scribner's Sons, 1993), Chapters 19 and 23.

111. Ronald Reagan, "Remarks on the Caribbean Basin Initiative to the Permanent Council of the Organization of American States," February 24, 1982, online by Gerhard Peters and John T. Woolley, *The American Presidency Project*, www.presidency.ucsb.edu /ws/?pid=42202.

Chapter 6 · *From the Cold War to the Global War on Terrorism*

1. Yuen Foong Khong, *Analogies at War: Korea, Munich, Dien Bien Phu, and the Vietnam Decisions of 1965* (Princeton: Princeton University Press, 1992), esp. 245–250. Epigraph citations, respectively, are to White House, *The National Security Strategy of the United States of America 2006* (March 2006), www.whitehouse.gov/nsc/nss/2006/, 1, and Kathryn Sikkink, *Mixed Signals: US Human Rights Policy and Latin America* (Ithaca, NY: Cornell University Press, 2004), xix.

2. Thus, Ellen Schrecker, "Introduction: Cold War Triumphalism and the Real Cold War," in *Cold War Triumphalism: The Misuse of History after the Fall of Communism*, ed.

Ellen Schrecker (New York: The New Press, 2004), 9, contrasts the public attractiveness of Cold War analogies with those of the Korean War.

3. See Richard Neustadt and Ernest May, *Thinking in Time: The Uses of History for Decision Makers* (New York: The Free Press, 1986), 5–8, 43, 88, 235; Robert Jervis, *Perception and Misperception in International Politics* (Princeton: Princeton University Press, 1976), 269, 280; Alexander George, *Bridging the Gap: Theory and Practice in Foreign Policy* (Washington, DC: United States Institute of Peace Press, 1993), 13.

4. Walter Russell Mead, *Power, Terror, Peace, and War: America's Grand Strategy in a World at Risk* (New York: Knopf, 2004), 111–112, 171, 181, 189–190. The parallels have limitations, though: for example, Mead, *Power,* 171, like the 2006 Quadrennial Defense Review (United States Department of Defense, *Quadrennial Defense Review 2006* [February 2006], www.defenselink.mil/qdr/report/Report20060203.pdf), 32, argues that deterrence will operate differently in the two conflicts.

5. See, respectively, *A Nation at War: Seventeenth Annual Strategy Conference, April 11–13, 2006,* ed. Colonel (Retired) John R. Martin (Carlisle Barracks, PA: US Army War College, January 2007), 2–3; White House, *National Strategy for Combating Terrorism 2006* (September 2006), www.whitehouse.gov/nsc/nsct/2006/nsct2006.pdf, accessed April 20, 2008, 19; *Quadrennial Defense Review 2006,* 21–22.

6. *National Security Strategy 2006,* 1.

7. Final Remarks for Deputy Secretary of Defense Gordon England, Center for Strategic and International Studies, February 1, 2006, St. Regis Hotel, Washington, DC, www.defenselink.mil/qdr/report/FinalCSIS.pdf, accessed July 10, 2008.

8. Paul Williams, "Security Studies, 9/11 and the Long War," in *Security and the War on Terror,* ed. Alex Bellamy (New York: Routledge, 2008), 13; Marilyn Young, "Still Stuck in the Big Muddy," in *Cold War Triumphalism,* ed. Shrecker, 271.

9. Richard Falk, *The Great Terror War* (New York: Olive Branch Press, 2003), xxvi, 4, 112, 114.

10. See Harlan Ullman, *Finishing Business: Ten Steps to Defeat Global Terror* (Annapolis, MD: Naval Institute Press, 2004), xix, 69, 83, 176; see also Robert Pape, *Dying to Win: The Strategic Logic of Suicide Terrorism* (New York: Random House, 2005), 280 n. 2. Examples include Richard Russell, "Saudi Arabia's Conundrum and the al Qaeda Insurgency," in *The Ideological War on Terror: Worldwide Strategies for Counter-Terrorism,* ed. Anne Aldis and Graeme Herd (New York: Routledge, 2007), 37; Young, "Still Stuck," in *Cold War Triumphalism,* ed. Schrecker, 273; Ian Shapiro, *Containment: Rebuilding a Strategy against Global Terror* (Princeton: Princeton University Press, 2007), 15.

11. On jihadi extremism, see Ullman, *Finishing Business,* xi; on islamofascism, White House, "President Discusses War on Terror at National Endowment for Democracy," October 6, 2005, www.whitehouse.gov/news/releases/2005/10/20051006-3.html; Christopher Hitchens, "Defending *Islamofascism:* It's a Valid Term. Here's Why," *Slate,* October 22, 2007, www.slate.com/id/2176389, accessed January 13, 2009; Mead, *Power,* 175–177; on Islamic radicalism, see *National Security Strategy 2006,* 36.

12. Jason Burke, *Al-Qaeda: The True Story of Radical Islam* (New York: I. B. Tauris, 2004), Chapter 1; Peter Bergen, *Holy War, Inc.: Inside the Secret World of Osama bin Laden* (New York: The Free Press, 2001), Chapter 10; Gilles Kepel, *The War for Muslim Minds:*

Islam and the West (Cambridge, MA: Harvard University Press, 2004), Chapter 4; Marc Sageman, *Leaderless Jihad: Terror Networks in the Twenty-First Century* (Philadelphia: University of Pennsylvania Press, 2008), 28–31, 71–88, 144. Formally, the June 2001 merger of Zawahiri's group with bin Laden's produced a joint organization named Qaedat al-Jihad, which perpetrated the September 11 attacks (Stephane Lacroix, "Introduction: Ayman al-Zawahiri, Veteran of Jihad," in *Al Qaeda in Its Own Words*, ed. Gilles Kepel and Jean-Pierre Milelli, trans. Pascale Ghazale [Cambridge, MA: Harvard University Press, 2008], 160). In this chapter, I use "al-Qaeda" as shorthand.

13. See Pape, *Dying to Win*, 15, 21–22.

14. Anonymous, *Through Our Enemies' Eyes: Osama bin Laden, Radical Islam, and the Future of America* (Washington, DC: Potomac Books / Brassey's, 2002), 207. On al-Qaeda as insurgency, see Russell, "Saudi Arabia's Conundrum," in *The Ideological War*, ed. Aldis and Herd, 38; Daniel Byman, "Measuring the War on Terrorism: A First Appraisal," *Current History* 102, no. 668 (December 2003): 412; David Kilcullen, "Countering Global Insurgency: A Strategy for the War on Terrorism," *Journal of Strategic Studies* 28, no. 4 (August 2005): 603–604; Robert Cassidy, *Counterinsurgency and the Global War on Terror: Military Culture and Irregular War* (Westport, CT: Praeger, 2006), 1–11.

15. See Ullman, *Finishing Business*, xiv; Paul Pillar, *Terrorism and US Foreign Policy* (Washington, DC: Brookings Institution Press, 2001), 55–56; Shapiro, *Containment*, 6, 60–61, 78–90.

16. Kilcullen, "Countering," 604; Bruce Hoffman, "A Counterterrorism Strategy for the Obama Administration," *Terrorism and Political Violence* 21, no. 3 (2009): 363.

17. See Vladimir Lenin, "What Is To Be Done?" in *The Lenin Anthology*, ed. Robert C. Tucker (New York: W. W. Norton, 1975), especially 24, 52–54, 63, 75–77.

18. Che Guevara, *Guerrilla Warfare*, with an Introduction and Case Studies by Brian Loveman and Thomas M. Davies Jr. (Lincoln: University of Nebraska Press, 1985), 50.

19. Burke, *Al-Qaeda*, 293 n. 3, suggests on the basis of an interview with a "Saudi intelligence source" that bin Laden initially set up, in 1988, a *database* ("base" serving as the root in both English and Arabic) of militants traveling through safe houses to Afghanistan to fight the Soviets. Lawrence Wright, *The Looming Tower: Al-Qaeda and the Road to 9/11* (New York: Alfred A. Knopf, 2006), 130, makes the vanguard point explicitly: "Azzam himself was in favor of forming a 'pioneering vanguard' along the lines called for by Sayyid Qutb. 'This vanguard constitutes the solid base'—*qaeda*—'for the hoped-for society,' Azzam wrote in April 1988."

20. *Al Qaeda in Its Own Words*, ed. Kepel and Milelli, 314–315.

21. See text in *Al Qaeda in Its Own Words*, ed. Kepel and Milelli, 140–141 (see also 101); see also Burke, *Al-Qaeda*, 2.

22. Bergen, *Holy War*, 201; quotation from text in *Al Qaeda in Its Own Words*, ed. Kepel and Milelli, 196, 200–201.

23. See text in *Al Qaeda in Its Own Words*, ed. Kepel and Milelli, 74.

24. See text in Brynjar Lia, *Architect of Global Jihad: The Life of Al-Qaida Strategist Abu Mus'ab al-Suri* (New York: Columbia University Press, 2008), 350–373, 476. Like Ayman al-Zawahiri, al-Suri had belonged to a "vanguard" organization (the Combatant Vanguard of the Muslim Brotherhood, a Syrian insurgent group) (Lia, *Architect*,

35–40). Similarly, see Lenin, "What Is To Be Done?" in *The Lenin Anthology*, ed. Tucker, 107.

25. See Daniel Byman, "Going to War with the Allies You Have: Allies, Counterinsurgency, and the War on Terrorism," (Carlisle, PA: US Army War College Strategic Studies Institute, November 2005), 6–7; Andrew Tian Huat Tan, *US Strategy against Global Terrorism: How It Evolved, Why It Failed, and Where It is Headed* (New York: Palgrave Macmillan, 2009), 160–164; Kilcullen, "Countering," 609.

26. See, e.g., Cole Blasier, *The Hovering Giant: US Responses to Revolutionary Change in Latin America and the Caribbean, 1910–1985*, rev. ed. (Pittsburgh: University of Pittsburgh Press, 1985), 300–304; Schrecker, "Introduction," in *Cold War Triumphalism*, ed. Shrecker, 8.

27. Sageman, *Leaderless Jihad*, 149–151; see also Shapiro, *Containment*, 6; Ullman, *Finishing Business*, 6, 85–89, 176.

28. Shapiro, *Containment*, xv, 34, 42–45, 290–291.

29. Shapiro, *Containment*, 8, 59.

30. Hoffman, "A Counterterrorism Strategy," 369; see also Tan, *US Strategy*. Further recommendations of counterinsurgency for US strategy towards al-Qaeda include Daniel Byman, "Al-Qaeda as an Adversary: Do We Understand Our Enemy?" *World Politics* 56, no. 1 (2003): 160; Kilcullen, "Countering," 606; Cassidy, *Counterinsurgency*, 2.

31. Ullman, *Finishing Business*, 89; see also Pillar, *Terrorism*, 56.

32. See Pillar, *Terrorism*, 68–69, 186; John Gearson, "The Nature of Modern Terrorism," in *Superterrorism: Policy Responses*, ed. Lawrence Freedman (Malden, MA: Blackwell Publishing/The Political Quarterly, 2002), 23. On multilateral issues in counterterrorism, see Nora Bensahel, "A Coalition of Coalitions: International Cooperation against Terrorism," *Studies in Conflict and Terrorism* 29, no. 1 (January–February 2006): 35–49.

33. Pillar, *Terrorism*, 118–119.

34. See Shapiro, *Containment*, 94.

35. Cassidy, *Counterinsurgency*, 127.

36. Nora Bensahel, *The Counterterror Coalitions: Cooperation with Europe, NATO, and the European Union* (Santa Monica, CA: RAND, 2003), 7, 17.

37. Ullman, *Finishing Business*, 107, 112 [sic].

38. On the limited institutionalization of US counterterrorism coalitions and the emphasis on bilateral partnerships, see Daniel Byman, "Remaking Alliances for the War on Terrorism," *Journal of Strategic Studies* 29, no. 5 (October 2006): 798–801; Bensahel, *The Counterterror Coalitions*, 22–24, 45, 52–54; Marilyn Young, "Still Stuck in the Big Muddy," *Cold War Triumphalism*, ed. Schrecker, 272.

39. Shapiro, *Containment*, 7, 87–88.

40. *National Strategy for Combating Terrorism 2006*.

41. Ibid., 19.

42. Ibid., 20.

43. Ibid., 21.

44. White House, *National Security Strategy 2010* (May 2010), www.whitehouse.gov/sites/default/files/rss_viewer/national_security_strategy.pdf, accessed February 20, 2012.

45. Ibid., p. 20.

46. US Department of Defense, *Quadrennial Defense Review Report 2010* (February 2010), www.defense.gov/qdr/images/QDR_as_of_12Feb10_1000.pdf, accessed February 20, 2012, iii, vi, x–xi.

47. White House, *National Strategy for Counterterrorism 2011*, www.whitehouse.gov /sites/default/files/counterterrorism_strategy.pdf, accessed February 20, 2012.

48. Byman, "Remaking Alliances," 768; Clyde Prestowitz, *Rogue Nation: American Unilateralism and the Failure of Good Intentions* (New York: Basic Books, 2003), 10, 253; Nadia Alexandrova Arbatova, "Russian-Western Relations after 11 September: Selective Cooperation versus Partnership (a Russian View)" in *Superterrorism*, ed. Freedman, 157.

49. Sageman, *Leaderless Jihad*, 126.

50. Ibid., 138.

51. See Kepel, *The War for Muslim Minds*, Chapter 3.

52. Kilcullen, "Countering," 599 (diagram included).

53. Richard A. Clarke et al., *Defeating the Jihadists: A Blueprint for Action* (Washington, DC: The Century Foundation Press, 2005), 16–18. Kilcullen, "Countering," 604–606, contrasts terrorism and insurgency.

54. Byman, "Going to War with the Allies You Have," 16.

55. Bensahel, "A Coalition of Coalitions."

56. See the text of *The Global Islamic Resistance Call* in Lia, *Architect*, 380.

57. Ibid., 378–380.

58. For this list, see Anonymous, *Through Our Enemies' Eyes*, 206–211.

59. See White House, "Fact Sheet: Combating Terrorism Worldwide. What the United States and Its Partners Are Doing to Fight Al Qaeda and Other Terrorists," August 6, 2007, www.whitehouse.gov/news/releases/2007/08/20070806-1.html; Eric Schmitt, "US Training in Africa Aims to Deter Extremists," *New York Times*, December 13, 2008, A1; David Sanger, "Revamping Pakistan Aid Expected in Report," *New York Times*, December 7, 2008, A28.

60. List of rivalries as of 1999 (most recent year available) from Colaresi et al., *Strategic Rivalries*, 38–50; data on religious affiliation from CIA *World Factbook* online, www .cia.gov/library/publications/the-world-factbook/fields/2122.html, accessed in 2008; list of rebellions as of 1999 from Heidelberg Institute on International Conflict Research, *Heidelberg Konfliktbarometer 2000*, www.hiik.de/de/konfliktbarometer/pdf/Konfliktbarometer_2000.pdf.

61. See Steven Cook, *Ruling but not Governing: The Military and Political Development in Egypt, Algeria, and Turkey* (Baltimore: Johns Hopkins University Press, 2007), 12; Ronnie Lal, "The Maghreb," in Angel Rabasa, Cheryl Benard, Peter Chalk, C. Christine Fair, Theodore Karasik, Rollie Lal, Ian Lesser, and David Thaler, *The Muslim World after 9/11* (Santa Monica, CA: RAND Corporation, 2004), 148–151, 161.

62. Peter St John, "Independent Algeria from Ben Bella to Boumédienne: II. Foreign Policy," *The World Today* 24, no. 8 (August 1968): 340.

63. I. William Zartman, "Foreign Relations of North Africa," *Annals of the American Academy of Political and Social Science* 489, International Affairs in Africa (January 1987): 18.

64. Zartman, "Foreign Relations," 15; Mary-Jane Deeb, "Inter-Maghribi Relations since 1969: A Study of the Modalities of Unions and Mergers," *Middle East Journal* 43, no. 1 (Winter 1989): 22; also John Damis, "The Western Sahara Conflict: Myths and Realities," *Middle East Journal* 37, no. 2 (Spring 1983): 170.

65. Robert A. Mortimer, "Maghreb Matters," *Foreign Policy* 76 (Fall 1989): 163; Zartman, "Foreign Relations," 21.

66. Zartman, "Foreign Relations," 21.

67. Zartman, "Foreign Relations," 21.

68. Damis, "The Western Sahara," 176.

69. See, e.g., Damis, "The Western Sahara," 170, 179.

70. Mortimer, "Maghreb Matters," 163–168.

71. Deeb, "Inter-Maghribi," 32–33; Mortimer, "Maghreb Matters," 168; Paul Balta, "French Policy in North Africa," *Middle East Journal* 40, no. 2 (Spring 1986): 244.

72. "U.N. Chief in Algeria to Discuss Western Sahara," The Associated Press, May 26, 1991.

73. "Chadli, Hounded by Islamic Fundamentalists, Prepares for Sahara Talks," *Agence France Presse—English*, May 27, 1991.

74. Ibid.

75. In the first round, the FIS won 188 out of the 430 seats outright, to the ruling FLN party's 15 seats and a socialist party's 25; the remaining 199 of 430 seats required a run-off, which easily would have given the ISF a parliamentary majority. See Ruth Marshall and Scott Sullivan, "In Algeria, 'The Victory of God,'" *Newsweek*, January 13, 1992.

76. Boudiaf had lived in exile in Morocco since 1964, referred to it as his "second homeland," and appeared vaguely optimistic about possible rapprochement, but there is no indication that he took steps to achieve it or that the relationship with Morocco motivated his assassination. See "Algeria Boudiaf Statements Prior to Arrival; Mission to Calm Situation," BBC Summary of World Broadcasts, January 18, 1992; Youssef Ibrahim, "Algerians, Angry with the Past, Divide over Their Future," *The New York Times*, January 19, 1992; "Algeria Interview with Boudiaf on His Role and That of Higher State Council," BBC Summary of World Broadcasts, February 6, 1992; "Boudiaf Comments to Moroccan Paper on Algerian Political Situation; Other Issues," BBC Summary of World Broadcasts, February 26, 1992; Youssef Ibrahim, "Hope, Too, Is Gunned Down in Algeria," *The New York Times,* July 5, 1992.

77. Marc Sageman, *Understanding Terror Networks* (Philadelphia: University of Pennsylvania Press, 2004), 61–73.

78. Hon. Tom Lantos, in US House of Representatives, Committee on Foreign Affairs, 110th Congress, Hearing, "US Policy Challenges in North Africa," June 6, 2007, transcript downloaded from www.foreignaffairs.house.gov, 10; Sageman, *Leaderless Jihad*, 129–130.

79. Susan Slymovics, *The Performance of Human Rights in Morocco* (Philadelphia: The University of Pennsylvania Press, 2005), 193.

80. Angel Rabasa, Peter Chalk, Kim Cragin, Sara Daly, Heather Gregg, Theodore Karasik, Kevin O'Brien, and William Rosenau, *Beyond al-Qaeda, Part I: The Global Jihadist Movement* (Santa Monica, CA: RAND, 2006), 119–124; Lal, "The Maghreb," in Rabasa et al., *The Muslim World*, 171–173.

81. Paul Schemm, "Morocco's Problem: Freelance Jihadis, Not al-Qaida," *The Associated Press*, October 16, 2011; "Morocco Says It Smashed Al-Qaeda–Linked Cell," *Agence France Presse—English*, September 23, 2011.

82. Some terrorism analysts take this threat particularly seriously, however. See, e.g., Yonah Alexander, "Special Update Report: Terrorism in North, West, & Central Africa: From 9/11 to the Arab Spring," Potomac Institute for Policy Studies, International Center for Terrorism Studies, January 2012, via http://moroccoonthemove.files.wordpress.com/2012/02/2012-special-update-report-full-report-terrorism-in-africa-from-9-11-to-arab-spring-icts-potomac-2feb2012.pdf.

83. C. David Welch, in US House of Representatives, "US Policy Challenges in North Africa," June 6, 2007.

84. Kingdom of Morocco, in ibid., 22.

85. Hon. Tom Lantos, in ibid., 10.

86. Cook, *Ruling but not Governing*, 22–24, 47.

87. Ibid., 60–61.

88. David Sorensen, "Civil-Military Relations in North Africa," *Middle East Policy* 14, no. 4 (Winter 2007): 105–106.

89. The term originally referred to a storehouse or sultan's treasury but now refers to the monarch's coterie of powerful advisors, relatives, and security agencies. See Marvine Howe, *Morocco: The Islamist Awakening and Other Challenges* (New York: Oxford University Press, 2005), 355; Neil MacFarquhar, "In Morocco, a Rights Movement, at the King's Pace," *New York Times*, Late Edition, October 1, 2005, A3, 1.

90. Sorensen, "Civil-Military Relations," 108–109; MacFarquhar, "In Morocco."

91. Damis, "The Western Sahara," 174.

92. Calculated from data from World Bank World Development Indicators Online, accessed March 12, 2012.

93. Data from ibid.

94. African Development Bank, *African Economic Outlook*, "Country Notes: Algeria 2011," www.africaneconomicoutlook.org/fileadmin/uploads/aeo/Country_Notes/2011/Full/Algeria.pdf, accessed in 2012; African Development Bank, *African Economic Outlook*, "Country Notes: Morocco 2011," www.africaneconomicoutlook.org/fileadmin/uploads/aeo/Country_Notes/2011/Full/Morocco.pdf, accessed in 2012; Souad Mekhennet et al., "A Threat Renewed," *New York Times*, July 1, 2008; Howe, *Morocco*.

95. "Moroccan Monarch Has Unusual Two-Hour Meeting with Algerian President," *Associated Press Worldstream*, March 24, 2005.

96. "Moroccan and Algerian Leaders to Hold Rare Talks at Arab Summit," *Associated Press Worldstream*, March 21, 2005.

97. Translated quotes appeared in "Morocco's King Wants Closer Anti-Terror Ties with Algeria," *Agence France Presse—English*, July 13, 2007.

98. Richard Cochrane, "Algeria and Morocco Discuss Strengthening Ties," *Global Insight*, November 21, 2011.

99. "Moroccan King Calls for Improved Ties with Algeria," *Agence France Presse—English*, July 5, 2010.

100. "Algerian Leader: Morocco Is Our Brother, not Enemy," *Associated Press Online*, April 17, 2011.

101. Cochrane, "Algeria and Morocco Discuss Strengthening Ties."

102. "Morocco Calls for Negotiations with Algeria over Western Sahara," BBC Summary of World Broadcasts, August 1, 2003.

103. "Algeria Foreign Minister: 'No crisis with Morocco,'" *Al-Bawaba Reporters,* via Comtex News Network, Inc., October 26, 2004.

104. Gala Riani, "Morocco Wants to Normalise Ties with Algeria, Says Foreign Minister," *Global Insight,* April 21, 2009; "Foreign Minister Accuses Algeria of Trying to Harm Morocco's Integrity," BBC Monitoring Middle East—Political, December 2, 2009. Fassi Fihri continued these arguments in 2010, accusing Algeria of following an "obstruction strategy . . . against the negotiation process" in Western Sahara, explaining that Morocco had sent a letter to UN Secretary General Ban Ki-Moon to that effect. "Morocco accuses Algeria of blocking W. Sahara talks," *Agence France Presse—English,* January 28, 2010.

105. "Algeria Denies Obstructing Resolution of Western Sahara Issue," BBC Monitoring Middle East—Political, April 27, 2010.

106. "Algeria-Morocco," *The Middle East Reporter (MER),* May 30, 2011; Jamie Ingram, "Moroccan Government Criticises Algeria's Comments over Border Dispute," *Global Insight,* June 2, 2011.

107. Ingram, "Moroccan Government Criticises."

108. Cochrane, "Algeria and Morocco Discuss Strengthening Ties."

109. "Morocco's Foreign Minister on Fence-Mending Trip to Algeria," *Agence France Presse—English,* January 20, 2012.

110. "Algeria Agrees to Briefly Reopen Border," *UPI,* January 16, 2012.

111. http://english.al-akhbar.com/node/4370, accessed February 23, 2012.

112. "Morocco, Algeria Agree to Set Up Political Consultation Mechanism," *MAP,* Rabat, February 18, 2012, via http://moroccoworldnews.com/2012/02/morocco-algeria -agree-to-set-up-political-consultation-mechanism/27856, accessed February 23, 2012.

113. Javier Pérez de Cuellar's proposal for an eventual referendum was accepted by all parties in 1988 and the Security Council created the MINURSO mission in April 1991.

114. On the Baker mission, see Anna Theofilopoulou, "The United Nations and Western Sahara: A Never-Ending Affair," United States Institute of Peace Special Report No. 166, July 2006; also www.pbs.org/wnet/wideangle/episodes/sahara-marathon/interview -james-a-baker-iii/873/.

115. United Nations Security Council, "Report of the Secretary-General on the Situation Concerning Western Sahara, April 13, 2009," S/2009/200, via www.independent diplomat.org/documents/unws, accessed February 23, 2012.

Chapter 7 · *The Organizational Politics of Conflict Resolution*

1. I do not claim that this is the only path to rapprochement (see chapters one and two). Epigraph citations, respectively, are to Joseph Schumpeter, *Capitalism, Socialism, and Democracy,* 3rd ed. (New York: Harper & Brothers, 1950), 245, and Max Weber, "Politics as a Vocation," in *From Max Weber: Essays in Sociology,* ed. H. H. Gerth and C. Wright Mills (New York: Oxford University Press, 1949 [1946]), 80.

2. See Jorge Domínguez, "International Cooperation in Latin America: The Design of Regional Institutions by Slow Accretion," in *Crafting Cooperation: Regional Interna-*

tional Institutions in Comparative Perspective, ed. Amitav Acharya and Alastair Iain Johnston (New York: Cambridge University Press, 2007), 97–99.

3. See John M. Hobson, *The State and International Relations* (New York: Cambridge University Press, 2000); Graham Allison, *Essence of Decision: Explaining the Cuban Missile Crisis* (Boston: Little, Brown, and Company, 1971); Peter Trubowitz, *Defining the National Interest: Conflict and Change in American Foreign Policy* (Chicago: University of Chicago Press, 1998).

4. For example, international relations scholars might profitably engage the "state in society" framework developed by comparativists (see *State Power and Social Forces: Domination and Transformation in the Third World*, ed. Joel Migdal, Atul Kohli, and Vivienne Shue [New York: Cambridge University Press, 1994]) as well as building on the disaggregational efforts of Matthew Evangelista, "Domestic Structure and International Change," in *New Thinking in International Relations Theory*, ed. Michael Doyle and G. John Ikenberry (Boulder, CO: Westview Press, 1997), 202–228; and Edward Mansfield and Jack Snyder, "Democratic Transitions, Institutional Strength, and War," *International Organization* 56, no. 2 (Spring 2002): 297–337.

5. The research design mitigated some of these concerns by sequentially analyzing closely comparable subsets of cases, considering Brazilian-Argentine relations over time and Central American rivalries at one point in time, rather than directly comparing the foreign policymaking of Nicaragua and Brazil.

6. Bruce Russett and John Oneal, *Triangulating Peace: Democracy, Interdependence, and International Organizations* (New York: W. W. Norton, 2001); Katherine Barbieri, *The Liberal Illusion: Does Trade Promote Peace?* (Ann Arbor: University of Michigan Press, 2002); Stephen Brooks, *Producing Security: Multinational Corporations, Globalization, and the Changing Calculus of Conflict* (Princeton: Princeton University Press, 2005); Emilie Hafner-Burton, "Trading Human Rights: How Preferential Trade Agreements Influence Government Repression," *International Organization* 59, no. 3 (Summer 2005): 593–629; Snyder, *Myths of Empire*.

7. Stephen Brooks and William Wohlforth, "Economic Constraints and the End of the Cold War," in *Cold War Endgame: Oral History, Analysis, Debates*, ed. William Wohlforth (University Park: The Pennsylvania State University Press, 2003), 275–278, though see Robert English, "The Road(s) Not Taken: Causality and Contingency in Analysis of the Cold War's End," 243–272, in ibid.

8. Several recent Latin American analyses explain foreign policy based on categories of development strategy, to say nothing of an earlier wave of Latin American *dependencia* scholarship emphasizing states' positions in the hierarchical global economy. See particularly Amado Luiz Cervo, *Relações Internacionais da América Latina: Velhos e Novos Paradigmas* (Brasília: Universidade Nacional de Brasília, Instituto Brasileiro de Relações Internacionais, 2001); Felipe A. M. de la Balze, "Política Exterior," in *Argentina y Estados Unidos: Fundamentos de una Nueva Alianza*, ed. Felipe A. M. de la Balze and Eduardo A. Roca (Buenos Aires: Asociación de Bancos de la República Argentina / Consejo Argentino para las Relaciones Internacionales, 1997); and Carlos Escudé, *Foreign Policy Theory in Menem's Argentina* (Gainesville: University Press of Florida, 1997).

9. See particularly Brooks, *Producing Security*; Etel Solingen, *Regional Orders at Century's Dawn: Global and Domestic Influences on Grand Strategy* (Princeton: Princeton

University Press, 1998); and Deborah Avant, *The Market for Force: The Consequences of Privatizing Security* (New York: Cambridge University Press, 2005).

10. Robert Burr argued half a century ago that non–Latin American scholars have tended toward this reductionism, and the point is still persuasive. See Robert Burr, *By Reason or Force: Chile and the Balancing of Power in South America, 1830–1905* (Berkeley: University of California Press, 1967), 1.

11. See David Mares, *Latin America and the Illusion of Peace* (London: Routledge / International Institute for Strategic Studies, Adelphi Paper No. 429, 2012); Miguel Angel Centeno, *Blood and Debt: War and the Nation-State in Latin America* (University Park: Pennsylvania State University Press, 2002); Federico Gil, *Latin American–United States Relations* (New York: Harcourt Brace Jovanovich, 1971); Abraham F. Lowenthal, "Latin America at the Century's Turn," *Journal of Democracy* 11, no. 2 (Apr. 2000): 41–55.

12. See David Mares, *Violent Peace: Militarized Interstate Bargaining in Latin America* (New York: Columbia University Press, 2001), 28; G. Pope Atkins, *Handbook of Research on the International Relations of Latin America and the Caribbean* (Boulder, CO: Westview Press, 2001), Chapter 1; Jeanne A. K. Hey, "Three Building Blocks of a Theory of Latin American Foreign Policy," *Third World Quarterly* 18, no. 4 (Sept. 1997): 631–657; and *International Relations Theory and the Third World*, ed. Stephanie Neuman (New York: St. Martin's Press, 1998). João Resende-Santos, *Neorealism, States, and the Modern Mass Army* (New York: Cambridge University Press, 2007), is a model here, as is Walt's defense (Stephen Walt, *The Origins of Alliances* [Ithaca, NY: Cornell University Press, 1987], 13–14), of analyzing variation in international politics within a region other than Europe.

13. See, e.g., Charles Kupchan, *How Enemies Become Friends: The Sources of Stable Peace* (Princeton: Princeton University Press, 2010); Kristina Mani, *Democratization and Military Transformation in Argentina and Chile: Rethinking Rivalry* (Boulder, CO: Lynne Rienner Publishers / FirstForum, 2011); Brooks, *Producing Security*; Solingen, *Regional Orders*; Arie Kacowicz, *Zones of Peace: South America and West Africa in Comparative Perspective* (Albany: State University of New York Press, 1998); Andrea Oelsner, *International Relations in Latin America: Peace and Security in the Southern Cone* (New York: Routledge, 2005); Gian Luca Gardini, *The Origins of Mercosur: Democracy and Regionalization in South America* (New York: Palgrave MacMillan, 2010).

14. Victoria Tin-Bor Hui, *War and State Formation in Ancient China and Early Modern Europe* (New York: Cambridge University Press, 2005).

15. See, for instance, the treatment of autonomy in Tullo Vigevani and Gabriel Cepaluni, *Brazilian Foreign Policy in Changing Times: The Quest for Autonomy from Sarney to Lula*, trans. Leandro Moura (Lanham, MD: Lexington Books / Rowman & Littlefield, 2009).

16. Alexander George and Andrew Bennett, *Case Studies and Theory Development in the Social Sciences* (Cambridge, MA: MIT Press, 2005), 181–185, 201; James Mahoney and Gary Goertz, "The Possibility Principle: Choosing Negative Cases in Qualitative Research," *American Political Science Review* 98, no. 4 (Nov. 2004): 653–669; David Welch, *Painful Choices: A Theory of Foreign Policy Change* (Princeton: Princeton University Press, 2005), is exemplary on these points.

17. See Michael Colaresi, Karen Rasler, and William Thompson, *Strategic Rivalries in World Politics: Position, Space, and Conflict Escalation* (Cambridge: Cambridge University

Press, 2007), 287; Kupchan, *How Enemies*, 9–12; Dan Reiter, *How Wars End* (Princeton: Princeton University Press, 2009), Chapter 4.

18. See Marc Trachtenberg, *The Craft of International History: A Guide to Method* (Princeton: Princeton University Press, 2006); Ian Lustick, "History, Historiography, and Political Science: Multiple Historical Records and the Problem of Selection Bias," *American Political Science Review* 90, no. 3 (Sept. 1996): 605–618.

19. Studies of diffusion address such challenges directly. See, e.g., Kurt Weyland, *Bounded Rationality and Policy Diffusion: Social Sector Reform in Latin America* (Princeton: Princeton University Press, 2007).

20. Other works raising these concerns include Deborah Larson, *Anatomy of Mistrust: US-Soviet Relations during the Cold War* (Ithaca, NY: Cornell University Press, 1997); Andrew Moravcsik, *The Choice for Europe: Social Purpose and State Power from Messina to Maastricht* (Ithaca, NY: Cornell University Press, 1998); and Richard Ned Lebow, "Transitions and Transformations: Building International Cooperation," *Security Studies* 6, no. 3 (Spring 1997): 154–179.

21. 2006 Quadrennial Defense Review (United States Department of Defense, *Quadrennial Defense Review 2006* [February 2006], www.defenselink.mil/qdr/report /Report20060203.pdf), especially 90–91; D. Michael Shafer, *Deadly Paradigms: The Failure of US Counterinsurgency Policy* (Princeton: Princeton University Press, 1988), 90–97; Hilton Root, *Alliance Curse: How America Lost the Third World* (Washington, DC: Brookings Institution Press, 2008), 13; Walter Russell Mead, *Power, Terror, Peace, and War: America's Grand Strategy in a World at Risk* (New York: Knopf, 2004), 170–171, 189–190.

22. For a particularly sobering discussion, see Daniel Byman, "Going to War with the Allies You Have: Allies, Counterinsurgency, and the War on Terrorism," (Carlisle, PA: US Army War College Strategic Studies Institute, Nov. 2005), 8–16.

23. Christine Fair, "Islam and Politics in Pakistan," in Angel Rabasa, Cheryl Benard, Peter Chalk, C. Christine Fair, Theodore Karasik, Rollie Lal, Ian Lesser, and David Thaler, *The Muslim World after 9/11* (Santa Monica, CA: RAND Corporation, 2004), 293–295.

24. Daniel Byman, "Remaking Alliances for the War on Terrorism," *Journal of Strategic Studies* 29, no. 5 (Oct. 2006): 805.

25. Harlan Ullman, *Finishing Business: Ten Steps to Defeat Global Terror* (Annapolis, MD: Naval Institute Press, 2004), xx, 76.

26. Seth G. Jones, Olga Oliker, Peter Chalk, C. Christine Fair, Rollie Lal, and James Dobbins, *Securing Tyrants or Fostering Reform? US Internal Security Assistance to Repressive and Transitioning Regimes* (Santa Monica, CA: RAND, 2006); Walt, *Origins of Alliances*, 221–224; William H. Mott IV, *Soviet Military Assistance: An Empirical Perspective* (Westport, CT: Greenwood Press, 2001).

27. Byman, "Going to War with the Allies You Have," 27–29.

28. Karin von Hippel, "The Roots of Terrorism: Probing the Myths," in *Superterrorism: Policy Responses*, ed. Lawrence Freedman (Malden, MA: Blackwell Publishing / The Political Quarterly, 2002), 28; Root, *Alliance Curse*, 32, 47.

29. Paul Pillar, *Terrorism and US Foreign Policy* (Washington, DC: Brookings Institution Press, 2001), 190.

30. See, e.g., Byman, "Remaking Alliances," 806.

31. Jeane Kirkpatrick, "Dictatorships and Double Standards," *Commentary* (Nov. 1979), 44.

32. Ian Shapiro, *Containment: Rebuilding a Strategy against Global Terror* (Princeton: Princeton University Press, 2007), 105, 115.

33. See Kalev Sepp, "Best Practices in Counterinsurgency," *Military Review* (May–Jun. 2005), 9; Byman, "Going to War with the Allies You Have," 23; Pillar, *Terrorism*, 194–197.

34. Edward Mansfield and Jack Snyder, *Electing to Fight: Why Emerging Democracies Go to War* (Cambridge, MA: MIT Press, 2005); Shapiro, *Containment*, 100; Byman, "Remaking Alliances," 805–806; though see Vipin Narang and Rebecca Nelson, "Who Are These Belligerent Democratizers? Reassessing the Impact of Democratization on War," *International Organization* 63, no. 2 (Spring 2009): 357–379.

35. Thomas Carothers, *Aiding Democracy Abroad: The Learning Curve* (Washington, DC: Carnegie Endowment for International Peace, 1999), 308; *Exporting Democracy: The United States and Latin America*, ed. Abraham F. Lowenthal (Baltimore: Johns Hopkins University Press, 1991); James Dobbins, John G. McGinn, Keith Crane, Seth G. Jones, Rollie Lal, Andrew Rathmell, Rachel Swanger, and Anga Timilsina, *America's Role in Nation-Building: From Germany to Iraq* (Santa Monica, CA: RAND, 2003), 2, 165; Mark Peceny, *Democracy at the Point of Bayonets* (University Park: The Pennsylvania State University Press, 1999), 187–190.

36. See Byman, "Going to War with the Allies You Have," 27–29; Pillar, *Terrorism*; Ullman, *Finishing Business*, 146–147; Shapiro, *Containment*, 49–51.

37. See Shapiro, *Containment*, 34–35, 39.

38. Byman, "Remaking Alliances," 802.

39. See the text in *Al Qaeda in Its Own Words*, ed. Gilles Kepel and Jean-Pierre Milelli, trans. Pascale Ghazale (Cambridge, MA: Harvard University Press, 2008), 201–202; see also Robert Cassidy, *Counterinsurgency and the Global War on Terror: Military Culture and Irregular War* (Westport, CT: Praeger, 2006), 18.

40. Stephen Walt, *Taming American Power: The Global Response to US Primacy* (New York: W. W. Norton, 2005), 223, 240–242.

41. Walt, *Taming American Power*, 243.

42. Christopher Layne, *The Peace of Illusions: American Grand Strategy from 1940 to the Present* (Ithaca, NY: Cornell University Press, 2006), 181–182.

43. Layne, *Peace of Illusions*, 189, 169 (emphasis in original); see also Shapiro, *Containment*, 92.

44. See, e.g., Edward Hallett Carr, *The Twenty Years' Crisis, 1919–1939: An Introduction to the Study of International Relations* (London: MacMillan and Co., 1940 [1939]), 196–197, 302; see also Shapiro, *Containment*, 103.

45. See Kirkpatrick, "Dictatorships," 38.

46. See Michael Colaresi, "When Doves Cry: International Rivalry, Unreciprocated Cooperation, and Leadership Turnover," *American Journal of Political Science* 48, no. 3 (Jul. 2004): 555–570.

47. See especially Stephen Rock, *Why Peace Breaks Out: Great Power Rapprochement in Historical Perspective* (Chapel Hill: University of North Carolina Press, 1989).

48. See, e.g., Miroslav Nincic, *The Logic of Positive Engagement* (Ithaca, NY: Cornell University Press, 2011); William Long and Peter Brecke, *War and Reconciliation: Reason and Emotion in Conflict Resolution* (Cambridge, MA: MIT Press, 2003); Tony Armstrong,

Breaking the Ice: Rapprochement between East and West Germany, the United States and China, and Israel and Egypt (Washington, DC: United States Institute of Peace, 1993).

49. See Kupchan, *How Enemies*, especially 13, 66–67, 394. Despite Kupchan's important and optimistic finding that neither joint democracy nor economic integration is necessary to overcome rivalry (3, 112, 399–406), the argument that rapprochement is generally driven by strategic necessity but contingent on several structural factors and on carefully coordinated reciprocal moves of accommodation and self-restraint still seems daunting (35–44, 73, 180, 389–398).

50. Economists refer to this as "opportunity cost," or what is given up in the pursuit of gains elsewhere.

Page numbers in italics indicate figures or tables. Entries for US presidents or other government leaders may refer to the individual, the administration, or both.